THE ALLURE OF LABOR

THE ALLURE OF LABOR

Workers, Race, and the Making of the Peruvian State

———

Paulo Drinot

Duke University Press   Durham and London   2011

© 2011 Duke University Press

Printed in the United States of America on acid-free paper ∞

Designed by Heather Hensley

Typeset in Warnock Pro by Keystone Typesetting, Inc.

Library of Congress Cataloging-in-Publication Data appear on
the last printed page of this book.

To my parents

CONTENTS

Acknowledgments   ix

Introduction   1

1. RACIALIZING LABOR   17

2. CONSTITUTING LABOR   51

3. DISCIPLINING LABOR   85

4. DOMESTICATING LABOR   123

5. FEEDING LABOR   161

6. HEALING LABOR   193

Conclusion   231

Notes   239

Bibliography   281

Index   305

ACKNOWLEDGMENTS

This book began as a doctoral dissertation completed at the University of Oxford in 2000. Over the last decade I have taken another look at the material that I amassed in the late 1990s, in archives and libraries in Peru and elsewhere, and rethought what it helps me and others understand about Peru's history. This book is the product of that process. Many people, and several institutions, have helped me to make the book what it is. I spent a decade at the Latin American Centre in Oxford, first as a master's student, then writing my doctoral dissertation, then on a post-doc (when I was also a member of the then Institute of Latin American Studies and now Institute for the Study of the Americas in London, which I have recently rejoined), and finally as a temporary lecturer. Those years in Oxford were life-changing, and I have the then staff of the Centre to thank for this, in particular Alan Angell, Malcolm Deas, Rosemary Thorp, and, above all, Alan Knight, who supervised the original dissertation. Alan is a shock-and-awe scholar; it is impossible not to feel at once in awe of, and, in turn, a little intimidated by, his intellect and the significance of his contribution to the historiography of Latin America. He has been a source of constant inspiration and support, and I am deeply grateful for this and for the *cariño* that he and Lidia have shown me and my family over the years.

I also have benefited greatly from the expertise and camaraderie of superb scholars at the institutions where I have worked in the past years. At Leeds my colleagues and especially Paul Garner and Richard Cleminson made me feel welcome and helped make the short time I spent there intellectually rewarding. At Manchester several of my colleagues in the history subject area and in the Centre for Latin American and Caribbean Studies commented extensively on earlier versions of the chapters in this book and contributed in important ways to its completion. I also want to thank the small community of *peruanistas* in the United Kingdom, in particular John Crabtree, Rory Miller, Patricia Oliart, Lewis Taylor, and Fiona Wilson, for their support. Fiona read an earlier version of the entire manuscript and provided very useful suggestions. I owe a special debt of gratitude to two fellow historians, James Dunkerley and Colin Lewis, who have given me plenty of *apoyo*, not least in the shape of countless letters of recommendation, for almost two decades now; in the case of Colin, since my undergraduate days at the London School of Economics. Beyond the United Kingdom, Carlos Aguirre, Diego Armus, Kim Clark, Carlos Contreras, Marcos Cueto, Iñigo García-Bryce, Paul Gootenberg, Steven J. Hirsch, Nils Jacobsen, Peter Klarén, Gerardo Leibner, Nelson Manrique, David Nugent, Scarlett O'Phelan, Steven Palmer, David S. Parker, José Luis Rénique, and Chuck Walker, among others, have provided valuable advice on this and other projects over the years. Ruth Borja was a wonderful guide to, and friend at, the Archivo General de la Nación. I acknowledge gratefully the help provided by the staff of the Bodleian Library, the British Library, the National Archives in London, the International Institute of Social History in Amsterdam, the Archivo General de la Nación in Lima, the regional archives in Arequipa, Cuzco and Trujillo, the Biblioteca Nacional del Perú, the Instituto Riva Agüero, the Pontificia Universidad Católica del Perú, the Instituto de Estudios Peruanos, SUR–Casa de Estudios del Socialismo, and the Universidad Nacional Mayor de San Marcos. The Economic and Social Research Council, the Hewlett Foundation, and the Leverhulme Trust provided the financial assistance that made possible the research upon which this book is based.

Sections of this book have appeared in print before. Chapter 4 is a revised version of "Food, Race, and Working-Class Identity: Populism and *Restaurantes Populares* in Peru," *The Americas* 62, no. 2 (October 2005): 245–70. Portions of chapters 2 and 3 appeared in "Fighting for a Closed Shop: The 1931 Lima Bakery Workers' Strike," *Journal of Latin American Studies* 35.2 (May 2003): 249–78, and "Hegemony from Below: Print Workers, the State, and the Communist Party in Peru, 1920–

1940," in *Counterhegemony in the Colony and Postcolony*, edited by John Chalcraft and Yaseen Noorani (London: Routledge, 2007), 204–27. I am grateful to the respective editors and publishers for permission to use this material.

Three anonymous readers provided invaluable critical evaluations of earlier versions of these chapters. I am deeply grateful to them. At Duke University Press, Valerie Millholland, Miriam Angress, and Neal Mc-Tighe have been model editors. Special thanks go to Maura High, who copy edited the manuscript. I also wish to acknowledge the many friends who have been a part of the long strange trip this book has taken me on, in particular those I met at St. Antony's College, Oxford (not least Sarah Washbrook, who read and commented on the whole manuscript), and in Peru. Special thanks go to the members of *Walrus*, the Beatles-tribute band that kept my archive fever in check by giving me an opportunity to scream into a microphone on many a Barranco night. I am especially grateful to my extended family in Lima, and in particular to my grandmother Teresa, for putting me up and putting up with me over the years. I was lucky to meet Jelke Boesten at the history workshop that Scarlett O'Phelan and Maggie Zegarra used to run in Lima. I thought Jelke was stunning, a little crazy, but, above all, wrong about *enganche*. She thought I was cute, pretty uptight, and, worse, much worse, a typical *miraflorino*. A decade and a beautiful son, Seba, later, we still feel pretty much the same, which just goes to show that love does conquer all. Jelke commented on many versions of these chapters and her critical readings have made this a much better book.

I dedicate this book to my parents in gratitude for, well, everything.

INTRODUCTION

Francisco Alayza Paz Soldán, the director of the Escuela de Artes y Oficios (School of Arts and Crafts) of Lima, in his 1927 valedictory address to the assembled audience of worthies and graduating students argued:

> Peru has entered an industrial age. The number of industries that it possesses and the quality and quantity of manufactured goods that it produces increases year by year. . . . I will outline the evolution and characteristics of modern industry, of great industry, and show the progress achieved by machines and the immense good that civilization has brought us. I will finish by discussing some ideas about the consequences of industry and about the dissolvent social doctrines derived from progress that have absolutely no reason to exist in this country.[1]

Of course, Alayza Paz Soldán was wrong: Peru had not entered an industrial age and would not do so, in a significant way, in the whole of the twentieth century.[2] His assertion was an expression not of an observable reality but of an aspiration shaped by two key beliefs—shared by progressive members of the elite—regarding the economic and political development of the country. First, these elites believed that Peru needed to industrialize if it was to become a modern and civilized nation. All modern civilized nations in the world were industrial, they observed. They concluded, perhaps naturally, that until Peru industrialized there could be no such thing as a civilized Peruvian nation. The editorial of the first issue of *Industria*, the newspaper of the Sociedad Nacional de Industrias (SNI, National Society of Industries), proclaimed in 1915: "We propose to demonstrate that to have industries is not to have an object of luxury or an object of vanity. . . . Without industry there is no nation."[3] Second, these elites agreed, although industry was key to nation building, industrialization had a dark side. The experience of industrial nations in Europe and North America demonstrated that industrialization invariably brought about the spread of subversive ideologies, which led to social unrest—what came to be called, in Peru as elsewhere, "the labor question."

Alayza Paz Soldán and other social progressives recognized that they faced a dilemma. Industrialization could transform Peru into a forward-looking civilized nation but, at the same time, it could sow the seeds of the nation's destruction. For these "modernizing" elites, this was a risk worth taking. In fact, as I show in this book, as far as they were concerned there was no choice. The reason was represented graphically on the cover of the second issue of *Industria Peruana*, the revamped and renamed periodical of the SNI, published in late 1931. The image on the cover, by A. G. Rossell, is of a worker wearing overalls and heavy boots standing next to a seated "Indian" figure wearing a poncho and a *chuyo* (an Andean woolen hat) and holding what look to be coca leaves in his hand. The worker, who is represented as being of white/mestizo phenotype, has placed his left hand on the Indian's shoulder and stretches out his right hand to draw the Indian's attention to the background, which consists of a factory with chimneys belching black smoke and fronted by cars and trucks. The image itself is flanked by more representations of industry, including other factories, oil derricks, and sugar cane, as well as a ship in the far background. To complete the allegory the caption "To protect national industry is to contribute to the country's prosperity" runs vertically on either side of the image.[4] To be sure, the editorial of 1915, Alayza Paz Soldán's speech, and the image of 1931 reflected and expressed the particular sectoral interests of Peru's industrialists. But they also illustrate more broadly, and more interestingly, the ways in which Peruvian elites in the early twentieth century understood the functions of industrialization, and the promise of an industrial future, in racialized ways.

These various "texts" combine to present an unambiguous elite proj-

FIGURE I Cover of the second issue of *Industria Peruana*, November 1931, revamped periodical of the Sociedad Nacional de Industrias (National Society of Industries). Drawing by A. G. Rossell. Source: Courtesy of Biblioteca Nacional del Perú.

ect of national redemption and civilization through industrialization and, more specifically, through the effect of industrialization on the Peruvian population. Industrialization, more than an economic project, emerges as a cultural aspiration. As the 1931 image suggests, Peruvian elites understood industrialization primarily as an embodied project of racial improvement. Like the propaganda posters of the European fascist and Soviet regimes, the image expresses the identification of national progress with the creation of a new man.[5] In the case of Peru, elites identified national progress with the creation of new *homo faber* expressive of a highly racialized understanding of "industrialization as progress." The image of the Indian and of the worker, as representing the past/present and the future, articulates the elites' belief in the transformative power of industrialization but clearly locates that transformation not in the sphere of the economy but in the sphere of race/culture. The power (magic?) of industry, the image suggests, resides in its capacity to transform Peru's backward indigenous peoples into civilized white/mestizo industrial workers. The image thus makes a claim for the nature, and conditions, of citizenship: it is nonindigenous, and therefore white/mestizo. The Peruvian nation would only constitute itself once industrialization had transformed Indians into workers. Put differently, the emergence of the industrial nation would bring about the elimination of the Indian.

The contention at the core of this book is that Peruvian labor policy in the early twentieth century reflected, and was shaped by, assumptions that were the product of a racialized understanding and construction of Peruvian society. Although it drew on transnational processes common to many countries in the first half of the twentieth century, labor policy in Peru was subject to particular local inflections and can only properly be understood when placed within a broader analysis of Peru's racialized process of nation-state formation. Specifically, labor policy in Peru was shaped by racialized ideas about the nature of work and the nature of workers and in particular by the racialized assumption, indeed the widely held and often expressed belief, that industrialization and the emergence of an industrial workforce would bring "civilization" to Peru. More specifically, this book argues that labor policy in early twentieth-century Peru was expressive of a set of beliefs that, at once, associated Peru's future progress and civilization with industrialization and the labor question, warts and all, and, in turn, associated Peru's present backwardness with the predominantly rural and indigenous character of its population and, consequently, with its inferior racial makeup or what came to be known as the Indian question or the Indian problem. Labor policy in Peru, in short, came to play a central role in a broader process of nation-state formation because of the way in which labor in Peru was racialized: in some ways, the labor question in Peru came to be seen as a solution to the far more worrying Indian question. This was the allure of labor that this book's title refers to.

With this book, I aim to contribute to and, in turn, suggest new ways to study Peruvian labor history, a field largely neglected in the last couple of decades. The Allure of Labor challenges the binary construction of Peruvian society as two worlds, unconnected and antagonistic, one coastal and white/mestizo, the other Andean and indigenous; a construction that, for the most part, historians of Peru, particularly those working on its twentieth century, and particularly those working on its labor history, have left unchallenged. Although it has made a major historiographical contribution in some respects, the growth of local or regional studies since the 1980s has helped to further this apparent disconnection between the "two Perus" because of its tendency to focus on either Andean regions or coastal ones.[6] Drawing on the work of anthropologists such as Deborah Poole and Marisol de la Cadena, who have shown how ideas about "race" firmly articulated these supposedly separate worlds, I argue that labor policy reflected racialized assumptions that were the product of ideas about the Peru of the coast *and* the Peru of the Andes, about urban Peru *and* rural Peru, about the white/mestizo *and* the indigenous.[7] *The Allure of Labor* explores the ways in which Peruvian elites envisioned and developed labor policy, and statecraft more generally, as a way to overcome the binary nature of Peruvian society by "incorporating" (both figuratively, and as the *Industria Peruana* cover image suggests, literally) the Andean into the coastal and the indigenous into the white/mestizo through the industrialization of the country and the making of "modern" workers.[8]

LABOR POLICY

The empirical core of the book consists of the analysis of four state "agencies" created to address the labor question in the 1920s and 1930s and to implement new labor laws and the labor provisions of the 1920 and 1933 constitutions. These agencies were (a) the Sección del Trabajo (Labor Section) of the Ministerio de Fomento (Ministry of Development), an agency set up in 1920 to grant official recognition to unions and to institutionalize conflicts between labor and capital through state-mediated arbitration and conciliation tribunals; (b) the "barrios obreros" or state-funded worker districts built to provide cheap and "decent" housing to workers; (c) the "restaurantes populares," a group of state-funded eateries whose function was to provide cheap food for a working-class clientele; and (d) the Seguro Social Obrero or worker social insurance law of 1936, which, through the Caja Nacional del Seguro Social (National Office of Social Insurance), provided workers with near comprehensive social insurance and access to free hospitalization. In my analysis of these agencies, I draw on a broad range of sources to examine both the official and celebratory narratives produced by these agencies and their intellectual architects and the critical counternarratives produced by varied actors, including workers, employers, political parties, "experts," and interested commentators. Drawing on an extensive comparative literature, I pay particular attention to the ways in which these agencies and the labor policies they were created to implement were, at once, part of a broader transnational "social politics" or processes of "social reform" reshaping "the social" in much of the early twentieth-century world and, in turn, expressive of particularly Peruvian circumstances.

Historians have paid limited attention to these state agencies and have tended to see them as little more than hollow "populist" measures of the authoritarian governments of the 1920s and 1930s aimed ostensibly at coopting organized labor. Several historians suggest that their function was not, say, to provide cheap and nutritious food, as in the case of the restaurantes populares, or affordable and decent housing, as in the case of the barrios obreros, but rather to undermine the growing popularity of new political parties of the Left, such as José Carlos Mariátegui's Partido Socialista (later Comunista) del Perú (Peruvian Socialist [later Communist] Party) or Víctor Raúl Haya de la Torre's Alianza Popular Revolucionaria Americana (American Popular Revolutionary Alliance—Peru's historic "populist" party).[9] According to this influential interpretation, the authoritarian governments of the 1920s and 1930s coopted workers by offering material benefits through these state agencies in exchange for political quiescence while at the same time, through repression, they broke up militant unionism and the political parties of the Left, thus neutralizing alternative political projects. Certainly, as contemporary documents reveal, both APRA and the Peruvian Communist Party saw the social measures of the governments of the 1930s as a thinly veiled strategy to weaken their political appeal to organized labor. APRA, in particular, claimed (with some justification) that many of the policies implemented by the governments of Luis M. Sánchez Cerro (1931–33) and Óscar R. Benavides (1933–39, his second term of office) had been lifted from its 1931 electoral program, while the Peruvian Communist Party denounced the policies (and the governments) as "fascist."

However, such an interpretation is incomplete. As several historians of labor in twentieth-century Latin America have shown, populism in the "classic period" was a dynamic process, shaped from above and below, and cannot be adequately accounted for by approaches that focus narrowly on "cooption" or "incorporation."[10] Populist politics in the 1920s and 1930s, and later, were the outcome of complex negotiations between leaders and clients, negotiations that involved the distribution of both material and, just as important, symbolic benefits. As I argue in the following chapters, workers were not simply duped into participating in collective bargaining, applying for worker housing, eating in the restaurantes populares, or registering for the Seguro Social. More generally, through their engagement with the state agencies, workers influenced and made their own the discourse and praxis with which the state sought to reshape labor relations. But the conventional interpretation of these state agencies is also incomplete because, by restricting their analysis to the agencies' supposed political function (the neutralization of the Left), historians have failed to recognize, or have underplayed, other equally important functions. In particular, as I show in this book, these agencies reflected and in turn constituted assumptions, practices, and projects of state formation shaped by the allure of labor, that is, by the belief that labor was an agent of progress and civilization, or, which amounts to the same thing, a means to overcome the Indian problem in Peru.

THE LABOR STATE

In Peru as elsewhere in the late nineteenth and early twentieth centuries, industrialization was consonant with civilization and progress. But, as Alayza Paz Soldán's speech made clear, industrialization was also consonant with social and political (and, indeed, biological) pathologies. The rise of the so-called labor question, or what Jacques Donzelot calls the invention of the social, reflected a growing perception among elites that the contradictions internal to capitalism (the fact that the gains of capitalist growth were unequally distributed) were creating social and political "forces" that appeared to be undermining capitalism and could end up destroying it.[11] These elites concluded that it was therefore necessary to protect labor from pernicious influences (anarchism, socialism, etc.). At the same time, driven by transnational ideological currents such as positivism and social Catholicism, they also believed that it was necessary to address the factors that made labor susceptible to these influences (such as low wages, poor housing, poor nutrition, and poor health). The labor question in Peru and elsewhere was therefore expressive of the way in which labor came to be seen as a problem (at once social and moral) that required a solution; a solution, an increasing number of commentators agreed, that in light of the scale of the problem could not be provided solely or indeed primarily by benevolent employers or charitable institutions. By the early twentieth century, social reformers viewed the state as the entity to be called upon to address the labor question both by protecting labor from pernicious influences and by improving the conditions that labor faced, in the workplace and in the community, and that made it susceptible to those influences. In so doing, an expanded social role was created for the state.

Historians who have documented this process, particularly in the European and North American contexts, emphasize that the responses to the labor question, that is, the emergence of social politics and the beginnings of the welfare state, amounted to more than the simple cooption of labor.[12] Instead, they argue, these responses typically involved a transformation in how the state and its role in regulating society were made sense of. This literature is characterized by an epistemological shift away from conceptualizing the state and social policy according to either modernization or Marxist paradigms. It is marked by two competing if not necessarily exclusive approaches: (a) an institutionalist (i.e., neo-Weberian) literature attentive to the role played by gender (and to a lesser extent, race) in shaping social policy and the origins of the welfare states (the so-called maternalist approach at once influenced by and in turn reacting to feminist interventions in debates on social policy); and (b) a culturalist literature that conceptualizes the state and social policy as a manifestation of what Foucault calls a new art of government or governmentality, that is, a project of rule focused on "the way in which one conducts the conduct of men."[13] Although Foucault viewed governmentality as originating in the eighteenth century, historians and other scholars concerned with the rise of social politics in the nineteenth and, increasingly, twentieth centuries have been particularly drawn to this approach because of the evident resonance for these periods of Foucault's key and influential insight that the end, or goal, of government was "certainly not just to govern, but to improve the condition of the population, to increase its wealth, its longevity and its health."[14]

Most studies of the emergence of social politics and the beginnings of the welfare state in Latin America have tended to privilege the institutional approach (in the sense that they typically envision the state as a more or less autonomous bureaucratic apparatus) and focus on the interplay between gender and the state (hence a tendency to view the state as a paternal or patriarchial state).[15] Such studies, which typically focus on labor, have done much to demonstrate the importance of gender to understanding the social and political history of several Latin American countries, and specifically, the gendered character of state formation in Latin America. However, with some exceptions, they have tended to pay relatively little attention to race and racialization.[16] In this study, I have privileged the governmentality approach for two reasons. First, governmentality provides a useful analytical framework for moving beyond the cooption or incorporation paradigm. From the perspective of governmentality, the state agencies I study are neither mechanisms of cooption nor simple expressions of autonomous bureaucratic rationalities or elite interests. Instead, from the perspective of governmentality, the agencies, and the state they constituted, are best understood as elements in, or dimensions of, a project of rule, or a governmental aspiration, invested by a broad range of social actors (elites but also workers) whose goal was to protect workers from pernicious influences and improve the immediate and mediate conditions workers faced in order to enhance the capacity of workers to contribute to the project of industrialization that would beget civilization and progress.

Governmentality therefore usefully captures the process whereby workers came to be seen as a valuable resource that needed to be protected and enhanced. Governmentality substituted concepts that Foucault had introduced earlier in his life, namely pastoral power and biopower. All these concepts expressed a similar insight: at some point, Foucault suggested, state reason, the rationality or "art" of government, became the management of the population and no longer its police (i.e., its disciplining): "It is now a matter of ensuring that the state only intervenes to regulate, or rather to allow the well-being, the interest of each to adjust itself in such a way that it can actually serve all."[17] In thinking about how these "regulating" agencies may be usefully approached through the analytical lens of governmentality, that is, through a perspective that envisions them as mechanisms to regulate and allow the well-being of workers for the benefit of all, Peter Miller and Nikolas Rose's distinction between rationalities of government and technologies of government is particularly useful.[18] By rationalities of government, Miller and Rose refer to the ways in which certain "objects" of government become knowable, calculable, and administrable and are rendered amenable to intervention and regulation. Once known and understood as amenable to management, such objects can become subjected to technologies of government, that is to say, to physical and symbolic mechanisms that operationalize rationalities of government. This is clearly discernable with regard to labor in early twentieth-century Peru. The rationalities and technologies of government reflected and in turn constituted by the state agencies I study here served to identify, and in the process to constitute, labor as an agent of progress.

The creation of the Sección del Trabajo, for example, was the culmination of a series of proposals that can be traced back to the late nineteenth century to make labor "legible": it identified, monitored, classified, and registered "labor"; it "inscripted" labor, as Miller and Rose put it. In so doing, it constituted labor, brought it into being, and framed it as an object of state action and intervention, a development that was reflected in the 1920 constitution, which contained a series of articles that identified labor as an object of statecraft and made its management a key concern of the state. At the same time, the Sección del Trabajo, like the other agencies I study, the barrios obreros, the restaurantes populares, and the Seguro Social, reflected and in turn constituted technologies of government. As a close reading of the agencies' own narratives reveals, their function extended beyond coopting labor to functioning as physical and symbolic mechanisms that were intended to "improve" Peru's laboring peoples through the disciplinary inculcation of specific values and habits but also, and perhaps primarily, through the governmental management of their immediate and mediate environment (examined here in relation to work, nutrition, housing, and health) in order to reshape them into modern homo fabers: that is to say in order to make them into self-regulating subjects of what I call the labor state, the conjunction of rationalities and technologies of government that composed a broader project of governmentality that placed labor, and the construction of a modern homo faber, at the center of Peru's quest for civilization and progress on the basis of industrialization.[19]

Of course, these agencies, and the labor state more generally, "failed" in the unsurprising sense that no modern homo faber was produced in Peru. Workers were not uniformly "improved" along the lines envisaged by the agencies' architects: the services that these state agencies were supposed to provide (modern industrial relations, cheap and nutritious food, hygienic and morally uplifting housing, decent health services and social insurance) proved highly deficient and inadequate even if some benefits accrued to some workers some of the time. The agencies proved incapable of addressing the opposition to their interventions from employers (who argued that the interventions were unnecessary and harmful to capital) and, in the 1930s, from new political forces on the left (who argued that the interventions were ineffective and harmful to labor). Moreover, targeted workers were not idle bystanders in these projects of improvement. The labor state, I argue, was mutually constituted by labor and the state: workers' reaction to projects of improvement was not one of simple or outright resistance; workers viewed the labor state as an expression of their own aspirations but felt betrayed by its failure to meet them.[20] Workers' engagement with the labor state combined acquiescence, accommodation, and occasionally resistance; all reactions that helped inflect the project of governmentality manifested in the labor state, at least momentarily. Finally, the project of governmentality failed more generally in the sense that the broader transformation that the state agencies were intended to bring about, the industrialization of the country, and the transformation of Peru into what elites envisioned to be a "modern" and civilized nation, proved to be more an aspiration than a reality.

RACE

The "failure" of the project of governmentality manifested in the labor state should not be taken to mean that governmentality as an analytics is flawed. Governmentality, by definition, is an unrealizable project, a utopian aspiration. As Miller and Rose note, "Government is a congenitally failing operation."[21] What is useful about interpreting the social politics of the early twentieth century as a project of governmentality is that it enables us to better understand how ideas about labor's role in inaugurating a new era of industrialization and civilization reflected broader racialized ideas about the sources of progress and backwardness in the country. This is the second reason for privileging the governmentality approach in this study. In contrast to much of Europe, North America, and some Latin American countries such as Argentina or perhaps Brazil (or São Paulo more precisely), where a sizeable proportion of the population was represented in the "labor" invoked by similar rationalities of government and targeted through analogous technologies of government, in Peru "labor" represented a very small proportion of the laboring population and of the population more generally. Why, then, did such agencies and the labor state more generally come to be? Why were resources, intellectual and material, expended on such a small sector of the population? Why did labor come to be seen as particularly amenable to improvement? This requires us to ask what the governmentalization of labor meant in the Peruvian context or, to put it another way, how particular social and cultural configurations prevalent in early twentieth-century Peru shaped the project of governmentality manifested in the labor state.[22]

In his now famous Collège de France lectures, Foucault suggested that governmentality had emerged as a form of power distinct from sovereignty, which he saw as having territory as its target, and discipline —or what he calls police—as its chief apparatus. Governmentality is perhaps best understood therefore as an *overcoming* of police in that the management of the population seeks not to maximize the power of the sovereign but rather that of the population, by extending, and guarantee-ing, freedom in the spheres of the economy and civil society.[23] Although Foucault's genealogy of governmentality suggests a teleological or "stag-ist" (as well as Eurocentric) process, in fact sovereignty and governmen-tality are better understood as forms of power that coexist in all types of societies.[24] For this reason, although Foucault, and others, see govern-mentality as exclusive to liberal societies characterized by free subjects and free market economies (in some ways governmentality is a liberal form of power or the form of power that liberalism assumes), in practice, as David Scott and Mitchell Dean among others suggest, governmen-tality is eminently transposable to (as an analytics), and evident in (as a form of exercise of power), colonial and authoritarian or, more generally, illiberal societies.[25] Foucault acknowledges as much in his discussion of Nazi Germany in his 1976 lectures, where he explores the interplay between the disciplinary and regulatory dimensions of biopower (the management of life or power over life—a concept first introduced in the *History of Sexuality*, vol. 1), that is, between the apparatuses of sov-ereignty and biopower (what he will refer to later as governmentality) and where he pays particular attention to biopower's "dark side."

In envisioning governmentality, in short, Foucault gave particular importance to racism as that which inscribes biopower/governmentality as a key mechanism of state power. As Ann Laura Stoler suggests, al-though the Nazi regime exemplified for Foucault "the sovereign right to kill and the biopolitical management of life," he recognized that racism was "intrinsic to all modern, normalizing states and their biopolitical technologies."[26] Although the development of labor policy and its coales-cence in what I call the labor state in the early twentieth century echoes transnational responses to the rise of the "social" and the labor question, this process had specific characteristics in Peru, which Foucault's thinking on racism and governmentality illuminates particularly well. Both the idea that industrialization was equivalent to civilization and progress and in turn the idea that labor was a valuable resource that needed to be protected and enhanced because it was essential to the project of industrialization were inflected locally by Peru's particular social and cultural configurations; namely, by the fact that Peru's predominantly white elites viewed the country's predominantly indigenous population as culturally and racially backward and as an obstacle to progress. As suggested above, and as I examine in detail in chapter 1, in early twentieth-century Peru the idea that industrialization was consonant with civilization existed in counterpoint to the idea that Peru's current lack of civilization, its backwardness, was a product of the predominantly rural and indigenous, and necessarily nonindustrial, character of its population and consequently of its inferior racial makeup. For this reason, in Peru labor came to be understood in racialized terms to a greater extent than in many other countries: labor was defined typically in terms that excluded the indigenous from the sphere of labor for the simple reason that if labor was commensurable with progress and indigeneity was commensurable with backwardness, it followed that labor was incommensurable with indigeneity.[27]

As I discuss in the chapters that follow, the racialization of labor in Peru is evident in the ways in which labor policy was devised. Implicitly and sometimes explicitly legislation and praxis excluded the indigenous from the sphere of labor policy. The incommensurability between labor and indigeneity is clearly expressed in the 1920 constitution, which established separate constitutional regimes for labor and for the indigenous. But this separation was also reflected in specific labor policy and in the activities of the agencies that dealt with labor. The Sección del Trabajo, for example, did not recognize or seek to intervene in disputes that involved the indigenous; a separate Sección de Asuntos Indígenas (Indigenous Affairs Section) existed for that purpose. Of course, indigenous Peruvians took their labor grievances to the Sección del Trabajo but they did so as workers, not as Indians. Similarly, the Seguro Social Obrero, at least at the beginning, explicitly excluded the indigenous from its coverage, not by virtue of the fact that the indigenous were not worthy of inclusion, but by virtue of the fact that as Indians they were not considered workers and therefore not amenable to coverage. Finally, both the barrios obreros and the restaurantes populares reflected implicit racialized understandings of workers (assumed to be nonindigenous) as agents of progress to be protected and improved through the provision of better housing and nutrition for the benefit of the nation. In short, all of these agencies constructed labor, implicitly or explicitly, as necessarily and inevitably nonindigenous. Labor in Peru was governmentalized because, as elsewhere, it was seen as an agent of progress. But in Peru, to a greater extent than in other countries, the governmentalization of labor was racialized.

To be sure, as historians of Peru and elsewhere have shown, like workers, Indians were also deemed amenable to redemption and were also subjected to a project of governmentality manifested in education, public health, and, indeed, labor policies. However, unlike redeemed or governmentalized workers, in Peru or in Mexico, Bolivia or Ecuador, Nicaragua or Guatemala, redeemed and governmentalized Indians (or, indeed, Afro-Latin Americans, the Chinese, etc.) were never envisioned as agents of progress.[28] Whereas workers were governmentalized in order to enhance their contribution to the industrial nation, Indians were governmentalized in order to reduce or eliminate the obstacle that they represented to the industrial nation.[29] The allure of labor in Peru coexisted with, indeed was conditional upon, the repulsion of indigeneity. As they had done since the colonial period, when the category Indian and its associations with backwardness were first established, throughout the period under study the indigenous in Peru challenged their exclusion and negotiated their governmentalization.[30] They continued to do so for the rest of the twentieth century, even after the allure of labor waned and new "alluring" solutions to Peru's backwardness were formulated (Odría's migrant squatters, Belaúnde's roads, Velasco's "revolution," Sendero's "time of fear," and Fujimori's entrepreneurial cholos; in addition, of course, to APRA's many ideological and programmatic iterations).[31] That such challenges and negotiations continue to this day reveals that despite the "failure" of the project of governmentality manifested in the labor state its underpinning racist fictions are powerful and resilient and continue to shape Peruvian nation-state formation.

Labor policy in the early twentieth century, this suggests, can only properly be understood when placed in a broader analysis of Peru's racialized process of nation-state formation. For even though the indigenous were excluded from the sphere of labor, they remained immanent to labor policy precisely because of the fact that labor was, discursively and in practice, conceived as not indigenous. This reveals how labor policy in Peru reflected a broader process of nation-state formation premised on the exclusion of the indigenous from a national project: the governmental projects of improvement that targeted labor need to be read not only as expressive of ideas about, and practices reflective of, labor's role in the attainment of progress but also as expressive of ideas about, and practices reflective of, the nonrole of indigeneity. They illustrate how the labor state was also, a fortiori, a racial state.[32] The analysis of labor policy explains the fundamental character of Peruvian nation-state formation in the twentieth century: the exclusion of the Indian, the Indian's evacuation from, and incommensurability with, conceptions of Peru's future. What I argue in this book, and what the study of state agencies that targeted labor counterintuitively reveals, is that the exclusion of the Indian from projects of nation-state formation was not the consequence of the Peruvian state's "failures," as is often argued. Rather, the exclusion of the Indian has been and is immanent to the project of Peruvian nation-state formation, which was and in many ways continues to be premised on the *overcoming* of indigeneity, that is to say on the de-Indianization of Peru.

1

RACIALIZING LABOR

In his 1913 annual report, the Peruvian minister of government included the following remarks on the new law regulating strikes introduced by the government of Guillermo Billinghurst (1912–14):

> The unusual frequency, lately, of conflicts between capital and labor, and the urgency to adopt measures that will make their consequences less disastrous, forced the government to introduce the supreme decree of 24 January regulating strikes, which has had, once applied, excellent results, making it possible to resolve disagreements between bosses and workers with a positive outcome for both, establishing in this way the harmony that had disappeared. All countries have labor legislation, and the time has come for this country to have it too.[1]

According to this view, Peru had entered a new phase of historical development, one in which conflicts between capital and labor henceforth would play a central role and, as such, one in which the state would need to intervene in order to create the conditions for such conflicts to be resolved. Indeed, a series of strikes had shaken Peruvian society since the 1880s, and urban workers had played a key role in the rise to power of President Billinghurst in 1912.[2] Labor militancy, the minister suggested, signaled at once Peru's entry into a new industrial age and its vulnerability to the less palatable consequences. The implication was that for reasons both of social order and economic efficiency it was imperative for the state to address the labor question. In this, Peru was but one part of a broader process. As Daniel Rodgers notes in his study of the transnational rise of "social politics" in the North Atlantic, strikes in the late nineteenth and early twentieth centuries "were the most unnerving sign of the new order ..., they grew in scope as the era proceeded, pulling the state more and more deeply into the role of policeman, negotiator, or military suppressor."[3]

As I show in this chapter, the minister of government's comments on the rise of labor militancy and on the need for labor legislation suggests that ideas about the causes and consequences of strikes and about the need for a state response to labor militancy circulated in the early twentieth-century world beyond the North Atlantic economies examined by Rodgers. I begin by examining the ways in which the rise of the so-called labor question in Peru, the coming into being of labor as a problem that needed to be addressed, resulted in new conceptions of the state, of the state's social role, and of labor.[4] I argue that these changes reflected both rationalities of discipline (the purpose of the state is to control and discipline labor, a threat to social order) and rationalities of government (the purpose of the state is to protect and improve labor, an agent of progress) that responded, at once, to elite fears of labor unrest and, in turn, to transnational currents that linked Peru to developments in "social politics" in Europe and North America, and more generally, to the coming into being in Peru of what I call the labor state. In a second section, I examine early labor legislation to show that, as elsewhere in Latin America and beyond, early social politics in Peru were shaped by, and were expressive of, gendered assumptions. The labor state was, in practice, a patriarchal state. However, to a greater extent than in many countries, as I show in the final section, in Peru the rise of the labor question was a racialized process.[5] Labor in Peru came to be envisioned in ways that excluded the indigenous from the sphere of labor and conceptions of progress or, rather, that included the indigenous in ideas of progress insofar as they ceased to be indigenous as a consequence of the civilizing effect of labor upon them. Either way, I argue, the study of the rise of the labor question in Peru reveals how the indigenous were perceived as incommensurable with the labor state, and more generally, with the project of an industrial and civilized nation.

Like their contemporaries in Europe, North America, and much of Latin America, a new generation of university-educated professionals in Peru responded to what came to be known as the social question by fashioning themselves as social reformers and seeking to influence and shape policy in various spheres. This group included engineers who hoped to map Peru's vast mineral assets and physicians who sought to modernize public health provision.[6] It also included a number of lawyers and budding social scientists who sought to address what they referred to as the labor question, by which they usually meant the tendency for workers to strike and their susceptibility to unpalatable social and political doctrines, but also the conditions in which workers worked and lived and which served to enhance that susceptibility. For much of the nineteenth century, Peruvian elites had agreed largely that it was the role of private philanthropy or the beneficence of religious orders to address society's, and more specifically laboring peoples', ills. However, by the early twentieth century many agreed that the state was better placed to address social problems and assume responsibility for social order, but also public health or education.[7] As elsewhere in the world, what George Steinmetz has aptly called the "regulation of the social" was expressed in Peru in an emulation and adaptation of European and North American examples of social "improvement."[8] Specifically, it was expressed in the expansion of the state's coercive and cognitive capacity through the enactment of legislation and the creation of institutions that equipped it with the tools to implement projects of social regulation and improvement. But it was expressed also in fundamental changes in ideas about labor and about the state.

For the most part, social reformers in Peru did not understand labor unrest as an aberrant phenomenon but rather as reflective and constitutive of an industrial capitalist age. In 1905, Luis Miro Quesada, then a young university graduate but soon to become a pioneer of Peruvian social thought, argued that the social question "is merely the expression of the evils produced by the profound division that exists between the two classes that seek to conquer the benefits of industry: that of capital and that of the proletarians; classes that mistakenly consider themselves enemies, and that, in open struggle, forget the more permanent interests of humanity as a consequence of selfishness in the case of one, and of

desperation in the case of the other."[9] In other words, for social reformers such as Miro Quesada the rise of the social question was the
consequence of the imperfections of capitalism. Along with several of his
contemporaries, Miro Quesada argued that it was the purpose of the
state to address these imperfections. Various observers reprised this idea
time and again during the first half of the twentieth century. On the one
hand, social reformers argued that the state should intervene in the
sphere of labor in order to ensure industrial peace and secure production, which meant addressing the conditions that produced labor unrest.
Typically, they identified unrest as a product of militant influences on
labor, which the state, naturally, needed to counteract. But social reformers also understood unrest as product of the conditions that workers faced in their mediate and immediate environments; that is, in the
workplace and in the home.

In 1906, for example, Alberto Elmore, the newly chosen president of
the revamped Peruvian Academy of Legislation and Jurisprudence, decided to dedicate his inaugural lecture to "the industrial and commercial
conflicts, veritable battles that pit capital either with labor or with consumers." Recalling the recent Callao dockworkers strike, Elmore noted
that Peruvian legislation did not even mention the terms "strike" or
"coalition" (by which he meant unions), but he argued that the right to
strike and the right to unionize needed to be accepted. However, although he saw these legislative developments as necessary in light of
developments elsewhere, he was concerned by the fact that such laws
were typically abused by those they were intended to protect. Workers,
he claimed, were susceptible to the influence of "socialist" agitators who
sought "political outcomes."[10] The idea of a corrupting external influence on otherwise peaceful Peruvian workers was reprised regularly in
government publications and the press. The minister of government's
warning in 1916 that foreign anarchists who had recently arrived in Peru
had begun to gain followers, set up organizations, and organize publications found echo in an article published in *La Crónica* on a series of
strikes in the northern ports of Salaverry and Pacasmayo that argued that
it was imperative to "find out whether behind all of this is the cowardly
hand of the foreign agitator." Significantly, the article allowed the possibility that the source of militancy was local but suggested that only
criminals would resort to such measures: "And if the agitators are our
own workers, it is the responsibility of the working class, which, for-

tunately, has in this country achieved a high level of culture, to name them and to present them to the judgment of public opinion as unconscious and perverted workers and creators of a criminal enterprise."[11] The implication, in this and many other texts on labor unrest of this period, was that workers had no legitimate cause to protest; indeed that workers who protested were not true workers.[12]

Labor militancy may have appeared to Peruvian elites as evidence of Peru's industrial progress, and as one of its inevitable and natural consequences, but its "othering" (its denaturalizing as foreign to Peru) served to legitimize its repression. In this way, labor militancy created a role for the state, which was called upon to protect labor from perverse foreign or militant influence, and more generally to bring order to, and regulate, conflicts between capital and labor, a role that expressed what I call rationalities of discipline. As Miro Quesada argued, "Given the difficult situation that society finds itself in today, recognizing the danger represented by that dull and persistent struggle that for many years has pitted capital and labor and that threatens to destroy . . . progress, peace and social institutions, we have to conclude that the state not only has the right to intervene to regulate labor, it has the duty to do so."[13] Similarly, Augusto Elmore argued that it was imperative for the state to act in order to repress the negative influences that labor was exposed to: "A special and vigorous legislation is needed, to be executed by an active and intelligent government aided by public opinion; only in this way will it be possible to avoid or reduce these dangers, guarantee more effectively the freedom to work, give greater protection to the involved public interests, and to put a brake on the unscrupulous complicity of political speculators."[14] This was the thinking that, as we saw, led the minister of government to argue in 1913 that the increase in conflicts between labor and capital had created "the urgency to adopt measures that will make its consequences less disastrous."

If intervention in the sphere of labor was justified by the need to protect labor from "political speculators," it was similarly justified by the belief that it was the modern and civilized thing to do. As the minister of government had noted, "all countries have labor legislation," by which he meant all "modern" and "civilized" countries. As this implies, social reformers believed that if the time had arrived for Peru to have labor legislation it was because Peru had arrived at a historical "moment" that made such legislation necessary. Indeed, as David Parker has argued in a seminal article on the general strike of late 1918 (considered to be the founding moment of the Peruvian labor movement), the strike may have contributed to President José Pardo's decision to extend the eight-hour day to all workers on 15 January 1919 (it had been granted to dock workers in 1913 and to women and children in 1918). However, the impetus for the law came from within the elite: from lawyers, academics, and politicians who had come to see labor legislation as a necessary component of "modernity."[15] The law was not a victory for anarchist organizers as some contemporaries believed and some historians suggest, but rather a top-down measure that reflected the anxieties and aspirations of Peruvian elites. Indeed, social reformers like Alberto Ulloa Sotomayor argued in 1919, perhaps overstating his case, that workers were only really interested in agitation and that "no law and no initiative of that order has been demanded by workers or their unions; those few that exist and those that are being debated have been given to them by the good faith of far-sighted men."[16] Certainly, Peruvian elites were aware of international developments in labor legislation and viewed progressive measures such as laws regulating the hours of work in a favorable light, since by adhering to them it became possible to proclaim, or so they believed, Peru's firm march down the road to "civilization." As Parker states, "Reformers felt that Peru needed an advanced labor code just as much as it needed railroads, electric lighting, bowler hats, and everything else in vogue across the Atlantic."[17]

Two seemingly contradictory transnational discourses influenced Peruvian social reformers' view that state protection of labor was evidence of a country's march toward civilization. The first of these was the social thought associated with the *Rerum novarum*, the papal encyclical of 1891, and later texts that developed social Catholic thought, such as the Social Code of Cardinal Mercier, which articulated a social philosophy in favor of a third way between capitalism and socialism. As David Rock suggests, *Rerum novarum* "wove an ambiguous synthesis of reactionary and outwardly progressive prescriptions." It criticized the selfishness and rapaciousness of capitalists and the subversive tactics of socialists. In particular it rejected the claim that class conflict was inevitable. Significantly, however, "its concept of the functions of government stood closer to socialist interventionism than liberal laissez-faire. . . . The encyclical called on the state to 'promote public well-being and private prosperity.' The state should curb the accumulation of excessive wealth, and seek 'distributive justice.'"[18] These ideas are clearly evident, for example, in the speech given by Francisco Cabré, a Franciscan missionary, at the Círculo de Obreros Católicos, in Arequipa in 1918, where he critiqued both "the absurdity of socialism, which seeks to alter God's work, thus upsetting the current social order," and the exploitation of labor by capitalists and called for the creation of institutions, such as mutual aid funds, that would improve the lives of workers.[19]

The impact of social Catholic thought on the debates over the labor question in Peru is most clearly expressed in Víctor Andrés Belaúnde's *La realidad nacional*, first published in 1931 and a response to José Carlos Mariátegui's *Siete ensayos de interpretación de la realidad peruana*. Belaúnde placed the social Catholic thought that had emerged from *Rerum novarum* at the forefront of social policy, noting that "it is unnecessary to restate the traditional position of social Catholic philosophy with regard to the right to strike, the work of children and women, industrial accidents, and so-called vocational or professional training." Social Catholicism, Belaúnde stressed, recognized workers' right to organize in trade unions, and, "as regards social conflicts, [social Catholicism] has always favored conciliation and arbitration, and has sought to avoid giving too much influence to capital in such processes." Moreover, Belaúnde stressed that in contrast to liberalism, social Catholicism envisaged a strong role for the state in addressing the labor question: "Social Catholic philosophy has not, like individualist philosophy, sought to keep the state outside of the country's economic life. On the contrary, it favors its intervention for the protection and maintenance of the principles previously discussed." For Belaúnde, social Catholicism's prescriptions with regard to the labor question were particularly suitable to Peru since they provided "a series of reasonable and just practical orientations that, in addition to the importance that derives from their universality, given that they are supported in the principal countries of Europe and America by eminent people, also correspond to the religious background and the traditional psychology that the Church has given our people."[20]

At the same time, social reformers' belief that labor was amenable to protection by the state was shaped by positivism, the influential view that society presented a series of problems that could be overcome rationally and through the application of the scientific method.[21] As a number of historians have shown, the early decades of the twentieth century witnessed the development of an elite gaze influenced by positivism on the poor, the marginal, the criminal, the "racially degenerate," the female, and the suicidal. This gaze led to growing state intervention in the spheres of public health, policing and imprisonment, and education; a state intervention that reflected the belief that scientific "progress" enabled the reordering and "improvement" of society.[22] This was no different with regard to the labor question. As Luis Miro Quesada argued:

> The state, in protecting labor, has to do so inspired by justice and the public good; it must seek to harmonize, wherever possible, the interests in conflict, subordinating individual interests when they conflict with those of the community. The implementation of these principles is the responsibility of legislators and of the men of state [*hombres de estado*] in each country, who are the only ones who, following a careful examination of the industrial laws of other countries, of the study of the race, character and customs of their people, can determine the level of intervention that is convenient and the means to undertake it in order to achieve peace and progress.[23]

Like Belaúnde, Miro Quesada too conceived of state action with regard to the labor question as a necessary combination of the universal (Catholicism; scientifically derived industrial legislation) and the local (a "religious background" and "traditional psychology"; "the study of the race, character, and customs of the people").

These transnational currents shaped the belief that the purpose of the state was not only to protect labor but also to "improve" it, to enhance its well-being by acting upon workers' mediate and immediate environments; a belief expressive of what Tania Murray Li calls the "will to improve" and Miller and Rose call rationalities of government.[24] Campaigning in favor of evening schools for workers, for example, the periodical *Ilustración Obrera* noted in 1917 that the creation of such schools "is an obligation of the state and not a favor given to the working classes, as some mistakenly believe."[25] That same year, Juan Angulo de Puente Arnao concluded his treatise on labor legislation by arguing that "only with interventionism will it be possible to achieve a true organization of labor, and the government who assumes this challenge will not only write a glorious page in the history of the Fatherland, but the name of its leader will be forever etched on the hearts of all Peruvian workers."[26] According to an editorial in the periodical *Mundial* in 1921, "To cheapen popular subsistence goods, to provide cheap, hygienic, and comfortable housing for the people, to provide ample work opportunities for workers, to discipline and educate the masses, constitute the urgent obligation of the modern state." Some years later, in 1937, Napoleón Valdez Tudela, who held the chair in social legislation at San Marcos University, explained that "the intervention of the state in capital-labor relations, which constitutes the primary contemporary social problem and whose roots are found in the evolution of human labor and industrial development, is the only means to bring about social justice, because it provides legal protection to the worker without prejudicing industrial progress."[27]

By intervening in the sphere of labor, the state not only protected workers from both rapacious capitalism and ungodly socialism, it also enhanced labor's capacity to contribute to the advent of civilization itself in Peru. These rationalities of government coexisted and cross-fertilized with repressive impulses, that is, with rationalities of discipline: the reformers argued that the state should intervene in the sphere of labor in order to protect labor from political influences because to fail to do so would be to allow labor to turn from an agent of progress into a threat to society. As Clorinda Corpancho argued in 1913:

> Let us not forget that the industrial element, which constitutes the soul of the modern world, and the worker, who is the breath that gives life to that soul, are as necessary to our existence as our daily water and bread. Destiny has tied them with indissoluble knots that are no less sacred than those that form Nature, because they carry within them the seed of great virtue and if we overlook them they are capable of causing the greatest calamities.[28]

Although the identification between workers and "peace and progress" and the "modern world" elevated workers into agents of progress, social reformers continued to perceive workers as a potential source of social danger.[29] In this way, social reformers represented the protection and well-being of labor as the very purpose of government and of an expanded social role for the state.

To be sure, not all elite commentators were in favor of increasing labor legislation or of an expanded social role for the state. Some employers, particularly those associated with the Sociedad Nacional de Industrias, argued that the state had a role to play in stimulating and protecting industry and thus in contributing to "the development of the nation and, as a consequence, the increase of its wealth" but rejected state intervention in setting wages or regulating working conditions.[30] According to one commentator, "the function of the state—its sole function—is to protect industry."[31] In an article published in early 1917, partly in response to campaigns in the press aimed at increasing wages in order to mitigate the impact of war-induced inflation, the industrialists argued that such campaigns were unnecessary since employers were perfectly aware that "a good wage guarantees to his collaborator, the worker, a high *standard of life* [in English in the original], contributing in this way to higher levels of production, quality, and quantity of goods." Enlightened employers, rather than civil society or the state, would decide adequate wages and working conditions, since "our industrialists know perfectly well that in each human it is necessary to cultivate the animal as Spencer argues; because a good animal is the necessary condition of intelligence and a good orientation." Moreover, the article stressed, what would ultimately lead to better wages and improved working conditions was neither pressure from strikes nor state intervention but the unimpeded growth of Peru's industries: "The future of the Peruvian worker depends on the development of national industry."[32]

Resistance to an expanding state role extended to the public sphere. In the mainstream press, several commentators reflected on the new social legislation and state intervention in the sphere of labor. Some viewed such measures as unnecessary, while others saw in them hollow posturing. An editorial in the periodical *Economista Peruano* argued in 1913 that most labor laws proposed in Congress were not relevant to Peruvian reality: "They are solutions that are presented to the government before the problems have arisen."[33] The article rejected the idea that the state was best placed to address the social needs of workers and claimed that the legislative proposals were little more than political maneuvers that had "imported socialism to a market with few consumers" and created "state socialism" in the country. For the editorialist, who claimed to raise the flag of economic freedom, "to pretend to solve the social question with regulations, with violence and the intervention of the authorities [. . . is] to disrupt social life and to maintain it in permanent disequilibrium." The social needs of workers, the editorialist claimed, would be met not by legislation but by "industrial education for the worker, by raising his moral level, by the efficiency of the tools of labor that make him more productive, and by the increase in the number of people dedicated to commerce and industry, to the sciences and the arts and to the cultivation of mutual respect between men." The state should refrain from trying to solve labor problems and limit its activity to "guaranteeing the work contract and the freedom to labor." A few years later, an article in *La Prensa*, a daily, on industrial relations in the United States, which focused particularly on the activities of Charles M. Schwab and Henry Ford, concluded that laws "cannot accurately regulate the fundamental organization of social justice" and argued instead that workers have gained far more from the "noble initiative" of capitalists than they ever could have from either legislation or through strikes: "social justice is a powerful force that emanates from the hearts of capitalists who see in their employees not mere machines of meat and bone but human beings, honest and loyal men, family men with a moral right to personal well-being."[34]

Although there was disagreement regarding the role and capacity of the state to protect the worker, what these comments reveal is the emergence of a consensus in Peruvian society that workers were a valuable resource that needed to be protected and improved morally and physically, that is, a consensus expressive of rationalities of government. What was debated was whether protection and improvement would result from the intervention of the state or from the benevolence or the rational actions of employers. But both social reformers, on the one hand, and industrialists attached to the SNI, on the other, as well as observers writing in the national press, acknowledged that workers had "social needs" and "a moral right to personal well-being" and that it was imperative that their needs be met and their well-being secured so that their productivity would be enhanced for the benefit of industry and, more generally, the nation. Of course, we should not take these comments too much at face value: after all, few employers would openly claim not to have the best interests of their workers at heart. And yet many employers in Lima and in the export industries in this period adopted what was often denounced as "paternalist" measures—by José Carlos Mariátegui among others—and implemented social welfare measures in their factories and plantations, providing housing, health benefits, and pensions for workers, as well as schooling for workers' children. More generally, as I show in this and the following chapters, although the state only rarely effectively protected or "improved" workers, rationalities of government were very much at the center of labor policy in the first half of the twentieth century.

The idea that the purpose of the state was to protect and improve labor was reflected in legislative changes that operationalized the rationalities of discipline and in government that shaped this idea. As many as twenty major laws, decrees, and regulations regulating work and workers' lives were introduced between 1900 and 1920.[35] These ostensibly progressive laws formalized the power of the state to intervene in the sphere of labor. The 1913 strike law, described by an English-language newspaper as "a most remarkable document, which is probably the first of its kind in South America," is a good example of how rationalities of discipline and government shaped intervention in the sphere of labor.[36] Following a wave of strikes (which led to the Callao dockworkers being granted the eight-hour day) in 1913, President Guillermo Billinghurst introduced a decree that recognized workers' right to strike. However, the decree also established a number of regulations limiting the use of the strike. Strikes could go ahead only after attempts at conciliation with employers had collapsed. Workers had to show that a majority was in favor of the strike and send a notice, indicating the names and addresses of strikers, to the police twenty-four hours before the strike began.[37] Whether the decree served to stifle or promote workers' use of the strike is unclear, but what is clear is that the decree positioned the state as the entity with the capacity and legitimacy to shape labor-capital relations in the workplace and beyond. In theory at least, workers now could strike legally and, at the same time, be afforded the protection of the state. On the other hand, the state could now legitimately repress wildcat strikes, while the regulations contained in the decree made striking a complex and time-consuming affair.

Two further laws illustrate how the idea that the purpose of the state to protect and improve labor translated into an expansion of the state's sphere of action. The first, the Ley de Accidentes del Trabajo (Work Accidents Law—Law 1378), decreed in 1911, was the culmination of a long process of negotiation in Congress in which Rosendo Vidaurre (discussed below) played a major role. The law had many defects and was easily resisted by employers and strongly criticized for its shortcomings by workers. Nevertheless, Peru was still "the first country in Latin America to have such a law, and with Canada, only the second in all of the Western Hemisphere."[38] The second law, the 1918 Ley sobre Trabajo de

Mujeres y Niños (Women and Children Work Law—Law 2851), regulated the work of women and children and sought to address "the considerable increase in women who work, a phenomenon that reflects the great economic crisis faced by poor households, where in order to reduce hunger it becomes necessary to alienate the efforts of the mother and the daughters."[39] The law limited women and children's workday to eight hours, prohibited the employment of women and children on nightshifts, granted women paid maternity leave, and forced employers to provide a nursery for children younger than one year of age.[40] It reflected a key aspect of the transnational development of social politics; the assumption, as Daniel Rodgers argues, "that women and child workers belonged in a separate, particularly helpless category of workers."[41]

Like similar laws enacted in this period in other countries, these Peruvian laws are best understood as elements in a gendered project of social and moral regulation. Like the laws in Germany studied by George Steinmetz, these laws embodied "certain assumptions about gender and the family" expressive of a "civilizing" patriarchal order.[42] In the more obvious case of the law on women and children, the state claimed to protect from exploitation in the workplace women and children who were forced by poverty to sell their labor.[43] One, admittedly not fully contemporary, commentator noted that the law regulating the work of women and children had, in the last instance, "to keep watch over morality, 'since the workshop is so often the first step towards prostitution.' "[44] Some contemporary observers, such as Luis Miro Quesada, went even further, calling, in a statement that invoked gender stereotypes, for the creation of state-run workshops where the state could intervene directly to annul the corrupting influence of the factory by freeing women from "the exploitation that results from their helplessness and the weakness of the female character, which is inclined toward resignation and sacrifice, that encourages the exploiter to use these virtues as weapons against women."[45] State intervention of this sort was framed in a rhetoric that associated "progress" with virility; Luis Miro Quesada justified the need to entitle women to pregnancy leave on the grounds that "this measure, of a highly humanitarian nature, is currently in operation in the United States, that great country whose harmonized sentiments of respect and consideration towards women explains the virile preponderance that it has achieved in the world."[46] In other words, the protection of women and children, and labor legislation more generally, was understood as expressive of a patriarchal order that would bring about "progress," as demonstrated by the fact that such laws were already in place in more "advanced" or "civilized" countries.

Like the law regulating the work of women and children, the accident law was expressive of a civilizing patriarchal order that purported to guarantee the well-being and social and moral "improvement" of workers. As early as 1901, Luis Miro Quesada argued that an accident law would mean that workers "would no longer have to receive, as a gracious concession, that which is owed to them by virtue of a natural right."[47] In 1903 the minister of justice noted in his annual report the need for legislation to protect workers from the "dangers in the great factories and centers of production created by modern industry" and that the fate of workers who had suffered accidents "should not, as it has been done until now, be left to more or less humanitarian sentiments of the boss, manufacturer, or entrepreneur, but be protected by the imperative mandate of the law."[48] In this way, the law constituted the state as a paternal figure overlooking the safety of his worker-sons and worker-daughters. It is worth pointing out that not everyone was convinced that such a law was needed in Peru. Salvador Diez Canseco argued in his doctoral dissertation in 1907 that the accident law was impractical, since neither workers, employers, nor the state could afford it, and that in any case the absence of modern machinery or, indeed, modern industry in Peru meant that such a law was unnecessary. Yet in his rejection of the need for the law, Diez Canseco, like the law's supporters, established a clear link between labor legislation and civilization: "Later, when Peru's industrial growth acquires the rate of that of European countries, when numerous productive enterprises are established, when the culture of the country is equal with that of the nations that stand at the forefront of civilization, then will we reap the fruit that, doubtless, produce the beneficial system of obligatory [accident] insurance."[49]

Clearly, we should be under no illusion as to the effectiveness of these laws. As Elizabeth Quay Hutchison correctly notes, "Like worker housing and sanitary laws, attention to labor legislation in [the early twentieth century] testified more to elite anxieties about the menace of anarchism and superficial humanitarian interest than to any concerted effort to better the lives of Chilean workers."[50] In Peru too, the passing of such laws reveals more about elite anxieties and, I would add, aspirations, than about the actual working and living conditions of laboring peoples. The law on women and children had far more to do with elite anxieties about women being, *pace* Mary Douglas, "out of place."[51] In Peru, as in Chile, "even the most progressive agenda for labor reform relied on a fundamentally domestic construction of women's role in society."[52] But those anxieties did not translate into the effective domestication of women. As late as 1932 the law had been implemented only partially. The general labor inspector's report on the Santa Catalina textile mill indicated that in the "silks" section "the women who work there, who represent the bulk of the workforce, work nine hours a day, and have no right to holidays [in violation] of Law No. 2851. In spite the long hours, they only receive ninety centavos a day."[53] Similarly, although Peru had pioneered accident legislation, few workers benefited from the law, including, one suspects, the two bullfighters who, as late as 1939, sought to obtain reparations for the "work accidents suffered during the *corrida* of Sunday 15."[54] As Ulloa Sotomayor confirmed some six years after the passing of the law, "its general implementation has been hampered by the bosses."[55] Similarly, writing in 1925, Mariano Echegaray and Ramón Silva noted that the law "is deficient and anachronistic, its clauses do not properly protect workers and leave plenty of loopholes through which unscrupulous employers can escape their responsibilities, leaving their victims and their families, who they support, in the most terrible misery."[56]

We must be careful, then, not to assume that the advent of labor policy resulted in an effective reshaping of society by an all-powerful state. The rationalities of government operationalized through such early legislation in Peru (as elsewhere) did not necessarily translate into an effective capacity to bring about change. Nevertheless, the analysis offered here suggests that early state responses to the labor question, as elsewhere in the world at this time, helped constitute a new understanding of the role that the state should play in shaping society. The laws discussed above, like the British National Insurance Act studied by Daniel Rodgers, "entailed no seismic shift in political culture.... Nonetheless it represented a small but important shift in thinking about the risks of labor."[57] As with education in Timothy Mitchell's study of colonial Egypt, in Peru labor became "the state's active and extensive concern, a field of organization, a major realm in which what is called 'the state' was to exist and build relations of power."[58] In this way, the regulation of the labor question became central to a broader process of the constitution of the state as a labor state, a state of and for labor. As I will discuss in the following chapters, the state came into being through the establishment of labor discipline in the workplace in order to guarantee social order and industrial progress. But it also came into being through its attempts at protecting and "improving" labor by acting in the sphere of public health, nutrition, housing, and more generally, social welfare. It was, in Peru, again, as elsewhere, as I have anticipated here and will discuss in greater detail in later chapters, a highly gendered process. But it was also, for particularly Peruvian reasons, a racialized process, as I discuss in the following section.[59]

THE RACIALIZATION OF LABOR

As elsewhere in the world, the legislative response to the labor question in Peru was subject to a local translation. As we have seen, both those influenced by positivism and those influenced by social Catholicism justified labor laws by stressing their modernity and universality (concretely, by pointing to the fact that they were the *dernier cri* in Europe and the United States). But the laws also expressed local assumptions about the character of Peruvian society and specifically about the character of Peru's population and reveal how these assumptions about the character of the Peruvian population shaped ideas about labor. As in the German and British cases studied by Richard Biernacki, in Peru too "a nationally specific understanding of labor" emerged.[60] In Peru the concept of labor "did not 'reflect' or 'express' economic conditions . . . , [it was] part and parcel of those conditions."[61] Put otherwise, labor legislation in Peru was not merely a response to the labor question. It was at once expressive of and constitutive of the very idea of "labor" and in particular of the idea of "worker" that predominated in Peru. Take for instance the worker accident law. As the journal *Economista Peruano* noted shortly after the law was passed, the law only covered those workers who worked with machinery. Yet the overwhelming majority of workers in Peru were employed in activities that did not involve the use of machinery.[62] Similarly, the law on women and children applied only to those employed in factory work, but the overwhelming majority of women and children worked not in factories but as domestic servants, in workshops, and in agricultural activities. As I have suggested above, the laws were intended to discipline, protect, and "improve" workers. But they also, in their design, constituted the very notion of "worker."

Labor legislation in early twentieth-century Peru helped fix the meaning of labor through its reference to a labor process that involved mechanized or factory production. It was a meaning that in the Peruvian context served to exclude the vast majority of the laboring population from the sphere of labor, that is, from the notion of labor immanent to the legislation, and, therefore, from the (highly deficient) protection afforded by labor legislation, according to criteria that, though framed with reference to the material sphere (machines, factories), in fact were expressive of the cultural sphere. Put simply, labor legislation fixed the idea of labor as machine-based and factory-bound and served to constitute labor as primarily industrial. By extension, it excluded all those laboring peoples who did not meet these criteria. These exclusions reflected broader hierarchical classifications based on gender and race. As Pierre Bourdieu notes, "Through the framing it imposes upon practices, the state establishes and inculcates common forms of categories of perceptions and appreciations, social frameworks of perceptions, of understandings or of memory, in short *state forms of classification*," but, he goes on to argue, such forms of classification only take root to the extent that they "*awaken* deeply buried corporeal dispositions outside the channels of consciousness and calculation."[63] In others words, as I argue in this section, labor legislation expressed, and at the same time helped reassert, ideas about the fundamental gendered and racialized differences between Peru's laboring peoples and, more concretely, between Peru's creole (coastal/white) and Andean worlds.

An early legislative project and the reactions it provoked can help to illustrate this. In 1903, Rosendo Vidaurre, a tailor and the first worker elected to the Peruvian Congress, proposed a "Labor Law."[64] The proposal is instructive because it points to the work regimes that characterized employment in Peru at the beginning of the twentieth century and that Vidaurre hoped to regulate. Its very first article, which forbade the employment of children younger than eleven years of age, suggests that this was a common practice. Article 27, which prohibited payment of salaries in the form of scrip, suggests that this too was usual. But the proposal also introduced some radical measures aimed at improving the well-being of the "proletarian classes," considered a "duty of the public authorities." Article 2, for example, established that employers would provide access to primary education to children in their employment. More generally, the proposal limited the hours of work to six for children, seven for women, and ten for men and established indemnities for workers injured on the job of a sum equivalent to three years of salary or no less than one hundred Peruvian pounds in the case of children and women and five hundred Peruvian pounds in the case of men. If a male worker died on the job, his widow would receive a lifelong pension of five Peruvian pounds per month, as would his children until they reached adulthood. Article 26, on the other hand, established that workers who were declared to be "habitual drunks" by a physician would lose the right to benefit from the law.

The proposal provoked a response from the Sociedad Nacional de Minería (SNM, National Society of Mines) that illustrates how employers approached the labor question in the early twentieth century. In a letter sent to the director of the Ministry of Development, the president of the SNM Alejandro Garland noted that the institution he represented "does not dispute the need for the law to regulate certain aspects of the relations that exist between labor and capital." Laws, he suggested, could help to conciliate the legitimate aspirations of workers and capitalists and contribute to the elimination of conflicts. But Garland formulated a series of objections to Vidaurre's proposal. He argued that the indemnities envisaged by Vidaurre would ruin the mining industry and threatened to halt further foreign investment. He suggested more generally that new legislation was unnecessary as the mining companies were self-regulating and had already implemented measures (regulating the work of children, providing indemnities to workers injured on the job, and prohibiting the payment of wages in goods) that the government had approved. Most important, Garland argued that laws that could conceivably be applied to industrial establishments in Lima and other manufacturing centers in the country were not applicable, indeed were "completely inadequate," in "the isolated and solitary Andean regions" where most mines were located: "The social condition, the level of culture and the Republic's topography are so diverse that a uniform labor law to fit all the political circumstances of the vast national territory would be an unjust law and a law that would prove impossible to implement."[65]

The SNM's objection to the proposal put forward by Vidaurre points to the assumptions that underpinned elite ideas about the differentiated nature of Peru's laboring peoples. If the "social condition" and "level of culture" of workers in the cities justified the implementation of modern legislation, it followed that in the "isolated and solitary" regions of the Andes—where, Garland implied, social and cultural conditions were inferior—such measures were not only unnecessary but also potentially counterproductive. The objections therefore reflected which sectors of the Peruvian population members of the elite like Alejandro Garland considered to be amenable to becoming the objects of "modern" labor legislation and which sectors they did not. Thus, the objections point to how elites like Garland viewed Peru's population in a differentiated way. As this document suggests, markers such as "social condition" and "level of culture," and therefore, as these categories imply in the Peruvian context, a racialized hierarchical conception of Peruvian workers, determined this differentiation. The urban worker was clearly deserving of the state's legislative oversight by virtue, it would seem, of the worker's urban residence and industrial occupation. By contrast, workers of the "isolated and solitary" regions of the Andes (to whom Garland refers in several places as "peons") were "inadequate" objects of legislative oversight, by virtue of their rural residence and nonindustrial occupation. What implicitly underpinned the SNM's objection was the belief that ultimately race differentiated these two types of worker, since race in Peru was and to some extent remains, firmly identified with, and defined by, urban/coastal or rural/highland residence.

The SNM's objections to Vidaurre's legislative proposal reflect the ways in which ideas about work and workers were deeply racialized in early twentieth-century Peru as several other documents reveal. Alberto Ulloa Sotomayor's "Social and Legal Organization of Labor in Peru," published in 1916, which one reviewer described as "a painful study because it lays bare the repugnant and sad sore that is our impossible mix of races, our social indiscipline, [and] the lack of direction of our imprecise and sporadic efforts," provides a privileged perspective on the racialization of ideas about workers.[66] Examining the relative aptitudes for work of the different "races" that composed the "working element," Ulloa Sotomayor noted that the Spanish Conquest "did not turn the vanquished race into a people apt for labor and civilization."[67] Although he had something to say about all five "races" (Indians, mestizos, whites, blacks, and Chinese), Ulloa Sotomayor focused on Indians and mestizos.[68] He rejected "the old dogma of the inferior races" and argued instead that the natural and historical environment shaped races. This was a widespread if not universal view, echoed some years later by Francisco Alayza Paz Soldán in his valedictory speech to the School of Arts and Trades: "We do not believe in the intellectual superiority of certain races. If the South American is relatively backward in terms of his political and industrial evolution it is not because of the mysterious influence of ethnicity, but for other reasons that the individual can overcome."[69] For Ulloa Sotomayor, the Indian's low aptitude for work owed to climatic conditions and the exploitation that Indians had historically suffered as well as to the ignorance in which they were kept (which contributed to their exploitation). The Indian, he suggested, had become practically devoid of morality (because for Indians religion too meant exploitation), and beholden to alcohol (in which they find "comfort and oblivion to make up for the harsh oppressiveness of life") and mind-numbing coca (which serves as "a palliative against tiredness and as a source of food").

Ulloa Sotomayor's views of the Indian as culturally and morally backward were not unusual for the time. They echoed the racist views of some of the most influential intellectuals of the early twentieth century in Peru, such as Clemente Palma, Alejandro Deustua, or the brothers Francisco and Ventura García Calderón.[70] They also echoed the views of Peru's "indigenista" intellectuals, such as Luis Valcarcel or Uriel García, who as Marisol de la Cadena, among others, has argued, rejected "biological" understandings of race and racial "degeneration" ("the old dogma" that Ulloa Sotomayor himself rejected) and favored cultural and environmental understandings.[71] More generally, his views reflected a broader racial thinking in Latin America. This thinking took various forms in different countries as several historians have shown. In countries with large indigenous populations, such as Mexico and Peru, it became characterized by the emergence of an "official" *indigenismo,* which combined a cultural exaltation of indigenous cultures (particularly those firmly situated in the past such as the Aztecs, the Mayas, and the Incas) with policies aimed at "redeeming" the indigenous by increasing access to education and public health (these policies were pursued with greater vigor in Mexico, where indigenismo became a rhetorical and political strategy of the revolutionary state, than in Peru). It also became characterized, in countries such as Mexico and Brazil, by the rise of a celebratory nationalist ideology of "mestizaje" or "racial democracy" or what we could call, more generally, racial hybridity, which sought to challenge the racial pessimism associated with European notions of racial purity by giving a "positive inflection . . . to interracial mixtures."[72]

Ulloa Sotomayor's views were not wildly original, but they are of interest because of the way in which he applied these racist and racial ideas to a discussion of the aptitude for work of different "races." He argued that the environmental and historical factors he delineated had

contributed to making "the Indian a bad worker, and . . . to the development of habits that make him avoid work during large parts of the year."
However, he insisted that this situation could be reversed through a
combination of protective laws and education. Here, again, we find reflected what historians, who have examined race and racism in the context of the rise of eugenics in early twentieth-century Latin America,
have argued convincingly: that racial thought in Latin America tended to
reject the rigid ideas of the permanent racial type and the degeneracy of
the hybrid (associated with Anglo-Saxon eugenics) and favored neo-
Lamarckian interpretations (associated with French eugenics), which
suggested that environmental factors could impact positively on genera-
tional inheritance.[73] But despite his rejection of the "old dogma of inferior races," Ulloa Sotomayor concluded his study in a way that illustrates how, in practice, "hard inheritance" and neo-Lamarckian "soft
inheritance" coexisted in the Peruvian context: "Since it would be utopian to expect that only laws, by suppressing inveterate abuses and pun-
ishing severely the system of exploitation today in use, could regenerate
the Indian and make of him an efficient component for work and the
national economy, let us look at ways of injecting into the aboriginal race
germs of improvement [gérmenes de mejoramiento], fostering his interchange and constant and incremental cross-breeding [cruce] with the
mestizo who, in the final analysis, must become the specifically Peruvian
product."[74]

The redemption of the Indian therefore, this analysis suggested, involved his transformation into a mestizo worker through the modification of his environment and of his genes. For Ulloa Sotomayor, the
mestizo (or "criollo"—he uses the terms interchangeably), who "constitutes the near totality of workers of the factories and workshops as
well as the agricultural population of the coast," is "a superior ethnic
type" compared to the Indian (mestizos, although inferior to Spaniards,
are, according to Ulloa Sotomayor, superior to their indigenous or African parentage and are not weakened noticeably by the contribution of
the Chinese to the racial mix).[75] These mestizo workers, however, are far
from optimal. Their dominant character is "a curious mix of servility and
haughtiness." On the one hand, they are perennially lazy, a probable
consequence of both an inheritance of Spanish indolence and the fact
that they have few needs. Mestizo workers have a tendency to work as
little as possible since most of their basic needs are easily met. Like the

Indian, they are prone to alcoholism, although in a lesser proportion, and are of low morality. This is particularly evident in the high proportion of illicit unions that characterize mestizo intimacy. But the mestizo worker is also prone to rebelliousness. According to Ulloa Sotomayor, the moment a mestizo worker identifies a "goal that he mistakenly believes he can attain," he becomes irascible and insolent "and since social and political exploiters often place before him the spectacle of absurd situations and goods, tense situations are brought about, and have been brought about lately, that, feigning a social question that does not exist, drag the working class into violent and sterile actions." However, Ulloa Sotomayor concluded that given a well-considered work regime and intensive education the mestizo worker could easily become "an element of progress and good."[76]

Like the cover of *Industria Peruana* discussed in the introduction, Ulloa Sotomayor's study points to how a highly racialized understanding of the Peruvian population shaped elite ideas about labor. As several historians have shown, early twentieth-century discourses on Peru were shaped by racialized views of the country that elites were intent on "modernizing," fueled by a desire to rebuild the country following the humiliation of defeat in the War of the Pacific (1879–84) and place it on a new path of "progress" by promoting the exploitation of the country's resources (particularly export commodities such as minerals, sugar, cotton, wool, and rubber). For Peru's elites the key obstacle to progress and modernity was located in the Andes and embodied by the Indian.[77] As such, given the dominant ideas about the sources and location of progress (the export and urban economy, the coast) and backwardness (the subsistence economy, the Andes), it is hardly surprising that, as Efraín Kristal has suggested, the Andes became increasingly invisible to Peru's coastal elites (hence, as discussed below, the repeated, and failed, attempts to promote European immigration in order to people an "empty" country).[78] Many agreed that Peru's indigenous communities deserved state protection from some of the more rapacious Andean *misti* landlords or *gamonales* and cultural redemption through education or "civilization." Others celebrated the glorious past of Andean civilizations.[79] But "the Andean" was largely absent from elite conceptions of Peru's future. In contrast to Argentina or Chile, or, indeed, the United States, in Peru the indigenous majorities were not physically eliminated in order to make way for "progress." However, they were eliminated from constructions of Peru's future or, as in the case of Ulloa Sotomayor and others, as I show below, incorporated insofar as they became, or could be transformed into, mestizo workers.

The idea that industrial work could redeem the Indian, by, in the final analysis, de-Indianizing him, played an important role in Peruvian social thought in the late nineteenth and early twentieth centuries, though scholars have tended to overlook this role.[80] In the 1880s, Luis Esteves challenged dominant racist interpretations of Peru's indigenous populations to argue that Indians could become, as Paul Gootenberg puts it, "the keystone of Peru's industrial future." According to Esteves, the industrial capacity of Indians needed to be "awakened," a task that required emancipating them from feudal oppression. Once free, their natural potential as workers would come to the fore: "It is no difficult task to make the Indian into an industrial being; [the Indians] enjoy gifts of imitation and patience, which are enough to transform them into useful workers, and their sobriety will keep them content with the most modest of salaries."[81] In the early twentieth century Francisco García Calderón reprised these ideas to argue in his celebrated *Le Pérou contemporain*, published in 1907, that the Indians, a "people of aged children," could be turned into productive beings, indeed into "remarkable workers," if governed by "wise tutelage." Once freed from their "local traditions, from their homes, from their monotonous and depressing surroundings" and placed in special schools and taught the Spanish language, the Indians' skills, "patience, attention to detail, a plastic precision," would help this "obeying race" with a real aptitude for discipline to overcome its ills, defined as "uniformity, a sterile monotony, and a secular somnolence." In this way, García Calderón suggested, the "Indian-agriculturalist" would be successfully transformed into an "Indian-worker."[82]

As this suggests, when Dr. Pedro Oliveira presented a paper at the National Congress of Mining Industry in 1918 in which he considered whether "work in the mines has been a factor of culture for the Indian laborers" he was addressing a question that many felt to be not only scientifically legitimate but of considerable national importance.[83] An article, entitled "The Indians: Their Economic Value," first published in the *Boletín de la Dirección de Fomento* (Bulletin of the Development Directorate) and reproduced in the journal *Economista Peruano* in late 1910, addressed this question directly: its author claimed that the Indian "still does not know work as it is understood in civilized nations." It followed that the duty of every state was to educate Indians "in modern physical work," not least because immigration could not realistically address the shortage of "hands." Moreover, one type of immigrant, the Asian, represented a threat to civilized countries, and in the final analysis, "the Indian race is superior and preferable to the yellow race." The education of the Indian would be achieved by placing foreign immigrants among the Indians ("Little by little they will become used to the pleasures that civilization offers if these are presented to them") and by forcing Indians to perform obligatory labor service, which, the author stressed, did not amount to slavery but rather to a civilizing enterprise that would teach Indians "the duties of man to his own person, to his fellow citizens, and to the state, which is to say the Fatherland." This education would include a demonstration of the superiority of the white race, which would enjoy certain privileges, "so that discipline may be exercised and authority represented." A racial division of labor would therefore ensue, with whites focusing on intellectual labor and Indians on manual labor. Finally, a combination of manual labor and good living and working conditions, to be guaranteed by the state and employers, would ensure that "Indians will soon become used to a life that, for now, they disdain."[84]

These ideas, and particularly the idea that the redemption of the indigenous involved the "awakening" of their capacity for labor, are particularly resonant in publications associated with Peru's agro-export sectors such as *El Agricultor, La Agricultura,* and the bulletin of the Sociedad Nacional de Agricultura (National Agricultural Society). Early in the 1900s, discussion of labor shortages emphasized the need for the state to implement an immigration policy that would favor the immigration of European laborers, "whose habits," one observer noted, "can adapt more easily to ours, and who possess all the attributes that will contribute to the improvement of the race."[85] Indeed, for many observers, European immigration promised to address not only the problem of labor shortages but the equally if not more important problem of the racial inferiority of the Peruvian population.[86] As Octavio Pardo argued in 1887, in addition to providing the labor to make productive Peru's fertile lands, "immigration must also contribute to improve the race, with a transfusion, if we may be allowed this word, of robust European blood; it is well known that in most of our [Latin American] countries we have white, Indian, and black races as well as the innumerable combinations and varieties that derive from them. How many of the so very serious obstacles that we have encountered in our political life result from our lack of [racial] homogeneity?"[87] Expressing a similar idea, another author replaced Pardo's blood metaphor with a reference to a plant's sap: "Unfortunately," the anonymous author lamented, "our western location, which places us at some distance from the Old World, has meant that, for a long time, we have not benefited from the sap that nourishes the organism of weak peoples." But the signing of an agreement between the Peruvian government and the Pacific Steamship Navigation Company to encourage Spanish immigration to Peru was a reason to celebrate, "because immigration leads to the improvement of the race, a truly transcendental issue, when we consider nations such as ours who are still in that incipient period of existence, when they need to nourish themselves with vital elements."[88]

By the 1920s, however, observers increasingly rejected immigration as a solution to labor shortages. Instead of Europeans, one commentator noted, Peru had received Asian immigrants, and this had contributed further to weakening the racial and social homogeneity of the country:

> Several of our coastal valleys were cultivated with the perverted assistance of exotic laborers, and this is why today their proletarian masses are constituted by heterogeneous elements who flaunt an unfortunate diversity in their physical vigor, in their sentiments, and in their ideals. If, in the ethnic realm, it is painful to observe the scene that our people compose, in the social realm, the future holds great difficulties. The nationalist ideal of *unity* [italics in original] will soon be a pretty utopia if a reactionary movement does not raise powerful barriers capable of impeding new imports of elements of those races.[89]

For this observer, the external solution to the problem of labor shortages had created new, and worse, problems. The real solution, he suggested, needed to be found locally:

> The Andean peon is strong, industrious, submissive, and has the stamina required for all types of labor tasks. Some have denied him intelligence, but experience and a serene and ample contemplation of his intellectual ability suggest to us that his lack of initiative and discernment are a consequence of the depressed and ignorant state in which he is kept. This is amply demonstrated when . . . he spends

some years on the coast where he adapts so well to the characteristics and requirements of various labor tasks that one has to ask why no one thought of solving the labor shortage problem with the great Andean proletarian mass whose migration to the coast would be easily achieved.[90]

Indians, then, could be turned into productive workers if removed from their backward environment.[91] It followed that the state had the responsibility to create conditions that would favor internal migration in order to provide labor to the agro-export sector and in order to "improve" the Indian: "It is the responsibility of . . . the state to study the best way to turn the large autochthonous population into a useful and efficient collectivity. Instead of pursuing exotic immigrations, we must raise the moral and social level of the Andean population."[92]

Other observers agreed: the time had come to harness the labor of Peru's indigenous masses, which were, in effect, yet another bountiful natural resource that Peru's elites were called upon to make productive for the greater glory of the nation. Rather than focus on foreign immigration, one commentator noted, Peru had to focus on the obstacles that had, in the past, stopped the country's indigenous people from becoming "a factor of industrial progress and an element to strengthen our nationality."[93] For this anonymous author, the obstacle that needed to be overcome was the "indigenous community," the sociolegal institution that many Andean people were members of, and within which they lived and labored as agriculturalists or pastoralists, a veritable barrier to progress because of the primitive production methods that characterized it, the fact that the members of the community failed to make full use of the land, that collective ownership meant that improvements to production were rarely made while it subtracted workers from other economic activities. However, the author warned that it was not enough to eliminate the indigenous community; the Indian needed to be educated in modern ways while markets and property rights needed to be created so that their modern production could find outlets: "Only in this way will the dissolution of the indigenous community succeed in incorporating the Indian into national life and will agricultural industries be able to profit from his valuable labor and effort."[94]

Although ideas about the Indian as a source of labor were beginning to change, some commentators continued to argue that Indians were only suitable for some types of work. In an article that considered the use of Indians in the colonization of Peru's Amazon region, Leopoldo Arnaud argued that the labor that Indians could perform was restricted: "I accept that a well-directed or ably led Indian can become a valuable and important assistant in the manual or mechanical tasks required by the agricultural industries, but given his current cultural level I do not think it prudent or sensible to give him responsibility for tasks that require a degree of inductive reasoning or leadership."[95] Among other reasons, Arnaud suggested, Indians would be unable to perform the work of a *colono* because they had no notion of the family, and by definition, colonization required the constitution of families: "The Indian ... is completely ignorant of the obligations that tie him to [the family] and to society." Indians would have to be restricted to basic manual labor. The Indian's role in the agricultural development of the country, Arnaud insisted, "is purely mechanical or purely material," by which he meant devoid of intellectual initiative. In particular, for Arnaud, the Indian was unsuitable for industrial labor.[96] Others, however, disagreed:

> Since the Indian represents the vast majority of our population, it is obvious that as long as he is barred from accessing better living conditions, which would allow him to change his parasitic ways, by including him in the life of progress, to which every man has a right, we will never be able to expect a significant development of the industries of our country. We must civilize the Indian, raise him to our level if possible, refrain from exploiting him, and we will have taken the first profitable and secure step for the benefit of our national industry.[97]

For this commentator, Indians could be usefully employed in modern industrial activities, but, like others, he believed that this could only occur after they had been "civilized."

Such views could be seen as mere justifications for the capture of Indian labor by either the state or capitalists eager to secure the cheapest form of labor and, as such, as yet another chapter in a long history of forced labor extraction that dates back to the early colonial period. Certainly, as a number of historians have shown, the belief that the Andean population was racially incapable of work combined with the limited capacity of a weak state apparatus to extract coerced labor forced Peruvian capitalists, particularly those engaged in agro-export sectors, to seek out alternative sources of labor. Early experiments with imported labor on the coast, particularly Chinese indentured laborers (who had first arrived in Peru during the guano boom of the mid-nineteenth century) and Japanese contract laborers, had mixed results, as we have seen.[98] As a consequence, the indigenous laborer, warts and all, was revalued in the eyes of the capitalist: "There is no better than our peon from Bamba-marca, even when drunk," one sugar plantation manager noted.[99] In the early decades of the twentieth-century, the sugar plantations and (to a lesser extent) cotton estates on the coast and the mines in the central highlands captured Andean labor through "enganche" or debt-peonage. This system of labor contracting was less opprobrious than some con-temporaries believed. It evolved as a byproduct of dynamic interregional economies linking, on the one hand, the northern coast and the highland regions of northern Peru and, on the other, the mines (particularly the Cerro de Pasco copper mine) and the valleys of the central highlands. A response to the needs of both planters and miners and of the Andean peasantry, by the 1920s seasonal enganche labor, which proved expen-sive and politically inconvenient, was abandoned gradually in favor of the constitution of a stable proletarianized labor force in the sugar planta-tions of the coast and mines of the central highlands, as a combination of push and pull factors (including environmental consequences of mining) drove peasants off their land.[100]

However, to interpret such views as mere instrumental justifications for the capture of Andean labor would be to overlook or misunderstand the powerful racialized assumptions that underpinned ideas about the differentiated nature of work and workers and about the role that Indians could play in Peru's industrial future. These ideas are reprised most clearly in a book titled *El problema del indio en el Perú*, by the director of Lima's School of Arts and Crafts, Francisco Alayza Paz Soldán, and pub-lished in 1928. In Alayza Paz Soldán's view, Peru's Indians were a source of backwardness, national weakness, and embarrassment. They consti-tuted a race "left behind on the march to progress, alien to our senti-ments, indifferent to our ideals, inert to our needs and suffering."[101] But they also constituted a "human capital," albeit a human capital "in a state of medieval uncultured backwardness, which exists in spiritual separa-tion from the rest of society." For Alayza Paz Soldán, who, as we have seen, believed passionately that industry and commerce were the source of a nation's greatness, it followed that "the problem of civilizing and incorporating the Indian into our national life is the deepest, most transcendental, problem we face." In solving this problem, he believed, Peru would become "a rich producer, a powerful entity."[102] He believed that, as descendants of a glorious civilization (the Incas), Peru's Indians were capable of overcoming their present backwardness. But they would need help, and that help would need to be provided in the shape of property rights, education, transport infrastructure, military service, and industrial work. In short, exposing Indians to a corrective environment would allow them to overcome their cultural backwardness.

In particular, Alayza Paz Soldán noted that Indians who were employed in industrial work were necessarily exposed to modern civilization, which "created interests and needs that radically modified their beliefs and habits." He commented with satisfaction that "the culture and civilization that the Cerro de Pasco metallurgical company . . . has developed in the apathetic Indian these last few years is truly remarkable. A veritable transformation has occurred at both the individual and collective level, particularly among the young. In being placed in civilizing conditions, the Indian has experienced a complete metamorphosis in ideas and sentiments."[103] Industry, in short, could redeem the Indian. As another author noted in 1930: "What the Indian needs, apart from land to cultivate, are factories, workshops, where he can learn to use all sorts of machinery, which is also a way of civilizing the Indian."[104] The extent to which such ideas were naturalized can be gauged from the fact that, some years later, the legal scholar Raúl Ferrero argued, in a study entitled "The Racial Destiny of Peru: Mestizaje" presented to the Twenty-seventh International Congress of Americanists: "Agrarianism turns the Indian into a base being, dominated by atavisms of rustic simplicity and servile and resigned submission. In contrast, the mestizo is an Indian redeemed of fatigue and automatism." Like others before him, Ferrero believed that if the Indian was removed "from the region he inhabits or his work system" he invariably changed for the better, though Ferrero warned that "when he returns to his land he is reabsorbed by his environment." For Ferrero mere contact with the "modern" world turned the Indian into a better being, into a mestizo: "Labor in the mines of the sierra and military service or debt-peonage in the haciendas of the coast, change the Indian. The pace of military life, the changed nutrition, or the new labor conditions experienced as an industrial wage earner force him to sharpen up in order to measure up to the agile temperament of the coastal dweller. The Indian who comes down to the coast is already a mestizo in spirit."[105]

The aspiration that such views spelled out, and which was unambiguously expressed in the cover of *Industria Peruana* discussed in the introduction to this book, was that industrialization would present Peru with a solution to its most pressing of problems: the inadequate nature of its population. As an article in the same journal noted, labor in most of Peru remained largely unmechanized and indigenous productive activities had changed little for a thousand years: "This is no longer backwardness, it is barbarism." The solution was to industrialize indigenous production for the good of the nation: "Peru will become strong when the Indian becomes apt."[106] These were not views exclusive to the oligarchy or to those who, like Ferrero, were firmly on the right of the political spectrum. José Carlos Mariátegui, Peru's most important intellectual figure of the twentieth century and the pioneer of Peruvian Marxism, shared many of the assumptions already examined. As is well known, Mariátegui rejected the openly racist views of Indians of many of his contemporaries even if he did not fully escape the racialized assumptions of the time.[107] But like his contemporaries, he viewed the condition of Indians, and indeed Afro-Peruvians, as a "problem" that needed to be solved.[108] For Mariátegui too, the resolution of the "problem" involved a transition away from a necessarily backward state to, in his case, socialism: "Whether the Indian rises materially and intellectually depends on changing the socioeconomic conditions. . . . His emancipation will be assured by a dynamic economy and culture that contains the seeds of socialism."[109] This transition, Mariátegui argued, could only be achieved through a phase of industrialization that necessarily involved the proletarianization of Peru's population.

Thus, although Mariátegui rejected the racism of his contemporaries, he nevertheless reproduced the idea of industry and proletarianization as factors of cultural redemption, as in this discussion on Afro-Peruvians: "The black or the mulatto, as artisans and domestic servants, represented the plebe that the feudal class could always count upon more or less unconditionally. By eliminating racial barriers between proletarians, class consciousness elevates the black man both morally and historically."[110] Similarly, Mariátegui presented the cultural redemption of Peru's Indians as dependent on the destruction of a feudalism that kept

Indians in a state of stagnation and servitude by a transition to socialism through industrialization:

> Without the material elements that modern industry creates, or to put it another way, without capitalism, is it possible to formulate the plan, or even the intention, of a socialist state based on the grievances and the emancipation of the indigenous masses? The dynamic character of this economy, of this regime that makes all relations unstable, and that opposes classes and ideologies, is without a doubt what makes possible the resurrection of the Indian, a fact that will be decided by the interplay of economic, political, cultural, and ideological forces, but not of racial forces.[111]

For Mariátegui too, then, the Indian *qua Indian*, as opposed to the Indian *qua worker*, was incommensurable with his vision of Peru's socialist future.

Such ideas were similarly integral to the political ideology and social philosophy of APRA, the political party that profoundly shaped Peruvian political life from the 1930s onward. In the foundational text, *El antiimperialismo y el APRA*, Víctor Raúl Haya de la Torre, the party's founder and ideologue, reproduced many of the racialized ideas of Indians as members of a fallen culture, whose "ignorance of the reasons that brought about their state of slavery forces them to be superstitious and mystical."[112] Indians, once members of a great civilization, he suggested, would be made productive again thanks to APRA's policies. Although he celebrated the collective means of production supposedly favored by indigenous communities, Haya de la Torre argued that these would only be made truly productive through the redemptive influence of APRA upon the Indians and their world: "The vindication of the Indian as a man and of his [social] system as method of production is imperative for economic reasons." This influence would incorporate the Indian into the national future that APRA would trace: "The basis [of the economic transformation of Indo-America] is to be found in the millions of agricultural and mine workers who champion as a sacred yearning for the future the reestablishment of a social system of the past. Reestablished in essence or modernized by modern technology, we will have used the past like no other people, in conditions favorable to accelerating the arrival of the future."[113] The Indian, in short, would be made into a productive, socially useful being through his effective incorporation into modern society as a consequence of APRA's social and economic policy.

The ideas about the Indian expressed by Haya de la Torre were formulated in a more explicit (and less rhetorical) way by Rómulo Meneses, a party cadre from Arequipa. Meneses died while in jail in the early 1930s, but managed to produce a short booklet that discussed several of the party's objectives. In considering whether "the indigenous class is a proletarian class," Meneses concluded, "No, obviously. It is a category of racial masses that lacks an authentic goal, [a category] devoid of culture, devoid of consciousness."[114] Meneses noted that Indians "do not even possess a revolutionary ferment of defined demands," as demonstrated by the fact that all indigenous uprisings had resulted in failure. For Meneses, the Indian could not be a proletarian because he could not sell his labor and lived in a semifeudal world. But this situation could change, Meneses suggested:

> When the Peruvian and neighboring Andes enter a phase of effective capitalization, when the system of exploitation of land and its products changes its methods, by means of its restitution to those who work it, when the large landholdings are parceled out, "promoting the most efficient use of the wealth produced for the benefit of society" (Haya de la Torre); that is to say, when we succeed in incorporating the indigenous as a modern factor of production and consumption, then, without needing to resort to the prosody of mentioning antislavery rights in constitutions that are honored in the breach, the material force of things will take care of resolving the medieval situation in which are found our great ethnic masses, amorphous in the terrain of class, by destroying their present servitude and transforming them progressively into true collectivized peasant classes.[115]

Again, in this understanding, Indians would be turned into productive and socially useful beings through their incorporation, indeed transformation, into something else, in this case a collectivized peasant class. Like Mariátegui, APRA's ideologues believed that little could be expected from Indians qua Indians. Indians had to be transformed into productive beings, into workers, and, in order to achieve this transformation they necessarily had to cease being Indians.

CONCLUSION

"Without industry, there is no nation." As this chapter has shown, this aphorism and the image on the cover of *Industria Peruana* discussed in the introduction illustrate how labor policy in early twentieth-century Peru was shaped by the ways in which Peruvian elites came to associate the "Indian problem" with Peru's backwardness and the "labor question," warts and all, with Peru's industrial, "civilized," and "modern" (as well as white/mestizo) future. The labor question, I have argued, was racialized in Peru to a greater extent than in many other countries. In considering the racialization of labor policy in Peru, I draw on David Theo Goldberg's suggestion that in making sense of the interplay of race and state formation we need to pay attention "not just [to] the way the state is implicated in reproducing more or less local conditions of racist exclusion, but how the modern state has always conceived of itself as racially configured."[116] For Peru's elites, to answer the labor question in Peru was not merely to address the problems that, in Peru as in other countries, came to be associated with the rise of industrialism and the formation of organized labor. In Peru, for social progressives such as Francisco Alayza Paz Soldán, conservatives such as Raúl Ferrero, and even radicals such as Mariátegui, to answer the labor question was to resolve the fundamental problem of Peruvian nation-state formation: the obstacle to progress represented by Peru's indigenous population. To answer the labor question in Peru was to eliminate the racial obstacles to progress thanks to the power (magic?) of industry to transform Peru's backward indigenous peoples into civilized white/mestizo industrial workers. For this reason, and despite the fears expressed at the social and political threat that the development of organized labor represented, workers came to play a central, if disproportionate, role in state formation and national politics in the first half of the twentieth century.

Although workers represented only a small proportion of Peru's laboring peoples, they were subjected to far more attention from the state (and from Peru's political parties), proportionate to their size, than Peru's far more numerous rural and indigenous peoples for most of the twentieth century because, unlike Indians, who were envisioned as obstacles to progress, workers were envisioned as agents of progress.[117] This is not to argue that the rural and indigenous population received no attention from the state or to ignore the various indigenista projects, whether top-down or bottom-up, that shaped social policy.[118] Rather, as the following chapters show, the interplay of race, labor, and the state in the Peruvian context reveals the ways in which "the modern state . . . founds itself not just on exclusions, those absences that render invisible, but on the internalization of exclusions."[119] As I discuss in the chapters that follow, the Peruvian state in the early twentieth century developed primarily as a labor state. That is to say, it developed as a state of and for labor, constituted by, and constitutive of, a project of governmentality that reflected the idea that labor was a valuable resource, an agent of progress, and that the purpose of the state was to protect and improve that valuable resource. It developed in a way that revealed the particular allure of labor in the Peruvian context. At the same time, it developed as a state expressive of the belief that Indians qua Indians were incommensurable with progress and, therefore, as a state whose ultimate, and fundamental, purpose was to redeem and rebuild the nation by eliminating the Indian.

2

CONSTITUTING LABOR

During the 1921 strikes in the Chicama valley, the main sugar-
growing region in northern Peru, employees of a newly created
state institution distributed a pamphlet that explained article 48
of the recently enacted 1920 constitution.[1] The article established compulsory arbitration in labor disputes. After detailing
the constitutional article, the pamphlet went on to point out the
benefits of arbitration, which, it noted, was merely a variant of
direct action. Strikes were unlikely to succeed if not properly
organized. However, those unions that embarked on a dispute
with the full support of the constitution could be guaranteed
success: "Only arbitration, which places the bosses and the
workers on an equal footing, makes it possible to discuss amply
and in detail each of the grievances included in your demands
and therefore contribute to the triumph of the worker's aspirations, which are almost always born of unsatisfied needs."[2] Interestingly for a government publication, the pamphlet echoed
anarchist themes and the polemical style common to worker
publications of the time. However, the message and the purpose
of the pamphlet were very different. At one level, as the quota-
tion above illustrates, the pamphlet, and the institution that had
produced it, sought to limit the systematic and highly disruptive
recourse to the strike that marked a number of labor disputes in
the late 1910s and early 1920s and to promote state-mediated
arbitration as an alternative. More broadly, the pamphlet, the
constitutional article it promoted, and the institution created to

implement that article are evidence of the consolidation of the new conception of labor policy that had begun to take shape in the 1890s, as examined in the previous chapter. The institution in question was the Sección del Trabajo of the Ministerio de Fomento (Labor Section of the Ministry of Development), created in 1919.

The creation of the Sección del Trabajo, and the labor policy that it promoted, would appear to confirm standard narratives that suggest that labor policy in early twentieth-century Peru, and particularly in the second presidency of Augusto B. Leguía (1919–30), the period known as the *oncenio* (eleven-year rule) or Patria Nueva (New Fatherland), was in essence reactive to the labor question, an attempt to placate or neutralize growing labor mobilization.[3] President Leguía himself argued in this manner, telling the Peruvian Congress in 1920 that "the multiplication of strikes and work stoppages, in tandem with the disorders that, thanks to subversive propaganda, tend to accompany them, has made it necessary to create the Sección del Trabajo, in the Ministry of Development, whose function is to impose the calming arbitration process, as indicated by article 48 of the constitution."[4] Certainly, an "atmosphere of class struggle," in Peru as elsewhere in the world, shaped the conjuncture that saw the creation of the Sección del Trabajo.[5] The general strike of December 1918–January 1919, which ended with the passing of the eight-hour day law on 15 January, and, perhaps more important, the May 1919 food riots, were pivotal moments in the history of Peruvian organized labor and in the history of Peruvian politics.[6] The role of labor agitation in shaping labor policy, or, concretely, in bringing about the creation of the Sección del Trabajo should not be easily dismissed. But, as I suggest in this chapter, interpretations that focus exclusively on the reactive character of labor policy, or that see labor policy as being brought about exclusively by labor agitation, are incomplete.

Although many historians agree that it was a pivotal historical period, there exist surprisingly few serious scholarly studies of the Patria Nueva or, indeed, of labor policy during Leguía's eleven-year rule.[7] The Patria Nueva continues to be understood as a flawed project of modernization expressive of an aspiration to reestablish and reorient the nation that had been humiliated by the catastrophe of the War of the Pacific (1879–84) on a new path to progress that marked a departure in terms of state-society relations. Historians typically argue that the political order that came to be known as the República Aristócratica (Aristocratic Republic,

1895–1919) was characterized by an incipient agent state dominated by an oligarchy represented by the Partido Civil (hence the oligarchy's identification as *civilistas*, that is, members of the Civil Party). In turn, they suggest that the Patria Nueva was characterized by the development of a relatively autonomous state and by the expansion of the state's cognitive and coercive capacity reflective of a modernizing project more socially inclusive than that pursued by preceding governments.[8] Some years ago, for example, Steve Stein suggested that the Leguía period established the conditions for the emergence of "mass politics."[9] More recently, Augusto Ruiz Zevallos has suggested that in the changes that resulted from the events of 1919 (that is to say the general strike for the eight-hour day, the subsistence strikes of early 1919, and the rise to power of Leguía on the shoulders of the urban working class) "we can find the beginnings of the populist state and the historical and social roots of the programmatic proposals of the main political movements of the twentieth century—such as APRA, Christian Democrats–PPC, Acción Popular and the left-wing parties."[10]

I suggest in this chapter that the transformations of the Patria Nueva are best understood not primarily as an expansion of state capacity but rather as the coming into being of a new project of rule that created, and was expressed through, a new role for the state.[11] In this project, the state was called upon to protect the population, enhance its well-being, to "improve" it, through the disciplinary inculcation of new habits and practices but also through the management of its immediate and mediate environment. The Sección del Trabajo, I show, illustrates how this project of governmentality unfolded in the sphere of labor. I begin by examining the early attempts to make labor "legible," which focused on creating institutions, in effect precursors to the Sección del Trabajo, and which expressed rationalities of government in the sphere of labor (i.e., expressed a project to protect and improve labor) and sought to frame labor as an object of state intervention. I turn next to examine how the 1920 constitution clearly envisioned such rationalities of government. I then examine how the Sección del Trabajo was key to making labor "technical" and show the importance of this process to the success of the labor relations promoted by the Leguía regime. I argue that the early success of the institution in channeling labor disputes is best understood as the outcome of labor's coproduction of what I call the "labor state" and that the Sección del Trabajo is best understood as a technology of government expressive, and in turn constitutive, of the labor state. Finally, I discuss the ways in which the Sección del Trabajo reflected, and reinforced, through its exclusions from the sphere of labor of certain laboring peoples, specifically of the indigenous, the broader racialized assumptions about labor that shaped labor policy in this period.

MAKING LABOR LEGIBLE

Although not created until 1919, the idea of a Sección del Trabajo was not new. In 1904, the labor code proposals drawn up by the educationalist and congressman José Matías Manzanilla included plans for a national labor board. Although the labor code proposals did not prosper, the following year Manzanilla persisted and presented to Congress legislation in favor of, again, a "National Labor Board." According to Manzanilla's proposal, the board would be composed of a senator, two lower-house deputies, and three academics (one from the Political and Administrative Sciences Faculty, another from the Jurisprudence Faculty, and a third from the Medicine Faculty at Lima's San Marcos University), as well as four workers and four employers. Whereas the politicians and the academics would be nominated by their "respective institutions," the executive would designate the workers and employers. All would serve for four years and would be entitled to renew their positions. The board's functions included providing advice to the government on labor issues, preparing labor laws, studying the legislation of foreign countries on labor matters, collecting statistical material on industrial employment, and undertaking investigations into "the moral, intellectual, political and economic state of the working classes." The law gave the board extensive powers: the authority to intervene in labor disputes and to resolve, in the last instance, those disputes that were taken to arbitration; the power to approve (or reject) the statutes of "industrial and worker societies" and to adjudicate on their legality; and the entitlement to fine anyone who contravened the labor laws.[12]

Manzanilla's labor board proposals seem to have been the model on which were based the *secciones obreras* (worker sections), established in 1913 by President Guillermo Billinghurst (1912–14). Later closed down by President Óscar R. Benavides (1914–15) during his first term of office, these secciones obreras were housed in the police stations of Lima and Callao.[13] As their statutes indicate, the secciones obreras had been set up in light of "the latest labor agitation and in consideration of public and social interest."[14] Their function was mainly to collect labor statistics but extended to the inspection of industrial establishments and granting official recognition to worker societies. In addition to registering the number of industrial establishments, the number of workers, and wage rates, the secciones obreras were also charged with reporting on the construction costs of worker housing and on the rent paid by working-class tenants, determining population density in working-class districts, and analyzing the cost of living and the prices of subsistence goods. Other statistical functions included the setting up of registers of work-related accidents and of unemployed workers (thus allowing the secciones obreras to "provide industrialists with the number of workers that they require"). The statutes also envisaged the creation of a "Labor Bulletin," to be published on a monthly basis, that would reproduce both the statutes of the worker societies and the regulations of industrial establishments and be made available free of charge to all. Finally, and importantly, the statutes established that it was the responsibility of the secciones obreras to "process and register" all the documentation related to strikes and stoppages that were now regulated by the recently enacted strike law.[15]

The secciones obreras did not prosper. But their brief existence points to the emergence of strong support for such an institution among certain sectors of the elite and, more broadly, for the idea that the state had to acquire and develop the capacity to make labor "legible" so that it could be acted upon.[16] Several of the social reformers encountered in the previous chapter contributed to the debates on the need for such an institution. As early as 1905, Luis Miro Quesada, a student of Manzanilla's and, like his teacher, one of Peru's pioneering social reformers, called for the creation of an industrial council, whose functions were to include overseeing the implementation of the new labor laws being discussed at the time, inspecting industrial establishments, and settling strikes by means of an "arbitration and conciliation tribunal."[17] In his 1916 doctoral dissertation, Alberto Ulloa Sotomayor, a young up-and-coming jurist, later to become one of Peru's most distinguished "internationalists," also picked up on Manzanilla's proposal, and argued that "there is no doubting the need for this National Labor Board." Ulloa Sotomayor suggested that in addition to the board, a Sección del Trabajo should be set up in the Ministry of Development, in order to administer all issues relative to labor and to keep statistics, without which, he insisted, it was impossible to assess the impact of existing labor laws or the need for new ones. He also called for the creation of a corps of inspectors to supervise industrial establishments and to determine whether the labor laws were being observed in various parts of the country.[18] In 1917, Juan Angulo de Puente Arnao, an eminent lawyer, suggested similarly, echoing the arguments put forward by Miro Quesada and Ulloa Sotomayor, that a General Directorate of Labor be set up within the Ministry of Development.[19]

These proposals, or "projects of legibility," held the promise of a "synoptic vision" of labor that would allow the state to act by disciplining labor—by establishing the parameters of acceptable behavior in the workplace as well as in the home and the community—but also through projects of "improvement." The proposals reflected rationalities of discipline but also rationalities of government that aimed to protect labor and enhance its well-being. In putting forward their proposals, the social reformers underlined the fact that the establishment of the institutions they envisaged would put an end to workers' highly disruptive recourse to the strike. Miro Quesada, for example, pointed out that the industrial tribunal that he envisaged would promptly resolve strikes "in the unlikely circumstances that they would arise once the indicated measures have been adopted."[20] Similarly, Puente Arnao concluded that his labor department would eliminate the likelihood of strikes: "Because once the capitalist, the worker and the state develop an intimate relationship through the administrative office whose creation I am proposing, all conflicts will be easy to resolve."[21] But the social reformers also pointed to broader functions of these institutions, and implicitly, of the state, in reshaping and improving the conditions that workers faced in the workplace and, to a lesser extent, in their communities. Typically, these new state roles were justified with reference to their existence in "more advanced" countries, that is, Europe and the United States. The evolution of other countries, Puente Arnao suggested, for example, showed that the state had a role to play in bringing the warring social forces, capital and labor, into a harmonious relationship.[22]

The fact that such rationalities of discipline and government with regard to labor were increasingly reproduced in the public sphere points to the extent to which they were becoming influential beyond a small coterie of legal experts and social reformers. In 1917, the newspaper *Ilustración Obrera* ran a number of articles lamenting the "groundless" decision of the Benavides government to close down the secciones obreras set up during the Billinghurst administration and argued in favor of their reestablishment. However, the periodical suggested that the envisioned "Labor Office" should not be housed in the police stations, as before, but rather be part of the Ministry of Government and that the ministry should organize a "great register or catalogue" of employed and unemployed workers. This statistical exercise would result in a "positive control" of the working classes as it would allow the state to weed out "the bad elements who infiltrate them, and who, for the most part, are foreigners [and] who hail from other parts with the goal of inculcating in them subversive and anarchist ideas that end up demoralizing them and pushing them to aggressive and dangerous excesses."[23] But while necessary, the newspaper stressed, this coercive role was insufficient. In order to avoid militancy, the periodical argued that it was necessary to establish a commission, "which by visiting the industrial centers and firms will gain an understanding of the life of the worker, his nutrition, the remuneration which must be in accordance with his needs, his housing which gives him shelter and of all such details that must be known in every collectivity that lacks protective laws and the guarantees to shield it from the abuse of despotic capital."[24]

Such rationalities were even shared by some workers who also saw the need for such an institution. Although there is limited information on whether it was put into operation, in 1914 the Confederación de Artesanos Union Universal (CAUU, Confederation of Artisans Universal Union), an umbrella artisan organization, set up a "Bolsa de Trabajo" (labor exchange) under the direction of Adrián Zubiaga, an artisan.[25] The CAUU's Bolsa de Trabajo clearly was intended to fulfill a similar role as the institutions envisaged by Manzanilla, Miro Quesada, and others, since it counted among its goals "to serve as an intermediary between the supply and demand of labor, establishing a permanent relationship between the interested parties and enabling the placement of workers and employees and organizing statistics and exact information on the labor market." In addition, the labor exchange would "contribute to the satisfactory solution of labor conflicts" and, perhaps more ambitiously, "help bring about the expansion of national industries." In short, the Bolsa de Trabajo saw its function as "undertaking all actions that will help ease the situation of the worker and to harmonize the interests of the two classes: capital and labor." Like Ulloa Sotomayor, Zubiaga justified his proposal with reference to developments in Europe, and noted that labor exchanges "are considered in the European nations to be one of the just demands of the working class."[26]

What such proposals and commentaries reveal is the growing consensus regarding the need to develop channels to protect and improve labor, or, put otherwise, the need to develop technologies of government in order to operationalize the now largely hegemonic rationalities of government in the sphere of labor. This is clearly in evidence in the second legislative project that Manzanilla presented to Congress in 1918, which called for the creation of a General Directorate and Inspectorate of Labor as a subunit of the Ministry of Development. Manzanilla justified the 1918 legislative project in light of "the current state of ideas and the realities of Peru" and of the fact that the peace treaty that had put an end to the war in Europe had established a permanent organization of international legislation "to favor workers."[27] This project echoed Manzanilla's earlier project, but it featured a series of changes and extensions that clearly incorporated the suggestions put forward by Miro Quesada, Ulloa Sotomayor, and Angulo de Puente Arnao, and indeed those expressed in the *Ilustración Obrera* articles and the CAUU's Bolsa de Trabajo project. These changes reflect how ideas about the labor question had evolved in a decade. Whereas the earlier project envisaged a broad representation on the labor board's executive (with politicians, academics, workers, and employers), the new law proposed a purely technical (perhaps even technocratic) membership (including a director, a secretary who doubled-up as chief of publicity, two section chiefs, two first-order officers, four second-order officers, two medical inspectors, two engineering inspectors, and a further number of inspectors to be determined by the executive). Precise indications that point to a clearer idea of the role that the state could and should perform in relation to the labor question now replaced the relatively vague functions of the labor board included in the earlier proposal.

Manzanilla's 1918 project still called for investigations "on the moral, intellectual and economic state" of workers, but "especially on their wages and salaries in relation to the cost of foodstuffs, housing and clothing." Similarly, the statistical functions of the new General Directorate were more clearly spelled out: it would "carry out a census of the working population and [produce] statistics on labor issues, particularly strikes, industrial accidents, and professional diseases." The new law also extended the functions of the General Directorate to the education and moralization of the working population: it would publish pamphlets attacking alcoholism and promoting safety and hygiene in the workplace and the home and would establish a museum that would house "models and protective apparatus . . . and statistical graphs on the consequences of a lack of personal care." Finally, the new law envisaged a far more active role for the General Directorate through its labor inspectors, who were given the power to enter and inspect all places of work, demand that industrialists observe labor laws, fine these industrialists if they failed to follow their orders, order the removal of women and children from establishments that infringed the laws pertaining to them, and finally close down establishments that broke the Sunday rest law.

The differences between the two proposals suggest a shift toward a more technical understanding of the role of the state in relation to the labor question. The technicization of labor relations envisioned by Manzanilla's second proposal reflected a growing consensus among social reformers that politics ought to be evacuated from the sphere of labor, as I discuss below. As Ulloa Sotomayor argued, it was necessary to establish an institution "that is as independent as possible from the actions of the government, not only in its constitution but also in its functioning," in order to avoid powerful influences "intervening in a pernicious way in labor issues."[28] But the most important aspect of Manzanilla's new proposal, which incorporated ideas put forward in the various commentaries to the original proposal, was the idea that the state, ultimately, had to fulfill not merely a disciplinary role but primarily a governmental role. Indeed, the General Directorate proposed by Manzanilla would seek not only to resolve conflicts between workers and employers but also actively to shape labor relations and workers (and employers) themselves by seeking to improve them. Such projects sought not only to make labor "legible" but to constitute labor as an object of state action. More generally, they sought to impose, as Bourdieu suggests, "a particular vision of the state, a vision in agreement with the interests and values associated with the particular position of those who produce them in the emerging bureaucratic universe."[29] But in so doing they also brought into being a particular idea of labor: labor as a factor (indeed, a partner) in the elite project of national redemption and "improvement"; labor as an agent of progress.

also contained several articles, grouped in a special section entitled "Social Guarantees," that outlined a new role for the state in the sphere of labor.[35] Article 47 established that it was the prerogative of the state to legislate on the organization of industrial work and on safety in the workplace, in order to safeguard life, health, and hygiene; to set the "maximum conditions" of work (i.e., the length of the working day) and a minimum wage; and made compensation obligatory for work-related accidents. Articles 48 and 49 established that conflicts between "Labor" and "Capital" would be resolved by compulsory arbitration and that conciliation and arbitration tribunals would be established for that purpose. Other articles pointed to a more overt governmental role for the state. Articles 55 and 56 established that the state had a duty to foment sanitation and public assistance through the creation of hospitals, asylums and institutes, and to protect children and the "needy classes" as well as to develop institutions of "social foresight and solidarity, savings and insurance establishments, and production and consumption cooperatives whose goal is to improve the condition of the popular classes." Article 57 established that in "extraordinary circumstances" the state would be entitled to act in order to reduce the prices of basic consumption goods, although "under no circumstances will it be able to expropriate goods without compensation."

The 1920 constitution represented a turning point from the point of view of the labor role of the state, since it expanded the power of the state by positioning it, both rhetorically and administratively, as the legitimate mediator between labor and capital while at the same time establishing a broader state responsibility for the protection and well-being of workers. As one contemporary commentator noted: "The new Peruvian constitution is inspired by the idea of a new scientific socialism; it favors the intervention of the state on behalf of those who need its protection while respecting the freedom of industry and commerce."[36] Arguably the impetus for this new role came from a combination of transnational and local developments. Certainly, international labor conventions agreed at the first annual International Labor Conference, which met in Washington beginning on 29 October 1919, inspired the articles included in the "Social Guarantees" section of the 1920 constitution. However, although the constitutional articles clearly made reference to the first six international labor conventions, which dealt with hours of work in industry, unemployment, maternity protection, night work for women, minimum age, and night work for young persons in industry, at least some of them had already, if recently, passed into law. Thus although transnational developments clearly influenced the 1920 constitution—it was a product of constitutional diffusionism—it also reflected local developments in relation to labor policy. As we have seen, the 1920 constitution in fact capped several years of social legislation and state intervention in the sphere of labor.

As critics of the constitution's "Social Guarantees" understood well, the constitution not only expanded the labor role of the state. It brought into being that which it identified as a legitimate object of state intervention: labor. The lawyer Carlos Aurelio León, for example, suggested that compulsory arbitration was "an idealism that is not applicable to Peru, where there is no industrialization, or real social questions." Its implementation, León suggested, was therefore unwarranted and, in fact, dangerous, since those who supported it also supported the workers' right to strike, and thus were sending out the message that the rulings of the arbitration tribunal could be ignored. Moreover, León argued, the incorporation of compulsory arbitration as a constitutional principle suggested that solutions needed to be found to social problems that did not exist: "This extemporaneous law creates artificial needs; and the labor problem, which is incipient only in Lima and Trujillo, more as a consequence of a spirit of imitation than because it reflects an urgent need for social betterment, does not exist nor will it ever attain in Peru, which is a country that has a small population but large and endless [natural] resources, the tragic character that it has acquired elsewhere." Indeed, León insisted, Peruvian workers enjoyed relatively high wages and had little reason to raise grievances with employers or to strike. The transitory conditions created by the European war and a "spirit of imitation" had led "the masses into a situation of intolerance and extreme demands that can undermine their own cause and the future of the country"; but, clearly, León seemed to suggest, this was no justification for the constitutional reform that aimed to address a problem that could easily be resolved by the direct intervention, violent or otherwise, of the political authorities.[37]

Like earlier labor legislation examined in the previous chapter, then, the 1920 constitution constituted labor by identifying it as an object of state intervention, an engendering legitimized by the universality of precepts that underpinned the articles that conformed its "Social Guarantees." But, just as important, it constituted labor by establishing a strict distinction—indeed a literal distinction, given the organization of the constitution's articles into separate sections—between "workers" and "Indians." What is remarkable about the 1920 constitution is the way in which it created completely separate constitutional regimes, and consequently separate, economic, political, juridical, and cultural "constitutional existences," for workers and Indians. These different regimes reflected not primarily ideas about what we could think of as the different realities that "workers" and "Indians" experienced (their experience of the material: factory work versus subsistence agriculture; the exploitation of the industrialist versus the exploitation of the landowner or *gamonal*) but rather ideas about the very essence of "workers" and "Indians." It was, indeed, the underlying belief in the incommensurable natures of workers and Indians, explored in the previous chapter, that made it imperative, and, in turn, natural and uncontroversial, for the state to develop separate spheres of action, indeed two distinct projects of legibility, with regard to them. This separation was confirmed, and made into institutional practice, with the establishment of the Sección del Trabajo and the Sección de Asuntos Indígenas as two distinct and separate institutions in the Ministry of Development.

MAKING LABOR TECHNICAL

There is little doubt that the immediate objective of Leguía's "prolabor" measures, and particularly of the Sección del Trabajo, was to limit labor unrest and reestablish labor discipline in the workplace. The Sección del Trabajo was created in a political context marked by severe instability. The relative success of the 1918–19 strikes, which coincided with the electoral process that resulted in the rise to power of Leguía, gave the incipient labor movement a newly found confidence: workers began to strike on an unprecedented scale in order to wrest concessions from employers. "During the last months," noted the British minister in October 1919, "strikes have been a daily occurrence. . . . Among the recent strikes have been the following: Central Railway, Southern Railway, tramways, light and power supply, textiles, dockmen, watermen, clerks, printers, telephone operators."[38] According to the British minister the wave of strikes resulted in a general rise in workers' wages of 25 to 30 percent. For some observers there existed a community of interest between striking workers and Leguía: in April 1919, for example, a police report noted that the campaign led by Carlos Barba, a shoemaker, to bring about a strike in order to force the government to reduce the price of subsistence goods was in fact a campaign in favor of Leguía's candidacy.[39] Certainly, once in power, Leguía was quick to introduce a series of measures to placate working-class discontent, including a decree that established that landowners had to devote at least 15 percent of their land to foodstuff production and that placed a price cap on meat sold in markets and in butchers' stores, and instituted greater controls aimed at eradicating price speculation. Taken together, the stipulations contributed to a fall in the price of most major foodstuffs.[40]

However, Leguía's prolabor measures and the creation of the Sección del Trabajo also reflected a fundamental change in the way those who newly governed the country understood the relationship between labor and the state and translated that relationship into policy. Measures such as the cap on food prices were part of a broader package of policies ostensibly aimed at improving the working and living conditions that urban workers faced and included the extension of the eight-hour working day law to all industrial workers; a cap on housing rents that did not exceed ten Peruvian pounds (Law 4123); and a law that projected the construction of a hundred houses for "native-born" blue-collar workers and public employees who had served the state for more than five years. The "revolutionary" tone (in evidence, for example, in the pamphlet distributed to the striking sugar workers in 1921), if not character of labor policy in the early 1920s, was a consequence of the purge of the civilista bureaucracy following Leguía's rise to power. Many of the incoming officials were, by comparison, social progressives, including the minister of government, Germán Leguía y Martínez, a cousin of the president, and Lauro Curletti, who became minister of development. Their presence in the higher echelons of the state bureaucracy created an intellectual climate that favored the introduction of new labor legislation. But the design and character of labor policy was largely the work of men further down the bureaucratic apparatus but also further along the progressive scale.

The key role played by progressives and even radicals in shaping labor policy in the early years of the Patria Nueva was most clearly in evidence in the Sección del Trabajo.[41] Erasmo Roca, a lawyer and erstwhile contributor to the anarchist periodical *La Protesta*, was largely responsible for the office's early organization.[42] In addition to the section chief, Roca, in the early 1920s the Sección del Trabajo was staffed by provincial intellectuals such as Hildebrando Castro Pozo, who went on to head the Sección de Asuntos Indígenas, and Agustín Haya de la Torre, whose brother, Víctor Raúl, was the founder and leader of APRA.[43] The incorporation of these "progressives" and "radicals" with strong ties to, and sympathies with, organized labor reflected the political moment (the purge of the civilista bureaucracy meant that a new bureaucracy had to be established). But it also reflected an attempt by the Leguía government to incorporate a "situated knowledge" on labor that would allow state officials further up the bureaucratic structure "to rule more effectively."[44] The incorporation of progressives into the government corresponded to a broader transnational pattern, particularly evident in the United States during the First World War, when, as Rodgers notes, the army recruited many social progressives for their expertise in hygiene, morale, and welfare and as "labor relations experts, mediators, industrial welfare specialists, or labor standards constructors."[45]

Ironically, the incorporation of progressives and radicals into the state apparatus coincided with, or perhaps contributed to, an attempt to present labor relations as at once technical and in turn nonpolitical.[46] Lauro Curletti, minister of development from 1921 to 1923, for example, justified the eight-hour day law in these terms:

> Experience has shown that the worker who dedicates eight hours to work, another eight to rest, and the remaining to himself, to sport and to study, can satisfy all the demands of his culture, remains healthy, and offers more efficient service to the industry that he serves. It has also been demonstrated that after eight hours it is no longer possible to maintain an adequate level of attention, and that beyond this time the fruits of labor diminish and accidents are more frequent. Thus the interests of capitalists and workers are conciliated in the indicated distribution of time.[47]

Curletti presented labor legislation (in this case legislation regulating hours of work) as a scientific and technical field of knowledge and practice. The eight-hour day was desirable not only from the perspective of the workers' well-being but also from the perspective of the capitalists since it was scientifically proven to increase productivity and was therefore of economic benefit to the bosses. According to this vision of labor policy, the state's role was to demonstrate to both workers and bosses the scientifically proven mutual benefits of cooperation. As in other fields where the state became increasingly active in this period, such as public health or education, in respect to the labor question too the invocation of "science," in this case an embryonic social science, served to justify and to legitimize state intervention. In this way, the Sección del Trabajo promoted itself as a purely technical solution to what its architects also envisioned and represented as largely technical problems in the labor sphere.

The key implication of the "technification" of labor policy was that "politics" had no role to play in the resolution of labor disputes. The officials at the Sección del Trabajo sought to present, indeed perform, the process of collective bargaining and state-mediated arbitration as an ostensibly technical process where politics did not interfere, as an article published in *Mundial*, a weekly magazine aimed at Lima's upper and middling classes, illustrates. Its edition of 28 January 1921 included a two-page spread, and several photographs, on the Sección del Trabajo's intervention in a dispute between the Federación de Zapateros (Shoemakers' Union) and several workshops in Lima. The article began by establishing its author's approval of the work of the Sección del Trabajo and noted that "the Sección del Trabajo . . . has justified its existence with the solutions that it has found for the various conflicts between capital and labor." The article then reported in approving terms how Hildebrando Castro Pozo had found a solution to the dispute that had come about when the workers requested a wage increase. In order to test the claims of both workers and employers, Castro Pozo had set up a small shoemakers' workshop in the offices of the Sección del Trabajo in order to observe the work process. As the article and the photographs that accompanied the article made clear, the solution to the dispute hinged on determining whether the request for a wage increase was justified in light of the work process involved in the production of the shoes. The dispute was taken to an arbitration tribunal composed of three lawyers, who ruled in favor of the workers and awarded them a 15 percent wage increase, among other benefits.[48]

A key aspect of the performance of dispute resolution as a technical process was the standardization of the procedure for dealing with collective disputes; a process that corresponds to what James C. Scott calls "state simplification."[49] First, the claimants submitted a list of grievances (*pliego de reclamos*) to the Sección del Trabajo. The claimants and defendants were then summoned to a conciliation meeting (*junta de conciliación*) within forty-eight hours. If no agreement was reached at the conciliation meeting, an *arbitro*, usually the chief of the Sección del Trabajo, would then rule on the dispute. If either of the parties disagreed with the ruling, then an arbitration tribunal was convened, composed of an arbitro representing each side and a third member (usually the president of the arbitration tribunal) designated by the judiciary. After hearing the case presented by each side and examining all the evidence, the tribunal would then give its ruling. Failure to comply with the ruling was punishable with a fine of between five and twenty Peruvian pounds or ten to thirty days in prison (although this rarely happened).[50] As this suggests, the immediate goal of conciliation and arbitration was to reduce the disruptive recourse to the strike as the chief form of labor struggle. But its aim was also to convince workers, and to a lesser extent bosses, that collective bargaining and state-mediated arbitration were fair and ultimately in their interest because they were technical processes outside, and impervious to, the sphere of politics.

This technification of labor policy, and the Sección del Trabajo itself, more generally served to "naturalize" power in the state.[51] The power of the state to arbitrate between capital and labor, the Sección del Trabajo suggested by its very existence and its procedures, derived from its privileged capacity to make labor relations technical and scientific and, in so doing, to place it beyond politics. Indeed, in framing state action with regard to labor within the sphere of the technical, the Sección del Trabajo constituted itself as the privileged, indeed necessary, "technology" for the regulation of labor relations. The interpellation of science and of the technical conferred upon the Sección del Trabajo a universal and disinterested character: in acting upon labor through science and the technical the state could claim to set in motion universal laws that existed outside the realm of personal or class interest and "politics" more generally. The power of the state accrued from, and was reinforced by, the idea that it possessed a privileged knowledge of, and capacity to bring forth, science. But it also accrued from the notion that state-mediated labor relations was itself a "science," universal and disinterested. Put differently, the naturalization of power in the state resulted from the fact that science gave the state a tool for the exercise of power but also, and perhaps primarily, from the idea—which the Sección del Trabajo sought to represent and, in turn, demonstrate by showing labor relations as an extension of a natural order—that the state itself, and its institutions and practices, were a type of science. As Carroll notes, "the point is that the modern state does not simply use science. Rather it is crucially constituted by science."[52]

It is therefore significant that worker opposition to collective bargaining and arbitration stressed that, far from being purely technical, arbitration was in fact a political device invented to favor the capitalist class. Anarchists such as the bakery worker Delfín Levano argued against "obligatory arbitration in conflicts between capital and labor, which forbids the worker, with the backing of the right to unionization, from putting a price on his labor and forces him to submit his demands for betterment to a bunch of ignorant lawyers [una rábula cualquiera] or to an arbiter who all hail from among the enemies of the worker."[53] Similarly, an article in the very first issue of El Obrero Textil, the newspaper of the recently established textile workers' federation, published in late 1919, claimed that arbitration was skewed in favor of capitalists: "In the arbitration tribunals, workers have one representative, whereas capitalists have two: the representative of the firm or industry affected by the workers' demands and the arbiter who always hails from the bourgeois class or who represents the authorities." Arbitration was designed, in its technical architecture, to favor the interests of the capitalist order, the article concluded.[54] It is therefore no surprise that in November 1920, textile workers on strike rejected compulsory arbitration, which they qualified as "bourgeois justice," while the First Workers' Congress, held in 1921, roundly condemned compulsory arbitration as a "trick law" (ley trampa).[55] In other words, for these critics of arbitration, the Sección del Trabajo, or arbitration more specifically, did not replace politics with a technical process. The technical process of arbitration was a simple reformulation of a system of politics that favored the capitalist class.

This opposition homed in on the rationalities of government expressed by the labor policy pursued by the Sección del Trabajo. The anarchists attacked the notion that the intervention of the Sección del Trabajo, and more generally, of the state, in the sphere of labor served (1) to protect workers by evacuating politics from labor relations and (2) to enhance their well-being by helping to create the conditions that would result in better wages, better working conditions, and, indeed, better living conditions. For the anarchists, and for later critics of the Sección del Trabajo, these rationalities of government had as their covert goal to obscure the simple reality that the state and its representatives, progressive or otherwise, always favored the interests of capital and that the well-being of labor could only be attained through class struggle. For the anarchists, the goal of the Sección del Trabajo was not simply to favor capitalists in labor relations but to "trick" workers into perceiving the type of labor relations favored and promoted by the Sección del Trabajo as being in their best interest. The anarchists were wrong about one thing: as I show in the following section, workers were not "tricked" into turning to the Sección del Trabajo to resolve their disputes with capital. They did so willingly. But they were right more generally: the Sección del Trabajo did indeed operate as a technology of government whose primary and overt function was to convince workers that its goals in the sphere of labor were commensurable with their own, and that in turning to the Sección del Trabajo rather than to the strike in order to resolve disputes, as Li puts it, they behaved as they ought.[56]

MAKING THE LABOR STATE

Despite cases of resistance to, and rejection of, the technification of labor policy, by at least two measures the Sección del Trabajo was a success in its early years. First, large numbers of workers turned to the Sección del Trabajo in the early 1920s in order to obtain official recognition for their unions and to negotiate collective work contracts with employers. This period saw a rapid unionization of both urban and, to a lesser extent, rural workers. The driving forces for unionization varied from case to case, but, as I discuss in greater detail later in this section, official recognition became a strong incentive to unionize since recognition could be a powerful tool for workers. According to the decree of 6 March 1920, the Sección del Trabajo was entitled to grant official recognition to unions "as long as their aims and statutes do not contravene the law and they comply with all the requisites established by law or special decree."[57] Procedure was straightforward and again expressive of state simplification: the unions submitted a letter requesting recognition and a copy of their statutes to the Sección del Trabajo, which then issued a ruling either granting or denying recognition. Once they obtained it, unions could point out to employers their recognized status as evidence of their legal personhood and legitimacy. Many boasted the recognized status on their letterheads.[58] In 1922, according to the British minister, 31 out of a total of 86 unions had been recognized. By 1929 the figure had risen to 272 recognized unions.[59]

Second, workers turned in large numbers to the Sección del Trabajo to settle disputes and consequently limited their use of the strike. According to one source, the Sección del Trabajo dealt with 89 disputes in 1920, 106 in 1921, and 77 in the first half of 1922.[60] In 1921, the minister of development boasted that "despite the short time that it has been in existence [the Sección del Trabajo] has been able to resolve fifteen labor conflicts and is in the process of resolving another seventeen."[61] In some disputes rulings resulting from Sección del Trabajo conciliation or arbitration provided little more than a small increase in wages or the payment of compensation. However, many workers, most but not all organized in unions, obtained comprehensive collective contracts regulating everything from wages to the length of the working day, as well as working and living conditions. In the railway industry, for example, three different collective contracts were signed on 27 September 1919 following a successful strike between the Central Railway, controlled by the Peruvian Corporation, a British firm, and the shopmen of the Factoría Guadalupe and its annexes in Chosica and La Oroya, the train crews, and the track workers. All workers obtained wage increases, ranging from 10 to 25 percent, and double pay on weekends and one and a half day's pay on holidays. In addition, the contracts obliged the company to undertake a number of health and safety improvements and to provide living quarters of better quality.[62] In Arequipa, the Southern Railway management and workforce agreed to a similar contract.[63] As a result of the collective contracts, wage payments on the Central Railway, amounting to 28 percent of gross receipts in 1918, rose to 37 percent in 1921.[64]

The "success" of the Sección del Trabajo, measured by the number of unions that sought official recognition and by the number of disputes that it handled, owed to a number of factors, but particularly to developments within labor itself. Clearly, workers were encouraged by the presence of familiar and friendly faces in the institution and, no doubt, by the broader political climate that favored state arbitration of disputes. Juan Pévez, a union leader from Ica, recalls the ease with which the Tahuantinsuyo Committee, a pro-Indian society, was recognized by the Sección del Trabajo: "It was lucky for us that Dr. Castro Pozo was authorized to grant official recognition to workers' unions and other institutions, since he was the chief of the Sección del Trabajo. And he was our friend. . . . It was therefore very easy for us."[65] In addition to their work in the Sección del Trabajo, both Castro Pozo and Roca served as legal advisors to a number of unions at this time.[66] But the success of the Sección del Trabajo was also a consequence of changes within the labor movement. In particular, it owed to the waning influence of anarchists, who were opposed to any dealings with the state, and to the emergence of a new leadership that came to see the Leguía regime as a potential ally in its dealings with employers. More generally, and importantly, it owed to a changing understanding, within organized labor, of the idea of the state and of the idea of labor itself; an understanding that coincided with the idea of the state and the idea of labor that the Sección del Trabajo promoted and with the rationalities of government that those ideas reflected.

Such changes need to be understood in light of the history of organized labor in Peru. Early forms of labor organizing can be traced back to the early 1860s, when artisans seeking protection from "free trade," the rise of "dishonorable trades," and incipient industrialization set up the first mutual aid societies.[67] The hardships brought about by the War of the Pacific (1879–84) boosted mutual aid membership throughout the country. By the 1880s there were mutual aid societies in Huacho, Lambayeque, Trujillo, Tarma, Cerro de Pasco, Zorritos, Cuzco, and Arequipa, in addition to those in Lima. By 1911 there were sixty-two societies in Lima alone, with an average membership of two hundred. They ranged from unions that restricted their membership to a specific trade to umbrella organizations like the Confederación de Artesanos Unión Universal (Confederation of Artisans Universal Union) or the Asamblea de Sociedades Unidas (Assembly of United Societies). Mutual aid societies established close ties with elite politicians, particularly the civilistas, and a number of workers joined the Partido Civil.[68] Some benefits accrued from these relationships, including limited labor legislation, as well as patronage and financial support for some mutual aid organizations. Despite these gains, many workers came to see the ties between the mutual aid societies and elite politicians as an unequal and unfavorable relationship, which benefited only the politicians and the *cúpulas* (leadership) of the mutual aid societies. Influenced to some extent by maverick intellectuals like Manuel Gonzalez Prada, but drawing more generally on the anarchist rhetoric and praxis shaping labor throughout Latin America, some workers came to see the wave of strikes in the 1890s and early 1900s as evidence that confrontation, as opposed to accommodation, could produce results.[69] In Lima, Manuel Caracciolo Levano and his son Delfín, both bakery workers, became both the staunchest critics of the mutual aid leadership, and of its relationship to elite politicians, and the staunchest proponents of confrontation, but anarchists began to play a role in the labor movement elsewhere in the country too.[70]

Historians have tended to see the rise of anarchism in Peru as a teleological process that culminated in the general strikes of 1919. True, in the 1910s a number of anarchist organizations were set up in various parts of the country and anarchist literature, in the shape of newspapers and pamphlets, started to appear in both the cities and countryside.[71] Anarchist workers played leading roles in both the eight-hour day movement and the Comité Pro-Abaratamiento de las Subsistencias (Committee for the Cheapening of Subsistence Goods) in 1919 with mixed results. However, anarchism's direct influence on the mass of workers was limited. The predominance of anarchist texts, primarily periodicals, in the 1910s has led some authors to interpret the period as one of anarchist hegemony in the labor movement. However, texts written by a few workers do not necessarily reflect the views of all workers.[72] Indeed, the anarchists' programs were often at odds with the bulk of the attitudes of laboring peoples in the early twentieth century. For example, the anarchists' internationalism and routine denunciations of "patrioterismo" (patriotic chauvinism) found little favor among large sectors of the popular classes.[73] Defeat in the War of the Pacific had begotten a culture of *revanchisme*. Government-sponsored "tiro al blanco" societies (rifle clubs) were ubiquitous and popular among urban workers who, at least rhetorically, were always at the ready to fight the Chilean enemy. Anarchists rejected all forms of nationalist symbolism and patriotic manifestations. By contrast, mutual aid societies participated regularly in patriotic festivities, particularly the 28 July (Independence Day) parades and the commemoration of the battle of Angamos (a pivotal point in the War of the Pacific, when Chilean warships destroyed the Peruvian navy). Moreover, the extent to which workers who self-defined as anarchists were fully committed to anarchism as a political project, in Peru or elsewhere, is unclear. As one construction worker, Isaias Contreras, remembers: "I spent all of the 1920s practicing sports and parts of my Sundays I dedicated to anarchism."[74]

In the early 1920s a new leadership composed mainly of textile workers progressively ousted anarchists, mostly bakery workers and shoe-makers, who had been at the helm of both the January and May 1919 general strikes.[75] Several of the new leaders, such as Julio Portocarrero, had previously been anarchists. However, they came to question increasingly the suitability of anarchism. As Temoche Benites notes, the anarchist-dominated Federación Obrera Regional del Perú (Regional Worker Federation of Peru), which grouped various Lima-based unions, was doomed by its sectarianism: "The FORP . . . was condemned to death, not so much by government repression . . . but rather by the internal polemics which defined the fields of ideology and action, by the evolution of methods of labor organization, by the creation of institutions that addressed the problems between workers and bosses, which the leaders of the FORP rejected indiscriminately."[76] The First Workers' Congress, held in 1921, debated whether to adopt anarchism as its ideological orientation. Though anarchists controlled the top positions at the Congress—Delfín Levano was elected secretary—the debate was postponed to a later congress as no agreement could be reached—evidence, Piedad Pareja argues, of anarchism's waning influence.[77] Following the congress, the FORP was reorganized into two local labor federations, the Federación Obrera Local de Lima (Local Worker Federation of Lima) and the Federación Obrera Local del Callao (Local Worker Federation of Callao). According to Temoche Benites, admittedly not a totally impartial observer, the sessions of these federations typically pitted anarchist workers, who "turned every meeting into a tribune for long and tedious dissertations," against workers who believed it was necessary to "find a way out, a solution to labor problems, to achieve a healthy understanding with the bosses, to establish tolerable relations between workers and bosses, using what they called the 'collective work contract.' "[78]

Many of the new labor leaders self-identified as "revolutionary syndicalists." They claimed to share many of the anarchists' ideas but rejected their violent methods (even if, in the Peruvian context, the use of violence by anarchists was rare). According to Arturo Sabroso, a textile worker and possibly the chief ideologue of revolutionary syndicalism in Peru (and later an APRA labor cadre), "the term 'revolutionary' refers to our concern for all that is progressive innovation and never to the adoption of terrorist methods that produce suffering and death."[79] Revolutionary syndicalists such as Sabroso saw the state as a potential ally in their quest for social justice. To some extent, the syndicalists' stance was a tactical response to the political climate of repression that I will examine in the next chapter: syndicalists pointed to the immaturity of the labor movement, to the need to build up its forces gradually. As such, they claimed to reject politics and act only in the sphere of economic demands. But syndicalists also put organization and unity, which they saw as key to wresting concessions from employers by taking advantage of the new labor laws, before ideology. In short, depending on your viewpoint, syndicalism was pragmatic or opportunistic. But, more important, it reflected the belief held by Sabroso and others that labor had a positive role to play in "progress" and specifically that achievement of social justice would benefit society as a whole.[80] Syndicalism was a perfect complement to the "technification" of the Leguía state. It reflected the view within organized labor that labor was an agent of progress whose contribution to progress would be enhanced by engaging in state-mediated labor relations.

Put otherwise, by the 1920s, organized labor in Peru shared the rationalities of government expressed, and promoted, by the Sección del Trabajo. Organized workers such as Sabroso reformulated the idea of labor and the idea of the state in terms that echoed the arguments put forward by social progressives such as Manzanilla or Curletti. This is evident not only in worker writings but more important in the way that workers approached the collective contracts that they obtained at the Sección del Trabajo. Workers understood the collective contracts as far more than mere agreements regulating work. They were a contract between workers, employers, and the state, in which the state played a crucial role as guarantor. The 1920 contract between the workers and management of the Santa Catalina Textile Mill, for example, signed "ante los poderes públicos" (before the state authorities), established a minimum wage for newly employed men and women, in addition to wage increases ranging from 5 to 15 percent. Workers would be given cloth, from which they could have a suit made, and waterproof clothing. In addition, the mill and the union established agreements regulating illnesses, accidents, holidays, and a half-yearly bonus.[81] The use of "ante" in the wording of the contract is revealing. It literally meant "before"; that is, the state official was present at the signing. But the significance of "ante" was clearly "guaranteed by." As the wording suggested, the collective contract brought the state within the mill's walls (but also brought the state into being more generally) as the power that guaranteed the contract, and therefore that guaranteed the workers' newly acquired benefits. In the absence of a labor code or specific legislation regulating working conditions and pay, these "guaranteed" contracts became the workers' principal bargaining tools. Through these collective contracts, the state and workers were drawn into a powerful alliance. Through the collective contract the state was constituted as a labor state and the Sección del Trabajo as a technology of government that had as its principal goal the protection and well-being of workers.

That workers came to view the state as the manifestation of a project of governmentality that was also their own is further evident from the way in which the collective contracts signed at the Sección del Trabajo became hallowed documents, reproduced and distributed widely, and often included in the unions' statute books. Indeed, workers viewed as a momentous event the bringing of bosses to the negotiating table with the state as overseer. For example, Juan Pévez recalls that the negotiations between representatives of the Comité Parcona, a labor organization in Ica, and the local plantation owners "[were] followed with interest by a great number of peasants, who constantly applauded our speeches. This gave us great confidence. This was the first time that Ica witnessed something of this nature, for the first time planters and peasants were openly confronting each other."[82] The success of the Sección del Trabajo in Lima and the neighboring valleys led workers in other areas to demand that the Sección del Trabajo attend to their needs too. Following the strikes in the Chicama valley, an umbrella union in Trujillo, noting "the importance of the Sección del Trabajo and . . . the efficacy of its work," requested that a delegation of the Sección del Trabajo be set up in the city. Only then, workers claimed, would plantation owners respect the labor laws, thus removing the need to strike.[83] For such workers, the idea of the state expressed by the Sección del Trabajo became a new, indeed the primary, channel of resistance because they came to see it, at least in part, as of their own making. The Sección del Trabajo as a technology of government at once reflected and in turn enabled the mutual constitution or coproduction of labor and the state as manifestations of rationalities of government.

The coproduction of labor and the state is most evident in the process of unionization that accompanied the formation of the Sección del Trabajo. Traditional histories of Peruvian labor movement have tended to interpret the rise of unionization in the early 1920s as the product of the development of class consciousness arising from the proselytizing efforts of anarchists and culminating in the strike wave of 1918–19. Certainly, between 1919 and 1921, as I have already noted, countless unions and federations were set up in quick succession, including the Federación Obrera Regional del Perú (Regional Workers Federation of Peru), the labor confederation that provided the organizational template for many other unions and labor federations. By the end of the 1920s Peru had acquired an organized labor "movement," with as many as twenty thousand "organized" workers, according to one estimate.[84] But this rapid unionization needs also to be understood as a reflection of an idea of, and practice toward, labor that was implicit in the development of the new form of labor relations represented by the Sección del Trabajo and expressive of the labor state, that is, of the idea of the state as the state of/for labor. From this perspective, unionization appears not as a process autonomous of, or, indeed, reactive to, the state, but rather as constituted by, and constitutive of, state formation. Put simply, the statutes of the Sección del Trabajo required workers to present their demands "collectively." Only "empleados" or white-collar workers could present demands to the Sección del Trabajo on an individual basis.[85] In this way, the Sección del Trabajo established a procedural framework that favored, indeed almost required, the unionization of workers. More important, it was a procedural framework that, like the 1920 constitution, constituted labor itself.

Not all the groups of workers who turned to the Sección del Trabajo were unionized. Agricultural workers, in particular, often approached the Sección del Trabajo united by a common grievance but not as a union. But it is apparent that many workers formed unions as a consequence of the need to present their grievances to the Sección del Trabajo as a collectivity. Among the unions that represented workers at the Sección del Trabajo between 1920 and 1922 were the following: Federación Gráfica del Perú (printworkers), Federación de Electricistas del Perú (electricians), Federación de Telefonistas del Perú (telephone operators), Federación de Obreros Zapateros (shoemakers), Unificación de Braceros de la Hacienda El Naranjal (agricultural workers), Federación de Obreros Panaderos "Estrella del Perú" (bakery workers), Sociedad Obrera y Auxilios Mutuos y Caja de Ahorros de Casa Grande (sugar workers), Federación de Carpinteros y Ramos Similares (carpenters), Federación del Gremio de Albañiles (masons), Federación de Empleados de Hotel y Ramos Similares (hotel workers), Unión Marítima Obrera de Auxilios Mutuos de Mollendo (port workers), Confederación Ferrocarrilera Obreros del Perú (railway workers), Federación de Mosaístas y Anexos del Perú (mosaic makers), Unificación de Campesinos de Carabayllo Alto (peasants), and Federación de Motoristas, Conductores y Anexos (tramway drivers and conductors). In short, in forming unions—unions that would represent them at the Sección del Trabajo—workers conformed to, and indeed reinforced, the idea of labor and the idea of the state that the Sección del Trabajo promoted but which they too saw as their own: the labor state.

LABOR CONSTITUTED

As this analysis suggests, the Sección del Trabajo operated as a technology of government that enabled the coproduction of labor and of the state. Who made their way to the offices of the Sección del Trabajo in effect tells us something about which laboring peoples came to see themselves, and came to be seen, as conforming to the idea of labor immanent to the labor state. To judge from the available documentation, labor was a large church in early twentieth-century Peru. As the documentation reveals, very diverse groups took their grievances to the Sección del Trabajo (or were targeted by Sección del Trabajo officials) in the early 1920s, including workers in the export industries like the sugar workers of the giant Casa Grande plantation in northern Peru, who complained about the banishing of some of their colleagues from the plantation; or the oil workers of the London and Pacific Petroleum Company in the northern oilfield of Negritos, who demanded the dismissal of the general manager, W. M. Young, and the construction of sporting facilities for workers; the miners employed by the "Sociedad Explotadora de Caylloma Consolidada" who submitted a series of demands; or, for that matter, the sharecroppers of the Carabamba hacienda in Otuzco in the highlands of La Libertad department.[86] Also associated with the export sector, transport workers similarly turned to the Sección del Trabajo to air their grievances. Among them were the stevedores of the port of Mollendo in the south (linked to Arequipa by the Southern Railway), who were concerned about work-related accidents; the port workers of Callao who complained about the firing of the "maestre de dique" (dry dock overseer) Eduardo Quesnel; or the workers of the Central Railway, who demanded an indemnity for one of their colleagues.[87]

Although the Sección del Trabajo was active in several parts of the country, most of the disputes in the documentation involved workers from the capital. Among the groups of workers in Lima who turned to the Sección del Trabajo were artisans such as the group of carpenters who complained that Abraham Barrera still owed the carpenter Raúl Vargas thirty soles for works, or the masons who complained that the "Ingeniero" José M. de Rivera had fired two masons called Pacora and Montoya.[88] Workers who tended to work in small workshops are also represented, including, as we have seen, shoemakers, who demanded wage increases from the owners of the shoe stores, printers denouncing the imposition of reduced wages at the Sanmartí printworks, bakery workers who protested about the dismissal of "national" workers and their replacement by Japanese workers at the Pampa de Lara bakery, or electricians complaining about the dismissal of some of their colleagues by the Empresas Eléctricas Asociadas (the company that provided Lima's electricity and ran the tramway network).[89] Finally, factory workers too were represented, including workers at the pasta factory of Ernesto Lavaggi, who protested about the dismissal of a worker called Genero, or, similarly, the textile workers of the San Jacinto textile mill, who complained about the dismissal of two workers.[90]

The records of the Sección del Trabajo also contain a relatively large number of documents from workers employed in agricultural estates near the capital or in neighboring valleys, such as the Negociación Villa and the Hacienda "La Estrella," both run by Chinese immigrants (Aurelio Pow San Chia and Pow Lung respectively), the Sociedad Agrícola Santa Barbara, or the Hacienda Puente Piedra, all of which produced foodstuffs for the local market.[91] Other workers to approach the Sección del Trabajo included urban transport workers, such as the streetcar drivers and conductors employed by Empresas Eléctricas Asociadas, who complained about unjustified dismissals, while their fellow workers employed at the various electrical power plants in the city demanded wage increases, the dismissal of some workers, and a bonus equivalent to sixty days' wages to be awarded to celebrate the centenary of Independence.[92] Finally, workers in more unusual sectors also turned to the Sección del Trabajo, including telephone operators in Lima, who complained about the dismissal of male workers and their replacement by female workers; hotel workers, who lodged a complaint against the administrator of the aristocratic Club de la Unión, the National Zarzuela Company, which lodged a demand against the administrator of the Mazzi Theatre; and, most intriguing of all, the

Comité Pro-Derecho Indígena (Committee for the Defense of the Indians), which complained about a certain Víctor Tapia, who seems to have owed some money to the indigenista organization.[93]

The Sección del Trabajo, then, reached, and was reached by, all types of workers in very different, and often distant, parts of Peru. Indeed, it is striking to note the sheer diversity in the workers and experiences of work that the employees of the Sección del Trabajo came into contact with, and, very likely, brought into contact with one another. In a sense, the Sección del Trabajo offices were a microcosm of the world of work in Peru, a place where sugar workers, many of whom were indentured laborers, from the northern departments of La Libertad and Lambayeque could run into miners from the Arequipa highlands; where Japanese sharecroppers from Huacho, to the north of Lima, could meet Afro-Peruvian agricultural laborers from Cañete and Chincha, to the south of the capital; and where largely mestizo industrial workers from Lima's textile mills could swap stories with also largely mestizo (bar the odd European or Asian migrant) printers, bakery workers, and electricians. In other words, from the point of view of the workers who turned up at the Sección del Trabajo, the idea of labor represented by, and constituted through, the Sección del Trabajo included workers who worked in the workshop and who worked in the modern factory, workers who cut the cane, picked the cotton, and mined the ore, workers paid by the hour and workers in debt servitude. And yet, while clearly extremely diverse, labor was constituted in the Sección del Trabajo as a unified *national* entity.

However, labor was also constituted through the absences or exclusions evident in the Sección del Trabajo documentation. Most of the workers who turned to the Sección del Trabajo were male. Available evidence suggests that only in a few cases did women seek the institution's mediation (or, just as likely, that Sección del Trabajo officials only rarely intervened in disputes that involved women). In late 1920, for example, a group of six women wrote a letter to the minister of development in representation of the Gremio de Empaquetadoras de la Compañía Salinera del Perú (Union of Packers of the Peruvian Salt Company) requesting wage increases and a change in their working hours. They noted that they were aware that several unions had already turned to the Sección del Trabajo in order to obtain improvements in their wages and that "as far as we know their grievances have been listened to and the justice of their claims has been acknowledged." They therefore hoped that they would receive similar treatment: "If it has been considered just, Minister, to accede to the demands of the male unions, bearing in mind that these had been motivated by the urgent need to address, even if partially, the disequilibrium caused by the rise in prices in the well-being of households who provide for themselves solely through their own efforts, we, who constitute a female labor union, are hopeful that our demands, which have exactly the same basis, will receive a similarly favorable acceptance."[94] These women were the exception. Most urban women worked as domestic servants or seamstresses and, despite their large numbers, remained outside, or rather were excluded from, the idea of labor.

The most glaring absence or exclusion was of course that of Peru's indigenous peoples, who, as we have seen, by virtue of the constitutional arrangements of 1920, were constituted as an object of state intervention distinct from, and incommensurable with, labor. To be sure, there is little doubt that indigenous people were among the many workers who visited, or at least among those represented by those who visited, the Sección del Trabajo offices to seek mediation in their disputes with the bosses. But they were there as workers and not as Indians. In establishing labor and the indigenous as two distinct objects of state intervention the 1920 constitution in effect constituted labor and the indigenous as two distinct and incommensurable categories of "the social." The Sección del Trabajo, along with the Sección de Asuntos Indígenas, institutionalized that incommensurability, and, in so doing, in material as well as ideological practice, excluded the indigenous from the idea of labor immanent to the labor state: labor as an agent of progress whose contribution to progress would result from its protection and improvement. In effect, the Sección del Trabajo at once reflected and in turn operationalized the broader exclusion of the indigenous from the national projects that Peruvian elites had begun to formulate in the wake of the defeat in the War of the Pacific (an exclusion that, needless to say, had deeper historical roots), and of which Leguía's Patria Nueva was a new version.

CONCLUSION

In this chapter, I have sought to show how the Sección del Trabajo was the culmination of a process begun in the late nineteenth century that arose from the problematization of labor, that is, from the labor question, and from the ways in which labor in Peru came to be identified with civilization and industrial progress. Early proposals to create labor boards and *secciones obreras* reflected rationalities of government that expressed new understandings of labor, and specifically of labor relations, as a field of knowledge and practice, a field amenable to becoming knowable, calculable, and administrable. In turn, such proposals expressed the perceived need to develop technologies of government that would enable the protection and the "improvement" of labor through action upon labor itself and the field of knowledge and practice that constituted labor relations. The Sección del Trabajo was the manifestation in the sphere of labor relations of such rationalities of government; rationalities that its early architects sought to turn into practice by evacuating politics from labor relations and presenting and performing labor relations as a merely technical matter whose very technicality guaranteed a favorable resolution to disputes for both workers and capitalists. Its early success, I showed, owed to the fact that the rationalities of government the Sección del Trabajo reflected were largely shared by the very "labor" that it sought to protect and improve.

Like the Inspection du Travail and the labor offices in French and British colonial Africa studied by Frederick Cooper, the Sección del Trabajo was among the era's "apparatuses of surveillance, shapers of discourse, definers of spaces for legitimate contestation."[95] But its coming into being reflected, as in colonial Africa, broader ideas about the nature of work and workers and more broadly still about the sources of progress and backwardness in Peru. The Sección del Trabajo, as a technology of government, expressed and operationalized a key idea that sustained the national project at the heart of Leguía's Patria Nueva: labor could, and indeed, should be constituted as an agent of progress; labor, once "improved," could and would engender civilization; this was the allure of labor. But through its exclusions the Sección del Trabajo also reflected another idea key to the national project of the Patria Nueva: that Indians, though amenable to redemption and civilization, were inimical, qua Indians, to progress. As such, labor and the indigenous became, in the 1920s as they had been in previous decades, logically incommensurable spheres of state intervention and management; an incommensurability that was normalized, as I have shown, by the 1920 constitution's establishment of distinct constitutional regimes for labor and the indigenous and by the Sección del Trabajo itself. As this analysis suggests, in the early twentieth century ideas about labor ultimately reflected ideas about race: labor could come to be understood as an agent of progress amenable to improvement precisely because it was conceived as incommensurable with indigeneity, invariably understood as inherently backward and incommensurable with progress.

3

DISCIPLINING LABOR

In early 1922, the prefect of La Libertad wrote to the minister of government to express his surprise and disagreement with the government's decision to put some thirty workers on a ship bound for Australia: "I cannot understand, Minister, the severity of the punishment inflicted on these Peruvian citizens, who only a little over a month ago [the state] had recognized as delegates of the diverse labor societies in the Chicama and Santa Catalina valleys."[1] The strikes that rocked much of the northern sugar regions of La Libertad in 1921 were one of the various contexts in which the newly formed Sección del Trabajo sought to implement the new labor policy enshrined in the 1920 constitution, or put differently, one of various contexts in which the labor state came into being. Lauro Curletti, the minister of development, traveled to the strike zones and met with the worker delegates. The elite press reported approvingly on his attempts to bring about a state-mediated solution to the dispute. But Curletti's efforts collided with a growing anxiety in elite sectors concerning labor unrest. As strikes multiplied and intensified around the country, much of the elite came to see the collective bargaining and state-mediated arbitration championed by the Sección del Trabajo, and which they had initially accepted and even celebrated, as unpalatable. This was a local manifestation of a transnational process. As Rodgers notes, "Just as the contagion of revolutionary ideas was worldwide in the years 1917 to 1920, so was the frightened reaction to it."[2] The consequence of the "frightened reaction" in terms of labor policy in Peru was quickly felt: the construction of the labor state gave way to repression combined with a far less consensual form of labor policy.

The idea that labor was a valuable resource that the state needed to protect and "improve," I have argued, shaped responses to the labor question in Peru. Workers came to see the Sección del Trabajo as a potential ally and, as such, participated actively in the constitution of the labor state. However, as I show in this chapter, the opposite is true of most employers. While some accepted the rhetoric of the labor state, most employers rejected the intervention of the Sección del Trabajo and the type of labor relations that it sought to promote, as I discuss in a first section. This had consequences for how labor related to the Sección del Trabajo, which, in most cases, proved unable to enforce its rulings in the face of employer resistance. Workers gradually came to see the Sección del Trabajo as ineffective and the labor relations it promoted as a sham. In the next two sections, I consider how both rationalities of discipline (expressive of a belief in the need to control labor and of the construction of labor as a social threat) and rationalities of government (expressive of a belief in the need to protect and improve labor and of the construction of labor as an agent of progress) shaped, at once, elite reactions to labor and, in turn, Leguía's labor policy. I argue, counterintuitively, that Leguía's systematic if selective repression of labor was envisioned as an integral part of the construction of the labor state. Finally, I turn to examine how labor negotiated the complicated field of labor relations in the politically polarized context of the early 1930s by exposing the tensions between the rationalities of discipline and government that shaped labor policy.

EMPLOYERS AND THE SECCIÓN DEL TRABAJO

Some workers saw the period of labor agitation of 1918–21 as favorable to revolution. A leaflet, circulated in late 1921, called on workers to rebel: "Revolt, worker, the time has come, the bourgeoisie agonizes and wants to drag you down in its fall, even the humble Indian understands this and rises to exterminate it; you should do no less, worker."[3] In most cases, however, the Sección del Trabajo succeeded in convincing the bulk of organized labor of the benefits of state-mediated arbitration, as I showed in the previous chapter. However, it was far less successful with employers. Many employers viewed workers' demands for higher wages and better working conditions as unjustified and indeed as tantamount to rebellion. As one flour mill owner noted, "Workers today are spoilt and fearlessly demanding and they use any pretext to strike."[4] Such views translated into a routine refusal on the part of employers to accept the rulings of the Sección del Trabajo. A 1925 study of recent labor legislation concluded that only employers flouted the rulings of the arbitration tribunals: "The records of the Sección del Trabajo do not include a single case of rebellion against a ruling from a union or labor organization."[5] Often employers opted to pay a fine rather than accept the tribunals' rulings. The Sección del Trabajo, as we will see, proved incapable of forcing employers to observe its rulings. As a consequence, labor came to see it as a lame duck institution and started to abandon its initial enthusiasm for state-mediated labor relations.

Workers succeeded in extracting considerable improvements in wages and working conditions from employers in the heady days of political uncertainty and rapid social and constitutional reform that characterized the rise to power of Leguía. This situation did not last. Following the collapse of sugar prices in 1921, which had dramatic consequences for the Peruvian economy as a whole, many employers tried to reverse some of the earlier concessions they had granted workers. Pointing to the situation of crisis, employers openly flouted the clauses of the collective contracts. They cut wages and bonuses. In some industries they forced workers to work longer hours for the same wage. In others they reduced the working week, thus reducing workers' incomes. Most of the documents in the Sección del Trabajo documentation dating from 1921 and 1922 concern protests by workers over employers' failure to comply with collective contracts as well as over wage reductions, failure to pay salaries, and reductions in the working day. In most cases, workers had little choice but to accept wage cuts, increased workloads, and worsening working conditions. In 1921, for example, workers at El Naranjal, a plantation on the outskirts of Lima, agreed to a 20 percent cut in wages, thus annulling the increase gained in early 1920.[6] Although many complained of increased workloads, for some workers the crisis resulted in less work and less pay. The peons of the Hacienda Puente Piedra complained in early 1922 that they were offered work only two or three days of the week.[7]

Examples abound of employers refusing to observe the procedures the Sección del Trabajo established. In June 1923, the mosaic workers' union complained that Francisco Gilabert had refused "with insulting and hurtful phrases about our Fatherland" to consider the list of grievances presented to him or to take the matter to the Sección del Trabajo.[8] A few months later, the electricians' union complained that the Empresas Eléctricas Asociadas (Associated Electrical Enterprises—the company that ran the electricity grid and streetcars in Lima) refused to observe the accident law.[9] Employers not only flouted the law, they also took the opportunity to purge their businesses of "uppity" workers. This occurred in all types of industries. For example, workers at the Hacienda El Naranjal complained in April 1921 that the hacienda owners were systematically firing those workers who had joined the recently formed union.[10] In early 1926, the pasta makers' union made a similar complaint about the Nicolini pasta factory.[11] In February 1921, the Electricians Federation of Peru noted that according to the collective contract between the Empresas Eléctricas Asociadas and their workers, which had been signed at the end of a strike in November 1920, management agreed not to fire any workers "without justification"; yet two workers had been fired in the previous five days at the Yanacoto Central.[12] A few months later, the management of the Ticapampa mines in Huaraz explained that "the complete anarchy among the workforce, and their continuous strikes and armed violence, has made indispensable the suspension of work for the time being so that we can get rid of the troublesome element."[13]

In addition to direct confrontation, employers made use of a number of different strategies to neutralize their workforce that effectively bypassed the Sección del Trabajo. In response to what they perceived to be an increasingly, and worryingly, organized labor movement, employers too began to organize. In Ica, for example, a Planters League was set up in 1921. Meanwhile, in an attempt to undermine militant labor organizations, employers organized rival, more pliant, unions such as the Federación Regional de Trabajadores de Ica (Regional Federation of Workers of Ica).[14] Similarly, following the 1921 strikes in the northern sugar regions, Víctor Larco, owner of the Chiclín hacienda, set up a paternalistic Unión de Empleados y Obreros de Chiclín (Union of Employees and Workers of Chiclín) to rival the more militant unions in the Chicama valley.[15] Such attempts to undermine perceived labor militancy were reproduced in the "symbolic" field. In 1926, a monument to "Work, Progress, and Life" was inaugurated at Chiclín. The marble monument, designed by "prestigious Roman artist" Ernesto Gazzeri, and which stood almost four meters tall, depicted "Labor represented by the majestic central figure, whose right hand lies on the shoulder of an adolescent, symbol of Progress. At his feet, on a bale of wheat, is Life: a mother who holds and caresses her tender child and has in her left hand a bouquet of roses." According to *Variedades*, the owners of the Chiclín plantation offered the monument to the local community, "as a homage to the conduct of the employees, artisans and workers of Chiclín, who, during the strikes of 1921 remained loyal and counteracted with personal efforts in the abandoned fields and wholesome principles in the meetings that took place during those days the misplaced and violent actions of the agitators." The report concluded: "Its symbolism and its function are thus equally to be celebrated and they raise up high the reputation that the small population of Chiclín has already earned for its exemplary industrial, cultural and patriotic activity."[16]

In Lima too employers sought to organize in order to counter the growth of unions. An employers' union, the Union Imprentas (Printshops Union), was set up as early as 1919, only a few months after the creation of the Federación Gráfica del Perú (FGP), the printers' union. The goals of the Printshops Union included the implementation of paternalistic measures or, as the employers claimed, "the betterment of the working class employed in the printshops."[17] But, its main goal was to put up a united front to counter the growing assertiveness of the print workers. They were relatively successful. Although employers claimed to be interested in "the betterment of the working class," they did little to improve working conditions in their shops. When, in 1924, the FGP wrote to printshop owner Carlos Fabbri to demand basic repairs in the workshop in order to improve hygienic standards, Fabbri replied that "workers' poor health is a consequence, in general, of their fragile constitution and of the lack of order in the lives they lead and not of [the conditions of] the establishments where they work."[18] Most famously, in early 1928, the manager of La Victoria textile mill in Lima Ricardo Tizón y Bueno set up a mutual aid union of which he was named honorary president and implemented a number of paternalistic measures in the mill. Tizón y Bueno sought to extend the mutual system he had created in his mill to the rest of the textile industry. He set up an Association for the Development of Mutuality in Peru. Tizón y Bueno became the object of fierce attacks by José Carlos Mariátegui and others, who saw these measures as a means to "constrict the class-based revolutionary impetus" and "divert workers from their own, economic and political, route in order to prolong the tutelage of the bosses on their organizations, deliberately halted in an embryonic phase and a composite type."[19]

The measures employers adopted benefited from a changed political climate, which had dire consequences for the type of labor relations that the Sección del Trabajo had been promoting. As his grip on the country strengthened, President Leguía backtracked on his early progressive measures. In early 1923, for example, the Lima print workers union complained to the mayor of Lima that the tenancy law introduced by Leguía to protect poor workers was not being observed.[20] That same year, Leguía dismissed Germán Leguía y Martínez from his position at the head of the Ministry of Government, and most of his supporters. Lauro Curletti, Erasmo Roca, and Hildebrando Castro Pozo, the architects of the government's early labor policy, all left the Ministry of Development at this time, either voluntarily or, in the case of Castro Pozo, as a result of enforced exile. The ministry's budget was slashed from 109,000 to 36,000 Peruvian pounds in 1921 and 1922.[21] But even before the departure of Roca and the others, as we have seen, the Sección del Trabajo had proved incapable of forcing employers to respect either the collective contracts that they had agreed to with their workers or, more generally, the new labor laws. Other government institutions, also previously willing to implement this type of progressive labor relations, were similarly weakened. In Ica, for example, planters managed to force the replacement of a prefect sympathetic to workers.[22]

In this new, less favorable context for state-mediated labor relations, workers began to shun the Sección del Trabajo. Although the Federación de Obreros Panaderos "Estrella del Perú" (FOPEP, Federation of Bakery Workers "Star of Peru"), the Lima bakery workers' union, had obtained a very favorable collective contract in 1920, by 1921 complaints about the Sección del Trabajo's ineffectiveness in resolving disputes had become commonplace in the union's meetings. As one member noted in 1922, "the arbitration law is counterproductive for the union's general interests."[23] In 1926 the FOPEP wrote to the prefect "to demand justice, as we have not found it in the Sección del Trabajo."[24] Even when disputes were resolved in favor of the FOPEP, the rulings were rarely implemented; as happened in 1927 to a worker who had yet to receive compensation for dismissal after obtaining three rulings in his favor.[25] Like the bakery workers, the textile workers too lost all hope of finding redress in the

Sección del Trabajo and refused to have anything to do with the institution. In May 1926, for example, the workers at the San Jacinto textile mill struck after managers told them they had to take their grievances to the Sección del Trabajo.[26] As late as 1929, a police spy reported that at a meeting of striking workers, a certain Guzmán had argued that "no matter how many grievances we, organized workers, take to the Sección del Trabajo of the Ministry of Development, we will always obtain negative results because the managers of factories . . . are intimate friends with the director of the Sección del Trabajo."[27]

The experience of the Lima print workers' union, the Federación Gráfica del Perú (FGP, Federation of Print Workers of Peru), further illustrates the change in workers' fortunes at, and perceptions of, the Sección del Trabajo. In October 1919 the FGP had presented its first *pliego de reclamos* (list of grievances) to the owners of forty-six print shops. Included in its demands were wage increases of between 50 and 80 percent, double pay on Sundays, the elimination of fines, and sick pay equivalent to 50 percent of normal pay. As the dispute unfolded, an arbitration tribunal was set up to settle the dispute. Dr. Pérez Aranibar, the government-designated *arbitro*, headed the tribunal. The dispute was a clear victory for the FGP. The collective contract signed between workers and employers granted workers on a per diem wage a 70 percent pay rise, while workers on piecework got specific increases. Other benefits gained included double pay on holidays, 50 percent extra pay for night work until 11 P.M., and double pay thereafter. The FGP concluded:

> No doubt about it; none of our comrades has been jailed; no traitor has been beaten up, no notes have been skipped, no one has sung out of tune. Social harmony has been our goal and victory our driving force. It is a modest material victory but a glorious moral victory. We have succeeded in organizing the most disorganized workforce that has ever existed. And if we did not obtain all that we strove for, we must take advantage of the edifying lessons that our struggle has left us.[28]

Dr. Pérez Aranibar was thanked for his intervention, and the union backed a motion sent to the National Assembly to create a Ministry of Labor. A few months later, in January 1920, the Sección del Trabajo granted the FGP official recognition.

The FGP's triumphant tone and enthusiasm for state intervention in its disputes was short lived. It soon became clear that although the printshop owners had signed a new collective contract they had little intention of respecting it and that the Leguía government, and its new bureaucratic institutions, had no interest or power to force them to do so. Between March 1920 and October 1921, the FGP sent several letters to the Sección del Trabajo pointing out that employers were flouting the collective contract. Some letters referred to the shortcomings of the contract's clauses. Humberto Ibáñez, president of the FGP, noted in March 1920, for example, that the wording of clause 13 relative to sick pay was lacking in precision, which allowed the printshop owners to evade it: "each time a worker falls ill he gets fired inhumanely as has happened with a union member who works at the Fabbri printshop."[29] Other complaints referred to lack of payment on holidays, poor hygiene in some print shops, "the scant security and the danger posed by machinery installed in locales that are unsuitable [for that purpose]," as well as workdays exceeding eight hours, and "unjust dismissal."[30] Although critical of the employers' behavior, the fact that the FGP produced these letters suggests that, at least initially, its members were willing to participate in, and help shape, the new system of labor relations that the Leguía government was promoting. This attitude did not last.

The FGP became increasingly dissatisfied with the Sección del Trabajo and convinced of its incapacity to enforce the contract in the course of 1922. In August 1922, the FGP protested at "the uselessness and incompetence of the Labor Office."[31] By mid-1923, the *Obrero Gráfico*, the union's newspaper, claimed that the Sección del Trabajo and the Concejo Superior de Previsión Social (Superior Council of Social Foresight), a short-lived institution with labor representation set up by Leguía but which had no effective power, "in theory and in practice, only fulfill decorative functions, because, to this date, we have not seen or heard of a single just resolution." According to the newspaper, the institutions served only the interests of capitalists: "They are bureaucratic entities created to protect the rich."[32] The growing dissatisfaction with the Sección del Trabajo led the FGP to seek the intervention of Lima's prefect when, in 1924, it issued a new list of grievances demanding a general wage rise in the industry. Teobaldo Sarmiento, the FGP's general secretary explained to the prefect: "We have not sought the intervention of the Sección del Trabajo because we have little confidence that this entity can achieve a fair resolution in our disputes. We speak from bitter experience. For this reason we ask you for an impartial and serene ruling."[33] During another dispute, in May 1925, the FGP rejected the mediation of the Sección del Trabajo, preferring instead to settle the dispute directly with the owner of Imprenta Scheuch on the grounds that "the conciliations promoted by that institution do not inspire confidence, as previous experience has shown its clear partiality and that is why we do not seek its intervention."[34]

As the experience of the FGP suggests, the labor relations envisaged by Curletti, Roca, and Castro Pozo collapsed quite simply because employers refused to accept the rulings of the Sección del Trabajo, and the Sección del Trabajo proved incapable of forcing them to do otherwise. As a consequence, workers who initially had been willing to engage in state-mediated labor relations, and, in so doing, participate in the construction of the labor state, gradually lost faith in the Sección del Trabajo, further weakening this institution. Available evidence suggests that its activities were severely reduced from 1922 onward. Economic calculation, no doubt, motivated employer resistance to the Sección del Trabajo: the collective contracts signed in the period 1919–21 represented a significant, and, from the employers point of view, unsustainable, increase in labor costs. But in order fully to understand employers' rejection of the labor relations envisaged by the Sección del Trabajo we need to set motivations shaped by interest alongside motivations shaped by how the elite viewed and in turn constructed labor. The labor state, I have suggested, reflected, and reinforced, elite ideas about labor as an agent of progress. Peru's employers largely agreed with progressives such as Manzanilla and Miro Quesada and labor leaders such as Sabroso that workers needed to be protected and "improved" if they were to contribute fully to progress. But most elites viewed labor demands for better wages or working conditions and particularly the use of the strike as a threat to social order that reflected the growing influence of nefarious political forces among labor; an influence that needed to be repressed actively and quickly.

ELITE REACTIONS

The wave of labor unrest and demands in 1918–21 produced a hostile elite reaction to labor. An article published in September 1919 in *La Revista del Foro*, the mouthpiece of the Colegio de Abogados (the Law College), observed: "what we are witnessing is a great upheaval among all social classes, propelled merely by practical interests, as a consequence of pure communism. This situation confirms that the pressure that socialists exercise on workers who do not want to belong to their organization is more fatal and has more terrible consequences for the people than the exaggerated oppression of the bourgeoisie." Labor laws, such as the law that gave workers the right to organize unions, the author of the article suggested, were necessary but potentially dangerous: "But, how many dangers [the law allowing unionization] contains if socialism uses it for its own ends employing its economic function to mask a profoundly revolutionary spirit!"[35] These sentiments were reprised in an article published two years later in the same journal, which argued that the general strikes that Peru had recently experienced had been declared "not in the interests of the labor movement, but for political goals."[36] The authors of both articles stressed that they recognized workers' right to strike and that they believed it was the duty of the state to prevent strikes by passing new laws that would protect workers in the workplace and by creating institutions that would resolve labor disputes, such as arbitration tribunals. But they clearly also believed in the need for the state to repress labor militancy, which they construed as increasingly violent in character and revolutionary in intent: "The violent behavior that all strikes provoke and that are the cause, we repeat, of its own loss of legitimacy, necessarily create the need to repress it with violent means."[37]

The strike wave brought to the fore ideas about labor that had shaped how Peruvian elites approached the labor question since the late 1890s. In the late 1910s and early 1920s, such ideas resonated in unexpected forums. Two publications aimed primarily at women of the elite included similar commentaries on the strike wave. In June 1919 *La Mujer Peruana* featured an article on the recent general strike that lambasted "demagogues" who sought only to awake "the bad instincts of the proletariat, firing up its hatred, and stirring up its unjustified ambitions."[38] The author of the article, clearly aiming for poetic effect, likened the "demagogues" to "hurricane winds from afar" while claiming that "fortunately our people are, at heart, peaceful, like the ocean that bathes our coasts," thus reprising the idea that the cause of the recent strikes had been imported from elsewhere. Similarly, the magazine *Hogar* published in 1920 an article titled "Long Live the Strike!" that commented ironically on the "absurd" strike wave and on the fact that "this phenomenon has become so widespread that it is impossible to find anyone who has not belonged to a strike committee." The absurdity of the strike wave was evident: it had raised the cost of living and everyone was worse off as a result.[39] Another article published in the same magazine commented on a recent strike in the Roma sugar plantation and noted that the only explanation for the strike was that nonworkers "had stoked [the workers'] spirits with perverse and dark intentions." The workers certainly had no reason to strike: the plantation owner Víctor Larco Herrera, a well-known "philanthropist, a friend of the people," had always provided his workers with all that they could possibly want "for their always simple but always also expectant lives," including a theater, a school, a hospital, and a library.[40]

The mainstream press too reprised these arguments. An article published in May 1920 in *Mundial* on the recent strike wave pointed to its illegitimacy, claiming that it expressed nothing more than "hatred and vengeance," given that Peru was enjoying a period of democracy and was free of "tsarism" and "militarism" (a choice of language that illustrates how the broader transnational context shaped local ideas about labor militancy). Strikes, ultimately, were counterproductive for workers, since they invariably led to price rises: "And thus the poor worker who dreamt for a moment that he would get some respite, finds that not only did it not come, but far from it, that his rebellious attitude only succeeded in making his situation, and that of his fellow struggling and sacrificed workers, worse."[41] *Variedades*, meanwhile, blamed the 1921 strikes in La Libertad on agitators, who "have undermined the spirit of the valley workers with the Bolshevik virus and with outmoded Proudhonian theories." For the author of the article, the labor "problem" did not exist in the Chicama valley: the plantations provided workers with all they could possibly need, including good wages, nutritious and cheap food, adequate housing, leisure, education, justice, and "buen trato" (good treatment). It followed that those who made demands were not workers but rather "revolutionaries," who sought only to destroy private property, and ne'er-do-wells, who "demand the right to a comfortable and productive idleness." The article concluded that it was the duty of the government to intervene with force in order to eliminate this threat to social order.[42]

These reactions point clearly to the social fear that the period of labor agitation from 1918 to 1921 produced in the elite. This fear generated a discourse that stressed the illegitimacy of the strikes (since, it was claimed, workers enjoyed optimal working and living conditions), that located the source of militancy in a nefarious political influence external both to Peru and to a "true" working class, and that called on the government to adopt strong-arm tactics to repress labor militancy.

Attempts by elites to construct a more congenial form of labor complemented their calls for the violent repression of labor militancy. The magazine *Variedades*, for example, included a "Workers' Page" that regularly reported on those worker societies that were deemed to be respectable and nonpolitical, such as the Sociedad 33 Amigos de Tejidos (a mutual aid organization opposed to the more militant textile federation), the Sociedad Unión Huaraz, described as being "completely distant of all political goals," or indeed, the Centro Católico Obrero, whose banner was blessed by the Apostolic Nuncio.[43] Receiving special attention were worker activities that were perceived to be edifying, such as a matinee performance given by the wives and daughters of the members of the Sociedad 33 Amigos de Tejidos, which included "tableaux vivants"; the "lunch" organized by the Sociedad de Auxilios Mutuos of Mollendo; or indeed the award of prizes by the Sociedad Nacional de Auxilios Mutuos.[44] Typically, the "Página obrera" featured photographs of well-turned-out workers, wearing suits, ties, and panama hats, sitting around a large table and often flanked by oversized Peruvian flags. The imagery was unambiguous: the real Peruvian worker was a respectable and patriotic member of society. But which workers and which worker societies fell within this category could change suddenly. In early 1924, *Variedades* reported approvingly of the "Fiesta del Arbol"(The Day of the Tree) held in the textile town of Vitarte, and included photographs of the "professors and students of the Popular University." One of these professors, clearly visible in one of the photographs, was José Carlos Mariátegui, who also wrote a regular column in the magazine.[45] However, four years later the police refused to grant permission to hold this festivity on the grounds that "the Fiesta de la Planta [the Day of the Plant— the fiesta's real name] represents an act of solidarity among the working element to reaffirm its subversive ideology; that is to say it is a clearly Bolshevik celebration."[46]

Elite attempts to construct a more congenial form of labor are equally in evidence in the competition that *La Crónica* ran in 1924 to elect a "labor queen." This election took place at the same time as the more traditional election of the "carnival queen," typically reserved for society ladies, but instead involved "the ladies who dedicate their energies to the noble struggle for life." The carnival queen elected that year was Her Majesty Carmen I, or Señorita Carmen Valle Riestra Meiggs, a young woman who combined in her surname that to which the Peruvian elite most aspired, an aristocratic Hispanic ascendancy invigorated by Anglo-Saxon blood.[47] The title of labor queen, meanwhile, went to Her Majesty Rosa I, or Señorita Rosa Ramos Rozas, who worked at the Jardín Estrasburgo, a restaurant. The portraits of both queens were included side by side in a two-page spread in the magazine. With 53,958 votes in her favor, Rosa I had defeated strong competition from twenty-odd candidates, including Amparo Barrios, who worked at newspaper *La Prensa*, and María Lucia Oquendo, employed by the Banco Anglo-Americano. All the candidates, none of whom worked in industrial locales, were featured in *Variedades* in photographs taken in their place of work, standing next to a sewing machine, a typewriter, a barber's chair, a sales counter, or a desk.[48] Whereas the carnival queen was described simply as "sovereign of beauty," the labor queen, the caption under her photograph explained, had been chosen for her "virtue and beauty."[49] The labor queen was awarded a number of prizes by several commercial houses of the capital, including an iron, a china tea set, a gramophone, a comb set, a couple of wristwatches, and two lamps.

The elite constructed its own idea of labor as a version of itself, sharing its values and aspirations but existing in a separate and subordinate social sphere. The fact that "virtue" in addition to "beauty" had been a criterion for the election of the plebeian labor queen but not of the aristocratic carnival queen suggests that it was considered intrinsic to the latter and only achievable in exceptional circumstances in the former. The photographs of the float on which the two queens paraded and the clothes they and their respective "damas de honor" (ladies-in-waiting) wore reflect this dual construction: they were similar but ostensibly different. The labor queen's float represented a beehive; the carnival queen's float was a regal throne complete with two crowned papier-mâché lions. The labor queen and her damas wore striped dresses and little antennae on their heads; the carnival queen and her damas wore grand white dresses, representing different historical eras, such as classical Greece and eighteenth-century France. This performance of class distinction denied the existence of a working-class culture or identity. Labor, the performance implied, existed as an inferior, subordinate, and ultimately dependent version of the elite. But though the performance constructed labor as subordinate and dependent, it nevertheless represented labor as existing within a common universe with the elite.

We find such a construction of a subordinate and dependent labor reprised, albeit in a different form, in an article published by *Variedades* on Rafael Larco's Chiclín plantation. The plantation was presented as a "social and industrial deed."[50] Larco was praised for providing his workers with all the "elements and comforts needed for life," including housing, education, nutritious food, and leisure. The outcome was "abundantly cordial" labor relations on the plantation based on "solidarity and mutual respect." For the author of the article, the success of Chiclín owed to the fact that "politics, as a system of life, is not practiced." Instead, Larco's focus, which was presented as a model to be universally copied, was on "the civic and moral reeducation of the people, [in order to prepare it] for the great democratic conquests." Indeed, the article implied that the real success of Chiclín was that it represented a social experiment in the making of workers. All children had to attend school, "where their intellectual, moral and physical education is provided, harmonically." Sanitation and health services were provided so that "public and private hygiene is admirable." Vices such as alcoholism had been "definitively eradicated" thanks to an effective campaign. Workers' good health, moreover, was a consequence of the "raw and cooked rations of chosen foodstuffs in proportions scientifically required for life" that they received. The implication was clear: the success of Chiclín owed to Larco's "social deed," that is to his engineering of proper workers through the application of scientific methods (methods, one assumes, though this was not mentioned in the article, that he had picked up while studying at Cornell University). In short, Larco's social engineering suggested that workers could be improved by acting upon their bodies and character, as well as their environment.

As this suggests, a combination of rationalities of discipline and rationalities of government shaped elite ideas of labor. Elites agreed that workers needed to be protected and "improved" so that their contribution to progress could be enhanced (although they disagreed about whether the state or employers were best placed to perform these tasks). But because workers were susceptible to nefarious political influences and could very easily become a threat to the social order, elites agreed that the state needed to carefully and forcefully repress labor militancy.

As I discuss in the following section, almost from the very beginning of his regime, Leguía and his police apparatus systematically if selectively repressed what they perceived as labor militancy. They employed a strategy that consisted of "othering" militancy as expressive of foreign or malign influences while at the same time promoting a bland form of unionism. But these measures expressive of rationalities of discipline were not antithetical with, or reflective of an abandonment of, the rationalities of government manifested in the labor state. Instead, Leguía and his supporters viewed and justified the repression of labor militancy, and the deepening of dictatorship more generally, as a means to further the project of governmentality manifested in the labor state. The rationalities of discipline espoused by the regime were integral, rather than antithetical, to the rationalities of government of the labor state.

LABOR POLICY

An editorial published in *Variedades* in 1924 on a recent strike of streetcar workers over working hours and overtime pay combined a critique of anarchism, "a bloody and violent but fortunately utopian approach," with a discussion of socialism, a doctrine that, according to the editorialist, was far better placed to achieve a "slow adaptation of social life to the severe and indestructible reality which characterizes the existence of civilized peoples." Interestingly, however, the editorialist pointed to an unexpected source of socialism:

> As the strongest and best placed entity to change social values and to establish the best relations between them, and to achieve the economic betterment of the proletariat and the improvement of the conditions and rights with regard to capital, the state must take responsibility, and takes responsibility in all progressive countries, for the mission of directing all the institutions under its aegis toward an efficient and reasonable socialism, which implies not the destruction of a class, entity, or social value but rather the harmony of all; [so that] those who have achieved the most advantages and success sacrifice some of it for the benefit of those less fortunate.[51]

As this suggests, the "socialism" that this editorialist had in mind was not the socialism that young intellectuals such as Mariátegui and Haya de la Torre had begun to reinterpret for the Peruvian context.

In formulating the idea of "socialism" as the true path for proletarian improvement, the editorialist reprised some of the ideas that shaped the elite view of labor as susceptible to nefarious political influences and as a threat to the social order. The editorial suggested that if workers struck it was because they had allowed themselves to be "dragged along" by "doctrines of division and anarchy," and it went on to justify the use of force by the state when repressing illegitimate strikes. But the editorial also reflected the view of state-mediated labor relations manifested in the Sección del Trabajo that expressed a new understanding of the role of the state as a regulator of society and of labor itself—what I have called the labor state. As we have seen, earlier discussions of the legitimacy of strikes had hinged on whether workers had any right to complain in the first place. In the interpretation put forward in this editorial, however, the state and not employers or the elites determined whether strikes were legitimate or not. Workers were perfectly entitled to strike, the editorial concluded, "when a union or a class of workers, whose rights and interests have been attacked, place themselves within the law that the state has decreed to regulate the right to strike, and inform the state—which then becomes a mediator in the conflict—painful pressure is exercised on the entity that denies the justice that is owed."[52]

In the context of the so-called communist plot of 1927, when the regime accused workers assembled at the Second Workers' Congress in Lima of plotting to overthrow government, the same *Variedades* editorialist, most likely Clemente Palma, returned to the idea of state socialism as a solution to inequality. However, he now argued that the progressive evolution in the well-being of the proletariat that "socialism" entailed had been broken by the war and the Russian Revolution. The spread of communism represented a threat that needed to be nullified through force.[53] Palma's comments reflect the social fear that marked those days, which led *Mundial* to claim that the Second Workers' Congress had proclaimed its adherence to the Third International in Moscow and that the "hatred of the bourgeoisie was such" that "in the chemistry lessons at the Popular Universities the professors explained the diverse formula and measurements to prepare explosives and bombs."[54] More generally, Palma's apparent abandonment of "socialism" and embrace of force as the principal means to deal with labor appear to reflect the standard narrative of Leguía's Patria Nueva as Janus-faced. Typically, historians contrast the early promise of social reform and political opening toward labor and indigenous communities with the later subservience to foreign capital, generalized corruption, and repression of popular forces.[55]

There is little doubt that union activity was progressively curtailed in the course of the 1920s, as was the form of labor relations that the Sección del Trabajo had sought to institutionalize at the beginning of the decade. In 1927, the Ministry of Development handled only twenty disputes. Of these only seven were found to be legitimate.[56] It is telling that while the budget of the Ministry of Development was slashed in the early 1920s, the resources directed at the police ballooned from 275,000 Peruvian pounds in 1917 to 731,000 in 1921 and 600,000 in 1922.[57] However, though the Leguía regime did not eschew violent repression, the bulk of the regime's repressive policies consisted of the selective persecution, imprisonment, and exile of labor leaders and prolabor intellectuals, as the Ministry of Interior documentation reveals. In 1921, as we have seen, the unrest in the Chicama valley was resolved by the deployment of troops, who proceeded to disband the unions and arrest the strike leaders, leaving several workers dead. Though rare, similarly brutal incidents occurred in later years during the Patria Nueva. However, more generally, repression was aimed at disarticulating militant unionism. Typically, union halls and labor newspapers were closed down and worker libraries confiscated. In 1923, for example, police officers raided the Centro Obrero Iqueño (Ica Labor Centre) and confiscated several "forbidden books," whose authors included Marx, Kropotkin, and Gorki, as well as the center's archives.[58] The following year, the chief of police wrote to the prefect of Lima regarding the circulation of a "manifesto of socialist ideas," which he saw as part of a campaign to perturb "the workers' spirit with subversive ideas" and requested that orders be given to intercept all such publications.[59]

Perhaps inevitably, the removal of "subversive ideas" implied the removal of those who produced those ideas. Though some, like Mariátegui and Haya de la Torre, settled into relatively comfortable exiles, for most opponents of Leguía, exile was a testing and difficult time. Nicolás Gutarra's exile took him to Argentina, Bolivia, Brazil, and French Guyana. In Venezuela, this former cabinetmaker requested help from the Peruvian consul, as he found himself "in the most terrible circumstances." Little over a month later, Gutarra was arrested by the Venezuelan authorities, jailed, and subsequently deported to Colombia.[60] Of course, the exile of

Peruvian labor leaders or student activists did not prevent them from continuing their activities elsewhere. As the Peruvian consul in Panama noted, the Peruvians Luis Bustamante, Nicolás Terreros, Esteban Pavlevitch, and Dagoberto Ojeda, along with a Spaniard named Blázquez de Pedro, were behind the Tenants' League, protesting at rising rents in that city.[61] The reputation of Peru's exiles preceded them. In 1926, the Cuban government refused entry to Samuel Vásquez, described as "a striker deported from the San Lorenzo island prison." The consul was left in the embarrassing situation of having to send Vásquez, a former general secretary of Federación de Choferes and soon to become an APRA labor cadre, back to Peru.[62] With such large numbers of exiles, it is not surprising that the repressive tactics of the Leguía regime did not go undetected outside Peru. In March 1924 the José Martí Popular University and the University Federation of Cuba made an official protest to the Peruvian consul in Havana for the arrest of José Carlos Mariátegui and the closure of *Claridad*, his printworks.[63]

While Peruvians with subversive ideas were sent out of the country, foreigners with subversive ideas had to be kept out. In 1922, instructions were sent out to coastal prefectures "to prevent the disembarkation in these ports of certain individuals, some of whom are wicked instigators of strikes while others are renowned pimps and thieves."[64] The following year, a Dane called "Crisp. S. Nor" described as a member of the "international labor association of the United States of America," along with a Romanian and a Dutchman, who possessed "subversive newspapers . . . that prove their support of the new tendencies among workers" were closely watched "in order to prevent them from disembarking or communicating with anyone" when their ship docked at Salaverry in La Libertad.[65] In 1926, the Ministry of Government issued the following directive to the prefectures: "Having discovered that so-called itinerant salesmen, of Turkish nationality, are agents of Bolshevik propaganda, charged with agitating the working classes; [you are ordered], by the Minister, to undertake the most assiduous investigation regarding the origins and personal circumstances of the foreign itinerant salesmen who are traveling in your department, to confiscate their papers and to send them to this Directorate, and to arrest those that you suspect of wrong-doing."[66] Some observers went as far as to blame labor militancy on a Chilean plot to destabilize Peru in the run-up to negotiations over the territorial claims arising from the War of the Pacific.[67] An editorial in

Variedades claimed that Chilean ships carried "individuals who have as a mission to stir up the labor unions by predicating that they must seek to obtain justice, thus radically altering social order, and imposing new labor laws that would make them the real owners of industries and the absolute beneficiaries of capital and its fruits." What these individuals were really after, the editorial suggested, was "political chaos and the rise of a government with which Chile can come to an 'agreement.'"[68]

As the above suggests, the discursive strategy employed by the Leguía regime involved "othering" militancy by stressing the foreignness of militant workers. But the regime also "othered" militancy by establishing a strict distinction between "real" and "false" workers. When, in 1923, the prefect of Callao was requested authorization for a *romería* (procession) to take place to celebrate 1 May, he stressed:

> This authorization, which, needless to say, applies to the honest and duty-conscious element, has at its core my absolute order that the *outsiders [aquellos que vienen de fuera]*, who, claiming to be unionists, introduce themselves among the healthy workers, and take advantage of these circumstances, to ruin them with their vices and pernicious doctrines, be followed and observed. To this end, I am sending you a list of these harmful elements, which you will treat with extreme severity, if they attempt to produce disturbances or any act that falls outside the correct behavior and composure, characteristic of *true* Callao workers.[69] [emphasis added]

Similarly, in 1922, the gobernador of Tinyahuarco in Cerro de Pasco accused Jacinto Rojas Vicuña, a "traveling salesman," of being an "exploiter of the very poorest workers; an agitator of the proletarian masses, [which is why] he was thrown out of this foundry for being one of the leaders of the 1917 strike. Neither Rojas Vicuña nor those who back him can boast the honorable title of workers."[70] The deputy for Cajabamba, remarking on events in Chicama in 1921, pointed to the sorry state of affairs created "not so much by the true workers, but rather by the agitators who have settled in the plantations, who do little else but stir up the workers."[71] In 1926, the "pseudo-worker called Chávez," ousted from Chicama, found his way to the Julcán hacienda in Otuzco, where, according to a local authority "he produces pernicious propaganda against social order."[72]

In some cases, the rhetorical "othering" of militants extended to attributing lunatic or even demoniacal characteristics to "agitators," "instigators," and "inciters" who influenced honest workers. Following the expulsion of the agitator Marcelino Zamalloa from La Libertad in 1922, the local prefect claimed that "workers are now dedicated to their daily tasks, free from the sick influence of the expelled agitators."[73] Some years later, Carmen López and Mario Naverrete, two so-called agitators, "possessed by a blind fury, led a mob, which, armed with machetes chased the plantation foreman called Segura, who managed to escape," according to the prefect of Lambayeque.[74] Naturally, employers shared (and, doubtless, fed) this official discourse of the militant worker as necessarily alien. When their condition as workers could not be denied, their significance, and therefore the extent to which they spoke for other workers, was of necessity minimized. Thus, the managers at La Union textile mill in Lima complained that "the tranquility of our mill is threatened by the subversive actions of a miniscule group of workers who seek nothing more than to stir up their coworkers."[75] These discursive operations were elements in a broader strategy to render illegitimate, and repress, all types of organized activity by workers. All grievances were presented as the work of agitators; all meetings were seditious.

Workers spent considerable time and effort trying to convince the authorities otherwise. In 1925, for example, Samuel Vásquez, of the Federación de Choferes, now back in Peru after returning from exile in the Caribbean (see above), wrote to the prefect of Lima to complain that the police was denying the union the right to hold sessions. He stressed: "Our meetings never take on political or, as is claimed, subversive overtones, they are clearly proletarian and with class-based goals [con fines clasistas], that is to say they are clearly worker meetings."[76] Similarly, when in 1927, the Federación Obrera Local de Lima wrote to the subprefect of Lima to request permission to hold the Second Workers' Congress, it noted: "Since our aim is none other than to study the problems that workers face we hope that you will provide us with the guarantees necessary for us to hold our second proletarian congress."[77] But for the authorities, the very fact that workers held union meetings or national congresses was evidence of subversive activity whose consequences were potentially disastrous. As the subprefect of Lima noted in his letter to the prefect regarding the organization of the Second Workers' Congress: "it appears that in these meetings revolutionary syndicalism is promoted, and, as a consequence, a dangerous propaganda takes place among the proletarian institutions and among the indigenous element, who must join the ranks of the army."[78] If revolutionary syndicalism was the natural complement to the labor relations put forward by the Sección del Trabajo, it was at odds with the antilabor discursive strategies of the Leguía regime.

At the same time that it repressed what it considered to be a form of militant labor, the Leguía government promoted a bland form of unionism through patronage of mutual aid societies, which, in exchange, campaigned in favor of the president's reelection efforts. The regime subsidized and paid the rents (though, to judge from available documents, not very regularly) for the locales of the Confederación de Artesanos Unión Universal (CAUU) and the Asamblea de Sociedades Unidas (ASU), two mutual aid organizations.[79] In exchange, both institutions spread government propaganda. In April 1927, the CAUU published a *Manifesto to the Working Class*. Half the pamphlet was taken up by Leguía's mustachioed portrait. After enumerating reasons to endorse Leguía's reelection, it concluded: "The Confederation of Artisans Universal Union turns to the people of the Republic and asks that we look favorably upon the action of the president, who, in all his activities, is energetic and has benefited the whole country. This nation, which desires greatness, must demand unconditionally with its vote the REELECTION of don Augusto B. Leguía, to the presidency of the Republic for the constitutional period 1929–1934."[80] In 1928, the ASU similarly urged workers to back Leguía's reelection and sole candidacy.[81] The CAUU went one better. It produced a *Memorandum to all Workers Societies of the Republic*, two thousand copies of which were given to the Ministry of Government to be distributed throughout the country. The memorandum, which noted that the working class "must thank our genial leader [Leguía] for the most efficient laws that protect it from worker accidents, unfair dismissal, worker insurance, the hygienization of factories and workshops, and for social prophylaxis," called on workers to vote for Leguía.[82]

However, Leguía's labor policy cannot be reduced to mere repression of labor militancy and coopted unions. To be sure, Leguía's repressive labor policy was implemented in a broader context of deepening dictatorship. As Julio Cotler has indicated, like other "order and progress" regimes in Latin America, Leguía justified his reelections in 1924 and 1929 by arguing that the country was not ready for democracy as a consequence of its economic, social, and moral backwardness. Democ-

racy in such conditions was tantamount to chaos. It was therefore necessary for a "caudillo constructor" to organize the country politically and to
set it on the path to economic development. Only then could "true"
democracy prevail.[83] These were precisely the arguments used, and developed further, by one of the regime's most ardent supporters, Clemente
Palma, in his editorials in *Variedades*. Palma argued, for example, that "in
young nations, which have yet to bring together integrally and harmo-
niously the [various] elements of nationality, systems of governance that
are strictly democratic are neither prudent nor conducive to that end
[democracy]." More specifically, Palma suggested, countries "that have
still to resolve the problem of ethnic homogeneity, who maintain elements of ancestral regimes at odds with the principles of democracy"
have tended to produce "ideological vices," as well as "incongruences
with the sociological reality" and a sterile "rhetorical derivation" that
leads to economic stagnation. Palma concluded that such ideological
vices "because they represent ideological failures . . . do not educate but
rather discredit the democratic ideals and confuse societies that march
towards progress."[84]

The justification of dictatorship that Palma and others put forward
focused on the argument that Leguía was constructing a modern and
industrial future that would help Peru overcome its economic, social,
moral, and indeed racial backwardness and therefore establish "true"
democracy. Palma argued for example: "There are a series of public
works being built and more planned that will strengthen our productive
capacity and increase general progress, that the country does not want to
leave partially completed."[85] Similarly, when Manuel Vicente Villarán, an
eminent progressive lawyer and educationalist, issued a manifesto con-
demning Leguía's reelection in 1924, in which he questioned the supposed achievements of the regime, Palma replied:

> There is no person in Peru who can ignore the new spirit that today
> predominates in the nation, the atmosphere of frenzied progress
> and improvement that is visible everywhere. Dr. Villarán need only
> stand on the roof of his house and look south to admire the splen-
> did asphalt avenue that links the city with Miraflores, making of
> that balneario an urban annex of the city; and towards the west, the
> new asphalt road that links Lima with the Republic's foremost port.
> Dr. Villarán need only look at the never-ending buildings, some

sumptuous, others modest, that are being built in all parts of the city, the new factories, the new industrial establishments, that are erected continuously.[86]

The establishment of a new congress dominated by regime supporters was similarly justified with reference to the modern future that it would help to build: "Burning problems of particular concern to one or another political group or interest will not be discussed; but [the congress] will discuss issues related to public health, hygiene, mining, agriculture, trade, ports, industrial development, the support of cultural institutions, public education, etc."[87]

One of the cornerstones of this justification of dictatorship was that the redemption of the Indian was an integral part of Leguía's project of modernization, "by means of cultural action, the passing of protective laws, and the better management of justice in their legal cases." Leguía himself stated in 1929:

> The redemption of the Indian and the irrigation of the coast have the same meaning for me. They are tasks that I undertake consciously, bravely, self-sacrificingly, in order to awaken the agricultural consciousness of the country, in order to democratize property, so that it ceases to be a privilege of the strong and becomes a right of the weak; in short, in order to destroy the final link in the enslaving chain that the glorious hammer of Ayacucho was unable to break and that tied the Indians of the sierra and the colonos of the coast to the yoke of a servile and intolerable tutelage.[88]

It is telling that Leguía viewed irrigation and the redemption of the Indian as the same thing: the goal in each case was to transform something barren into something productive; to turn desert into cane fields and Indians into workers. Interestingly, Palma viewed this aspect of Leguía's broader project as one of the more difficult tasks that the regime set itself: "In our opinion this task will be difficult and take a long time to complete, because it will require us to struggle with the passive resistance that the Indian race puts up. Perhaps better and more permanent results would be obtained through the contact with superior races and the rigid application of special work legislation for the Indians."[89] Leguía thought otherwise. Immigration, though welcome, could not replace the need to redeem the Indian: "Before we promote immigration and inject new blood into our people our duty is to make the most of the potential of our own population."[90] As this reveals, the debates over labor and indigeneity examined in the first chapter clearly informed, indeed provided the rationale for, Leguía's project of modernization.

The influence of these debates on the policy of the Patria Nueva throws new light on one of the more controversial aspects of Leguía's regime: the Ley de Conscripción Vial (Law of Road Conscription). Scholars have tended to see the law, which, in practice, obliged indigenous people to provide corvée labor for road building, as a simple mechanism for the extraction of Indian labor; even, some argue, as evidence of an alliance between the central state and Andean landlords and gamonales. By contrast, a recent reinterpretation has suggested that, in fact, the law gave the indigenous the possibility to exercise a degree of agency, pitting the state against local gamonales.[91] But the law needs also to be understood as a reflection of the widely shared idea, shared even by Leguía, that labor could redeem Peru's indigenous people, and that Indians, once civilized (i.e., once de-Indianized) by their transformation into workers, could contribute to progress. This idea was graphically illustrated in 1925 in a magazine called *Ciudad y Campo y Caminos*, which included a photograph of a "group of Indians." The photograph's caption reads, "These men are the same men who, just a few days ago, were working on the construction of the road and now we can see them running, amazed and enthusiastic, after the cars, machines completely unknown to them but which will contribute to their civilization."[92] A few years later, the same magazine carried another photograph of two smiling indigenous men in traditional clothes. The idea that working on the roads was helping to civilize these men was repeated: "With the increase in road building and the popularization of the automobile, [these Indians] are assimilating civilization, which combining within them with the strength of their race, their healthy morality, and special aptitude for heavy work, transforms them into valuable and effective elements in the present era of prosperity that the country is experiencing."[93] In this way, elite observers, echoing Leguía's own rhetoric, reimagined, and justified, corvée labor in road-building schemes as a civilizational strategy.

On the surface, Leguía's labor policy would appear to have been characterized by a short period of labor relations envisioned by the Sección del Trabajo replaced by a longer period of labor relations characterized by repression. Put differently, the rationalities of government manifested in the labor state were abandoned in favor of measures that reflected rationalities of discipline. To be sure, Leguía repressed organized labor systematically if selectively, "othered" forms of labor deemed militant, and sought to mold a compliant labor movement. Other than the workers and organizations subjected to repression, the principal victim of this policy was the Sección del Trabajo—turned into an ineffective institution ignored by employers and shunned by workers—and more generally the labor state, the state of and for labor, which workers had embraced in the early 1920s. But as the analysis above suggests, rationalities of government continued to shape Leguía's broader labor policy even after the Sección del Trabajo's capacity to shape labor relations had been severely undermined. Leguía viewed the repression of militant labor, and the deepening dictatorship on which his rule depended, as a necessary condition for the successful implementation of a project of governmentality that posited labor as an agent of progress and as the key dimension of a civilizational and redemptive strategy aimed at the indigenous. Like the elite ideas of labor examined in the previous section, Leguía's labor policy was shaped by both rationalities of discipline and rationalities of government that reflected constructions of labor as a social threat but also as an agent of progress. In turn, this combination of rationalities of discipline and government expressed more generally the ways in which labor in Peru was immanent to a project of racialized nation formation.

REBUILDING THE LABOR STATE FROM BELOW

In the 1930s, both rationalities of discipline and rationalities of government continued to shape labor policy. Following Luis M. Sánchez Cerro's "Arequipa Revolution" (August 1930) and the fall of the Leguía regime, the Sección del Trabajo was reorganized during the brief interim governments presided by the government juntas led by Sánchez Cerro (August 1930–March 1931) and David Samanez Ocampo (March–December 1931). Erasmo Roca was reappointed as director of development, and a number of progressives and radicals, including Angela Ramos, a member of the Peruvian Communist Party, were employed at the Sección del Trabajo. Among the earliest activities of the revamped Sección del Trabajo was the organization of a labor exchange (Bolsa de Trabajo) in the locale of the CAUU to help Lima's growing army of unemployed workers.[94] Roca was particularly preoccupied with expanding the reach of the Sección del Trabajo beyond Lima. In September 1930, a decree ordered the creation of regional labor inspectorates (*Inspecciones Regionales del Trabajo*), to fulfill the same functions of the Sección del Trabajo in the major provincial cities of the country. By 1933, there were inspectorates in Talara, Trujillo, Cañete, Huacho, Oroya, Callao, Arequipa, and Chiclayo.[95] At the same time, Roca set about establishing a basic statistical understanding of Peruvian labor relations.[96] At the Sección del Trabajo, the new chief Manuel Chávez Fernández sought to recapture the spirit that had guided the Sección del Trabajo in the early 1920s. During a dispute between the Federation of Print Workers (FGP) and a print shop, Chávez Fernández remarked to the minister of development: "The print shop argues that when the workers struck, they abandoned their work, and have, as a consequence, lost all their rights. This medieval reasoning is unacceptable because the government exists as a regulatory power for just such cases. To accept the argument put forward by the printshop is to return to a no-holds-barred war between capital and labor and this is legally impossible given that constitutional and governmental precepts exist that establish the procedure and resolution of conflicts."[97]

Much as in the early 1920s, the combination of labor-friendly faces in the Sección del Trabajo and a climate of political and economic uncertainty appear to have convinced workers to turn again to the Sección del Trabajo to bring employers to the negotiating table. This was a local dimension of a transnational process. As Rodgers notes, in most North Atlantic economies in this period, "as jobs evaporated in the early years of the crisis . . . union coalitions that had long resisted government adjudication of the terms of collective bargaining turned to the state to broker new pacts between labor, government, and stability-seeking employers."[98] This increase in activity at the Sección del Trabajo did not go unnoticed. In May 1931, the prefect of Lima wrote to the Ministry of Government regarding "the frequent labor disputes handled by that Office" and requested that the Sección del Trabajo's rulings be transcribed to him.[99] According to the surviving documentation, the Sección del Trabajo handled some twenty-six disputes in 1930 and another twenty-two in 1931, although the actual figure is likely to have been higher in both cases. The rise in disputes created an "industry" built around dispute resolution. A number of lawyers, such as Luciano Castillo and Edgardo Rebagliati in Lima and Francisco Mostajo and José Luis Bustamante y Rivero in Arequipa, who had honed their skills as labor lawyers in the 1920s, began to specialize in advising unions during disputes and representing them at the negotiations at the Sección del Trabajo.[100] Booklets, such as R. Costa y Cavero's *Workers' Grievances Presented to the Ministry of Development*, were published and presumably bought by workers involved in disputes. The booklets contained all the relevant laws regarding labor disputes and explanations of the roles of the Ministry of Development and the Sección del Trabajo. In addition, the booklets provided copies of all the necessary forms.[101]

This climate of political opening during the early phase of Samanez Ocampo's interim government was short-lived. A strike wave begun in 1930 in the mines of the central highlands culminated in the general strike of May 1931 called by the Confederación General de Trabajadores del Perú (CGTP), the labor central controlled by the Peruvian Communist Party, in the context of a deeply acrimonious taxi drivers' strike.[102] During the general strike, the government issued a decree that suspended all civil liberties the moment a strike was declared.[103] Following the election of Sánchez Cerro to the presidency in late 1931, the repressive climate grew. In early 1932, congress passed the so-called Emergency Law, which handed the government extensive powers to repress labor and political opponents. A network of police informants was quickly put in place. Following the Trujillo Aprista "revolution" of mid-1932, the repression of labor increased significantly.[104] In a climate of increased repression of union activities and persecution of labor leaders, as in the 1920s, unions were forced to reassert their apolitical character if they wished to continue to operate.[105] For the authorities, however, again as in the 1920s, the very fact that workers sought to meet socially, let alone organize, represented a potential threat to social order. In 1934, the authorities denied workers permission to hold the annual Fiesta de la Planta, as they had done six years earlier (see above), on the grounds that "as regards this celebration, while it is true that the people of Vitarte, in particular the textile workers, and the people who go from Lima have a day of leisure, it is also true that it is used to remind [those attending] that on that day the struggle against bosses must be reaffirmed and that they must not allow themselves to be exploited, ideas that, evidently, only serve to revive the antagonism that is created between capital and labor, and which, if it is not countered, can have fatal consequences."[106]

In this context, the Sección del Trabajo was reorganized for a second time and Manuel Vigil was named chief in August 1932. Almost immediately, Vigil set about altering radically the tone of labor relations that

Roca and Chávez Fernández had favored. He requested a list from the prefecture of "dangerous individuals, particularly . . . those who propagate subversive, divisive, and communist ideas," so that the Sección del Trabajo would be "informed about the precedents of those who present grievances or provoke conflicts between capital and labor."[107] His request was denied on the grounds that police archives were secret. But Vigil's repressive instincts were not easily appeased. In October 1932, when the streetcar workers struck, Vigil wrote to the minister of government requesting that orders be given "so that the unacceptable situation is repressed."[108] Vigil's strong-arm tactics appear to have coincided with a sharp reduction in labor disputes in 1932, although it is unclear if the two were directly connected. By 1934, however, labor unrest was again increasing. The number of disputes handled by the Sección del Trabajo rose in 1934 to fifty-eight, more than one a week. Of these, fifty-two were settled by conciliation (i.e., both sides came to an agreement) and six by arbitration (i.e., the arbitration tribunal issued a ruling).[109] In spite of his apparent hostility to labor, under Vigil's stewardship, the institutional profile of labor issues was raised. The Sección del Trabajo was transferred from the Ministry of Development to the newly created Ministry of Public Health, Labor, and Social Foresight, and a Labor Directorate was created. The Sección del Trabajo expanded its functions to include an office that provided legal advice to workers in order to speed up resolution of disputes.[110]

The raised ministerial profile of labor issues reflected their raised constitutional profile. If the 1920 constitution had introduced a separate "Social Guarantees" section, the 1933 constitution grouped the articles related to labor in a single "National and Social Guarantees" chapter, as if to suggest that the social and the national were indistinguishable.[111] Such a suggestion seems to be confirmed by the inclusion of article 53, which outlawed "internationally organized political parties," a thinly veiled reference to both APRA and the Peruvian Communist Party (PCP). The articles refering to labor reprised the main points of the 1920 constitution. Thus, article 46 established the state's power to legislate on the organization and "general security" of industrial work, the length of the working day, and a minimum wage. Articles 48, 49, and 50 pointed to the state's role as guarantor of public health and provider of, in effect, social security, establishing that "the law will create a foresight regime [*régimen de previsión*] to address the economic consequences of unemployment, old age, sickness, disability, and death and will develop social solidarity institutions, savings and insurance establishments, and cooperatives" and gave the state the power to "cheapen" subsistence goods. Although the 1933 constitution made no mention of compulsory arbitration in labor disputes (an aspect of the 1920 constitution), it nevertheless included a number of innovations. Article 43, possibly inspired by the Italian corporatist Carta del Lavoro of 1927, established that the state would legislate on the collective labor contract, although article 44 prohibited the inclusion in collective contracts of any restrictions to civil, political, and social rights. Finally, article 45, possibly drawing on article 123 of the 1917 Mexican constitution, established that the state would favor a profit-sharing regime for workers.

Despite the raised institutional and the reasserted constitutional profile of labor issues, the governments of Sánchez Cerro and, from 1933, Óscar R. Benavides (1933–39) did little to address the problems that had plagued the Sección del Trabajo in the previous decade. In early 1931, one newspaper complained of the Sección del Trabajo's inefficiency in dealing with disputes and urged less bureaucracy.[112] However, the queues and delays that the newspaper criticized are more likely to have been the result of a *lack* of bureaucracy. The Sección del Trabajo's growing institutional presence was not necessarily reflected in an increased capacity to deal with the problems it was created to address. In 1896 the Ministry of Development had 30 employees, of which 11 worked in the Directorate of Development. By 1919, the Ministry's workforce had risen to 654 employees, and by 1929 it stood at 1,257.[113] But the Sección del Trabajo accounted for a very small proportion of this bureaucracy. In 1929, the Sección del Trabajo's workforce stood at 6 employees. The inspectorate employed another 5.[114] With a staff of 6, the Sección del Trabajo was not equipped to deal with the growing number of disputes. Though its budget is unknown, the Sección del Trabajo was clearly underfunded.[115] In addition to limited resources, the Sección del Trabajo suffered from a crippling lack of power. Sección del Trabajo officials regularly complained of employers' open flouting of their rulings. In 1936, the inspector in Cuzco admitted: "Unfortunately, many of my rulings are flouted by persons who lack scruples or who have a certain social position, [and] who disregard the laws that protect both the bosses and the workers."[116]

The problems faced by the Sección del Trabajo were compounded by the critique, formulated by the new political forces on the left, of the labor relations it sought to promote. Both the PCP and APRA encouraged workers' distrust of the Sección del Trabajo. The Communist-controlled CGTP called for the abolition of the Sección del Trabajo. It claimed that the Sección del Trabajo itself recognized that it could not impose its rulings on employers and that "the Peruvian proletariat never saw in the Sección del Trabajo anything other than a means to contain and halt the surge of the great worker masses."[117] APRA's newspaper *La Tribuna* routinely ran articles that pointed to the Sección del Trabajo's ineptitude, with titles to match: "Irrefutable Proof of the Uselessness of the Sección del Trabajo"; "The Lethargic Sección del Trabajo Allows Employers to Mock the Labor Laws."[118] Both parties sought to present the Sección del Trabajo as a mere appendage of employers' interests. Whether the Sección del Trabajo was indeed biased toward employers is unclear. As in the 1920s, the Sección del Trabajo continued to use union recognition as a tool to control unions. In 1934 it recognized seven new "societies"; in 1935 another twenty-six.[119] The bulk of these new unions, as indicated by their names, were mutual aid societies. But available evidence suggests that selective union recognition was intended to undermine union militancy rather than favor employers. Despite worker protests to the contrary, the documentation shows that the Sección del Trabajo employees saw themselves as impartial pillars of a state-endorsed form of social justice. But workers disagreed. As in the 1920s, workers in the 1930s soon began to shun the Sección del Trabajo. In 1934, for example, the textile federation complained of the attitude of Vigil in a dispute with *El Progreso* textile mill.[120] In 1936, the streetcar workers refused to negotiate at the Sección del Trabajo, arguing that "the Sección del Trabajo chief made scornful comments about the workforce (all the streetcar workers are thieves) and in this way made clear his bias with the company."[121]

In spite of the negative perception of the Sección del Trabajo among organized workers, the surviving documentation and, as we have seen, official figures published by the Ministry of Development suggest that many workers continued to take their disputes to the Sección del Trabajo. More than 160 separate disputes from 1930 to 1939 survive in the Sección del Trabajo documentation. As in the 1920s, as I discussed in the previous chapter, they concern a broad range of workers, although Lima textile workers, bus drivers, streetcar workers, shoemakers, bakery workers, and printers, as well as sharecroppers (a fair number of them Japanese sharecroppers pitted against Japanese landowners) from the valleys near the capital, dominate. The groups bringing their grievances to the Sección del Trabajo include theater workers from Callao, hospital orderlies employed by the Hospital Italiano, olive pickers employed by the Lima Jockey Club, the Arequipa hairdressers' union, and a group of disgruntled Poles contracted to colonize parts of the Cuzco jungle requesting that their return passages to Poland be paid by the Sindicato Polaco-Americano de Colonización del Sepa.[122] The relative dearth of disputes involving workers outside Lima may in part be a consequence of the creation of the regional inspectorates, which now dealt with disputes locally. One exception is a dispute involving the tenants of the Sangual and Unigambal haciendas in La Libertad.[123] Still, there is much to indicate that the documentation is largely incomplete. As in the 1920s, most of the disputes concerned attempts by employers to transfer the cost of the economic downturn to their workforce, by firing workers, cutting wages, increasing hours of work without increasing remuneration, reducing working hours without consultation with workers, failing to observe onerous labor legislation regarding days of rest, paid holidays, protective equipment, and hygienic conditions, and failing to observe collective contracts. Although the economy had recovered by 1933, most disputes continued to revolve around the same issues. But the dispute also reflected how labor policy in the 1930s continued to be shaped by both rationalities of discipline and rationalities of government.

One dispute, the 1931 dispute between the Lima bakery workers union, the Federación de Obreros Panaderos "Estrella del Perú" (FOPEP), and the bakery owners illustrates this well. Ostensibly over whether the union or the bakery owners were entitled to determine who worked in the industry, the dispute was acrimonious and long and was taken to an arbitration tribunal. The bakery owners argued that the 1920 industry-wide collective contract, which created a closed shop and which they were trying to rescind, established a monopoly that restrained the freedom to work and to contract, the "greatest" of all freedoms. Such a monopoly was unwarranted. For one thing, the work carried out by bakery workers could be performed by just about anyone: "The bakery worker is a worker like any other, he is not a professional, he has no special skills, he is a simple worker who acquires basic knowledge in a workshop, and who, with our existing mechanization, as incipient as it is, no longer performs any mental or physical labor, but rather merely executes a simple mechanical action."[124] Bakery workers, therefore, were mere appendages to machines, and, as such, had no right to a say in how the industry was run, or, more precisely, in who worked in the industry. Moreover, the bakery owners argued, bakery workers enjoyed some of the highest wages in Peru. The bakery industry, on the other hand, was poor: "We are not talking about large industrial establishments, run by large capitalists, but of simple kneading machines in which the owner lives right next to his workers, and shares their yearning and weariness." Indeed, the majority of bakery owners took an active part in the everyday work of the bakeries. By presenting themselves as little more than workers, the bakery owners created an image of an industry where both owner and worker were equals, where no exploitation could occur for it would affect the owner as much as the worker.

However, the bakery owners' key argument was that a ruling in favor of the FOPEP would be a victory for communism. The FOPEP members, the bakery owners argued, were unpatriotic troublemakers who sought simply to upset the social order, and who did not represent the majority of bakery workers: "Those who promote this impossible social reform are professional agitators, firebrands who upset social order, who put forward ideas that are at odds with the Fatherland and its institutions; they are, in the end, those who, in exploiting the good faith of our people and of their own comrades, hold the country in a constant state of agitation and alarm."[125] If the tribunal ruled in favor of the FOPEP, only the small group of workers who held "utopian and devastating ideas" would be able to work. Both capital and the state would suffer: "The freedom and capital of the bakery industry, as well as the respectability and prestige of authority would come under the control of an invariably passionate and violent union." Indeed the effects of such a ruling would have deep repercussions beyond the bakery industry and would amount to a radical overhaul of economic and social organization: "It would be the beginning of a substantial transformation in the present system and organization of work and of industry in Peru."[126]

The bakery workers' representative at the arbitration tribunal, Jorge R. Gutiérrez, made a spirited rebuttal of the bakery owners' accusations. He rejected the claim that the FOPEP did not represent the bakery workforce. Most bakery workers, he pointed out, were members of the union. The FOPEP had been officially recognized by both the national and city governments, clear proof of its legitimacy. Moreover, recognition had been granted for a very sensible reason: the FOPEP fulfilled a key social and sanitary role. The FOPEP did not seek a monopoly. Bakery workers were in favor of freedom of work "as long as that freedom does not undermine good practices and public health, just as the state constitution itself has established." How else, Gutiérrez asked, can we stop the "morally and physically diseased, assassins and thieves" from working in bakeries? Moreover, the FOPEP demanded that workers join the union not merely for the well-being of society as a whole but because unionization amounted to private well-being, or, "discipline, order, [and] the inculcation of method and culture of man by man [*la metodización y la culturización del hombre por el hombre*]."[127] Gutiérrez went on to claim that the bakery owners, who restricted competition by imposing a minimum distance between bakeries, held the real monopoly. Competition would benefit the consumer. The owners' claims that the industry was in crisis were bogus: the price of flour had fallen to half its 1919 price, wages had not been raised since 1920, demand had grown considerably, and owners had become rich enough to purchase property for themselves.

More important perhaps, Gutiérrez turned the bakery owners' key argument on its head. The FOPEP, he noted, played a key mutual aid function: it protected workers in an industry characterized by unhygienic conditions and high mortality, where workers were exposed to illnesses that were not considered in compensation legislation. However, unionization not only helped improve the organization of work but was a key factor in preventing "deviations of a political or other nature, which are not relevant to work and just work." The FOPEP was not a militant organization. On the contrary, Gutiérrez argued, it represented the last defense against communism. Moreover, the FOPEP, and unions generally, embodied progress itself. The League of Nations, Gutiérrez noted, had recommended to "civilized" governments of the world "the creation of worker corporations or guilds, in the different areas of human activity." Gutiérrez went on to argue:

> Today the state is not an abstract figure or an entity without substance. Today the state is a living thing; it is the summary and compendium of the way of thinking of the productive class. Today the state is the people themselves, creating the laws that favor their improvement and their legitimate life rights. Today the state is the aggregate of all guilds and unions, which account for all licit human activity. Nothing and no one can destroy these unions and

nothing and no one can stop them from regulating work, within mutual and reciprocal respect, within liberty and social harmony.

Unions, then, worked not against the state, but within it and together with it.

The debates at the arbitration tribunal clearly illustrate how rationalities of government and rationalities of discipline provided particular idioms with which workers and employers sought to shape labor relations. Typically, employers sought to present workers as dangerous to their businesses and to society more generally. During a dispute at the El Escritorio printshop in 1930, for example, the printshop owner refused to take back workers who had struck on the grounds that "because of their conduct they have become a danger to the calm and disciplined atmosphere that is necessary for the proper functioning of this business."[128] Similarly, in 1933, the manager at the Huaico textile mill in Arequipa wrote to the prefect to denounce the activities of a worker who had been behind the latest strike. This worker, the manager noted "has been in Germany and even in Russia and . . . has told us about conditions in São Paulo and we think it is very likely that during his travels he has come into contact with Communists and that he remains in contact with them; there is no other explanation for his behavior. In sum, he is a dangerous individual and his influence on the people is extremely negative."[129] Workers, by contrast, typically sought to present their grievances as consonant with, and conducive to, the objectives of the labor state. During a dispute at the San Jacinto textile mill in 1930, for example, the union pointed to its 1922 collective contract and to the legitimacy that the contract conferred on its demands: "The existence of a collective work contract means that it is impossible to deny our legal right. Contracts are legally binding for those who enter into them, this is a basic principle of classic jurisprudence, and, in the relations between bosses and workers, the collective contract represents a social guarantee to avoid a reduction in wages, which employers often attempt."[130]

As this suggests, in the early 1930s many unions invoked the rationalities of government expressive of the idea that labor was an agent of progress as a strategy to counteract the deployment by employers of rationalities of discipline expressive of the idea that labor constituted a threat to social order; that is, the two ideas about labor became idioms through which labor disputes, and the very idea of labor relations, were negotiated. In what amounted to an attempt to reestablish labor relations envisioned by the Sección del Trabajo from below, that is, to rebuild the labor state from below, workers used this idiom to invoke the labor state and the broader project of governmentality that it reflected. In most cases, such attempts backfired. Even when disputes were resolved in favor of workers, the Sección del Trabajo typically proved incapable of enforcing the rulings of arbitration tribunals. Many unions were severely weakened by this process and workers, understandably, sought alternative ways to resist the attacks of employers on their working conditions and livelihoods. In some cases, these alternatives lead to a radicalization of unions, as they came into contact with the political projects of the Peruvian Communist Party or APRA, a process that in many cases served to legitimize, in the eyes of the authorities, the accusations of employers regarding the danger represented by workers making demands for better wages or better working conditions. In others, it led to attempts to establish accommodations with the authoritarian regimes in power.[131]

Yet, as the bakery workers' dispute shows, labor proved adept at connecting the ideas of labor as an agent of progress and labor as a threat to social order in ways that helped to strengthen its position in the political context of the 1930s. Another example may further illustrate this. In 1939, the Lima print workers union was reorganized after a number of years of inactivity that came about because of repression. According to an editorial in the *Obrero Gráfico*, the union's newspaper, its aims and values were those of a moderate institution:

> We do not pretend to engage in a senseless struggle in the terrain of social demands; no, respectful of order and of the protection of the law, we aim to reconquer the rights that have been denied us, request the enforcement of those laws, and, respecting also the rights of others, while defending with justice and serenity our own rights, advance down that rugged road without wavering, with the sure footing that print workers know and can demonstrate and with the certainty that we will know how to defend our present and our future.[132]

With this editorial the union leadership hoped no doubt to signal to the authorities that it rejected radical projects, and, in particular, that its own flirtation with radical projects, namely the Communist Party, which had had considerable influence in the union in the early 1930s, was in the past. But while the editorial emphasized the moderate character of the union, it also stressed the type of legal and institutional framework of labor relations required in order to achieve a successful labor relations policy in the new, freer, political climate that the new government of Manuel Prado (1939–45) was promoting. The themes that the editorial flagged, the protection of the law, labor rights, and justice, and the implication that these had in the past been denied, all indirectly pointed to the causes of (and responsibilities for) the "senseless struggles" of the past. Like the bakery workers' rebuttal of the bakery owners' accusations, this editorial points to a sophisticated reformulation of the labor state from below. The editorial implied that the senseless struggles of the past were a direct consequence of the absence of effective labor relations, that is, of the absence of the labor state that the Sección del Trabajo had promoted but failed to deliver. In this way, Lima's print workers mobilized both rationalities of government and rationalities of discipline to formulate, at once, a critique of the state's failings and a proposal for a new social order based on the reestablishment of the labor state.

CONCLUSION

In this chapter, I have explored the interplay of rationalities of discipline and rationalities of government in shaping the labor policy envisioned in the labor state in the 1920s. The "failure" of the Sección del Trabajo to impose its rulings on employers and its gradual shunning by workers who had first been drawn to its promise of state-mediated arbitration and collective bargaining would appear to suggest that the Leguía regime quickly abandoned the project of governmentality that seemed to have come into being with the creation of the Sección del Trabajo and the 1920 constitution. Employers rejected the Sección del Trabajo's rulings because they perceived them as onerous but more generally because they, and Peruvian elites more generally, came to see worker demands for better working conditions as unjustified and as invariably influenced by militant tendencies that threatened the social order. However, in constructing labor as a threat to social order they also constructed a more congenial version of labor, inferior to, but dependent upon, a paternalistic elite; a construction that reprised and reproduced the rationalities of government that formed the basis of the labor state. Similarly, while the Leguía regime actively repressed labor, it construed repression as integral and necessary to the realization of the project of governmentality manifested in the labor state, which envisioned the governmental regulation of labor as a means of overcoming indigeneity; in this way the rationalities of discipline deployed in the Leguía period are better understood not as an abandonment, but rather as another dimension of the labor state; that is, of a racialized project of national redemption and civilization.

In the 1930s, in a context of intense repression and despite the bitter experience of the 1920s and the increasingly present critique of the state-mediated labor relations emanating from the Left, workers turned again to the Sección del Trabajo. In so doing, they sought to exploit the tension between the rationalities of discipline and the rationalities of government shaping labor policy in order to gain some concessions from employers as part of a broader attempt to reestablish the labor state from below. Like the elites in the 1920s, workers construed militancy as a social threat. But they argued that the threat would be most effectively combated by fulfilling the aspirations envisioned by the labor state rather than by repression alone. Militancy in this view was reelaborated not as a product of foreign or sick influences but as expressive of the failure to fully implement the labor state and more concretely as an inevitable consequence of employers' resistance to the project of governmentality manifested in the labor state. This discursive strategy reveals the extent to which workers viewed the labor state as an expression of their own governmental aspirations. But it also reveals how workers effectively reelaborated the rationalities of government envisioned by the labor state as a key dimension of their critique of the failures of the projects of nation-state formation of the elites.

4

DOMESTICATING LABOR

When, in 1935, the Junta Departamental Pro-Desocupados de Lima (Departmental Unemployment Commission of Lima) published a book showcasing the public works it had carried out since its creation four years earlier, it chose to depict on the book's cover a projected new bridge over the Rímac River. The book authors explained that the bridge was a project of "great technical and economic magnitude" that would make a major contribution to the urban development of the capital, "creating for the first time in 64 years a new structure that links the N. W. INDUSTRIAL ZONE with the S. W. WORKER POPULATION ZONE."[1] The symbolism of the image was clear. The Junta Pro-Desocupados, and through it, the state, undertook to enable industrial progress by linking physically and symbolically capital and labor. To put it in the terms of the image employed, the state's role, the book suggested, was to bridge the divide that kept labor and capital apart. The symbolism employed was revealing of the ways in which the authors of the book understood this "bridging." The image invoked the state's technical capacity, its ability to literally and metaphorically "engineer" the bridge between labor and capital; the divide between labor and capital was understood as a problem that could be addressed through the application of science and technology. But the image also invoked the role of the state as the mediator between labor and capital and as the entity in which the power to harness and make productive labor and capital in order to bring about progress ultimately resides. The image invoked what I have called the labor state.

This chapter and the next two examine the development of the Peruvian labor state in the 1930s. As in the 1920s, the technification of labor relations in the 1930s invoked by the image of the bridge reflected an attempt to evacuate politics from labor relations and protect labor from pernicious influences. But the development of the labor state in the 1930s also reflected the perception that labor was a necessary and key element in the constitution of an industrial order that would help Peru overcome its backward character: as in earlier periods, in the 1930s too labor was understood as an agent of progress and civilization. But labor was also seen as in need of civilizing. In the 1920s, as I have shown, elites came to see labor as endangered by foreign ideologies. In the 1930s that danger materialized in the shape of the Peruvian Communist Party and APRA. Labor policy was designed to counteract the influence of both parties on labor. Initiatives such as the worker housing projects discussed in this chapter, or the "popular restaurants" and the 1936 Social Security Law discussed in the next two, were "weapons of the strong" (to invert James C. Scott's famous term), which the 1930s governments used to undermine the support of labor for the parties of the Left.[2] The worker housing projects, or "barrios obreros," were elements in a broader strategy to undermine the appeal of the new political parties purporting to represent and lead labor. The new houses provided work (unemployed workers were used in their construction) and a decent place to live. By building these houses, the governments of the 1930s could claim to have the interests of labor truly at heart.

However, as historians who have studied worker housing in other contexts have argued, worker houses were not only intended to house workers and in so doing weaken the appeal of "revolutionary" projects. They were also intended to create the "right" type of worker.[3] Like their counterparts elsewhere, Peruvian social reformers too saw worker housing as a civilizational strategy or, as Lewis Mumford saw it, as civilization itself.[4] Drawing on such approaches, I argue in this chapter that the barrios obreros reflected rationalities of government and functioned as a technology of government in the sphere of housing; that is, they reflected the belief that the state should protect workers and seek to "improve" them by acting both directly upon them and upon their mediate and immediate environments. By building worker houses, social reformers hoped to "domesticate" workers, that is, to instill certain gendered values and habits in those who lived in them. Owning a house would encourage the male worker to settle down and start a family and to develop a new interest in thrift and economic responsibility. The architects of the housing projects believed that these new values and habits would keep militancy at bay. But the barrios obreros primarily reflected the belief that worker housing would protect workers from disease, immorality, and exploitation from unscrupulous landlords and that in so doing they would enable them to constitute themselves as the physical and moral agents of Peru's "civilization." In this way, worker housing, much like the Sección del Trabajo, reflected the rationalities of government manifested in the labor state, which hinged on the constitution of labor as a subject capable of redeeming the Peruvian nation and leading it down the path to progress.

BEYOND INCORPORATION

The 1930s were years of major economic and political upheaval in Peru. Although the economic downturn was relatively short-lived and did not contribute to a major structural overhaul of the country's economy, the world depression had a deep impact on the country, resulting in high levels of unemployment in cities and the export industries. The period was also characterized by severe political instability, which has led some authors to represent it as a "revolutionary crisis." In part, this instability was shaped by the formation of new "modern" parties, the Peruvian Communist Party (PCP), the Alianza Popular Revolucionaria Americana (APRA), and the Unión Revolucionaria (UR), the party of President Luis M. Sánchez Cerro (1931–33), and by the emergence of new political discourses (communism, populism, fascism), which, together, significantly expanded and polarized the political arena.[5] In this context, labor unrest increased considerably (as measured by the number and intensity of strikes), culminating, as discussed in the previous chapter, in the May 1931 general strike, which involved several thousand workers from a series of industries and which had a nationwide impact. As occurred with other strikes in this period, such as the October 1930 strikes in the central highlands, the PCP tried to transform the 1931 general strike into a catalyst for revolutionary action. Arguably, these were quixotic revolutionary ventures, which alienated much of organized labor and helped legitimize, in the eyes of many, state repression. However, these actions, and, later, a series of APRA-led strikes, set the tone for labor relations in much of the later 1930s. In this context, both the governments of Luis Sánchez Cerro (1931–33) and Óscar Benavides (1933–39) introduced a series of measures aimed, according to government propaganda, at easing the impact of the world slump on labor.

There is little doubt that the labor policy of both the Sánchez Cerro and Benavides governments, in the shape of barrios obreros, restaurantes populares, and the Seguro Social (among other measures), had a clear political intent. This "social action" of Sánchez Cerro and Benavides formed one part of a two-pronged strategy aimed at curtailing industrial unrest and labor militancy. As is well known, the other part consisted of intense but selective repression of labor organizations and of the political parties of the Left. During the general strike of May 1931, for example, the government issued a decree that suspended all civil liberties whenever a strike was declared. More important, in early 1932, congress passed the Emergency Law, which handed the Sánchez Cerro government unlimited powers to repress labor and political opponents. The political tension was raised as confrontations between the government and the parties of the Left became increasingly violent. The massacre by the military of hundreds of Apristas in Trujillo in April 1932 was followed in 1933 by the assassination of President Sánchez Cerro by an Aprista militant. In this increasingly volatile context, the "social action" policies became increasingly political, that is, increasingly perceived and used as political tools to coopt or "incorporate" a working class thought to be increasingly militant and potentially revolutionary.[6] Both APRA and the Communist Party claimed that the state's social action was strategy to weaken their political appeal to organized labor. According to Gonzalo Portocarrero, "the point was to show that the state could do what APRA was demanding."[7]

Like Perón in 1940s Argentina, but also like most interwar governments in the North Atlantic economies (from Mussolini's Italy to Roosevelt's New Deal United States), the Peruvian governments of the 1930s "preached the need to harmonize the interests of capital and labor within the framework of a benevolent state, in the interest of the nation and its economic development."[8] The Benavides government in particular presented its "social action," or "corporatism," as being above partisan politics:

> In general terms, [corporatism] represents the middle ground between individualism and socialism. It harmonizes the rights of man

with the permanent interests of the state. Corporations, the unitary organizations of the productive, cultural, or other forces, are the foundations of social organization. The state protects private initiative, which it considers the most efficient instrument for the [pursuit] of the national interest, but, at the same time, it subordinates individual goals to the higher goals of the nation. It organizes production according to a rational plan and with the invigoration of the nation as its purpose, [thus] eliminating conflicts between capital and labor.[9]

Rather than representing elite interests, the state thus claimed to stand above them and politics more generally and adopted a role as arbitrator between the two great social actors, capital and labor.[10] In this discourse, the pursuits of social justice and state autonomy meshed to form the supporting structures of new and "modern" (rational) state-building and nation-building projects that aimed at revitalizing the nation-state ("the invigoration of the nation as its purpose") by suppressing class conflict in favor of class harmony.

A speech Benavides gave in March 1939 may help illustrate further some of the ideas that underpinned his regime's labor policy. Benavides began by noting that Peru was undergoing a process of change that was occurring beyond the material sphere: the country had experienced a veritable transformation in its moral character. Thanks to his intervention, pessimism, "our most incurable disease," had given way to an optimism based on "our wealth, our capacity to exploit it, in the profound and true faith that leads Peruvians towards the great reality of Destiny."[11] One of the cornerstones of this new optimism was a new approach to social problems. Benavides suggested that those who believed that the just aspirations of well-being and improvement of the working class could be postponed indefinitely, or only partially satisfied, were blind accomplices of sectarianism (of APRA). He now realized that social problems were intimately tied to questions of security and progress. Although he made sure to stress that those who manipulated the legitimate aspirations of the working class for personal ambition deserved nothing but condemnation, Benavides declared:

I once said: "I do not know, nor do I want to know, whether I am or not, a socialist. I am, above all, human." Though this should not be interpreted as a rectification of my own thinking, I want to say that if socialism is heightened, compassionate and ample social justice, [in tune with] the supreme interest of the nation and the untouchable authority of the state, I not only share these principles, I have put them into practice, with deep faith, in these five years of government. And not with empty words and easy promises. With laws that function and that are now an inseparable part of our collective existence, which harmonize the legitimate interests of all classes; with useful and long-lasting public works, whose existence cannot be denied or disfigured.[12]

Had "la secta" (APRA) taken power when he had done, Benavides stressed, none of the social deeds he had undertaken would exist and Peru would have been plunged into chaos.

Although Benavides attributed the successes of his regime to his personal actions, he also emphasized the importance of the state in achieving what he called "social equilibrium." He suggested that the increase of wealth at the expense of human capital represented a threat to the nation. Similarly, if labor became too expensive, a drop in entrepreneurship would result; capital would flee the country, economic depression would ensue, and unemployment would increase. Because of its vast natural resources, Peru could look forward to many centuries of prosperity and increased collective well-being. However, Benavides implied, this prosperity would result only from the abandonment of class struggle in favor of class cooperation. New sources of capital would bring about the development of industry and commerce and create new sources of employment. However, the key to national greatness was the protection of human capital: "With a laboring class that is fed deficiently, forced to live in unhygienic housing, incapable of providing education to their children, condemned to live in misery by disease, and in the outmost helplessness by disability and old age, it was impossible to create that state of confidence, of faith, of permanent security that is necessary for the progress of nations."[13] These social problems, Benavides claimed, had been addressed by the social action of the state through the creation of the "restaurantes populares," the "barrios obreros," and the Seguro Social Obrero, among other measures. More generally, the state had initiated "an era of solidarity between classes and . . . instilled in them a consciousness of their responsibilities and duties to the nation."

As I discussed in the introduction to this book, like the APRA and

Communist critics of the Sánchez Cerro and Benavides regimes, historians have typically viewed this discourse as little more than empty rhetoric and portrayed the social policies that derived from it as no more than ploys to undermine support for the new radical political alternatives represented by the Left, that is, as elements of a broader populist politics based on the cooption of labor and the neutralization of the Left. There is little doubt that the "social action" of the Sánchez Cerro and Benavides governments had such a function. But the cooption or incorporation paradigm is incomplete. For one thing, historians of experiences of "populism" elsewhere in Latin America have shown that the cooption or incorporation paradigm does not properly capture the character of the relationship between populist leaders and their clients, particularly organized labor.[14] In this literature, populism appears as a negotiated political but also cultural process, shaped from above and from below, rather than a one-directional process of cooption or incorporation.[15] More generally, to reduce such policies to cooption is to misunderstand or underplay the rationalities of government that such policies represented. The belief expressed by Benavides in the need to protect "human capital," as the president termed it, in order to bring about "the progress of nations" reflected a broader and widely held belief in labor as an agent of progress and in the need for the state to protect, improve, and harness that source of progress. It reflected what I call the labor state.

WORKER HOUSING, 1900–1930

Concern with the poor housing conditions of Lima's workers can be traced back to the early twentieth century, if not earlier. By the middle of the nineteenth century a new group of professionals began to view the city as a source of biological and moral contagion in need of reordering.[16] Public health interventions against epidemic disease went hand in hand with the discovery of the poor as objects of study by Lima's small but influential cohort of physicians and lawyers concerned with the social question.[17] These professionals, foremost among which were the so-called *higienistas*, developed a strongly racialized understanding of Lima's problems, as racial mixing and the presence of "inferior" races (particularly Chinese immigrants, but also Afro-Peruvians and the indigenous) came to be seen as one of the key sources of the city's "backwardness."[18] Peru's higienistas pathologized the city, that is, came to view it as diseased. But they also deemed the city susceptible to sanitary reform and moral redemption. As elsewhere in Latin America, in Peru a new cohort of professionals (lawyers, physicians, architects, and planners) came to believe and forcefully argue that the pathologized city could be turned into a civilized city: bodies and buildings would be improved through the application of scientific methods and the inculcation of civilizing mores and practices.[19] In Latin America as elsewhere in the early twentieth century, as Daniel Rodgers has noted, social reformers agreed "that the core values of a society should be written in its street designs and public buildings, its shelters and its cityscapes."[20] In Lima, the houses of Lima's working peoples were one of the key urban spaces on which were "written" the "core values" of the Peruvian society that social reformers were trying to construct.[21]

The earliest projects to address the poor housing conditions faced by most working-class limeños were framed in terms that mixed ideas about urban regeneration with moral uplift. In 1900, for example, the former president Nicolás de Piérola and his associates set up a construction company, La Colmena, which promised to offer cheap housing to those who, according to the company's prospectus, "live off a wage," and in so doing turn people who rented into people who owned capital. The company sought not only to change the type of building that characterized the city but also, through its new constructions, to change "the city and the general condition of its inhabitants." According to the prospectus, the goals of the company addressed the economic, aesthetic, and moral needs of the city and its population. Thus in addition to "combat mud, ephemeral and unhealthy decoration, and [to fight for] the use of better, more protective and long lasting materials," the company sought to "build healthy and comfortable homes rather than unhealthy and poorly built ones" and "to replace buildings constructed without technique or art, by buildings that can be appreciated, and that make our cities more beautiful." Finally, the company aimed to stimulate the growth of associated industries, increase savings among the population, and more generally, "to open a field of action benefiting the working men." The ambitions of the company were truly revolutionary: "We are motivated, no less, by the intention to have a transformative influence on the habits, character, and way of being of the nation, in order to stimulate and initiate its development."[22]

Piérola's project expressed perfectly what David Parker has called the "fantasy of workers housing" of Peruvian reformers such as Pedro Paulet and Enrique Léon García among others in the early twentieth century.[23] Ideas about housing, according to Parker, reflected two elite objectives with regard to their broader goals of "improving" the working class: "On the one hand it had to provide the poor with clean, spacious, well-ventilated buildings that would resist the incubation of microbes; on the other hand, it had to educate the poor in cleanliness, hygiene, childrearing methods, savings, and temperance." The solution was to turn workers from tenants into proprietors, since elites believed that in so doing both objectives would be met: "Not only would workers live in sanitary homes and no longer be at the mercy of landlords, but they would also develop the habit of saving (rather than spending their paychecks on drink) and by becoming homeowners would supposedly learn the joys and responsibilities of domestic life."[24] Such goals were never met for two simple reasons: few houses were ever built with working-class proprietors in mind, and few workers could afford to pay mortgages as opposed to rent. During the early twentieth century much of the worker housing was built not by private investors such as Piérola but by charities such as the Sociedad de Beneficencia de Lima (Lima Beneficence Society), and only occasionally by the government, as happened during the Guillermo Billinghurst administration (1912–14) when a state-sponsored worker housing project was begun in the Malambo area of the city. However, this project remained unfinished in 1916. Only eight houses had been built and one of these was unlivable.[25] In this context, critics of the fantasy of worker housing began to voice their concerns: "No; let's not mislead ourselves," argued one critic in *La Crónica*. "To build fifty, a hundred, five hundred houses for workers in Lima, will not solve the problem of worker housing." At best, such a scheme would result in the creation of "fifty model workers" who, with time, would join the ranks of the middle class and become "pacific bourgeois, founders of a sort of worker bourgeoisie."[26]

During the 1920s, various elite commentators reprised the "fantasy of worker housing." In late 1921, Carlos Enrique Paz Soldán, a pioneer of social medicine in Peru, gave a talk in Lima's Teatro Mazzi titled "The Worker House, the Basis of Democracy," in which he argued that "the happiness and greatness of nations emanates from the greatness and tranquility of families, and it follows that it makes sense to provide comfortable and cheap homes for the less wealthy, and to create laws that will give each family ownership of the house they live in, with guaranteed fresh air, light, water and sanitation."[27] Similarly, E. S. Dávila Cárdenas, who suggested that there was a need for an "architect general" to oversee the urban transformation of Lima, argued that the city's housing problems needed to be approached from the perspective of science and social medicine. Rather than spending millions on a battleship, the state could build hundreds of modern houses, which would serve as models for further construction of houses and serve as a source of "positively civilizing capital" for workers, who would benefit from living in "physically perfect homes."[28] These ideas were reprised in the very first issue of the magazine *Ciudad y Campo*, in 1924, which suggested that cheap housing would give "modest families" the opportunity to access hygienic living conditions and to become proprietors over time. The magazine stressed that the houses needed to be built in such a way that they would confer a set of values and practices that were hygienic and moral: "Every apartment in the modern affordable house must include the necessary number of rooms for a family in accordance with the limits of relative well-being and with no communication of any kind with contiguous apartments or houses: communal toilets must be avoided, as should be internal corridors that encourage a mix of families that is inconvenient, both from a hygienic and a moral point of view." The magazine also noted that bedrooms should not be used for other purposes during the day and that children and parents should sleep in separate rooms.[29]

Workers were not merely objects of the elite housing "fantasy." They also sought to escape the dire housing conditions they faced in many of the *callejones* ("a blind alley lined generally with one-room dwellings and a single water tap at one end") or the *casas de vecindad* (tenements; usually large colonial houses subdivided into small rental apartments) in which they tended to congregate.[30] In 1921, a group of some fifty white- and blue-collar workers wrote to President Leguía to suggest a solution to the housing crisis in the capital. They pointed to the conditions that they faced: unhygienic housing, high rents, and landlords out for a quick profit. However a solution to this situation had presented itself with the arrival in Lima of "portable houses made of wood" imported by a U.S. company, which was happy to sell the houses on credit. The houses, built by the Portable House Company of Seattle, at the time showcased in Lima's Parque Zoologico, were described in glowing terms by the magazine *Variedades*, which noted that the prefabricated houses allowed anyone, "no matter how meager their income," to become a house owner, "thus satisfying the imperious need for housing."[31] Introducing themselves as "padres de familia," the workers requested that the state grant them land on which to establish these prefabricated homes in the Santa Beatriz district, halfway between Lima and the district of Miraflores. In this way, the signatories noted, "the idea long cherished by your government, a true worker neighborhood" would become a reality.[32] Some historians have seen the *callejón*, Peru's version (in symbolic rather than architectural terms) of the Argentine "conventillo" and the Brazilian "cortiço," as a privileged site of working-class culture and of particular forms of working-class sociability.[33] It has been somewhat romanticized in popular culture; perhaps as a reaction to its pathologization in elite discourse. But it is fair to speculate that most workers would have moved out of the *callejones* if they had been able to afford to do so.

As discussed in previous chapters, Leguía adopted a series of measures shortly after coming to power to address the housing problem. However, these measures appear to have done little to address the problem and may have exacerbated it. According to a study by Alberto Alexander, an architect, the rent controls introduced by Leguía helped stop construction of new housing.[34] For Alexander, the high cost of housing was a consequence of supply-and-demand forces and of the high cost of construction and not of landlord speculation as many believed. Alexander calculated that whereas there had been a 10.3 percent rise in housing supply between 1908 and 1920, the rise in population had been 25.3 percent. This had resulted in a 100 percent increase in the cost of the built square meter in some parts of Lima, an increase to which higher labor and building materials costs had contributed (the former of which Alexander partly blamed on "communist theories"). Rather than attempt to control rents in the city, Alexander suggested, it was imperative to begin a project to build, and build cheaply, in the city. He viewed this as a task in which the state would have to play a key role: "It is evident that the government must be capable of financing a project of intensive construction. It is not a question, naturally, of undertaking a program [of construction] for purely altruistic reasons. [It must be guided] by an economic goal, which would cover, in addition to the cost of the building, some interest and the costs of subsequent organization and management."[35]

Of course, the 1920s did witness a significant expansion of the city's built area. The Leguía regime gave the Foundation Company, a U.S. firm, an exclusive contract to widen and pave the city's streets, modernize its urban infrastructure (electricity, water, sewage, parks, and monuments), and more generally to turn Lima, through a process akin to Haussmann's transformation of Paris, into a "modern" city that would impress foreign visitors and limeños.[36] At the same time, a number of construction companies were given contracts to urbanize different parts of the city. The regime's boosters presented the urbanization undertaken by Leguía as a social deed. The urbanization of Santa Beatriz, previously agricultural land, was showcased as a particular success, thanks to a combination of the low cost of plots and the availability of cheap credit. As a consequence, so the boosters claimed, "it is impossible to count the number of persons who, in this way, have achieved the long-ambitioned dream of owning their own home. Army and navy officers, white-collar workers, veterans, pensioners, manual workers and intellectuals own up to 70 percent of all the plots that have been sold in Santa Beatriz."[37] In addition, the regime built a number of houses for workers in Callao.[38] At their inauguration, Leguía argued that the building of the houses reflected the belief that "social assistance is no longer a favor given by men and becomes an obligation of the state."[39] Similarly, a government report claimed that the seventy-two houses "constitute a model neighborhood. [The worker houses] surely represent the greatest effort made in this country to provide the working class with affordable and hygienic housing. These houses are built with first-class materials and include indispensable comforts and sanitary services."[40]

However, these initiatives did little to address the worker housing question, and their failure led some commentators to frame their concerns regarding the poor housing in Lima within a broader, if veiled, critique of the regime. In 1927, an article in *Variedades*, normally friendly to the regime, noted that the boom in construction was of benefit only to a small sector of the city's population:

> The problem is that houses are built only for the wealthy. Comfortable and spacious chalets; mansions with several floors surrounded by picturesque gardens. For the poor, for the laboring citizens who contribute with their personal effort, with their daily labor, to the well-being of the nation, there are no houses. They are forced to live in the so-called callejones, whose owners do little more than demand prompt payment of the disproportionate rents they charge for miserable, unsanitary, and unhygienic little rooms.

The article went on to describe the appalling conditions of housing in Callao, which it illustrated with a series of photographs. The indignant tone of the article is striking:

> How can we expect their infirmities [*raquitismo de la raza*] to disappear if our people cannot live in homes that have the most basic conditions for the conservation of their health? What use is propaganda in favor of sports, what function can soccer pitches, model stadiums, and lessons in physical culture have for beings that are forced to seek their reinvigorating sleep, after their daily energy expenditure produced by work and sports, in places where water is distributed by the spoonful and where there are no hygienic services?

The author of the article called on the government to urgently build houses for workers in Callao and concluded with what amounted to a thinly veiled critique of Leguía's urbanization projects—a critique that reveals how labor policy was increasingly understood in ways that expressed rationalities of government: "We have no right to boast about our beautiful and modern avenues, or to repeat with a parrot's insistence that *mens sana in corpore sano*, when our people cannot maintain a healthy mind or body given that they have nowhere to sleep according to the most basic principles of hygiene."[41]

Similarly, the magazine *Mundial* ran a series of articles on "the problem of worker housing." One article, which linked poor housing to the spread of tuberculosis, noted that the disease represented a threat not only to those who lived in poor quality housing but also to the rich in their comfortable homes. It gave the example of a woman, a Peruvian version of Typhoid Mary, who cares for her sick children at night but during the day works as a domestic servant in the home of a rich family, "taking with her the germs of this terrible disease, and the whole world knows that these germs do not respect either the poor or the rich . . . !"[42] Another article, written by Federico Ortiz Rodríguez, who penned a regular "Worker's Page," noted that while several countries in Latin America had initiated major worker housing projects, Peru lagged behind "in a matter that is today in all parts of the world the principal question of the modern state." The irony was that Peru had been one of the first countries to initiate worker housing projects. The article listed a series of initiatives: the houses built by Enrique Meiggs in the 1880s in what became the Calle de los Artesanos near the Santa Catalina barracks, the houses built in 1895 by Glicerio Joya in La Victoria district, and the houses built by Guillermo Billinghurst when he was mayor in 1910 (in the Santa Sofia neighborhood) and president in 1913 (in the Malambo neighborhood). None of these had been more than experiments. Like the author of the *Variedades* article, Ortiz Rodríguez concluded in a way that, again, invoked rationalities of government: "The best school for humanity, for patriotism, for hygiene, for thrift, for love and solidarity is a home where man can evolve because as long as our workers have for houses disgusting hovels where fresh air, ventilation, and water cost an arm and a leg, we will never obtain the citizens strong of body and spirit that our fatherland needs in order to achieve its aspirations."[43]

WORKER HOUSING AND THE JUNTAS PRO-DESOCUPADOS

In the 1930s, the worker housing situation remained largely unchanged, and arguably worsened as a consequence of the significant migration that occurred in the 1920s, when some 65,000 migrants moved to the capital, contributing to a general increase in the city's population from 223,807 in 1920 to 376,097 in 1931.[44] As in the previous decade, calls for state investment in worker housing were common. In early 1931, a series of articles in the periodical *Alma Obrera* urged the government to facilitate the construction of worker housing through various fiscal measures, including the elimination of import taxes on construction materials, the granting of a five-year tax moratorium, and the establishment of credit facilities that would allow workers to pay for the houses in monthly installments. The articles further suggested that the workers who benefited from the new housing could themselves provide the labor required during the construction phase. Such measures would address the dreadful housing conditions that most workers faced, particularly as concerned the poor hygiene conditions they had to put up with and the usurious rates of rent that they were forced to pay. They would also encourage and expand private ownership.[45] Another article, which called for other measures to protect workers, and particularly unemployed workers (such as a ban on dismissals of workers unless a very serious fault had been committed, state-run food distribution facilities for unemployed workers, and a moratorium on rent payments for unemployed workers), framed these broad appeals for state intervention in a rhetoric that highlighted the dangers posed by the rise of class struggle in the country: "Such measures have become necessary; they are the only way to help the unemployed proletariat and to neutralize the divisive propaganda of extremist elements who seek to create moments of chaos and anarchy very dangerous to the country."[46]

The belief that adequate housing for workers could help stop the rise of militancy was not limited to Peru, as several historians have shown.[47] In Peru as elsewhere, such concerns made worker housing a key political battleground, as the early house-building programs initiated by the Junta Pro-Desocupados in Lima in 1931 demonstrate. Founded on 10 April 1931, the juntas pro-desocupados were the Peruvian state's response to the unemployment created by the world slump. Their main function was the distribution of funds levied through new taxes. A central entity, the Comisión Distribuidora (Distribution Commission), assigned monies to the various juntas departamentales (departmental commissions) that were set up gradually during the course of 1931 and 1932. Initially, the membership of the Comisión Distribuidora was politically varied and included a leading APRA cadre, Manuel Seoane. The membership of the departmental juntas tended to include local worthies. In Lima, the junta was led early on by José de la Riva-Agüero, a historian and leading conservative figure. The junta's resources were considerable. Between July 1931 and December 1934, the revenues of the junta totaled some 7 million soles, of which 2 million was spent on roads and bridges, 1.11 million on hospitals and worker housing, 1.6 million on paving and sanitation, and 1.22 million on school buildings.[48] Between 1931 and 1943, a total of 32,018 workers registered with the Lima junta and received some support in the form of employment in public works.[49] In addition to public works, the juntas provided more immediate forms of relief. As late as April 1933, the Lima junta's soup kitchen fed some 500 persons a day.[50] The Lima junta, moreover, helped a fair number of those *provincianos* unable to find employment in Lima to return to their place of origin: some 8,060 between 1931 and 1934, 1,957 between 1935 and 1936, 615 between 1937 and 1938, and 836 between 1939 and 1941.[51]

The worker housing built by the Lima junta was inaugurated in August 1931.[52] Built on the old "camal" or slaughterhouse grounds, the new edifice, which cost 225,785 soles to build, covered a total area of 3,869 square meters and included six small houses, forty-nine small apartments, and two warehouses. Some 1,400 workers were employed in the construction phase. The junta's first report published in 1935 included the following description, illustrated with several photographs, of the new houses and apartments:

> The little houses have either two or three rooms, a corridor, an interior patio, a W.C., and a bathroom. The apartments have two rooms, a patio, a kitchen, and a bathroom. The rooms have wooden floors, and the patios and corridors are tiled and made of concrete. The walls are made of brick, the doors and window frames of Oregon pine, and they boast an adequate provision of fresh air and light. For the comfort of the dwellers, the [complex] also possesses a large interior patio.[53]

The emphasis on the quality of materials used (brick instead of adobe, for example, and tiles), the attention to the circulation of air and lighting and to the comfort of residents, points to the ways in which the architectural design of interiors and exteriors was considered an important aspect of these worker houses, and echoes some of the key themes of European social modernist architecture; an evident influence in the architectural design of the junta's worker houses, and a point to which I will return below.[54] Once completed, the new houses and apartments were handed over to the Lima municipality, although the junta had selected the new tenants from "those members of the working class with honorable reputations." This worker housing, the junta's report concluded, represented a new and permanent source of income for the city council. However, though the juntas continued to operate for over a decade, they undertook no additional worker housing. As we will see, the failure of the Lima junta to continue the worker housing projects became a political issue used by the emerging political forces on the left, and particularly by APRA, to attack the juntas and the Sánchez Cerro and Benavides regimes more generally. But the motivation for the building of the worker houses was largely political in the first place.

The creation of the juntas seems to have been partly inspired by the initiatives undertaken by the mayor of Lima, Luis Antonio Eguiguren, who took office on 1 September 1930. Faced with growing hardship among Lima's population, the mayor decreed a series of measures aimed ostensibly at helping the hardest hit. The price of electricity was cut, popular food fairs were organized, and meat was "municipalized." In late March 1931, a census of Lima's unemployed was begun when a vending kiosk in the Parque de las Tradiciones was opened for the purpose. Shortly thereafter, Eguiguren announced a series of work creation schemes, including worker housing construction and road building, and according to one document some two hundred or so workers were benefiting from these schemes by the time the juntas pro-desocupados were established. Eguiguren seems to have succeeded in raising funds from Lima's well-to-do to cover the costs of these schemes, perhaps in part because they, like the editorialist of *El Comercio* who commented positively on these measures, believed that "to give jobs to the unemployed is to contribute to killing the root of possible future disorder, because those who have the means to sustain their homes are unlikely to run the risk of dangerous adventures that could end tragically."[55] The editorial noted that hunger and desperation created fertile conditions for the spread of "dangerous propaganda" by agitators. As this suggests, the creation of the juntas pro-desocupados clearly responded to a fear among the elite that unemployment would heighten social tension and strengthen the appeal of radical political options among labor.[56]

Peruvian workers certainly faced difficult employment conditions as a consequence of the depression. The impact of the slump on Peru was severe but, in comparison to many Latin American countries, short lived. Between 1929 and 1932, real GDP (1941 = 100) fell from 84 to 65, while total exports fell from 134 million U.S. dollars to 38 million, a 68 percent drop. Though not all sectors were adversely hit by the slump, most employers sought to cut their workforce or reduce labor costs by other means, as discussed in the previous chapter. No national unemployment figures are available. The figures collected by the Lima Junta Pro-Desocupados are suggestive at best as they merely indicate the number of workers who registered as unemployed. According to its figures, between 1931 and 1934 some 22,151 workers registered. Of these 9,230 were from Lima, another 1,380 from Junín, 1,881 from Arequipa, 1,540 from Ancash, and 355 from Cuzco.[57] According to the 1931 Lima census, drawn up by the Lima junta (and created, in part, to provide employment for white-collar workers), some 31,139 men between the ages of fourteen and sixty-nine, or 25 percent of the working population, were unemployed. Construction workers, 70 percent of whom were unemployed, fared particularly badly. Significantly, workers in highly unionized industries, such as textiles, appear to have fared considerably better than those in nonunionized industries. Unemployment in the heavily unionized textile industry, for example, stood at 12 percent.[58] However, the accounting used by the census takers was poor, women were not considered, and, as the census takers admitted, many who declared themselves unemployed, such as commercial or state employees, had found employment in other areas, as salesmen or manual laborers. In addition, many workers considered by the census as unemployed worked in industries where work was irregular or seasonal, such as construction.[59]

However, following the default on the country's international debt in 1932, Peru's economy recovered relatively quickly, spurred by export growth in cotton, which, thanks to a high returned value and powerful income effects, had strong multiplier effects on the economy. By 1934, Peru's GDP had recovered its 1929 level.[60] Still, the economic recovery was not necessarily reflected in an improvement in unemployment. Some observers, such as the Lima Chamber of Commerce, claimed by 1933 that unemployment "has not shown alarming symptoms in this country."[61] Similarly, according to the British minister's 1935 economic report:

> For the past two years there has been little real hardship due to unemployment in this country and little available surplus labor. Except for seasonal periods between crops, practically all unemployment is concentrated in the large cities such as Lima, Callao, etc. Even at its worst in 1931, it has never amounted to more than 20,000 or 30,000 persons and, under present conditions is largely due to personal misfortune or improvidence of the workers of whom about 5,000 may be considered as unemployed.

The minister added that during the preparations for the country's centenary celebrations in January, when four thousand men were employed in Lima on street and park improvements, "there was an acute scarcity of labor in the district for ordinary building purposes."[62] However, others claimed that unemployment, or rather underemployment, remained a problem faced primarily by the middle classes: "Though it is true that only a few are jobless, there are many who have positions that are inferior to their capabilities and who receive salaries that are very much below what they require to meet their necessities, leading to a life of bitterness and sadness, which amounts to a veritable unemployment, even if it is partial." As David Parker has argued, and as this magazine article confirms, many observers saw the middle classes as particularly vulnerable to the effects of the slump; to maintain a "respectable" living standard, and therefore middle-class status, required a substantial income and the capacity to demonstrate the status that that income afforded. But for the working class too, the magazine article suggested, employment was no guarantee of even bearable living conditions: "As far as workers are concerned, their daily wages do not allow them to rise above a life of want and suffering, eating very bad food, wearing rags, and living in hovels."[63]

Regardless of whether the original reason for their existence had disappeared or been reduced, the juntas continued well in the 1940s to initiate and oversee a broad range of public works in Lima and throughout the country, channeling resources to major infrastructure projects, including road building and irrigation works. And yet, the juntas were very unpopular. Both employers and workers refused to pay the taxes to fund them, and fraudulent administration within the juntas was not unknown. More important, the bulk of the public work schemes were temporary. As the historian Jorge Basadre noted: "There was no real interest, in general, to promote economic activities that would create permanent jobs or bring about a reduction in living costs."[64] Criticism of the juntas abounds in the archival record. Some critics claimed that the juntas were slow to set up programs. In June 1931, for example, a group of unemployed workers in Arequipa complained that the local junta pro-desocupados had yet to undertake any work creation programs.[65] Funds were in short supply and, as soon became clear, there were many competing claimants. Because the funds were centralized, different departments vied for a limited budget. In Trujillo, the provincial council demanded that the funds levied in the department be invested locally.[66] Within departments, moreover, different workers vied for the same funds. In September 1932, a group of unemployed workers from the city of Arequipa complained that the junta was providing work for "peasant people," who benefited from access to land, whereas they—the workers— had no work and still had to pay rent and other costs.[67] Ironically, the juntas may have contributed to the general pauperization of the period. Public works administered by the juntas paid a daily wage of two soles, leading some industrialists to attempt to lower their own wage rates.[68] Moreover, labor leaders such as Arturo Sabroso considered the two soles wage largely insufficient to cover the everyday needs of Lima's workers.[69]

Part of the unpopularity of the juntas owed to the fact that they were seen as, and to considerable extent were, political instruments, tech-

nologies of discipline perhaps, of the interim Samanez Ocampo government and, later, of the Sánchez Cerro government. Given copious coverage in the government-friendly press, the public works that they initiated
were clearly intended to undermine the campaigns of both the Communist Party and APRA by dampening potentially explosive situations
through the injection of state funds.[70] Local authorities evidently were
aware of this function of the juntas and exploited it to obtain additional
funds. Noting in October 1932 that the situation of a hundred or so
unemployed workers in Mollendo was "hopeless, as well as dangerous
for public order," the subprefect of Islay requested that measures be
taken to ensure the prompt initiation of the works on the Mejía-Tambo
road by the junta pro-desocupados of Arequipa.[71] Similarly, when they
requested funds from the Comisión Distribuidora, the juntas departamentales often pointed to the threat of labor unrest. The Lima junta
noted in April 1932 that if it failed to receive additional funds, it would be
forced to "immediately cut the number of public works, thus reducing
the number of employed workers, which will, doubtlessly, produce serious conflicts and disturbances that can affect public order and which it
is urgent to avoid, especially at this time, so close to 1 May, a date that
tends to produce agitation among the working class."[72] Similarly, the
junta in Arequipa pointed out that the shortage of funds "worsens . . . the
unemployment problem [and] seriously threatens the maintenance of
the present social order."[73]

Perhaps inevitably, labor organizations associated with the political
parties of the Left denounced the juntas, precisely, as instruments of
political manipulation. In particular, the CGTP, the labor central controlled by the Peruvian Communist Party, mounted a scathing attack on
the juntas. It criticized the juntas for refusing to incorporate unions in its
operations—a position that, it claimed, confirmed its "fascist character,
its bourgeois and reactionary composition." The CGTP proposed a number of concrete measures to remedy unemployment: a 1.50 soles subsidy
for each unemployed worker, to be borne by the state and employers; free
rent, tax, electricity, water, and transport for workers; the use of public
buildings to house the jobless; a seven-hour working day without a reduction in wages; and a six-hour working day for women and children, as
well as a minimum wage of five soles for agricultural workers. Less concrete measures demanded by the CGTP include "the revolutionary solution to the crisis."[74] It is not clear whether the CGTP attempted to under-

mine the juntas directly. According to the Lima junta, its public works programs were hindered by "divisive elements" that infiltrated the groups of unemployed, and made "unjustified and immoderate demands that are beyond the capacity of the juntas to solve or address."[75] Clearly such denunciations should not be taken at face value but such tactics were part of the Communists' repertoire of action.

The Socialist Party and APRA too weighed in against the juntas. *El Socialista*, the newspaper of the Peruvian Socialist Party led by Luciano Castillo, concluded in 1934 that the juntas had "never been of any benefit to unemployed workers."[76] APRA claimed that most of the public works undertaken by the juntas were of little benefit to labor, the road to the exclusive Ancón beach resort and the refurbishing of the Parque de la Exposición being perfect examples. Very little money, by contrast, was channeled to address sanitation needs in working-class districts such as La Victoria.[77] Moreover, APRA argued, most of the juntas' money was being spent in Lima, with no funds designated to works outside the capital, largely on the mistaken assumption that no unemployment existed outside Lima.[78] *La Tribuna* went so far as to claim in late 1931 that the juntas misused their funds by hiring a large number of managers who were cronies of the president of the Lima junta so that "nothing is left for the rank and file of workers looking for jobs." In addition, some 28,000 soles had been spent on office supplies, "which have nothing to do with the tools that workers should be using," further proof of the misuse of funds that ought to be invested in giving "bread and work to the proletarians of this capital."[79] It is indeed likely that the juntas handed out work selectively, favoring workers sympathetic to the government. In April 1932, the Arequipa section of the Unión Revolucionaria (UR) requested of the president of the junta that its five hundred members be given priority when jobs were handed out.[80] In response, the president of the junta departmental, also mayor of the city of Arequipa and vice president of the UR, urged members of the party to sign up to the work rota administered by the junta, though, he added, "This presidency will do all that it can in order to meet this request."[81]

Like its other initiatives, the worker housing undertaken by the Lima junta became an intensely politicized issue. At the inauguration of the group of houses built by the Lima junta in 1931, José de la Riva-Agüero, the head of the junta and also mayor of the city, noted that not only did the houses provide employment to previously unemployed workers, they also stood now to provide "hygienic and comfortable homes to a fraction of the proletarian class" and that further house building would be guided by the aim to achieve "civilized goals of public health and social justice." But, crucially, he went on to argue:

> There is no immediate panacea to this Peruvian disease. The marvelous drugs, which very likely would worsen it, amount to ruses of charlatan healers. From these, fortunately, we are safe. The only secure method to consolidate the convalescence that is already evident depends on the intensification and guarantee of work, on a stimulus and respect for effort, on the cheapening of subsistence goods, on sobriety, on careful saving, and on the loyal acceptance of mutual help between the various productive classes.[82]

By counterposing the "marvelous drugs" of the "charlatan healers" to the "secure method" undertaken by the juntas to cure the "Peruvian disease," Riva-Agüero, who was clearly referring to the Communist Party and APRA and to their ideologies, made sure to frame the house-building program undertaken by the juntas, and indeed housing policy more generally, in the broader political struggle that was polarizing Peruvian society.

Housing became a key political issue in the run up to the October 1931 elections. APRA used its periodicals to mount a campaign to denounce the poor housing in the city. In July 1931 *La Tribuna* noted that the expiration of the rent control law would result in hardship for the working class and urged government action: "It is imperative that the state decree immediate and radical measures to defend the homes of workers, [not to do so would indicate that] it has abdicated its tutelary functions and lost all sentiments of justice."[83] The newspaper ran a series of articles on the appalling living conditions of Lima's workers. According to one piece, "What once was used for cows and mules is today a 'common house' that has no more habitable conditions than a sloping floor and the pseudo construction of rooms with used wooden planks and sacks. . . . Here live the families of our comrades, who have been placed in the worst possible degree of misery by capitalist rationalization." To make things worse, workers paid rents of between ten and fifteen soles.[84] Other articles claimed that the "corralones" where workers lived helped spread tuberculosis and plague.[85] This claim was repeated in 1932 in *El Socialista*, the newspaper of the Peruvian Socialist Party, which pointed out that houses that had not too long ago been rented out for five or six soles were now priced at fifteen, twenty, or more soles, and noted that "every callejón, in addition to being a source of corruption, because of the presence of all types of people, are also places where disease takes root."[86]

APRA's interventions were not restricted to critiquing the inaction of the government. It also put forward concrete proposals, such as those included in a two-page article, apparently prepared by Aprista architects, illustrated with copious photographs, published in the weekly APRA in early 1932.[87] Titled "The Basic Home and the Immediate Action Plan of the Peruvian Aprista Party," the article included drawings of several low-cost worker housing projects in Germany, the United States, and the Netherlands. The article explicitly rejected the accusation that APRA was politicizing the housing problem by stating that the problem was political to begin with. Whereas APRA viewed housing through the lens of social justice and believed that the working poor had the right to "a simple, but healthy and decent home," for the Right it was a question of convenience or "fuerza mayor" (force majeure). Critiquing the argument put forward by the architect Alberto Alexander that investment in housing was justified because it helped combat socialism and made workers healthier and therefore better able to carry out their work, the article claimed: "For APRA it is not necessary for there to be HEALTHY ELE-MENTS for work; for APRA the WORKING ELEMENTS have a right to HEALTHY housing. The conservatives need the spread of 'feared tendencies or doctrines' to think about improving the filthy hovels in which the productive classes live. We argue that as a matter of principle men have the right to live like men." Whereas in Europe, the article continued, worker housing had been developed since the 1860s, in Peru the rich built palaces for themselves, "while the productive classes lived and live sunken in horrible callejones, in old and dark *casonas* [dilapidated mansions], and, worse, in the insulting *rancherías* [barracks] of our mines and haciendas." In this way, APRA attacked the very ideas that, so it claimed, underpinned "conservative" housing projects while claiming to represent the true, unadulterated, interests of Peru's working peoples.

These attacks on the government's housing policy, or lack of policy, were reprised in mid-1934, when APRA publications again were allowed to circulate during the brief period of political opening following the rise to power of Benavides. In June, *La Tribuna* published a series of interviews with a number of workers, under the title "They Don't Want Hovels, They Want Houses." According to a twenty-year-old *canillita* (newspaper boy) named Antonio Galindo: "We lack adequate houses. I have been reading for some time in the newspapers advertisements of special houses for workers, but so far we have had to take refuge in old callejones or in places that they call houses but that are in reality hovels." Similarly, an artisan, Manuel Galdos, argued: "For many years we have seen projects related to this issue but nothing much has been done so far. Meanwhile the majority of the population lives without a single comfort and without having in their homes the most basic comforts." Andrés Carranza, an empleado, meanwhile stated that "a longing for the middle and working class is the housing problem. In other countries, the government takes action, and demands that affordable but hygienic and comfortable houses are built in certain neighborhoods."[88] These interviews were pure propaganda, of course. But whoever read them knew that the deplorable housing conditions that these workers and other workers faced and that APRA made sure to highlight in its newspaper, as well as the failures of present and past governments to do anything about them, were real enough.

As in previous years, APRA's critique of the government's housing policy focused on the unsanitary conditions and overcrowding that workers were exposed to. One article on insalubrious callejones included a photograph of a man described as "palúdico" (suffering from malaria).[89] Another article compared the "casas de vecindad" where many workers lived to prisons.[90] The criticisms homed in on the Lima Junta Pro-Desocupados. According to one article, for example, the sewage works along the Rio Huática, in the worker district of La Victoria, had not been repaired by the junta, as had been planned.[91] In fact, as we have seen, APRA accused the juntas of ineptitude and corruption and, more to the point, of having failed to use the revenue from the new taxes to address the housing situation in the capital:

> The initiative of the Junta Pro-Desocupados has not been very successful. It has not given thought to our working class. Only one or two buildings for workers have been built. Thereafter, it has undertaken other types of public works, some of which were unnecessary. And the people who have paid for some years now these taxes see agricultural land turned into military barracks, into ex-

pensive clinics, and have no hope of escaping the punishment of living in semiderelict and unhygienic houses.[92]

As this comment suggests, the worker housing project undertaken by the Lima junta had backfired. It provided employment for some workers and housing for others, but this amounted to very little in the context of Lima's dismal housing provision for its laboring peoples. It served not to undermine the appeal of the political parties of the Left among labor, but rather to further illustrate the failure of Peru's ruling elites to address the basic material and welfare needs of the country's population. There is little doubt that such considerations contributed to the decision of the Benavides government to channel significant resources from the Ministry of Development for the construction of five "barrios obreros" (worker districts) in the late 1930s.

BENAVIDES AND THE BARRIOS OBREROS

The barrios obreros were not the only worker housing built during the Benavides presidency. The Sociedad de Beneficencia de Lima (Beneficence Society) built twenty-two "casas de obreros" beginning in 1928 but built mostly after 1934. Designed by the architect Rafael Marquina and located largely in peripheral parts of the city, each of these "casas," which were in fact housing complexes of varying designs, contained a number of small housing units.[93] The largest, the "Casa de Obreros No. 8," had eighty-seven units and housed some 435 people, while the smallest, the "Casa de Obreros No. 15" had only six units and housed only 30 people.[94] In addition, five "barrios fiscales" were built in Callao, providing housing for some 4,660 people in 932 housing units.[95] But I want to focus here on the five barrios obreros built between 1936 and 1939 in Lima. To some extent modeled on the "Barrio Obrero Modelo" built in 1934 to house the workers of the Frigorífico Nacional in Callao, the five barrios obreros housed a total of 4,859 people in 1,001 housing units. The first four, located in La Victoria (Barrio Obrero No. 1), Rímac (Barrio Obrero No. 2), and San Martín de Porres (Barrio Obrero Nos. 3 and 4), were designed by the architect Alfredo Dammert, and the fifth by Roberto Haaker Fort (Barrio Obrero No. 5). (The last three barrios are adjacent to each other and constitute, in effect, a single barrio.) These architects were strongly influenced by German social modernist architecture and its functionalist aesthetics, which were incorporated in the architecture of the barrios

FIGURE 2 Views of worker housing in the barrios obreros. Source: *Progresos del Perú, 1933–1939, durante el gobierno del Presidente de la República General Óscar R. Benavides* (Buenos Aires: Editorial Guillermo Kraft, 1945), 226.

obreros.[96] A lottery helped choose the new residents. The first 120 or so owner-occupiers of Barrio Obrero No. 2, all men (although presumably, men with families), included mechanics, tailors, drivers, gardeners, textile workers, masons, electricians, train workers, and print workers.[97]

During the inauguration of the first barrio obrero, in La Victoria, President Benavides presented the new housing as concrete evidence of his government's effective "social action" in favor of labor—a social action that stood in stark contrast to the promises of APRA: "In contrast to the false demagogic promises that lead fatally to regression and misery, the worker sees here, with the strength and evidence of reality, the real and promising result of national peace, the solid result of public order, the creation of new sources of well-being, consequences of the methodical channeling of work energies supported by the indestructible solidarity that must unite all Peruvian workers who long for a prosperous, great and joyous fatherland."[98] Benavides's speech rejected the "false promises" of APRA and others but implicitly recognized that poor housing provision created conditions for the rise of labor militancy, as *La Crónica*, the daily that covered the inauguration graphically illustrated: a caption next to a photograph of worker housing noted that "those who live in these miserable houses of the callejón de Milano have plenty of reasons to look with sympathy upon Bolshevikism."[99] Similarly, the minister of development and public works, Federico Recavarren, stressed in his speech at the inauguration that "it is not necessary to have leftist tendencies or to sympathize with exotic and discredited doctrines to feel in one's heart and to appreciate fully the pain and anxiety felt by the needy."[100]

The construction of the barrios obreros corresponded in some ways to a classic attempt to control particular population groups, in this case workers susceptible to the propaganda of left-wing parties, through the establishment of disciplinary processes of surveillance and isolation. Like the houses built by the Sociedad de Beneficencia, the barrios obreros were all built in the periphery of the city and in areas with low real-estate value. The Barrio Obrero No. 2 was built on the site of a rubbish dump, while the Barrios Obreros Nos. 3, 4, and 5 were close to the old leprosarium. According to Thomas Crupi, the location of the barrios in these peripheral low-cost areas of the city corresponded to an ongoing elite project to establish a class-based spatial demarcation in the city, or "class segregation": "These projects built in the opposite direction from where the formal, upper-class urbanizations were located, further segregated the population and solidified Lima's dichotomized development."[101] The idea that the emplacement of the barrios obreros corresponded with a project of top-down social control seems further confirmed by the fact that the Barrio Obrero No. 1 in La Victoria was built opposite a new National Guard Barracks, which suggests that this location reflected "the government's interest in social order." Crupi concludes: "This direction of urban development demonstrates an obvious preoccupation with controlling the location and lifestyles of the working class and fulfilling the Benavides regime goal of transforming the working class into model citizens."[102] As an editorial in *La Crónica* noted, the worker houses in the barrios obreros helped turn workers into responsible citizens and more generally into "elements of order and valuable factors of production." Such workers were not susceptible to the "fallacious incitements to revolt or to strikes."[103]

As this editorial suggests, the disciplinary project reflected in the emplacement of the barrios obreros coexisted and in many ways cross-fertil-ized with a project expressive of rationalities of government that focused not so much on social control as on protecting and enhancing the well-being of workers conceived as agents of progress. As the inauguration speeches by Benavides and Recavarren suggest, the sixty-two worker houses built in La Victoria's new barrio obrero, which had provided em-ployment for some three hundred workers, were intended not only to house workers. They would also constitute them.[104] President Benavides noted in his speech that it was his hope that the barrio obrero "will be-come, in miniature, the real image of our great and efflorescent worker populations of the future, which we see from this vantage point rising up in all the horizons of the Fatherland." According to Recavarren, the new houses stood at the polar opposite of the callejón and the casa de vecindad "with its dismal retinue of diseases, shadows, and misery." However, the houses were not mere substitutes for the callejón. They fulfilled various roles. For one thing, they were designed in order to strengthen family ties, since their design would help instill in "the working masses the love of the home, of the small garden full of light and happiness, of the clean and welcoming house in which are tightened and strengthened the ties of the family." Similarly, the houses were intended to encourage small owner-ship, which would help foment further values: "In this way, the habit of saving is implicitly encouraged and the sense of economic responsibility that is so important for the development of our society is created." Finally, the houses and the broader housing complex sought to impact directly on the workers and their families' well-being, since a sport field, swimming pool, and small athletics stadium had been built (see figures 3 and 4) in order to provide an opportunity for workers to participate in a "methodi-cal and advantageous plan of physical improvement."[105] A report in a Ministry of Development publication summed up these sentiments: "the nation should feel satisfied as it contemplates such a beautiful deed of positive collective benefit [that] improves in an effective way the living conditions of the popular classes, guaranteeing the future well-being of workers, a human capital that the present government watches over with great interest."[106]

The idea that the construction of the barrios obreros was helping to constitute "human capital" further illustrates the ways in which housing policy reflected rationalities of government and in which the barrios obreros were envisioned as a technology of government. A series of

FIGURE 3 Aerial photograph of the sport field and swimming pool of one of the five barrios obreros. Source: *Progresos del Perú, 1933–1939, durante el gobierno del Presidente de la República General Óscar R. Benavides* (Buenos Aires: Editorial Guillermo Kraft, 1945), 226.

FIGURE 4 The swimming pool of one of the five barrios obreros. Source: *Progresos del Perú, 1933–1939, durante el gobierno del Presidente de la República General Óscar R. Benavides* (Buenos Aires: Editorial Guillermo Kraft, 1945), 225.

commentators remarked on how worker housing improved the worker both physically and morally. One article in *La Crónica* noted in early 1937 that the construction of worker housing meant that "the unsanitary, dark, and miserable callejón that so harmed the physical vigor of the race will be a thing of the past."[107] Writing that same year, Elvira García y García focused on the moral uplift that the worker houses represented:

> Our people need to learn to live properly, to develop an awareness of cleanliness and comfort . . . in order to become owners of a home, which brings only good things and can be considered a true gem, not only because of the comfort it brings, but because of its attractiveness it leads [the worker] to seek to safeguard the happiness of his family and his own. When sufficient new neighborhoods are built and when all workers, or those who do not spend their energies in the *cantina* [the bars], can have access to a house that is fully to their satisfaction we will have advanced considerably not only in the material sphere, but also, and this is most important, in our spiritual values, which will be the goal of each one's personality, adding value and peacefulness.[108]

Similarly, the journal *Mundo Peruano* applauded the measure to build worker districts and noted that "the worker who contributes with his personal effort and with the capital of his energies constitutes the most legitimate and valuable source of national wealth. This is the reason that all governments are keenly interested in solving all the social assistance and welfare problems of workers in tune with our present needs and the postulates of humanity and justice within social order."[109]

Such rhetoric emphasized the making of *male* human capital and male-headed worker families, which would produce conventional, that is, bourgeois, family patterns. A report in *Cascabel*, another periodical, reproduced a similar discourse. The barrios obreros gave workers an opportunity to abandon the life that they had led in the unhygienic callejones, where many were drawn, understandably, to alcohol and the cantina:

> Now, with a home that dignifies and extols him, knowing that in a few years it will be his own thanks to the protection of the state, [as well as] saving money, since the monthly payment is capital that he accumulates and that represents the value of the house, he leads a

life that is completely different to the life of yesterday. Absent the tyranny of the weekly rent payments, he decorates his home with nice furniture, and has no reason to envy the comforts of others, while his children can play and grow strong in the sport fields, [and enjoy] hygienic services that are properly installed, with plentiful water, fresh air and light, the life of the worker has changed radically. He begins to love his home, which he is purchasing with small payments that do not affect his budget. He feels proud of the home he owns and is satisfied to be the "dueño del hogar" [the master of the home], where he will live out peacefully his old age.[110]

In order to confirm the constitution of the male "dueño del hogar," the report included an interview with two of the new residents, a linotype operator called Eugenio Ascencio and Jorge Iturriaga, the president of the tobacco state monopoly workers' union. Both confirmed that they were very happy with their new houses, for which they paid very little, and emphasized that the barrio was a healthy place to live.

The idea that workers and labor more generally were being constituted in the new barrios obreros is perhaps expressed most clearly in the ways in which the literature that accompanied the inauguration of the worker districts discussed the inclusion of sport fields. In his speech during the inauguration of the barrio obrero in the Rímac district, the minister of development and public works noted: "Like the schools, these fields are powerful factors of resurgence. In them is forged the sporting brotherhood, a live source of sincerity and affect; in them grows team spirit [el espíritu del team], the solid base of collective discipline and precious root of racial pride [precioso germen del orgullo racial]; in them blood is enriched, the muscle is strengthened, the mind is sharpened, the character is educated."[111] The sporting facilities built in the barrios obreros were thus imagined not primarily as places of recreation but as a technology of physical and moral improvement. The impact of these sporting facilities was even presented as beneficial not merely to workers but to the Peruvian nation itself: "Outside, fresh-air activity represents vigor and health. From this point onward, we have outlined the road to progress that must be followed in sporting activities, so that Peru will be dignifiedly represented in international competitions, where it will be possible to gain new and positive victories that will increase markedly the prestige and value of the race."[112]

In this way, workers improved through the action of the state would come to represent Peru on the world stage: the workers being made in the barrios obreros were not merely better workers; they were representatives of the ideal of Peruvian nationality. Peruvian workers, this discourse suggested, were to become the very defining essence of the Peruvian nation.

Workers, then, were being constituted as the very essence of the Peruvian nation as well as housed in the barrios obreros. This literal engineering of worker housing and metaphorical engineering of workers is highly resonant in the literature that the Benavides government produced to trumpet its social programs. As in the cover of the book discussed in the introduction to this chapter, the state emerges in this literature as uniquely able to address social problems through the application of science and technology. Thus, in the construction of the barrio obrero in the Rímac district, "the construction . . . has followed special technical specifications, different to those that are usually employed, given that it was necessary to make deep excavations in order to lay the foundations on which rests the structure of the building."[113] Yet this technical success is also expressed in aesthetic terms: the barrio obrero of Rímac, we are told, "looks stunning and the arrangement of buildings is a success," while the barrio obrero of La Victoria is described as "harmonious" and its sports grounds as "beautiful."[114] This combination of technical and aesthetic achievement, resonant of the social modernist architecture and its functional aesthetics that clearly influenced the barrios obreros architects Dammert and Haaker Fort, is especially in evidence in the detailed discussion of the quality of the materials used in the construction of the houses:

> The condition of the newly inaugurated houses . . . could not be better. They are built with noble materials and their structure is complete. The walls sit on concrete foundations. The outside walls are made of brick and the roofs of lightened cement, covered with rooftiles, with the exterior covered in pebbledash. In the interior all the rooms have proper ceilings and tiled floors covered with wood or tiles. The electrical, water, and sewage installations and the sanitary equipment are magnificent and the kitchen and bathrooms are tiled.[115]

The attention to the details and aesthetics of construction in the barrios obreros had a clear purpose. Eve Blau has suggested that the architects of the Viennese *Geimendebauten* were above all interested in ensuring that the worker housing they were designing "should be radically different in formal aspect to the despised 'Mietskasernen' of the prewar era."[116] Similarly, the houses in barrios obreros of Lima had to be as different as possible from the despised callejón and casa de vecindad. In fact, the focus on science and aesthetics in the literature on the barrios obreros points to the more general ways in which architectural design was considered an element in the "civilizing" of workers. In this way, developments in Peru echoed architectural developments in Europe.[117]

The extent to which the barrios obreros did, in effect, produce better Peruvians through the social modernist architectural design and functionalist aesthetics remained a matter of elite concern well into the next decade. In 1947, Elvira García y García, for example, noted with some sadness that although the residents were forbidden to keep domestic animals, "we are told that it is common to find on the rooftops and inside the houses, all the little animals that these families are willing to shelter, both because they are keeping with tradition, and because they represent a business opportunity that can produce an income."[118] In spite of this, she was happy to note that when visiting one of the barrios obreros with a group of "American friends," they were welcomed into houses that were clean and comfortable. This confirmed, in her view, the belief that "if the poor are given the means to be decent and comfortable, it is certain that they will cherish and take care of them [the houses], because they represent a unique source of pleasure."[119]

Generally, however, contemporary observers were in broad agreement that the worker houses of the Benavides era had done little to address the problem of poor and insufficient housing in the city or in the country more generally. In 1940, M. V. Merino Schroder acknowledged the efforts of various governments, pointing to the "two little houses" that were built during the Billinghurst administration, the worker district in Bellavista during the second Leguía government, and the four hundred or so houses built during the Benavides regime. But, he argued, these were largely insufficient and did little to address the contradiction in government policy, which built new and shiny hospitals but largely failed to change the living conditions that most limeños faced and that forced them to "live while preparing their bodies for tuberculosis, typhus, and so many other diseases."[120] A decade later an article in an architectural review noted that most of the houses that had been built in the previous twenty years were of little consequence; from 1933 to 1945, this commentator noted, the state had initiated worker housing projects and had succeeded in building twelve "barrios fiscales" with 1,991 houses and a population of some 10,149 people. These barrios, however, had been poorly planned, "with no urbanistic criterion," and they lacked many essentials, including "communal services that can bring about the development of an integral and organic life."[121]

A unique statistical study can help us to get a sense of the housing situation faced by Lima's workers who did not benefit from access to one of the barrios obreros. Leoncio Palacios's 1940 study of 81 families, or 395 persons, included 21 seamstresses, 20 mechanics, 17 textile workers (eleven men and six women), 14 masons, 14 washerwomen, 13 domestic workers (nine male and four female), 13 carpenters, 13 laborers ("obreros"), 7 drivers, 6 cooks, 6 street-vendors, 5 agricultural workers, 3 printers, 2 bakery workers, and 2 empleados (white-collar workers).[122] He found that 41 of these families (or 173 persons) lived in callejones (where typically residents shared a single water tap and conditions were poor), 21 (117 persons) in casas-tiendas (described as stand-alone houses with a door that opens into the street and which has its own adequate water and electricity services); 16 (88) in corralones (described as closed-off fields with no real houses, other than poorly constructed shacks made of sugar cane with mud or wood planks); and 3 (17) in departamentos (described as apartments in subdivided houses, usually with adequate hygienic services and their own water and electricity).[123] In addition to living, for the most part, in poor quality accommodation, most of the working-class families in Palacios's study lived in cramped conditions. The families, which averaged just fewer than 5 members, overwhelmingly lived in one- or two-room accommodation (22 and 34 families out of 81 respectively). Only 9 families lived in either four- or five-room accommodation, and 13 in three-room accommodation.

The families in Palacios's study would have been the obvious targets for the worker housing projects: they spent a significant amount of their income on poor quality housing. But few would have been able to afford the houses in the barrios obreros. Overall, the families spent 12.70 percent of their income on housing, considerably less than they spent on food (50.70 percent), and marginally less than on clothing (13.60 percent).[124] But actual expenditure on rent varied considerably from family to family. Some families paid no rent, either because they owned their dwelling (six families), lived in accommodation paid by their employers (two families), or were provided with housing on account of being guards of the establishment where they worked (two). Of the sixty-nine families that did pay rent, six paid less than 10 soles per month, eleven paid up to 15 soles, twelve paid up 20 soles, fifteen paid up to 25 soles, seven paid up to 30 soles, ten paid up to 35 soles, and eight paid more than 35 soles.[125] Overall, Palacios estimated that the average rent paid by his sample of families was 21.56 soles. As this suggests, only the richer families would have been able to afford the 20 to 30 soles monthly mortgage payments or the initial deposit of between 100 and 140 soles that were required to access one of the dwellings in the barrios obreros.[126] In this respect, the Peruvian experience was similar to the experience of worker housing initiatives elsewhere in the Atlantic economies. Much of the new-build housing in 1920s and 1930s United States and social modernist worker housing in Germany was priced beyond the reach of all but the wealthier workers.[127]

Clearly, far too few barrios obreros were built to address the poor housing conditions faced by Lima's workers. But even if more had been built, it is unlikely that many would have been able to afford the houses in the barrios obreros. One of the consequences of this failure was the rise of the so-called "barriadas," or shanty towns. A study published in 1950 noted that although the old working-class housing, which consisted of solares, callejones, and casas de vecindad, was no longer considered acceptable, a significant number of workers continued to self-build "with no technical principles and no assistance from the city authorities" in various parts of the city, including Manzanilla, Surquillo, Ascara, and Pinonate. These areas were described as "veritable diseased centers of the city," in what amounted to a rhetorical transfer of the identification of Lima's privileged site of disease from the callejón to the self-built improvised home. The study went on to argue that the city had seen the rise of an even more basic form of housing, which used poor quality materials such as old wood and adobe, and which was built on stretches of land that belonged to the state, "with no official control and in such a way that they now occupy large areas." Such structures could be found in "in the shanty towns of San Cosme, Leticia, San Pedro, Matute, El Agustino, Mirones, etc., which now house a population of some 25,000 people."[128] A study published in 1958 concluded that 54 percent of families in Lima were poorly housed and that some 147,200 new homes were needed.[129]

As is well known, this emerging form of housing heralded the beginning of the famous "popular overflow" associated with large-scale internal migration that profoundly transformed the character of the capital and, more generally, of Peruvian society.[130]

CONCLUSION

In what sense, then, did these "governmental" housing projects "fail" in 1930s Peru? In two senses. Only a small minority of workers were housed in the new barrios obreros. Whether the new worker houses succeeded in "improving" these workers physically and morally as the architects of the worker housing projects intended is unclear. To ascertain it would require an examination of the "experiential side of housing," which is beyond the scope of this study.[131] But there is little doubt that the barrios obreros, as reflections of rationalities of government and, in turn, as a technology of government, did little to improve the lot of the majority of Lima's laboring peoples. In this sense, the failure of worker housing projects owed to their "timid" nature: they were too small, too underfunded, and too easily abandoned. In his study of public health campaigns in mid-twentieth-century Asia, Sunil Amrith recognizes "a tension between evidence of the governmentalization of colonial and post-colonial states, bolstered by international organizations, and the equally compelling evidence for the weakness, the absence, and the ineffectiveness of repeated interventions—colonial, national, and international—to govern the health and welfare of large populations."[132] This tension is equally observable in Peru in the 1930s, between evidence of governmentalization of the state as seen in its housing policy, and as I will show in the next two chapters, in its nutrition and social insurance and public health policies, and the equally compelling evidence for the weakness, the absence, and ineffectiveness of repeated interventions to govern the health and well-being of, not large populations, but rather small populations of mostly urban workers.

The form that this tension took in Peru is crucial. It reflects what I call the allure of labor: the fact, as argued in the preceding chapters, that Peruvian elites viewed workers as agents of progress. In this, as I have argued, highly racialized view, workers came to be seen as the solution to Peru's nature as a country populated predominantly by a racially and morally degenerate indigenous population. In this sense, the failure of the worker housing projects owed also, and perhaps primarily, to the ideas that they expressed and helped to reinforce: concretely, as Benavides put it, that the workers being constituted in the barrio obreros reflected "the real image of our great and efflorescent worker populations of the future, which we see from this vantage point rising up in all the horizons of the Fatherland." The failure of worker housing was, arguably, unsurprising. The worker housing projects were shaped by a transnational belief in the necessity and capacity of the state, in Peru as elsewhere, to "produce an environment which enabled help to take place efficiently—and, in particular which minimized resistance to that help when it had been offered, and which was conducive to restoring order in either the social or individual body," as Leif Jerram has aptly noted.[133] But they were also shaped by a very local racist fiction that exalted the worker as the agent of Peru's physical and moral redemption and as the agent of the destruction of the Indian—the despised perceived cause of the nation's backwardness. The allure of labor coexisted with, and, in turn, reflected, the repulsion of indigeneity.

5

FEEDING LABOR

And tell me, which president looked to the future? It was, believe it or not, [Sánchez] Cerro. I fully recognize that he was able to look to the future and . . . he grabbed the rich [by the neck] and took part of their wealth, you there [he said], you're going to give me potatoes, you're going to give me yucca, you're going to give me sweet potatoes, he told them, to feed the poor neighborhoods, you bring me rice, meat, you tell me you have five hundred cows, well then, kill only five cows, otherwise, slash-slash, I'm going to snuff you too, and then, no!, you have to do what Nine-Fingers [Sánchez Cerro, who lost one of his fingers during a military uprising] says. He was a strange president. What did he do? He'd bring out the military officers, the soldiers, [and he would say] you here, you're going to cook, and he'd go off with the trucks to the poor neighborhoods with the food, all ready to eat, the people should not be dying of hunger he would say, but *he saw that that too was indecent*, so he built the *comedores populares*. Who inaugurated them? One-eyed Óscar R. Benavides. But who started them? [Sánchez] Cerro.

—ANDRÉS DELGADO

This chapter focuses on a number of eateries, known as *restaurantes populares*, created in the 1930s. These eateries were conceived, funded, and run by the Peruvian state in order, according to the state's own propaganda, "to solve the urgent problem of [the provision of] easy, comfortable, and healthy nutrition to the popular classes."[1] These restaurantes populares should not be confused or conflated with the *comedores populares* that shanty-town dwellers organized in the 1970s (as the author of the above testimony does). They differ in a number of important respects and the restaurantes are not the historical precursor of the comedores. For one thing, from the very beginning the restaurantes populares were state-run eateries and not a community initiative. The fact that they were conceived as *restaurants*, and not something else, is particularly important, as I will show. Like the barrios obreros, these eateries provide a useful perspective from which to examine the labor policy of the governments of the 1930s. Historians have paid little attention to the restaurantes populares and have tended to see them, like the barrios obreros, as mere instruments in a broader policy of cooption (or "incorporation") and repression of labor. In so doing, historians have echoed contemporary interpretations, particularly those formulated by APRA and the PCP but also by more neutral observers such as the British minister to Peru who noted in 1936 that the real objective of the restaurantes populares was "to combat labor discontent and communistic ideas."[2] Yet, as the testimony reproduced above suggests, some contemporaries saw the restaurants in a different, far more positive, light.

The study of the restaurantes populares needs to be placed within the broader historiography of food and nutrition. In recent years, historians have started to recognize the importance of food and food consumption as subjects of inquiry. In particular, influenced by the work of anthropologist Arjun Appadurai, historians have paid special attention to the interplay between food and (national) identity.[3] Other historians, working at the intersection of the history of medicine, public health, and state formation, have focused more explicitly on the growth of food and nutrition science and the increasing role of the state in regulating the production and commercialization of food.[4] Combining such perspectives, historians such as James Vernon have turned to examine the cultural meanings of hunger: how hunger came to be viewed and managed as a social problem, how it shaped the way the state addressed the provision and regulation of food, and, more generally, how it can serve "as a critical locus for rethinking how forms of government and statecraft emerge and work."[5] In particular, historians have begun to pay attention to the ways in which "communal" forms of dining were organized and the various meanings that were attached to communal eating. As Vernon and others have shown, the examination of forms of state-organized communal eating offer a privileged perspective on how food and nutrition became central to projects of governmentality in various parts of the world.[6]

Like the barrios obreros, the restaurantes populares can indeed be seen as part of a political process of "incorporation," as other historians have stressed. They were intended to undermine the appeal of the parties of the Left among the working class by providing work for the unemployed (during the construction phase) and cheap meals (once they were operational). But as I show below, they were also intended to address what their architects perceived to be the poor nutritional habits of Peru's workers and were designed in such a way as to confer a set of values, such as respectability, sobriety, punctuality, and cleanliness, through their architecture, furnishings, and service. As such, the restaurantes populares were indeed elements in a political project that sought to combat "communistic ideas." However, like the barrios obreros, they also reflected rationalities of government and functioned as a technology of government; that is to say, they instantiated the project of governmentality manifested in the labor state. Like the barrios obreros, the restaurantes populares were attempts by a state increasingly concerned with the fields of nutrition and public health to act directly upon the biological and moral makeup of workers but also on their mediate and immediate environments. Like the worker houses examined in the previous chapter, the restaurantes populares were intended to protect and "improve" workers by providing nutritious and healthy food as well as civilized values that would help constitute workers, and help workers constitute themselves, as the agents of Peru's industry-led civilization.

FOOD, RACE, AND WORKERS

Food in Peru in the early twentieth century was at the center of a number of conflicts shaped by class, race, and gender. In particular, in the first decades of the twentieth century the price, quality, and availability of food played a key role in shaping the politicization of the urban working class. Nowhere is this role more salient than in the food riots that gripped Lima in May 1919, provoked by rising food prices. Although historians disagree about the causes of the rise in prices, there is little doubt that the events of May 1919, alongside the general strike of December 1918–January 1919, were a pivotal moment in the history of Peruvian labor.[7] President Augusto B. Leguía, who rose to power that same year on the shoulders of Lima's workers, was quick to introduce a series of measures, including a decree that established that landowners had to devote at least 15 percent of their land to foodstuff production and instituted a price cap on meat sold in markets and in butchers' stores, as well as greater controls aimed at eradicating speculation; these measures contributed to a fall in the price of most major foodstuffs.[8] As this suggests, the food riots of 1919 provide clear evidence of how food and nutrition contributed to the coming into being of labor as a political force to be taken seriously by the Peruvian government. But just as important, the food riots, which were a local variant on a global development brought about by price inflation induced by the First World War, illustrate how the "politics" of food were intimately linked to class conflict but also racial conflict in the city.[9]

According to Vincent Peloso, though the Peruvian coastal diet had traditionally been nutritious, rising food prices in the early twentieth century contributed to a worsening of the average urban worker's diet.[10] The coastal diet had included large quantities of meat, transported to Lima from the central highlands. However, as pasture land in the highlands was turned to wool production for export, meat became increasingly scarce and expensive. According to Ruiz Zevallos, the "subsistence" movement led by the so-called Comité Pro-Abaratamiento de las Subsistencias (Committee for the Cheapening of Subsistence Goods), as well as the riot of May 1919 and their concrete political goal—a greater say in the production and commercialization of foodstuffs—was, in the final analysis, the result of a desire to retain the popular diet rather than a response to a situation of famine.[11] The movement reflected a (class) struggle that pitted the dietary traditions of urban workers and the urban poor against the interests of the agro-exporting elites. In contrast to the way in which famine in Ireland and India served to turn hunger into a political critique in the context of British colonialism, as studied by James Vernon, in Peru it was diet, rather than—or perhaps in addition to—hunger, that served as a vehicle of political protest.[12]

These struggles to preserve the popular diet were explicitly racialized: invariably, elite and plebeian commentators blamed Asian, and particularly Chinese, merchants for the rise in the price of meat. As one newspaper article noted: "The Chinese merchants who have monopolized the provision of meat constitute a vast parasitic organization, which is fed and encouraged by the tribute paid by the majority of consumers. The profits of these Chinese merchants represent a large sum that radically increases the price of meat."[13] As I show below, as in Paris, New York, and Mexico City, in Lima too the commercialization of meat and "the unfettered marketplace clashed with principles of subsistence, health, and hygiene."[14] In Mexico City, the "sausage rebellion" of 1910 studied by Jeffrey Pilcher took on nationalist overtones as Mexicans sought to resist attacks on their diet and foodways when U.S. investors attempted to monopolize the provision of meat and introduce U.S. methods of centralized meatpacking and refrigeration.[15] In the Peruvian capital, however, the clashes over the "traditional" diet were shaped less by nationalism than by xenophobia and anti-Asian racism. Claims about Chinese merchants and the rising price of meat reflected broader racist assumptions among Peruvians about Asians in Peru and about Chinese and Japanese "culture" more generally.[16]

Ideas about the causes of the scarcity of meat were also highly gendered and sexualized. Culinary discourse tends to represent meat as male and associates its consumption with manliness. For this reason it is not surprising that the debates on the changing character of the popular diet in Lima dovetailed with a broader anti-Asian racism that constructed the Chinese and Japanese, on the one hand, as morally and sexually degenerate (and therefore of questionable manhood), and, on the other, as threats to Peruvian masculinity (given the tendency to represent them as seducers and exploiters of women but also because, by keeping meat prices high, Asians threatened the vitality and virility of Peruvian males). An article published in *El Obrero Textil* in late 1919 illustrates this well:

> Do not forget that this degrading race is in large measure the cause of our misfortune. It hoards and monopolizes all the principal goods, and feigning a fictitious scarcity, employs it to squeeze us at will and to deny us another piece of bread for our little ones. It makes its money from those centers of vice, perdition, and gambling where many of you go to leave the sweat of your brow, your tiredness, your sorrows, and your week's hardships; in this way, a short time from now, you will end up in jail, in hospital, or in the cemetery while it returns to its country to enjoy a fortune so easily acquired at the expense of innumerable victims.[17]

A month later, a similar article in the same newspaper suggested that:

> the people and the proletarian class see very little difference between a Chinaman and a Japanese; both constitute a degenerate and harmful plague for the people. There you have the hairdressers who lowered the old prices so low that they pushed out the Peru-

vian hairdressers and then increased prices by a factor of four. There you have our sisters and daughters dragged into prostitution by one group [of Asians] and squeezed out by another of their jobs as seamstresses, with which they helped us to feed our little ones. There you have the poor ice cream makers and juice makers replaced by those disgusting Japanese *raspadilla* [an ice-based refreshment] makers of cadaverous complexion and slitty eyes, with blackened nails and swarming with flies.[18]

As these and other sources reveal, workers typically represented Asian immigrants as racially degenerate, as direct competitors for jobs, and, more generally, as exploiters of the working class.[19]

Although these views were formulated in the heated context of the food riots of 1919, they reflected a deeper racialized conflict associated with food and nutrition. In the early twentieth century, restaurants run by Chinese and, to a lesser extent, Japanese immigrants, became one of the main sources of food for the urban poor. In 1907 Abelardo Gamarra penned a description of one of the Chinese "fondas" that peppered the city: "a single Chinaman serves two hundred patrons and from a whole street away one can hear his beckoning call, rice on its own, meat with rice, steak, pudding [*aló solo, cane con aló, cane sola, bite, dulce requesón*]. One can see the throng of people coming and going, hardly sitting down, fed in one minute. Dishes are set down and taken way and everything is presented [to the customer]: the menu, the bread, the tea, all is presented as if moved by a spring."[20] However, far from recognizing the contribution that Asian restaurants made to the popular diet and to the nutrition of the poor, both elite and working-class observers typically associated Asian food with disease.[21] According to an article published in the elite *El Comercio* in 1901: "In those fondas, which, unfortunately, are used by those who—because of their poor economic situation—cannot afford to go elsewhere for food, everything, from the crockery to the utensils employed by the Asians in the kitchen, lack the necessary and indispensable cleanliness required to avoid them becoming sources of infection."[22] Similarly, the Confederación de Artesanos Unión Universal, an umbrella artisan organization, called for regular inspections of these establishments: "This measure is requested clamorously, since the working class, which, for the most part, consumes those meals, suffers the consequences of the poor-quality ingredients that are used in those restaurants."[23]

These denunciations reflected a broader public debate about food quality and safety that transcended the Peruvian context. As Michael French and Jim Phillips have noted, this debate shaped state intervention in the regulation of food preparation and consumption in Europe and North America between 1890 and 1914, where it revealed broader "concerns about poverty and health" and regarding the "health of the race."[24] In certain contexts, such as the United States, immigrants, and their food, came to be seen as a threat to public health and national cohesion. For U.S. food reformers, "nutritional science reinforced what their palates and stomachs already told them: that any cuisine as coarse, over-spiced, 'garlicky,' and indelicate-looking as the food of central, eastern, and southern Europe must be unhealthy as well." Attempts to change the immigrants' food habits became central to their "Americanization," since many believed that "the immigrants could never be weaned from their old country attitudes toward work, society, and politics until they abandoned their old-country ways of living and eating."[25] In Peru, such concerns similarly expressed a broader anxiety regarding the negative impact of Chinese immigration on Peru's "racial makeup" (though there was no analogous attempt to "Peruvianize" the Chinese). As a consequence, Chinese food, like the Chinese themselves, came to be seen as a poison threatening the integrity of the Peruvian nation.

In the 1900s, articles in the Lima press regularly invoked the association between Chinese eateries and poisonous, unhygienic conditions that threatened the health of the worker. As Fanni Muñoz notes, "In several issues of the magazine *Fray K. Bezón*, edited by the progressive and liberal Francisco A. Loayza and published from 1907, one can find several caricatures that ironically portray the lack of cleanliness of the Chinese. One can see images of food prepared in Chinese restaurants made with rat, cat, and dog meat. The Chinese are presented as rachitic persons with long hair, dirty nails and a sinister gaze."[26] Other periodicals reproduced the same tropes. In 1909, *Variedades* reported that a sweet shop in the Callejón Otaiza was selling *mumpao* made with rat meat: "Good or bad, scarce or plentiful, until recently our people consumed beef and had no reason to distrust what they were served in the fondas, but the subtle Asiatic ingenuity of the *macacos* [Chinks] who live and reproduce among us has led them to discover that the meat of disgusting animals is more profitable for their businesses and they have started to introduce it clandestinely in the small pastries that they sell."[27] According to the magazine, this incident had helped convince the mayor of Lima, Guillermo Billinghurst (who later became president for the years 1912–14), to close down the Callejón Otaiza and build in its place a "decent and hygienic street," in what, arguably if perversely, amounted to a form of state-initiated consumer protection.[28] A cartoon on "meat scarcity" published in 1928 similarly depicted highly racialized Chinese cooks wielding large knifes in pursuit of fleeing dogs, cats, and mice.[29]

Not everyone shared these views of Asian food. Anarchist proselytizers writing in *Los Parias*, a libertarian periodical, suggested that far from undermining the economy, health, and morality of workers, Asian businesses had become an integral and necessary part of the working-class economy, by providing not only the cheapest food available, but also a number of other goods and services at affordable prices:

> The worker, who today kills his hunger for twenty centavos in a Chinese eatery, could not do so for forty or fifty centavos in a national or European diner [*fonducho*]. And what we say about food goes for footwear, clothes, etc. The people know, they can always sense it; and yet, because of that lack of logic so common among sectors of the rabble, some turn against those who favor them by blindly seconding the plans of their exploiters. The laborer and the rich artisan who scream stridently for the heads of the macacos have filled their bellies in a Chinese restaurant and draw the energy for their screams from the Chinese stew. The Sinophobe magnate who cannot be cured by the medical doctor, the healer, or the waters of Lourdes, turns for help to the Chinese doctors.[30]

As another article in the same periodical noted, poverty in Lima would be greater "were it not for the Chinese traders, who, sober and content with little gain, sell cheap goods, making them accessible to the poorest of all."[31]

At the other end of the political spectrum, the periodical *Cascabel*, run by Federico More, no friend of Asian (particularly Japanese) immigrants, published a long two-page article in May 1935 on Lima's Chinese eateries. More argued in unequivocal terms that "thanks to the Chinese, Peru, which completely lacked a culinary tradition, is learning the science and art of eating."[32] Focusing on the so-called *chifas* of Capón Street, visited, he claimed, by thousands of customers every day for lunch and dinner, but especially at night, More described some of the more popular, including Thon Pho, Kuong Thon, Kamlen, and San Joy Lao. These chifas, which served healthy and hearty food, catered for all types of clients, from those who paid 40 centavos for offal soup or stir-fried beef ("lomo revuelto") to those who could afford to eat with silver crockery and enjoy dishes such as boneless chicken, swallow-nest soup, or bamboo duck. Although the rich and the poor ate different dishes, and were subject to a different "topography and ritual" (with the rich eating in "boxes" and using ivory chopsticks and the poor eating next to the oven in the main dining hall and using black chopsticks), "they all eat under the same ensign and, when they enter and they leave, they pass through the same customs." "Heaven," More concluded, "cannot be too different to a chifa." For More, far from routinely poisoning their customers, the Chinese were teaching Peruvians how to eat: "Until now, our people ate empirically, if it is possible to use the expression. The Chinese are teaching them to eat scientifically and artistically." In a rhetorical operation that, given the prevalent anti-Asian racism in Peruvian society, amounted to an elevation of the Chinese to a superior status of civilization, More argued: "Each race has its role, we do not doubt it: the Saxons teach us corporeal hygiene; France mental hygiene; the Chinese the important hygiene of the stomach and palate."[33]

As More's comments suggest, a growing concern among sectors of the elite with nutrition, and particularly the nutrition of workers, as a field of study and a matter for state intervention underpinned the food-related anti-Asian racism discussed above. Peru, in this respect, was part of a global pattern, which, from the mid-nineteenth century saw a growing consensus develop regarding the idea that, as Harmke Kamminga and Andrew Cunningham suggest, "it is the state's duty to create the conditions under which its citizens can be helped, educated or even coerced to be fit." This consensus led to state support for the scientific study of nutrition and the link between health and diet, as, increasingly, the state came to define "health and fitness in relation to what it expected from its citizens, whether it be as workers, mothers, soldiers or wealth creators."[34] This is evident in Ignacio de la Puente's 1899 study "The Nutrition of the Worker," which argued that a scientific approach to nutrition would produce a better type of worker. De la Puente held that nutrition, or rather, the lack of proper nutrition, above other biological, cultural, or environmental factors, explained the inferior quality of Peruvian workers: "The lack of dependability of Peruvian workers in their labor, their lack of punctuality in accomplishing contracted tasks, must not be attributed to a lack of aptitude, an invincible laziness, and particularly not to the nervous effect of the climate; the overwhelming cause, in my opinion, is rooted in the deficient and poor quality of foodstuffs."[35] For de la Puente, as for the U.S. food reformers studied by Levenstein, "the main obstacle to elevating the standard of living of . . . workers seemed to be the workers' own ignorance regarding their food."[36] However, de la Puente suggested that if workers were taught to eat properly and to avoid alcohol they could easily become model citizens: "Teach our artisans properly, let them learn as children manual tasks in the school, to eat properly and avoid alcoholic drinks, and there will be no lack of hands for industry, no lack of an intelligent and virile population prepared [to fulfill] the functions of citizenship."[37] For de la Puente, the staple of the working class, the "sancochado," a meat stew with yucca that, he believed, was of low nutritive value, posed the principal problem. He noted that hospitals in Sweden and Britain had banned this meal and replaced it with "asado" or roast beef. He suggested that Peru follow suit: "Let us break this tradition, let us abandon the sancochado, and I can assure you that we will gain in population, in physical vigor and in intelligence."[38] Ironically, in light of local reactions to Asian food discussed above, de la Puente included Japanese foodstuffs such as "misso" and "tafou," which he considered highly nutritious and eminently adaptable to the coastal diet, among a number of alternatives to the sancochado.[39]

The idea that the careful control of the nutrition of workers would improve workers' aptitude for work and general capability to act as morally upstanding citizens points to how, already at the start of the twentieth century, nutrition was understood in ways that reflected rationalities of government. De la Puente went so far as to propose a specific diet for workers. For breakfast, which was to be taken at 6:30 A.M., workers would eat two pieces of bread with fried pork (chicharrón) and brown sugar cake (media tapa de chancaca), as well as water. For lunch, to be taken at 11 A.M., De la Puente recommended rice and beans, boiled or fried potatoes, maize or yucca porridge, more brown sugar cake, and two pieces of bread. Dinner, to be taken at 6:30 P.M., would include a noodle soup, rice, and beans, or alternatively lentils, and a dessert. De la Puente stressed that workers should eat heartily ("hasta saciarse"). He suggested that workers should avoid tea and coffee, or indeed yerba mate, which had little nutritive value and were "exitantes," better suited to those who performed intellectual labor, such as students, lawyers, and writers. Indians, by contrast, he suggested, should be allowed to continue to chew coca. Alcohol, which he saw as the main source of calories for workers, had to be avoided at all costs, not so much for reasons linked to nutrition, but for moral reasons: "Where there is alcoholism, there is no saving, no health, but disease, no virtue but clumsy and disgusting vices: when virtue is lacking and vices abound, the home, the constitutive molecule of the social organism is not produced, it degenerates and dies. When homes die, the Fatherland dies."[40] In this way, de la Puente echoed familiar ideas about alcohol's deleterious effects on the working class and the increasingly eugenic "scientific" thought that shaped such ideas.[41]

This preoccupation with worker's nutrition translated into calls for a more systematic attention to the matter from the state. In an article published in *Mundial* in 1927, Federico Ortiz Rodríguez reprised the common complaints about the quality and high price of food that was available to workers. He noted that it was impossible to pay less than one sol for a meal in the various establishments that workers used to feed themselves such as fondas, *cocinerías*, and *cafetines*, most of which were owned by Japanese and Chinese, and that most dishes were of poor quality: "In winter the meats are almost always raw and cold and in summer they are undergoing fermentation." Ortiz Rodríguez argued that the state should provide proper nutrition to Lima's workers in "salas-comedores." Like de la Puente, Ortiz Rodríguez presented this argument in a way that echoed the rationalities of government manifested in the labor state. Workers, he argued, were a key source of human capital that needed to be protected and enhanced: "It is well known that man as a human engine is subject to physical attrition; it follows that it is in the interest of the state to look after this human capital and of capitalists to maintain the strength and energy of that productive machine, which with an insufficient and deficient nutrition, which produces an inevitable attrition, will produce much less than it would produce if its physical and moral forces were not undermined."[42] This reasoning, as I discuss in the following section, formed the basis for the establishment of state-run eateries in the 1930s.

During the 1930s and particularly the 1940s, the poor nutrition of Peru's working peoples became an increasingly urgent concern for a growing cohort of nutrition and diet specialists. A number of studies were published that focused on the causes and character of malnutrition and possible solutions. In the late nineteenth century, de la Puente had identified workers' ignorance as the source of their poor nutrition. By the 1930s, as elsewhere in the world, Peruvian nutritionists typically viewed poverty rather than ignorance as the main cause of malnutrition. But like de la Puente they were concerned with the "quality" of the population's diet and with how to change its dietary habits. A study of Limeños' diet published in 1942 concluded that though the intake of calories was sufficient, it was far from adequate. There was a marked lack of meat, milk, eggs, cheese, fruits, vegetables, and bread.[43] A detailed statistical study published in 1945 confirmed this view: Peruvians ate too little and they ate the wrong foodstuffs—the problem was quantitative and qualitative.[44] A 1943 study of eighty-one poor families in the Rímac area of the city, a traditionally working-class neighborhood, concluded that soups and rice made up of the bulk of their meals. The study noted that greater nutritional advantage would result if the families substituted potatoes for rice and concluded that malnutrition was acute in the sample of families surveyed, a situation that explained the presence of tuberculosis.[45] A few years later, another study focused on the protein deficiency characteristic of the Peruvians' diet owing to a lack of meat consumption. Noting that meat consumption had dropped sharply in the first half of the 1940s, the authors of the study argued that since mass imports of meat were not possible, consumption of fish should be encouraged.[46]

Leoncio Palacios's study of Lima's working-class households in the 1930s adds support to these conclusions about the nutritional deficiencies of Peruvians.[47] As Palacios shows, food represented half of a typical working-class family's total expenditure, with housing and clothing together amounting to a quarter. Among the poorer families in Palacios's sample, expenditure on food reached as much as 58 percent of total expenditure. When expenditure on food is broken down we find that 26 percent of the food budget was spent on cereals; meat and fish accounted for 20 percent; while vegetables represented another 19 percent. If we take into consideration the price differentials between meat and bread or rice (in 1930 a kilo of beef cost 1.07 soles, a kilo of bread 0.34 soles, and a kilo of rice 0.43 soles), it is not surprising that meat was consumed only sparingly.[48] Palacios estimated that on a weekly basis the average working-class family consumed some three kilos of beef, four liters of milk, eighteen kilos of vegetables (potatoes, sweet potato, manioc, and greens), and twelve kilos of cereals (bread, rice, pasta, corn, and flour). In addition, these families used three kilos of sugar and twelve kilos of firewood. According to Palacios, average meat consumption in Peru (i.e., not just Lima, where consumption is likely to have been considerably higher than the average), at ten kilos per person per year, was a third of that of France, and a fifth of that of Norway. Moreover, again not surprisingly, Palacios found that the better-off working-class families had a better diet than the poorer families: as incomes rose, certain food groups, typically meat and milk, replaced others, such as potatoes and bread. The diet of most workers in the sample, however, was "almost exclusively energetic," meaning that a greater consumption of cereals compensated for the lack of meat or vegetables in the diet.[49]

As the above suggests, as elsewhere in the world, the unbalanced and nutritionally deficient diet of urban workers was a result of their low purchasing power and of the high prices of food products. Yet, revealingly, the nutritional experts blamed the unbalanced diet of Limeños not only on poverty but also on a shift in food culture toward "Asian," particularly Chinese, food. As one commentator noted: "In no small measure, the excessively calorific nutrition of the citizens is a product of the growing importance of Asian nutritional customs among the population (an excess of rice over bread, potatoes, and greens, etc.)."[50] In the 1900s Asian food had been perceived as a source of disease; in the 1930s it was also blamed for the malnutrition of the poor. As has happened with other minority groups in other historical and geographical settings, Asian immigrants and their "culture" in early twentieth-century Peru were targeted both by elite and popular sectors as the source of a variety of problems that ostensibly had little to do with their presence in the country, or (ironically) that in some cases, as with the provision of cheap and nutritious food, they were helping to solve. That such targeted (and often violent) discrimination happened is hardly surprising given that it was legitimized by elite racial discourse and that, in most cases, attacks (both verbal and physical) on Asians went unpunished.[51] Yet at the same time the targeting of Asians served an obvious, if perverse, purpose for urban workers. In constructing Asian immigrants as immoral, disease-ridden, and exploiters of women, urban workers sought to affirm their own morality and decency, in short, to construct a sense of collective identity in contradistinction to an "other" provided by Asian immigrants. In so doing, the Asian food, and the Asian restaurants, that they had come to rely on were "othered" as unhealthy and nonnutritious, in the first case, and filthy and contaminating in the second.[52] In this way, as I discuss below, workers too participated in placing food and nutrition at the center of the project of governmentality manifested in the labor state.

THE POLITICS OF FOOD AND NUTRITION

Along with the barrios obreros, the work-creation schemes of the juntas pro-desocupados, and the Seguro Social, the restaurantes populares were part of a number of measures directed at organized labor implemented by the Sánchez Cerro (1931–33) and Benavides (1933–39) governments. The original law creating the restaurants in 1932 projected the construction of eight restaurants in Lima, two in Callao, and one in each of the *balnearios* (the seaside districts of Miraflores, Barranco, and Chorrillos). Meals were to be priced at 0.30 soles.[53] In addition to raising a loan of 500,000 soles, the state introduced a tax on cigarettes to fund the restaurants.[54] By April 1936, three had been built in Lima and one in Callao. In 1938, the Dirección de Previsión Social reported that some 8.6 million "comensales" had made use of the restaurants.[55] By 1941, the mining town of La Oroya too boasted such a restaurant.[56] The construction of the restaurantes populares dovetailed neatly with the state work-creation schemes. Responsibility for the budget, construction, and operation of the restaurants was given to the Lima Junta Pro-Desocupados, the state agency charged, as I discussed in the previous chapter, with addressing the rise in unemployment in the capital, and which, Benavides claimed, was better placed to "make use of such works to reduce unemployment."[57]

The restaurantes populares and, more generally, the provision of cheap food for urban workers, became one of several arenas of political contestation between the Sánchez Cerro and Benavides governments and APRA and, to a lesser extent, the Peruvian Communist Party in the 1930s. It was both a symbolic arena and a brick-and-mortar one, since, for a while at least, workers were able to choose between the state-run restaurants that were situated in central Lima, in the districts of La Victoria and Rímac, and in Callao, and an APRA-run *comedor*. That choice ended during the political closure of late 1934 when the authorities closed down APRA's comedor indefinitely. That the restaurantes populares were understood as "weapons of the strong" in the struggle against APRA is illustrated by a report published in August 1935 in the

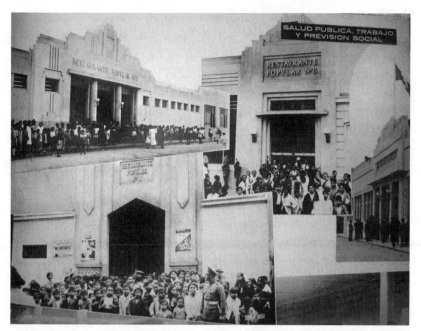

FIGURE 5 The main entrances of three restaurantes populares in Lima. Source: *Progresos del Perú, 1933–1939, durante el gobierno del Presidente de la República General Óscar R. Benavides* (Buenos Aires: Editorial Guillermo Kraft, 1945), 227.

government-friendly periodical *Cascabel* on the inauguration of the Restaurante Popular No. 2, in Rímac, which argued that the restaurant demonstrated that "the economic problems of the proletariat can be solved without books, without red flags, without demonstrations, without the cadavers of workers."[58] It is no surprise that for the far Right too, the provision of cheap and nutritious food became a key political concern. In the campaign for the 1936 presidential election, which was cancelled by Benavides, the Unión Revolucionaria, by then openly "fascist," called for a further expansion of the state's role in overseeing public nutrition and for an expansion in the number of restaurantes populares: "We want a strictly supervised public nutrition; the prohibition of excessive speculation and profit associated with the sale of foodstuffs; severe penalties for those who adulterate food; that the Public Nutrition Agency [Dirección de Alimentación Pública] be given sufficient power [to] take control of the production, transport, and commercialization of foodstuffs; and the large-scale expansion of restaurantes populares, milk programs, and school refectories."[59]

APRA's response to the restaurantes populares perfectly illustrates the ways in which the problem of food and nutrition became deeply politicized in the 1930s. On the one hand, APRA mocked such measures. In 1934, Carlos Manuel Cox, one of Haya de la Torre's lieutenants, argued: "Unemployment increases and the government thinks that it can calm the people's hunger by creating restaurantes populares!! This reminds me of the story of the disingenuous queen who upon learning that the uprisen people demanded because they were dying of hunger, answered: 'If they ask for bread, and there is none, let them eat cake.'"[60] At the same time, APRA claimed that the government's restaurantes populares were a mere copy of its own Comedor Aprista No. 1, which it had set up in November 1933 at 1073 Pobres Street, and which was first shut down by the government on 31 January 1934. In the political opening of mid-1934, the Comedor Aprista was allowed to reopen, enabling the party to make improvements to its "comedor" while two new "comedores" were planned. The party boasted: "With financial resources A HUNDRED TIMES SMALLER than those available to the restaurante popular of the Ministry of Development, we are successfully developing an organization plan to address the very real need of the people to have access to cheap, abundant, and hygienic food." The party claimed that the Comedor Aprista had been a success; it had even been profitable, despite the fact it had been set up with almost no money at all (according to one document the "capital" of the comedor was a mere 1,223.31 soles while the Restaurante Popular No. 1 in Huaquilla Street had capital of 154,874.59 soles): "Results so far: a constant increase in customers, which we cannot meet because of a lack of economic resources; very high satisfaction among both natives and foreigners, because of our technical organization and nutritious food; achievement of profits . . . which will be used to establish new comedores and to serve as a fund for the 'Tahuantinsuyo' National Cooperative, as well as to improve our services in benefit of the needy classes and to establish other cooperatives."[61]

APRA presented its "comedores apristas" as evidence of its capacity to address the fundamental problems faced by Peru's workers better than the Benavides government could; in this case the lack of cheap and nutritious food. On 7 April 1934, the APRA mouthpiece *La Tribuna* published an article reporting the creation of a second "comedor aprista" on Colón Street in the neighboring port of Callao. Meals were priced at 25 centavos, that is, five centavos cheaper than in the restaurante popular, and consisted of "two hearty dishes, with bread and tea."[62] The article stressed that, as in the comedor in Pobres Street, "service is personal," and that the comedor was proving a success among the port and customs workers, five hundred of whom made use of the facilities several times a day, and who, in so doing, "sense the effectiveness of Aprista promises." Together with similar comedores in the cities of Huacho and Huánuco, the newspaper concluded, the comedores in Lima and Callao "are an example of social organization and efficiency. In this period of crisis, APRA contributes in this way, with irrefutable deeds, to alleviate the economic penuries of the modest classes of the country."[63] Another article, announcing the reopening of the comedor in Pobres Street, declared that all customers would become stakeholders in the restaurant, emphasized the high quality of service and meals, and publicized the special menu prepared for the opening, which included "Genoese soup, goat stew, rice, fruit, tea and bread."[64] The report published on 26 June, the day of the comedor's reopening, noted that interest in the comedor had been so great that long queues had formed, the food that had been prepared had run out, and that it had been necessary to prepare more. As this suggests, APRA made sure to present its comedores apristas as places characterized by high standards in the quality of food, service, and, indeed, "experience." The comedor aprista on Pobres Street had been carefully decorated for its reopening and "pretty flowers" had been placed on tables. At the same time, the article noted, discipline and proper behavior was maintained in the comedores: they were invigilated and smoking was forbidden. In addition, the article emphasized the didactic functions of the comedores. Upon entering the comedor customers were given a booklet that explained to them, among other things, how to chew their food. More generally, the newspaper sought to present the comedores as places where workers could develop new forms of sociability and solidarity: "Camaraderie is created there, shoulder to shoulder, diner to diner. The *compañeros* feel a little closer to each other during the duration of the pleasant meal."[65]

By contrast, APRA sought to present the restaurantes populares as poorly managed, inefficient, and offering a poor service, and, as such, a reflection of the incapacity of the Benavides government to address the problems faced by Peru's workers. An article published on 21 June reported that two workers, José Gutiérrez and Alfonso Velardo, had come to *La Tribuna*'s offices to protest about the poor service offered at the restaurante popular on Huaquilla Street. They had brought with them a portion of rice that they had been served at the restaurante. The newspaper report confirmed that the rice was uncooked.[66] More generally, APRA argued that—despite the "numerous resources" that Law 7612 provided and the fact that "with these resources one would have expected that most of the problems associated with the provision of food to the working classes would have been solved"—the government's Restaurante Popular No. 1 had been a failure. Although two thousand people made use of it on a daily basis, this restaurante popular was losing money and failing in its objective to provide cheap food for the working class, as indicated by the fact that one congressman had requested that Restaurante Popular No. 1 be sold off "because it is chipping away at the national budget": "This congressman's request indicates that the management of the restaurant has failed to come up with a carefully studied plan to provide cheap and nutritious food to the people, without it resulting in the bankruptcy [of the restaurant] or the shrinkage of resources required to expand that project."[67] As late as 1941, in an article on the growing food shortages faced by the capital, *La Tribuna* pointed to the poor quality of the meals prepared in the restaurantes populares, described as "sometimes inedible."[68]

APRA's campaign against the restaurantes populares ultimately failed. Although it may be true, as APRA claimed, that the government's restaurantes populares were uneconomical and that the food they served was inedible, in the late 1930s workers made use of them in large numbers as some photographs, admittedly produced by the Benavides government, illustrate (see figure 6). If available figures are to be believed, in the first three months of 1937, some 536,300 *comensales* (customers) ate in the four restaurants in Lima.[69] In 1938 alone, as noted above, some 8.6 million comensales made use of the restaurants.[70] How can this be accounted for? One could argue, with the traditional historiography, that the success of the restaurantes populares was the result of the capacity of the governments of the 1930s to mobilize state resources to (a) repress the political opposition and (b) to create labor laws and agencies that, in helping to improve, however marginally, the material conditions of urban workers, effectively neutralized militancy and undermined the appeal of APRA, and to a lesser extent the PCP, among labor. The fact that workers were drawn to, or duped into, making use of the services that the restaurants provided would be evidence of the limited development of their class consciousness, of the failure of APRA's labor policy and cam-

FIGURE 6 Customers at one of Lima's restaurantes populares. Source: *Progresos del Perú, 1933–1939, durante el gobierno del Presidente de la República General Óscar R. Benavides* (Buenos Aires: Editorial Guillermo Kraft, 1945), 227.

paigns against the restaurantes populares, and of the success of the labor policy of Peruvian governments whose aim was to "incorporate" labor into a new "populist" relationship.

However, the restaurantes populares were not designed merely to undermine labor militancy and the appeal of APRA, as I show below. Their principal function was to "improve" the workers by providing them with better nutrition and by transmitting a set of values that workers would make their own. These values would indeed weaken workers' susceptibility to militancy and revolutionary influences. But, along with providing them with better nutrition, the restaurantes populares would also make them into workers that could effectively perform their role as agents of progress. As historians such as James Vernon have suggested, "collective feeding" in the twentieth century, of which the Peruvian restaurantes populares were but one example, was seen by its champions as "a new social form capable of producing greater health, efficiency, civility, and social solidarity."[71] Like the barrios obreros, the restaurantes populares are best understood as elements in a broader project of governmentality manifested in the labor state. They at once expressed rationalities of government in the sphere of food and nutrition, that is, the understanding that it was the duty and purpose of the state to ensure that workers were sufficiently and properly nourished, and in turn represented a technology of government, that is they represented the means of making that understanding into policy. However, in Peru, as in twentieth-century Britain, the restaurante popular like the factory canteen "helped engineer a new vision of society, even though at the same time if fell short of bringing it to fruition."[72] The analysis of a particularly rich document can help us to understand how and why.

FOOD AS CIVILIZATION

The Restaurantes Populares of Peru: A Contribution to the Study of the Problem of Popular Nutrition, published in Santiago, Chile, in 1936, was prepared by the Peruvian government and presented at the Labor Conference of the States of America (Conferencia del Trabajo de los Estados de América), organized by the International Labor Organization.[73] The book—which is fifty pages long and includes a number of photographs, illustrations, and text—was used to showcase one aspect of the Benavides government's statist social action to an international conference on labor. The book trumpeted the restaurantes populares as a success and as a blueprint that other governments in Latin America could copy: the book had been prepared as a result of "the fact that the organization of the Peruvian restaurantes populares is considered worthy of imitation or study in other countries (*Los Restaurantes Populares*, 9)."[74] In this sense, the book provides an invaluable perspective on how the Benavides government sought to present its achievements in relation to labor to an international audience, and specifically, to the ILO. According to the book's "Presentación [Introduction]," the restaurantes populares were conceived as both "true laboratories for the study of the effects of an adequate nutrition" and "schools of hygienic education for the people (9)." As this suggests, notions of science, education, and public health were uppermost in the minds of the architects of the restaurantes populares. The restaurantes populares offered, on the one hand, an opportunity for controlled experimentation and the application of science to the nutrition of the working class, and, on the other, ideal settings for educating workers in notions of proper nutrition and public health.

The idea that the restaurantes populares could "improve" workers is made explicit in the book through three central themes: science, dignity, and quality. Throughout the book emphasis is placed on how scientific principles underpin the conception and organization of the restaurantes populares. The location of the four restaurantes, according to the report,

FIGURE 7 Restaurante Popular No. 2 in the Rímac district, a traditional working-class area of the city. Source: *Los Restaurantes Populares del Perú: Contribución al estudio del problema de la alimentación popular* (Santiago de Chile: Imprenta Universitaria, 1936), 22. Courtesy of the Collection of the International Institute of Social History, Amsterdam.

had been "subject to careful study (15)." Similarly, the purchase of food was subject to precise estimations and "results from a calculation based on its consumption in a short period of days (from eight to twelve) and its conservation in perfect conditions," as were the meals: once a menu was approved, "we proceed, immediately, to calculate the rations, in conformity with our size and weight tables, which are deduced, experimentally, from individual consumption, which is constantly observed and corrected, taking into account the average daily attendance of customers (33; 46)." Like the purchase of food and the preparation of meals, the design of the restaurantes was a result of scientific study: the plans of restaurants (included in the book) allowed "a swift functioning and efficient distribution which facilitates the inspection of services, the attention to customers, and the movement of the restaurant staff." Indeed, "when calculating the structures [of the building] we have tried to keep obstructions to circulation to a minimum"; "the dining hall, the kitchens and the service corridors are sizeable and bereft of columns"; "in the rooms where a need for more light would have represented a considerable cost, we have reduced the number of columns (17; 19)." It is worth noting that although the absence of columns and, more generally, of

FIGURE 8 The male dining room of the Restaurante Popular No. 1 in Huaquilla Street. Source: *Los Restaurantes Populares del Perú: Contribución al estudio del problema de la alimentación popular* (Santiago de Chile: Imprenta Universitaria, 1936), 34. Courtesy of the Collection of the International Institute of Social History, Amsterdam.

obstacles to the circulation of waiters and customers was presented as resulting from a careful scientific assessment of how to provide the most economic and efficient service, it also facilitated supervision. This idea is similarly found in a section entitled "Customer Service—Control Measures," where one of the roles of the service staff is defined as "the strict vigilance over the integrity and conservation of all service utensils in use." Meanwhile, all the restaurantes employed a "guardianeria," whose function was to "[avoid] agglomerations and [ensure] the calm circulation of customers." Finally, we learn, "the doors of the restaurant are subject to a strict vigilance (39; 37)."

The other idea that is present throughout the book is the notion that the restaurantes populares would help dignify workers, both men and women, by providing them with an environment where a series of values were upheld and honored and where they could learn to espouse those values by making them their own. Indeed, the function of the restaurantes was not only to "provide workers with healthy, abundant, and cheap nourishment" but also to provide them with the means to "easily preserve their physical and moral patrimony (9)." In this, the restaurantes populares echoed other forms of communal feeding, such as factory canteens in interwar Britain, which were conceived as social laboratories or tools of social engineering and seen as places "where workers meet, make friends, and learn to be part of, and take part in, the life of what should be a valuable humanizing experience—their industrial home."[75] In the restaurantes populares, the food was not only cheap; it was "pleasant, comprehensive, adequate, and *harmonious*" (emphasis added). The conferment of values was both explicit and, more important, implicit or subliminal. In all four restaurants, "notices have been put up discretely on walls in different areas, inviting customers, courteously, without judgment: to take care of the building 'that belongs to the people,' to remove their hats, to wash their hands, to not spit on the floor, etc. (21)." Nationalism, or indeed, xenophobic tendencies were given a nod: "Both in the construction and in the installation of the restaurants we have given priority to native-born workers, artisans, white-collar employees, suppliers, and managers, as well as to locally sourced building materials (21)."

Workers' experience of the restaurants would also serve to confer certain values. In this respect, the restaurantes populares were seen as capable of transforming workers by providing in their experience of the restaurants an image of what they could become. In Britain, the architects of factory canteens argued: "Give workers a canteen to be proud of and the canteen will soon be proud of its workers."[76] A similar assumption seems to have guided the architects of the restaurantes populares. Hygiene was underlined throughout: in the *almacén* (storeroom) "the most exacting hygienic precautions" were to be observed; food was placed on shelves that "ensure its ventilation and isolation from the floor and all types of contamination (35)," while "the cleanliness of the restaurant and the observance of strict hygienic conditions in its maintenance, [which are] uppermost concerns of the management in accordance with regulations, have been maintained to this day, a fact that has met with the warm approval of customers and visitors, and resulted in highly favorable comments in the press (47)." Punctuality was similarly stressed: food was served from 11 A.M. to 2 P.M. for lunch and 6 to 9 P.M. for dinner, "precise times (37)." In combining scientific organization and values such as hygiene and punctuality, the book suggested, a dignified atmosphere was achieved in the restaurants. The "mood" of the restaurants was described as "dignified and hygienic," while the architectural style was "sober and beautiful (17)."

Yet a third and perhaps more surprising theme is present in the book:

quality. Quality is central both to the restaurants as structures and to the restaurants as a service offered to workers. The use of high-quality materials is stressed throughout: "All building material—of the highest quality." The toilets "can compete with the best in establishments of this type"; "electric services have been installed with first-class materials"; "the furnishings and appliances can be classed as top quality (17; 19)." Similarly, the quality of the service is emphasized. Each employee was assigned a separate uniform ("Cooks: white jacket and hat, blue khaki apron; controllers: white overalls; dining hall waiters: white jacket and apron, with a numbered badge on the lapel; cutlery waiters: black jacket and white apron, also with a numbered badge (29; 31).") As photographs in the book reveal (see figures 8 and 9), waiters were impeccably attired and the service was carefully choreographed:

> After being welcomed at his arrival to the restaurant, the customer is guided by the porters to the ticket window, and thereafter to the dining hall, and shown to his table. Two waiters approach the customer. The "dining hall" waiter takes the customer's ticket and the "cutlery" waiter sets down five pieces on the table: a spoon, a fork, a knife, a teaspoon, and a paper napkin. [After the meals and coffee or tea are served] the waitressing operations terminate, under the strict vigilance of ad hoc employees, who will have verified the order and exactitude of the service personnel's movements, either in the opportune revision of the cutlery and meals served to each customer, without omission or delay, or in the observance of the utmost politeness with the clients, receiving in a friendly manner every request, complaint or observation, which they will try to address to the best of their abilities (39; 41).

The careful planning involved in waiting on customers responded to various goals: "On the one hand, the greatest customer satisfaction, resulting not only from the quality and abundance of the meals, but also from the courteous and affable treatment that is provided, without distinctions or preferences" and "the precise, speedy, and opportune nature of the personalized service, exempt of mortifying delays (39)." As this suggests, the restaurantes populares were conceived as *restaurants* and not as canteens, cafeterias, or other forms of eateries, and this original conception was clearly important to the way in which their architects sought to attract a clientele of workers.

FIGURE 9 The entrance hall of the Restaurante Popular No. 1 in Huaquilla Street. Source: *Los Restaurantes Populares del Perú: Contribución al estudio del problema de la alimentación popular* (Santiago de Chile: Imprenta Universitaria, 1936), 26. Courtesy of the Collection of the International Institute of Social History, Amsterdam.

FIGURE 10 The soft drinks sale counter at the Restaurante Popular No. 1 in Huaquilla Street. Source: *Los Restaurantes Populares del Perú: Contribución al estudio del problema de la alimentación popular* (Santiago de Chile: Imprenta Universitaria, 1936), 43. Courtesy of the Collection of the International Institute of Social History, Amsterdam.

Why the insistence on science, dignity, and quality? No doubt it helped to "sell" the restaurantes populares and more generally the state's "social action" to the international audience at the Santiago conference, by presenting it as undeniably modern and enlightened. The conference gave an opportunity to the Benavides government to showcase the progressive character of his regime: by emphasizing the care and attention that had gone into designing, building, and running the restaurants, Benavides sought to make a point about his government's policies toward labor more generally, and indeed, about the nature of his government and its achievements in other fields. Delegates to the conference are likely to have read the book in this way. For historians, the book offers a more interesting interpretation. As suggested above, and as my analysis of the discourse that dominates the book—with its insistence on science, dignity, quality—seems to confirm, the restaurantes populares can be seen as an element in a broader set of measures expressive of rationalities of government manifested in the labor state. Like the barrios obreros, the restaurantes populares reflected the increasing "biologization of the social": the process whereby elite social reformers came to see social problems, through an increasingly medicalized gaze, as problems affecting individual bodies. Social problems would be best addressed, it followed, through labor policy focused on "improving" bodies, improving the mediate and immediate environment in which that bodily improvement could occur, and producing the "right" type of worker.

This suggests a more complex interpretation of the motives behind the creation of the restaurantes populares. At one level, the restaurants did fulfill a "populist" political role. By providing employment to workers and cheap meals, it was hoped, the restaurants helped to neutralize the appeal of radical alternatives. But, at another level, the restaurantes populares were clearly the product of a confluence of ideas about (a) labor and the nature of workers, increasingly perceived through a scientific or "medicalized" gaze, and (b) the role of the state, and of modernizing elites associated to the state, in "improving" workers through the inculcation of specific values and habits, such as cleanliness, punctuality, and respect for order, but also through the governmental transformation of workers' mediate and immediate environment in order to allow the coming into being of workers as agents of progress. Naturally, the political and governmental rationalities that shaped the restaurantes populares overlapped and reinforced each other, since the restaurants' architects assumed that the restaurantes populares provided an environment that would allow the urban poor to become model workers, who, once in possession of the values conferred by the restaurants and their environment, would rationally shun the radical political alternatives.[77] But, contra traditional historiography, the governmental rather than the political rationalities go further in explaining the success of the restaurantes populares, as I discuss in the next section.

PERFORMING DIFFERENCE

In November 1935, an article appeared in the periodical *Cascabel* arguing that the restaurantes populares should be renamed. The article noted that the restaurants were operating at less than full capacity. Although they could feed some 6,000 people a day, on 28 October only 1,181 people had made use of their services. According to the author of the article, this underutilization owed to two factors. On the one hand, the term "popular" in "restaurante popular" put off the better-off potential customers, those belonging to the middle class. On the other, workers were put off by the fact that the restaurants were clean and that the waiters were well turned out. Intimidated by these unfamiliar surroundings, the article suggested, many preferred the Chinese and Japanese eateries. As a consequence, the article estimated, only 15 percent of those who attended the restaurants were, properly speaking, workers. The others were, broadly speaking, members of the middle class: "petty employees, master artisans, journeymen, etc. The diners in the restaurantes populares tend to be located in the shadows between each class."[78] Still, despite this regrettable failure to attract more workers, the article went on to argue, the restaurantes populares fulfilled a clear nationalist function. Some 1,359,418 diners had made use of the restaurants since their inauguration. This was equivalent to 679,709 soles that had not been spent in Japanese or Chinese eateries: "As a result, the people have not paid this fabulous sum, which by now would be in Osaka or Peiping."[79] The restaurants, the article concluded, which gave one the "feeling of being in one of the great hotels of New York," should be made available to all social classes and renamed restaurantes nacionales, instead of "populares."

The restaurantes populares were not renamed. But their original function, to provide cheap and nutritious food to workers, was modified. By the early 1940s, the restaurants were being used to feed Lima's growing population of schoolchildren. According to one set of statistics, the three central restaurantes populares in the capital had provided meals to more than half a million schoolchildren per year between 1942 and 1944.[80] Still, workers continued to eat there and available statistics suggest that many overcame the initial reticence identified by the author of the *Cascabel* article as arising from unfamiliarity with cleanliness. Of course, it is difficult if not impossible to get into the minds of Limeño workers in the 1930s and to know with any certainty what considerations influenced their decisions to eat in one of the four restaurantes populares that existed in Lima. Naturally, there are obvious reasons why workers ate in the restaurants. They were cheap, and some meals, such as breakfast, were free for children.[81] But, by itself, the cheapness of the restaurants cannot explain why workers were drawn to them, since cheap food was available elsewhere (in street stalls, markets, and Asian restaurants). In order to understand, therefore, why workers chose to eat there, we need to consider what the restaurantes populares represented for Lima's workers.

As the *Cascabel* article suggested, and as my analysis of the book presented to the ILO conference in Santiago illustrates, elites presented the restaurantes populares as all that the Chinese restaurants were not: their antithesis. There is some evidence that at least some workers shared this view. According to an article published in 1937 in the newspaper of an artisan organization:

> One of the most feasible concerns of the present government is to provide the people with good and cheap food. This has been the motivation for the creation of the restaurantes populares. But the Japanese continue to run a series of diners [*fondines*] and most cafés in Lima. Especially in Lima, the Japanese have monopolized this type of business. But what worries us is not that they are monopolists. It is, rather, the way that they work. These people, their businesses, and the products they sell, show little sign of hygiene and of a concern for cleanliness and of the beneficial effects of salubriousness. The conditions in their businesses leave a lot to be desired and represent a great danger for *those who have become accustomed to frequent them*. Hence the need to exercise a strict control in order to ensure that all these businesses are run in such a way that they provide excellent hygienic conditions.[82]

Of course, this article was yet another example of the generalized anti-Japanese sentiment in the late 1930s. The same newspaper had claimed in an earlier article: "The Japanese eateries [*chicherías*] constitute centers of abjection. Within them, the future of our race and the decorum of Peru is attacked."[83] But it also provides some clues as to why workers might have been attracted to the restaurantes populares. Unlike the backward or degenerate Asian restaurants, this article appeared to suggest, the restaurantes populares were modern and scientific. They were comfortable, clean, and hygienic. The food was nutritious and healthy. The atmosphere was dignified.

As this suggests, the emphasis on science, dignity, and quality implicit in the architectural design and operational structure of the restaurantes populares may have helped sell them to the international audience in Santiago, but it may also explain why workers were drawn to them. As I argued above, although workers became increasingly dependent on Asian restaurants for cheap food in the first decades of the twentieth century, these workers reproduced elite racial discourses about Asian degeneration, immorality, and disease. In stressing their racial and moral distance to those who, in the end, provided them with an affordable means of subsistence, workers attempted to affirm a sense of collective identity based on the absence of those negative characteristics assigned to Asian immigrants. Asians became all that "Peruvian" workers were not, or aspired not to be. The logic that underpinned the construction of difference between "Peruvian" workers and Asian immigrants was the same logic that underpinned the construction of difference between the restaurantes populares and the Chinese restaurants. It is significant that, as the epigraph to this chapter shows, Limeños' recollection of the restaurantes populares half a century after their creation still associated the restaurants with notions of decency. This seems to confirm that what attracted Limeño workers, at least a considerable proportion of them, to the restaurantes populares was not merely the fact that cheap food was available there.

In a context in which urban workers had become largely dependent for affordable food on eateries run by Asian immigrants, the restaurantes populares provided an alternative place for workers to eat and socialize but also, and perhaps more important, where certain values central to the construction of a working-class identity could be reaffirmed and reinforced. This identity—based on values such as decency, respectability, sobriety, and (notwithstanding elite ideas to the contrary) cleanliness—was constructed experientially and discursively in various spaces, such as the workshop, the factory, the union hall, and the worker press. But it was also constructed in contradistinction to a racialized Asian identity, characterized (according to Peruvian workers) by degeneracy and uncleanliness. In being (or being represented as) the very opposite of supposedly unhygienic and indecent Asian restaurants, the restaurantes populares provided workers with an environment in which their desire for respectability and their aspiration to decency could be performed and therefore further reaffirmed. Indeed, it could be argued that eating in the restaurante popular became, in the late 1930s, one of the most accessible and affordable ways for Lima's workers to proclaim their decency. In this sense, the restaurantes populares could be seen as having become indispensable to the affirmation of a working-class identity that depended, in large measure, on the construction of difference with Asian immigrants. In short, the restaurantes populares were racialized through their construction as antithetical to Asian eateries, and this racialization helps to explain their success in attracting working-class customers. Workers were drawn to the restaurantes populares because they aspired to be, or believed that they already were, the workers that the architects of the restaurantes populares wanted them to be. The rationalities of government manifested in the labor state and, more specifically, in the restaurantes populares were the workers' own rationalities of government.

In a final twist to this story, the racialization shaping the politics of food and nutrition was put to political use by APRA in the late 1930s. One of APRA's strategies to attack Benavides in the late 1930s was to argue that the president was facilitating the penetration of "fascist imperialism" in the country; specifically that he was handing over control of key economic and military assets to Italian, German, and Japanese imperialists. As a consequence, APRA reframed its various policies as elements in a broader campaign to stop fascist imperialism in the country. This extended to what the party perceived to be a Japanese dominance of petty commerce in the country, which it claimed represented a rapacious and disloyal competition from which Peruvian nationality needed to be protected: "Neither in Lima nor in the other important cities in Peru is there a single street where one does not run into the impenetrable faces with oblique eyes." As part of this rhetoric, APRA reframed the origin of, and rationale for, its "comedores apristas": "Only Haya de la Torre, and Peruvian Aprismo, from their tenacious opposition and heroic clandestine existence, have put forward concrete and scientific solutions to this serious and dangerous problem that transcendentally affects the country. We have seen how, in order to counteract the actions of the Japanese restaurants, which harmed the nutrition of our people, Aprismo created for the first time, restaurantes populares, where a worker could find healthy, nutritious, hygienic, and exceptionally cheap food."[84] Although APRA claimed that "fascist imperialism" was intrinsically racist, given that fascists viewed the "Indoamerican" race as inferior and sought to attack it in the same way that they attacked "the Jewish race," its own attacks on Japanese immigrants and their businesses drew on and, doubtless, helped to exacerbate the anti-Asian racism prevalent in Peruvian society.

CONCLUSION

Like the barrios obreros, the restaurantes populares were more than a simple ploy to undermine the appeal of the political parties of the Left or to weaken labor militancy. Like the worker houses, they expressed rationalities of government and functioned as a technology of government. They were conceived as social laboratories in which model workers could be constituted: the provision of proper nutrition and the instillment of certain "civilizing" values would enable workers to constitute themselves as agents of progress and civilization. At one level, the restaurantes populares were a success. If official statistics are to be believed, the restaurants attracted a large number of customers. This success, I suggest, owed to the fact that the values that the architects of the restaurantes populares sought to inculcate in Lima's workers and hope that they would see as their own were precisely the values that the workers saw as their own; indeed, that they saw as the values that made them different from or superior to the Chinese and Japanese. The restaurantes populares, then, proved successful because they provided spaces where the construction of difference with Asian immigrants could be performed and, therefore, reaffirmed. But this performance of identity was possible because *in their design* the restaurants emphasized the same values that workers viewed as essential to their identity: the rationalities of government of the architects of the restaurantes populares were also the rationalities of government of the workers who ate there.

Of course, in other respects the restaurantes populares were not a success. Although they may have drawn many working-class customers through their doors, like the barrios obreros, the restaurants failed to "improve" workers in the ways envisaged by its architects. For all that they attracted customers, they reached only a small proportion of Peru's laboring peoples. Most Peruvian workers, in Lima as elsewhere, continued to depend on other sources of food, including food prepared by Asian immigrants. Nor is there any evidence that the restaurantes populares succeeded in addressing the malnutrition of the poor that so concerned Peru's nutritionists. By the 1940s, criticisms of the management and quality of service provided by the restaurants became increasingly common.[85] More generally, like the barrios obreros, the restaurantes populares reflected a governmental "fantasy," which, it should be noted, was equally expressed by the boosters of the APRA "comedores." The model workers that the restaurantes populares were supposed to create were little more than reflections of the elite's racist fictions—fictions that, as I have argued in previous chapters with regard to labor relations and housing, and that I explore with regard to public health and social insurance in the next, found expression in the allure of labor, that is, in a racialized understanding of the sources of progress and backwardness in the country that elevated the worker as the embodied redemption of the socially and racially degenerate Indian and as the salvation of the nation.

6

HEALING LABOR

In 1935, the periodical *Cascabel* published a drawing titled "A Frightening Ghost," which depicted the APRA leader Víctor Raúl Haya de la Torre lying in his bed while a monstrous figure, identified with the words "Compulsory Social Insurance," hovered over him. The drawing's caption explained that "without having to read Marx or burn the midnight oil trying to understand Hegel, there are those who, shortly, will present an integral project of Compulsory Social Security. For this reason the *líder Máximo* [the supreme chief] is jumpy. Because once this happens you can say goodbye to his [political] program! Goodbye to APRA! Goodbye líder Máximo!"[1] The drawing illustrates neatly how contemporaries, and, subsequently, many historians, perceived the Compulsory Social Insurance Law (Seguro Social Obligatorio), enacted by President Benavides in 1936. This law provided workers with near comprehensive social insurance, including free hospitalization, and helped raise the funds that allowed the state to invest in the construction of new public health facilities, including a new hospital for workers in Lima, the Hospital Obrero, completed in 1940. Like the barrios obreros and the restaurantes populares, the Seguro Social has tended to be seen as a policy devised by the Benavides regime in order to undermine APRA, and the forces of the Left more generally, by providing the very things that the Left claimed it would provide. Certainly, social insurance had been on the Left's agenda since the late 1920s. In early 1929, Mariátegui's *Labor*, the fortnightly newspaper aimed at workers, published two articles on social security systems. One focused on social security systems in capitalist countries and argued, somewhat contradictorily, that they were both a means to swindle the working class and a class conquest. The other, reproduced from the Comintern's Latin American newspaper *El Trabajador Latinoamericano*, focused on social security in the Soviet Union, which it presented as "the model and the goal toward which must be oriented the struggles of proletarians" in Latin America.[2] In late 1930, the Confederación General de Trabajadores del Perú (CGTP), the labor central controlled by the Communist Party, set as one of its objectives the establishment of "comprehensive Social Security (unemployment, disability, work accidents), paid for by a sliding-scale tax on capital and the confiscation of the Church's property."[3] APRA included a proposal in its 1931 "minimum program" for a comprehensive social security system. The Socialist Party of Luciano Castillo, similarly, included a plan for social security in its 1933 political manifesto.[4]

As with the barrios obreros and the restaurantes populares, however, the motives that explain the creation of the 1936 Seguro Social cannot be reduced to an attempt to incorporate labor and neutralize the Left. As the recent historiography on social welfare suggests, welfare reform is best understood as a process shaped by diverse social forces and ideologies.[5] As Stephen Kotkin aptly notes:

> In part a conservative response to the rise of the working class and the dangers it supposedly represented, especially those of contagious disease and political militancy, the welfare state also emerged from the variety of concerns articulated by experts pursuing such varied goals as workplace efficiency, psychological normalization and healthy populations. Industrialists, concerned about obtaining a reliable, docile supply of labor, and social reformers, crusading for what they took to be the best way to minimize social costs and maximize social benefits, shared a logic, even if their aims often appeared divergent.[6]

In the Latin American context, studies of social welfare reform, such as those by Weinstein on Brazil, Hutchison, Klubock, and Rosemblatt on Chile, Ehrick on Uruguay, and Guy on Argentina, have tended to privilege gender as an interpretative lens.[7] Historians of the region have paid less attention to how race, and racism, similarly shaped welfare reform. This chapter, while attentive to the ways in which gendered assumptions

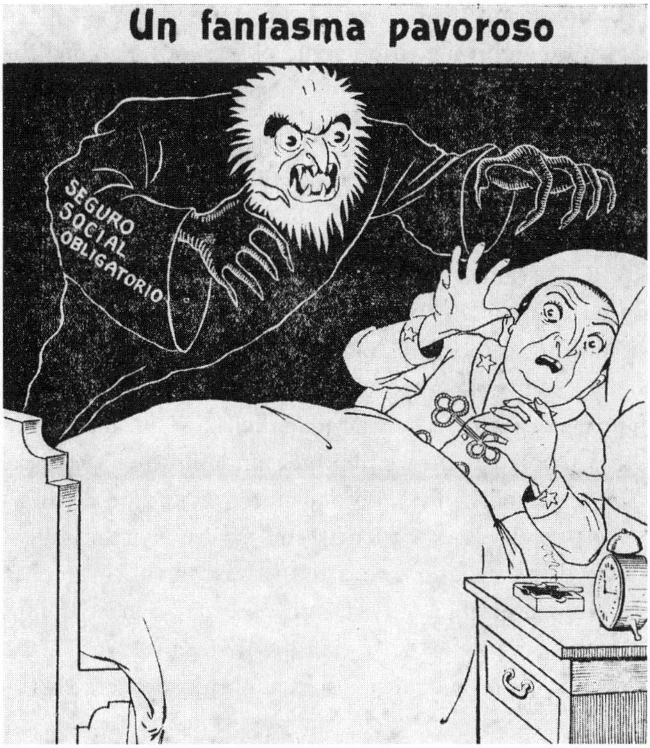

Un fantasma pavoroso

FIGURE 11 "A frightening ghost: Compulsory social insurance." Source: *Cascabel*, 17 August 1935. Courtesy of Biblioteca Nacional del Perú.

undergirded the constitution of the Seguro Social is equally focused on how racialized assumptions shaped its design and function. Recently, while admitting that advances in our understanding of welfare reform have been "breathtaking," Hacker has expressed concern that "the welfare state has become a convenient window into some larger relation of power—between blacks and whites, between women and men, between capital and labor."[8] A different, and more positive, way of seeing these changes is to argue that categories such as race or gender offer a uniquely useful window into welfare reform and, more specifically, its role in projects of governmentality.

The genealogy of the Seguro Social, and the various reactions that its implementation produced, that I trace in this chapter suggests that many contemporaries did indeed see the policy as a political strategy to neutralize labor militancy and the appeal of the Left, with APRA claiming that the Seguro Social was in fact its initiative. But reactions were more diverse than this suggests: physicians seem to have been opposed to the Seguro Social, employers were ambivalent, and some observers welcomed the measure. The ways in which the architects of the Seguro Social sought to convince both workers and capitalists of the benefits of social insurance reveals the rationalities of government that the initiative manifested. As several documents show, the architects of the Seguro Social were primarily motivated by the belief, formulated in a highly gendered manner, that labor constituted a valuable human capital that needed to be protected and "improved" through the intervention of the state. Like the barrios obreros and the restaurantes populares, the Seguro Social was conceived as a technology of government; specifically, as a means to resolve the health problems that workers faced in their mediate and immediate environments, that is, as a means to protect and "improve" workers, specifically male workers, both physically and morally. But the exclusions that the Seguro Social established, particularly the exclusion of the indigenous, as I discuss in a final section, points to the ways in which broader racialized understandings of labor and of the promise of national redemption to which workers became associated in the Peruvian context—the allure of labor—shaped the project of governmentality instantiated in the Seguro Social.

THE ORIGINS OF THE SEGURO SOCIAL

In early 1936, the periodical *Mundo Peruano* published a devastating critique of the hospitals run by the Sociedad de Beneficencia Pública de Lima (Public Beneficence Society of Lima), the religious institution that since the nineteenth century had provided what little hospital care was available to the city's population. The article noted that the hospitals were in a poor state and regularly failed to provide basic medical services. "This situation cannot continue," the article stressed, "the people have a right to social assistance, because the state receives taxes created by law, which it then transfers to organizations whose role is to safeguard public health." The article went on to argue that the Sociedad de Beneficencia was an anachronistic institution and that the time had come for the state to take over the running of the city's hospitals, "in order to place them at a level similar to that which exists in other countries."[9] A few months later, another article in the same periodical called for the creation of a "Seguro Social de Maternidad [maternity insurance]." Written by Susana Solano, a prominent activist in the campaign to abolish regulated prostitution in the city, the article claimed that infant mortality was a grave problem that needed to be addressed if the state of the country's population was to improve: "Providing assistance, rest, and economic security to mothers of all social classes during pregnancy, birth, and the lactation period, will destroy without a doubt several of the factors that conspire against the nation's population growth."[10] As this statement suggests, the idea that the state had to take responsibility for the health of the population, an idea established in the first years of the twentieth century, began by the 1930s to extend to calls for better state-backed hospital provision and social insurance. It was an idea that, in Peru as elsewhere, was highly gendered.[11]

Concern with the quality of hospital and medical care for Lima's growing population can be traced back to the early 1910s if not earlier, when physicians such as Carlos Enrique Paz Soldán, a pioneer of Peruvian social medicine, argued that responsibility for the provision of hospital care should be transferred from the beneficence societies to the state and that a ministry to oversee public health matters be created: "Social assistance, according to modern concepts, is a duty of the state, and the basis for individual and collective growth."[12] By the 1920s periodicals such as *Mundial* had reprised the idea that the Sociedad de Beneficencia was not capable of providing the medical attention needed by the capital.[13] An article by Antonio Alba in 1925 extended this critique of beneficence as charity and argued that it was the function of the state to provide social security (*asistencia social*) to the population: "Social security, provided by the state in a scientific and systematic manner, will produce a healthy, productive and conscientious population." Alba formulated his argument in explicitly governmental and racialized terms. He argued that it was the duty of the state to "protect every member of the social mass," to make them fulfill their obligations, and "to maximize the good that they bring to the commonweal." In favor of immigration, which would bring "healthy and honest people" to Peru, he also suggested that social security would help "incorporate" the Indian into "civilization and culture." For this reason, he concluded, upon social security depended "the future of our nationality, the selection of our ethnic components, the elimination of social blemishes that threaten to undermine the vigor of the race and to break its spirit." In short, Alba understood social security as a key element in a civilizing project that hinged on the "physical structure of the race."[14]

In the 1930s, medical doctors continued to argue in favor of a shift away from the Beneficence Society system toward a "modern" social security system. In 1930, *La Crónica Médica*, Peru's flagship medical journal, published a report written by doctors employed by the Lima Beneficencia Pública and prompted by a 1928 decree that established that the hospitals of the Beneficencia would henceforth offer free treatment to the "indigent." After making a number of observations on the decree, the doctors noted the limitations of the present system, which made it impossible to practice "preventive or prophylactic" medicine, and pointed to the development of obligatory social security systems in more "advanced" countries such as Germany. Although Bismarck's introduction of social security in that country was a political measure whose purpose was to combat socialism, the authors argued, "it had surprising results: a sharp reduction in mortality rates, a remarkable organization of [social] assistance and prophylactic institutions, and the might and social stability of that great country." The doctors suggested that a special commission within the Sociedad de Beneficencia be set up to study whether such an institution was timely in the Peruvian context, on the grounds that "to safeguard our human capital, to move from the simple healing of the sick to an institution of real assistance, which presupposes the idea of relief and prevision, it is necessary to overcome the stumbling blocks of misery, of indigence, [and] prepare the organization of social security, and especially of medical insurance."[15] In the years that followed, Peru's medical journals continued to publish articles in favor of more active state intervention in public health and preventive medicine in order to protect "human capital," further critiquing the inability of the sociedades de beneficencia, accused of being "colonial" and "aristocratic," to provide the medical assistance the country needed, and weighing the benefits and drawbacks of a social security system, seen as inevitable and necessary, for the medical profession.[16]

Physicians and other commentators put forward similar arguments in several public forums. In an interview published in the periodical *Suplemento* in mid-1933, Dr. Alfonso Pasquel reprised the critique of the beneficence societies, which, he suggested, based hospital provision on charity and religion rather than science. Pasquel argued that public health was a duty of the state; it represented, he stressed, the source of its power and the basis for the well-being of the population.[17] Similarly, the periodical *Cascabel* led a very vocal campaign in mid-1935 against the Lima Sociedad de Beneficencia along similar lines (see figure 12). It argued that the time had come to bury the cadaver called Beneficencia Pública and "and on its tomb we will build the Ministry of Social Assistance" and stressed that public health services needed to be modernized and that modern health facilities needed to be built.[18] According to the periodical's editor, Federico More, the proliferation of beggars in the city was a consequence of the absence of adequate and modern social insurance: "Lacking social insurance, lacking social foresight, lacking ample and well-supplied humanitarian institutions, and with an opulent class that dodges its contributions to the state, Lima is swarming with beggars."[19] According to More, it was the responsibility of the state to address such problems by implementing adequate measures. The campaign appears to have worked. That very year, in October, President Benavides created the Ministry of Public Health, Labor and Social Foresight. As this suggests, by the 1930s, most Peruvian elites shared the belief—increasingly common in countries with political regimes as diverse as the United States, Germany, Italy, and the Soviet Union—that the state was the entity called upon to provide and oversee social security for the population and that private charity was something that had served its purpose but that belonged to another age.[20]

The birth of the Seguro Social can be traced back to 1934, when Benavides charged the lawyer Edgardo Rebagliati and Franz Schrüfer, an actuary, with preparing a social security law proposal. In 1932, Rebagliati, who had worked as a labor lawyer in the 1920s, started to publish and edit a periodical titled *Revista de Seguros*.[21] Its very first issue included an article that discussed the shortcomings of Peru's accident law, although the periodical focused more broadly on the legal dimensions of various forms of insurance, both public and private.[22] Between 1933 and 1934, *Revista de Seguros* published reports on the social security systems of several countries, including France, Australia, Spain, and Chile, reproduced articles from foreign publications on specific issues (including an article on "The Problem of the Female Worker"), and began to include theoretical studies on social security systems. In 1935, Rebagliati traveled to Uruguay, Argentina, and Chile, to study the social security laws of those countries. An article in *Revista de Seguros* noted that Rebagliati's South American trip, which had received extensive coverage in the Lima press, was evidence of the growing consensus regarding "the need to establish a social security system as soon as possible."[23] Rebagliati would later refer to the Chilean system, established in 1924 and which, he claimed, covered some 800,000 workers by the mid-1930s, as a "true

Esta es una escena que ocurre todos los días en casi todos los hospitales.

FIGURE 12 "Hospital: There are no beds." *Cascabel*, 20 July 1935. Courtesy of Biblioteca Nacional del Perú.

continental model."[24] However, given that the Chilean social security law was not applied consistently until 1935–36 it is likely that Rebagliati's ability to study the Chilean system in practice was limited.[25] In fact, Rebagliati's Seguro Social was influenced not just by the Chilean model, or other Latin American models, but also by the broader transnational "social politics" shaping social insurance systems in the North Atlantic economy. The British minister in Lima, for example, suggested that the Peruvian system was based on both the Chilean and British models.[26]

On 2 September 1936, President Benavides signed the project prepared by Rebagliati and Schrüfer into law. Law 8433 established that all workers, male and female, under sixty years of age, working for an employer (including domestic workers) or independently and earning less than three thousand soles per year had to register. Workers would contribute 3.5 percent of their wages, employers 4.5 percent of their payroll, and the state 1 percent of daily wages and salaries, to be raised via additional taxes on receipt stamps, tobacco, and alcoholic beverages (in the case of the self-employed, the state contributed 2.5 percent and the worker 3.5 percent of daily wages).[27] The law guaranteed those who registered medical attention, hospitalization, maternity payments, a pension for those afflicted by a chronic disease, a pension for those who reached the age of sixty years and who had contributed under the scheme for twenty years, and finally, funeral expenses and death payments to the next of kin. The administration of the Seguro Social would be the responsibility of the Caja Nacional del Seguro Social (National Office of the Social Security), which a Consejo Directivo (Executive Council) that included two worker representatives would manage. As this suggests, the Peruvian Seguro Social, like all social security systems based on the German model, and, indeed, Beveridge's National Health Service, was not focused on the very poorest of society. Like the other systems the Seguro Social was designed "in order to socialize a portion of the risks of labor, not so that the abjectly poor could be assisted, but to make it less likely that the expected hazards of a working life would push the regularly employed wage earner either into the arms of political radicalism or onto the tax-financed rolls of poor relief."[28] In Peru, of course, there was little poor relief to speak of. But, as I argue below, motives other than fear of political radicalism shaped the Seguro Social.[29]

Rebagliati's Seguro Social met with significant opposition at first. Physicians, such as Ovidio García Rosell, who seems to have been irked by the fact that the medical profession was not consulted in the formulation of the project, suggested that as a consequence of the implementation of the Seguro Social the quality of patient care would diminish.[30] García Rosell was voicing what appears to have been a general resistance among physicians confronted with social security reform in this period. The American Medical Association similarly opposed any form of public health insurance in the run-up to the 1935 U.S. Social Security Act.[31] However, opposition to the Seguro Social hinged primarily on the idea that the law had been devised "with a view to vote-catching," as the British minister put it.[32] Certainly, the Seguro Social was but one element in a prolabor legislative flurry in the run-up to the 1936 elections that included an increase in the compensation law in case of dismissal from two weeks to one month's pay in the case of white-collar workers and from one week to two weeks in the case of blue-collar workers.[33] As the Peruvian Corporation, the British company that ran most of Peru's railways, noted, "These bills are obviously electioneering propaganda"; though, it added, "it needs only the '*cúmplase*' ["carry it out"] of the president for them to be turned into law."[34] Luis Antonio Eguiguren, a former mayor of Lima and presidential candidate for the 1936 elections (annulled by Benavides when it appeared that APRA support would hand victory to Eguiguren), similarly argued: "Is it even necessary to discuss its imperfections, its trickery, its condition as a wet nurse charged with paying political services? This institution, living from an exaggerated propaganda and which overpays its directors and employees, is first and foremost an organization planned and established in order to propagate within and outside the country that 'philanthropic socialism' of Señor Benavides, a mix of cynicism and theatricality and of profound ignorance of the real national problems." Eguiguren went on to add that he doubted that the Seguro Social would be able to fund new hospitals without raising the tax burden considerably.[35]

APRA echoed these views: the Seguro Social, it claimed, was "created for electoral purposes." Confusingly, it claimed that the initiative for the Seguro Social was both stolen from its 1931 party program and possessed "a wording slavishly copied from the Chilean law."[36] According to APRA cadre Manuel Seoane, writing some years later, the Seguro Social was only one of many proposals included in the party's 1931 program that Benavides had stolen. For Seoane, popular pressure had forced Benavides to implement the Seguro Social: "The idea put forward by the party, which the people soon embraced, became, in turn, a forceful demand on the government and a certain president was forced to submit to popular pressure initially given impulse by the Partido del Pueblo [APRA], and the Seguro Social was created. Although it carries the name of another creator, it has an owner who has clearly demonstrated its chronological title to justify its foresight."[37] In fact, the Seguro Social met with significant opposition from labor. Workers contended, and the British minister appeared to agree, that given the "smallness of their remuneration," the new charge should be met by solely the employer. A general strike was threatened, and the government decided to defer implementing the Seguro Social until November 1936, after the elections.[38] The Peruvian Corporation put the delays down to the need "to allow for further organization of the administration department, the Caja de Seguro Social." However, it acknowledged that "the law is being met by a certain amount of opposition from the laboring classes."[39] APRA picked up on the general objections to the Seguro Social emanating from labor circles: "Without union freedom and without worker representation on the commission that will draft the law and in the Bank Directory [presumably, the Executive Council], the Seguro cannot come into being." Triumphantly, APRA claimed that the implementation of the Seguro Social had been pushed back four times by worker opposition: "The people understand that they are being tricked again and again!"[40] In the 1940s, APRA continued to attack the Seguro Social and now claimed that, in addition to being in the hands of incapable and unscrupulous people, it was rife with nepotism (Mariano Peña Prado, the deputy director, was the son-in-law of Benavides and nephew of current president Manuel Prado) and corruption (some four million soles had been stolen).[41]

Employers' reactions to the Seguro Social appear to have ranged from outright rejection to tepid acceptance. The Sociedad Nacional de Industrias (SNI) expressed the ambivalent concerns of capitalists in an editorial published in July 1935 in its mouthpiece, which praised the initiative to provide Peru with such a "worthy institution" as well as the designation of Rebagliati, "a capable lawyer," as the person charged with drafting the Seguro Social. It recognized that in those countries where social security had been established, "the results could not be better," particularly as far as the state was concerned, since the measure provided it with the resources to address "its primordial duty [which is] to protect human capital, to look after the health and welfare of the working classes." However, the editorial also warned that the costs associated with employer contributions could destroy businesses, particularly small-scale industrial concerns, which could barely support the costs of already existing social legislation. More generally, it warned that the contributions that were expected from business "bear no relation with the margins that they can support."[42] In this, Peruvian business leaders echoed the objections of their U.S. counterparts to the social insurance proposals leading up to the 1935 U.S. Social Security Act.[43] Later that year, the SNI's mouthpiece published the legislative proposal in full, "so that, known to all members of the society, they will be able to present, when appropriate, the observations that its study suggests to them."[44] As this indicates, employers' reactions to the legislative proposal reflected an evident tension between a desire to project an enlightened and progressive attitude toward labor policy and the belief that social legislation while desirable was ultimately unaffordable.

These sentiments were reprised in a letter sent in early 1936 by Augusto Maurer, the president of the SNI, to the Constituent Congress, which was at the time deliberating on the proposal. Maurer restated the claim that social security legislation constituted "a step forward ... that no civilized nation can elude." However, whereas earlier SNI pronouncements had suggested that social security systems had been successful wherever they have been established, now Maurer severely qualified this argument and suggested that they had in fact been established "more or less successfully in some countries" and that in others they had "failed." Its successful implementation in Peru, Maurer went on to argue, depended therefore on a "careful study of the context in which it will operate." Maurer argued that the employers' contribution envisaged by the legislative proposal needed to be reconsidered in light of the other costs that employers faced. These costs were a consequence of other social legislation, such as paid holidays, dismissal compensation, occupational accidents, and the extra wage of 1 May, which in total amounted to 13.08 percent of the payroll—an amount that rose in the textile industry, where additional bonuses were paid, and in those industries where women and children, "privileged workers," were employed, as they were entitled to three paid hours of rest per week. Maurer thus concluded: "We must consider whether, in practice, the law will face serious and irresolvable difficulties, arising from insufficient capital [resources]"; he noted that in countries with more highly developed economies and a higher rate of industrialization, the contributions demanded of employers were lower than those envisaged by the legislative proposal.[45] Faced with the prospect of the higher labor costs that the Seguro Social and other new legislative initiatives such as the compensation law implied, many of the large employers, including the Peruvian Corporation and the Cerro de Pasco Copper Corporation, as well as the chambers of commerce of the larger cities, were by June 1936 "preparing protests to prevent the promulgation of these new laws."[46]

In the midst of worker opposition and employer ambivalence, some approving voices were heard nonetheless. Edilberto C. Boza, a lawyer writing in the journal *La Nueva Economía*, which declared itself in favor of a "controlled economy," and an admirer of developments in Italy and

Germany, published a couple of articles that praised the legislative pro-posal. Boza noted that those who viewed social security as a "socialist dogma, a threat to capital, a grave danger of bankruptcy for the treasury, an obstacle to the development of industry" would do well to look at the German experience, where the introduction of social security had coin-cided with industrial growth and the conquest of new markets, and that this owed to the fact that "the taxes that result from the protection of the worker, increasing his productive force, benefit industry and the Father-land."[47] For Boza, the benefits of social security needed to be understood in moral and even biological terms. Reminding readers of "the biological law discovered and enunciated by the genius Darwin," Boza stressed the positive effect that social security had on human capital through its remedial action at both the biological and environmental levels: "Social or collective diseases are reduced or tend to disappear, thus cleaning the internal medium, that is to say increasing the vital resistance of man, and cleaning the external medium, that is to say the soil or the subsoil, the air, the water, housing, and nutrition."[48] Boza's comments reflect the grow-ing influence of eugenic thought in the formulation of social policies. Given the avowed admiration of the journal for developments in Ger-many, this should not be surprising. But it is worth remembering that eugenics in the 1930s was considered a progressive and bona fide science in most countries of Latin America and, indeed, in the most "advanced" countries of the world.[49] In fact, as Daniel Rodgers suggests, eugenic considerations were characteristic of all social insurance schemes in the North Atlantic: "[Their] mark was a concern with national vigor, with efficient development of human resources, with conservation of the 'hu-man wreckage' as Theodore Roosevelt put it, 'which a scrap-heap system of industrialism had brought about.'"[50]

But the eugenicist justifications for the Seguro Social were joined by more conventional but no less important economic justifications. Shortly after the law was passed, *La Nueva Economía* continued its support of the measure by publishing an article that argued that "Peru has taken a major step which honors its present leader." The article applauded the fact that the Seguro Social established that *"the sole patrimony of wage earners, by Law, is safeguarded,"* and that it viewed those it protected *"not as a means to produce assets; instead it views assets as a means to serve the individual"* (emphasis in the original). The Seguro Social thus represented a rebuke to those critics who viewed workers as mere factors of production and failed to recognize their "particular and intrinsic value" and those who rejected state intervention "in matters alien to political functions, fiscal matters and administration." But the article also praised the fact that the Seguro Social created a new source of capital that would have a significant impact on the financial market, on the interest rate, and on the national economy. Armed with these new financial resources, the state would be able to play an important economic role, particularly in times of economic downturn when private investment tended to recede. In such contexts, the article suggested, the state would be able to intervene in the economy by investing in public works with social goals, "reducing in this way unemployment."[51] As this suggests, these articles argued that whether seen from the perspective of eugenics or economics, the Seguro Social made perfect scientific sense. The shortcomings of the Peruvian economy and deficiencies of Peruvian workers and by extension of Peruvian society, these articles seemed to suggest, "were to be transformed by the dynamic activity of technical development, which required the application of scientific and social scientific expertise."[52]

In early September 1937, the Benavides government introduced Law 8509, which modified substantially the original Seguro Social law. Certain categories of workers, specifically domestic workers, were now no longer required to register (they could do so, however, if they wished to). This change meant that, in effect, most employed women would not be covered and suggests that such exclusions reflected both material considerations (employers of domestic servants were likely to be unwilling to contribute) and gendered understandings of labor (a domestic worker was not a proper worker). In addition, the contributions of workers and employers were substantially reduced to 1.5 percent and 3.5 percent respectively, while the state's share was maintained at 1 percent. Moreover, the new law established that the income generated by the Seguro Social was to be invested in the construction of hospitals, and other health establishments, worker housing, in social disease prevention, and in the purchase of land on which "agricultural colonies" could be built (presumably in the Amazonian regions of the country). Finally, the new law established that workers would not be required to pay their contributions until health and maternity services were available in their localities. Naturally, the full effect of the Seguro Social would not be felt for some time. Old-age pension payments would not commence until twenty years after the Seguro Social came into operation, since workers had to

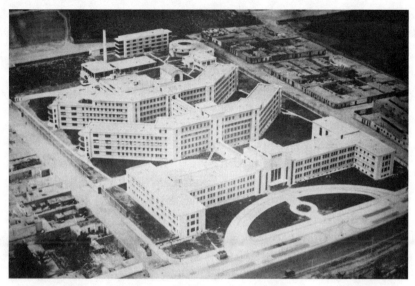

FIGURE 13 Aerial view of the Hospital Obrero. Source: *Progresos del Perú, 1933–1939, durante el gobierno del Presidente de la República General Óscar R. Benavides* (Buenos Aires: Editorial Guillermo Kraft, 1945), 228.

contribute for at least twenty years before they could benefit from a pension (which they only received upon turning sixty). Similarly, although workers did not need to pay contributions until health services were available to them, in most cases this meant that workers had to wait a number of years before they were able to benefit from the health provision. The first hospital built with Seguro Obrero funds, Lima's Hospital Obrero, was not opened until 1940. Still, by late 1939, the Seguro Obrero covered some 275,000 workers.[53]

As the above suggests, the implementation of the Seguro Social could be seen as little more than an attempt to weaken the Peruvian Communist Party and APRA by doing what they had been promising to do, a claim recently repeated by a historian of Peruvian social policy.[54] Similarly, the modification of the Seguro Social could be interpreted as evidence that the state had no choice but to push through a watered-down version of the law to placate opposition from both workers and employers. However, as I discuss in greater detail in the following section, and as the arguments put forward by Boza and others in *La Nueva Economía* suggest, motivations and ideas other than simple "vote catching" shaped the establishment of the Seguro Social. This is not to deny that the

Seguro Social was envisaged with political gain in mind in the context of the 1936 elections. With the elections annulled, some business sectors approached Benavides to ask him to repeal the recently enacted labor legislation.[55] However, as the Peruvian Corporation representative reported following a meeting with Benavides, "the president . . . unreservedly said that he was most anxious to avoid trouble with labor."[56] This was probably a sensible decision, since, as the Peruvian Corporation acknowledged, any attempt to repeal the legislation (irrespective of the fact that workers had opposed it) could have had dire consequences: "Should [the government] dare to take such a risk it might lead to their downfall with the result that more damaging laws would be immediately enforced by a revolutionary government."[57] The Seguro Social, this suggests, did, in part, reflect a social fear of labor; a fear shared by both the government and business sectors.[58] But as the discussion above indicates, and as I discuss in greater detail below, the Seguro Social primarily reflected an increasingly governmental understanding of labor—that is, an understanding of labor as a valuable resource to be protected and improved through the actions of the state.

SELLING THE SEGURO SOCIAL

As had happened with the Sección del Trabajo a decade and a half earlier, the architects of the Seguro Social actively sought to sell the project to workers. A series of documents, most of which were likely drafted by Edgardo Rebagliati, and some of which were directly aimed at workers, reveal both how Rebagliati understood the Seguro Social and how, he hoped, workers and, indeed, capitalists would come to see it. Like the New Deal reformers in the United States studied by Peter Swenson, Rebagliati too knew that "success and durability of reform depended on employers 'getting sold.' "[59] Indeed, to judge from the literature that survives, the Benavides government actively sought to publicize the new law but also to generate consensus around it. The Caja del Seguro Social even produced a monthly journal, *Informaciones Sociales*. The cover of its first issue carried an unambiguous message. It showed a mother carrying a child in her arms with the caption "The Seguro Social protects children and mothers."[60] That Rebagliati chose to represent the Seguro Social in such terms points to the gendered understanding of welfare that undergirded the project. The message was clear: the Seguro Social created a new stage on which (male) workers and capitalists would be able to perform, through the state, their gendered roles as protectors of women and children. The patriarchal state placed the interests of a feminized nation (*la nación*) above class interests, as was clearly stated on the second page of the journal issue: the Seguro Social had transformed "the traditional bases of our social organization" and made it possible "to rise above group interests and the general incomprehension of the moment and to concentrate on the supreme needs of the nation, from the superior vantage point of the statesman."[61]

Although President Benavides, and "politics" more broadly, appears in the texts that aimed to sell the Seguro Social, the measure was primarily presented as a *state* project. The first issue of *Informaciones Sociales* also carried a photograph of Benavides with a caption that suggested that the establishment of the measure was "one of his greatest achievements," while a piece on the history of social security provision firmly located the Seguro Social within the government's broader "social deeds."[62] But the government's role with respect to the Seguro Social was primarily presented as that of an enabler. The government, according to one article, had created conditions favorable for the establishment of the Seguro Social by providing "the ambient serenity of a firm and calm regime of rule."[63] Similarly, APRA and the Communist Party appear in these texts, but only through veiled references to "mirages and tendentious promises" and the implication that the political projects behind these promises are inevitably harmful to the worker, since they are counter to the Seguro Social, which workers recognize as being in their best interest: "Foolish are the attempts to veer the worker off the road of sympathy toward the system; those responsible ignore the reality of the labor problem or deliberately try to play around with workers' sacred interests."[64] Overall, the establishment of the Seguro Social was presented as occurring outside or above politics. It represented, Rebagliati claimed, "a completely new situation [characterized by the emergence of] the social function of the state as the regulator of the consumption of human energy in the field of labor."[65]

Although he sought to present the Seguro Social as being above politics, Rebagliati was aware that the Seguro Social had generated resistance among both workers and capitalists, and he tried to address their misgivings, which early on appear to have translated into a slow registration. In May and June 1937, Rebagliati wrote two letters, one directed at workers and the other at capitalists, which sought to convince both groups of the benefits of the Seguro Social. The fact that Rebagliati wrote these letters tells us something about the key role that he played in the successful implementation of the Seguro Social. There is much to suggest, as I discuss below, that Rebagliati understood the Seguro Social as an expression of a social philosophy. He argued repeatedly, as in an article published in *Informaciones Sociales*, that the Seguro Social signified a new phase of social evolution and indeed of human evolution: "Anything that contributes to the diffusion and establishment of Social Security systems in the world, also contributes to cement national consciousness over an institution that is today the most perfect of those created by man in his legitimate aspiration to lay down the rules, on the basis of social justice, for the pace of his march towards progress."[66] But Rebagliati was astute enough to know that those whom the Seguro Social targeted needed to be sold on its material rather than its philosophical merits. In addressing the workers, Rebagliati employed a class-conscious and gendered rhetoric that sought to present the Seguro Social as, at once, a class conquest (but a conquest that hinged on an aseptic notion of class) and a gendered male conquest (since the Seguro Social allowed male workers to fulfill their roles as providers and as protectors of their women and children). In addressing the capitalists, meanwhile, Rebagliati focused on the capacity of the Seguro Social to enhance the productivity of workers, who were, in the final analysis, simply another form of valuable capital, while raising the threatening specter of labor militancy fueled by pauperization.

The letter to the workers began by acknowledging that registration had been disappointing and, in what amounted to a veiled criticism, noted that the failure to register could only be a consequence of an "oversight," since the law established that registration was compulsory and that in any case failure to register did not exempt workers from paying their contributions to the Caja (contributions were deducted automatically from pay sheets). By contrast, failure to register did mean that workers would not be covered by the Seguro Social and would not, therefore, benefit from it. More generally, workers' failure to register meant that the information required to establish where new hospitals or other services should be provided was not gathered. But Rebagliati went on to argue that "there can be no worker who ignores the value of the class conquest that the Seguro Social Obligatorio represents." Workers could feel proud of the Seguro Social, Rebagliati implied, since it represented a class conquest to add to those other class conquests, such as the

eight-hour-day law, that the labor movement had won in the past. However, Rebagliati was quick to add that this was not a conquest "as a
consequence of struggle" but rather "a conquest of social culture, of
civilization," which had come about because "society" had recognized
that workers deserved to be protected while they worked, as well as later
in life. At the same time, Rebagliati stressed that the Seguro Social represented a "conquest that distances the wife and daughter from the equivo-
cal shadows of midnight doorways," thus playing on male anxieties regarding the failure to perform male gendered roles. The Seguro Social,
Rebagliati stressed, protected not only the worker's dignity as a worker
but also as family patriarch: "It is the conquest that keeps the worker's
head held high even when he reaches the age when his back starts to
curve, because he can now await calmly his old age and cheerfully put up
with his seclusion as a grandfather, without fearing for his wife's or
children's tomorrows."[67]

The letter to the capitalists began by acknowledging their concerns:
namely, that the Seguro Social favored workers; that existing legislation
already adequately protected workers; that many businesses could not
afford the new contributions. But Rebagliati went on to argue that whereas previous legislation had sought to improve the lot of workers (by fixing
working hours or establishing industrial accident legislation) and the lot
of employers (by regulating strikes and unions), structural changes in
society had created new problems ("unemployment as a consequence of
the rise of machinery, sickness as a consequence of exhaustion, poverty as
a consequence of meager salaries") that required laws that went beyond
the narrow interests of workers and employers in order to address "the
supreme social interest . . . the problem of human energy consumption." It
was for this reason that the state, "in representation of society," had begun
to legislate "in defense of that supreme capital, man," and had created a
series of social assistance institutions, such as nurseries, restaurantes
populares, and worker housing. But these institutions could not address
the problem of "exhaustion [desgaste]" of human labor, and this is where
the Seguro Social came in; it was necessarily of interest to the capitalist,
since the "exhaustion" of labor reduced productivity, and therefore it
followed that "measures that prevent, avoid or reduce the causes of the
devaluation [desvalorización] of the worker, are measures that favor the
employer." Rebagliati pointed to the compelling reasons for investing in
human capital, reasons that played at once on capitalists' social fears and

on their profit motive. A worker who faced miserable working and living conditions, Rebagliati argued, was a worker in whom "the germination of pain and of want will sprout in his spirit sentiments and impulses that employers have an interest in avoiding." By contrast, "a healthy worker who has no problems at home" was necessarily a more productive worker but, Rebagliati went on to argue, also a worker capable of expanding his purchasing capacity. Thus, Rebagliati concluded, "employer's contribution" to the Seguro Social was in reality an investment that would allow employers to reduce costs through gains in worker productivity and (in line with a Fordist logic) to increase sales, thanks to the increase in the population's spending power.[68]

At one level, these letters suggest an astute attempt by Rebagliati to convince both workers and employers of the benefits of the Seguro Social by arguing that it furthered their broader class interests. But along with a number of other documents, the letters show that the Seguro Social was influenced by ideas about nation, gender, and state formation that produced a particular understanding of the role of the state in shaping society; the Seguro Social, in short, expressed rationalities of government. Three themes are clearly evident in this literature. First, the Seguro Social was presented as corresponding to a universal process of statist intervention in society and, as such, as clear evidence of Peru's growing modernity but also, crucially, as a continuation of a distinctly Peruvian tradition. One document, for example, noted that social security had started out in Germany in 1883 and had been adopted subsequently in the "principal countries in the world," so that it now covered some 130 million workers. It stressed moreover that Peru's relatively late adoption of social security was in fact a bonus, given that since its inception social security provision "has improved its technical capacity so that it has now reached the perfection with which it has been incorporated in Peru."[69] In another document, Rebagliati similarly stressed the universality of the measure, noting that its more immediate origins lay in the Treaty of Versailles. As a consequence of the treaty's "social justice postulates, all subsequent political constitutions have taken into consideration social assistance and foresight as imperative functions of the state."[70] Naturally, these postulates had been incorporated into articles 42 and 56 of the 1920 constitution and articles 46, 48, and 50 of the 1933 constitution, and indeed, in the new Civil Code of 1936, which stated that the labor contract supposes, among a number of other things, "los seguros obligatorios." Thus, it followed, the

Seguro Social had been drafted taking into consideration a series of relevant precedents from around the world (which included ILO documents and the social legislation of Germany, France, Italy, and Chile) upon which it presumably improved.[71] The literature promoting the Seguro Social went on to argue that the perfection of Peruvian social security, based on its successful incorporation of the most advanced ideas in the sphere of social security from around the world, could clearly be surmised from that fact that it was now being copied in the American continent by Bolivia, Mexico, and Venezuela.

At the same time, the literature stressed that the Seguro Social had a distinctly national lineage. Indeed, Peru, one document noted, "has enjoyed, from the Inca Empire onward, social assistance and foresight laws that benefit the poor and disabled."[72] In another document, Rebagliati began by tracing "the state organization of social foresight" back to Inca times and through the colonial period and early republican period, emphasizing historical antecedents to the law, such as Viceroy Toledo's ordinances regarding *mita* labor, of which Rebagliati claimed "It is clear that this measure contained in embryonic form Old Age Insurance [Seguro Social de Vejez], because it established already at the time the right to rest and the retirement age as well as a cash transfer."[73] Finally, Peru had implemented in the previous twenty-five years a series of laws that had pioneered social legislation in the American continent. As a consequence, Peru was well placed, for historical reasons, to implement social security legislation and its citizens were well disposed to participate in its development and take advantage of its benefits: "Gradually a juridical and social conscience has formed, which is amenable to receive, as a corollary, this Seguro Social Obligatorio law."[74] As this suggests, Rebagliati was keen to present the Seguro Social as an inherently Peruvian institution, with deep roots in the country's history. The idea that the Seguro Social had, in fact, a local genealogy, appears to have found an eager audience. It was reprised by Germán Muñoz Puglisevich in a paper presented at the 1939 Congress of Americanists, in which he argued that "the oldest record of the Seguro Social Obligatorio is found in the Peruvian Inca Empire."[75] Like the South Asian nationalists studied by Gyan Prakash, Peruvian social reformers too, this seems to suggest, sought to uncover "another reason" that could indigenize the universality of social policy. By claiming that its roots were in fact local, Rebagliati sought to challenge the claim that the Seguro Social was unsuitable for Peru.[76]

The second theme developed by the literature promoting the Seguro Social was that social security was not an act of charity. Charity, this literature suggested, had arisen as a natural response to human suffering. Its origins were sentimental and pious. However, social security was based on very different premises. In contrast to charity, which focused only on the "external manifestations" of the problems that workers faced, the Seguro Social addressed their causes. In contrast to charity, which tended to entrench bad habits in workers, the Seguro Social helped to stimulate workers to improve themselves and did not harm their dignity, as charity often did when it proved to be less than discreet. Moreover, charity, whose effects were understood in overtly gendered terms, did not always reach those who were in greatest need, hidden away in homes "where work that supports the family has ceased, where disease has caught its prey, and where disability or old age have shut the doors of the factory to the father or husband." Charity, in other words, was not an adequate mechanism of social support to maintain a male gendered order and a familial system.[77] More generally, social security differed from charity in that it corresponded to an evolved stage of culture that had produced a new understanding of human worth. According to this view, each individual was an integral part of a great human capital. If one significant portion of this capital weakened, it affected the whole. It followed that it was in everyone's interest to protect human capital.

The final theme concerned the role of the state as a regulator of capital and labor and as the protector of labor. With the intervention of the state, social assistance based on needs met by charity gave way to social assistance based on rights met by social security. As Linda Gordon has noted, the rhetorical shift from needs (associated with the private sphere and women's social activism) to rights (associated with the public sphere and male legislative action) in welfare thought in the United States was a gendered process.[78] This is evident to some extent in the Peruvian case. In the rhetoric of rights featured in the Seguro Social literature, the state emerged as the paternal protector of the weak and, through social legislation ("derecho social"), sought to establish an equilibrium between labor and capital. In so doing, it was claimed, Peru was merely adhering to a general movement in the civilized world. The Treaty of Versailles had established that social justice was a requisite for world peace: as long as working conditions persisted that produced injustice, misery, and want for a large sector of the population world peace and harmony would be under threat. It followed that the worker is "a social problem in the workplace, AND BEYOND THE WORKPLACE" (emphasis in original), and that therefore the state had to regulate the conditions that workers faced in and beyond the workplace, that is, in the workers' homes and communities. By ensuring that the best, fairest, and most balanced laws and systems of social assistance were the result of the actions of a government "that senses the needs of the governed and prepares the future of the nation," rather than "the imposition of a desperate and anxious demand," Peru demonstrated to the world its civilization. If the country had only an incipient industrial sector, this was no reason not to implement measures that would help Peru stand at the "vanguard of civilization."[79]

As the above suggests, the Seguro Social reflected a new conception of the state that equated progressive labor policy with modernity and civilization (through its claims of—Western—universality) but that anchored that modernity in a distinctly Peruvian lineage and a gendered social order. The Seguro Social, this suggests, reflected more than political maneuverings. Rather, the Seguro Social reflected rationalities of government and in turn constituted a project of governmentality manifested in the "labor state," the state of and for labor. In the past, elites largely agreed that private philanthropy or the beneficence of religious orders was sufficient in order to address society's ills. By the twentieth century, and certainly by the 1930s, most agreed that a state with responsibilities for areas such as public health, education, and social order was required. This belief was clearly expressed by Guillermo Almenara, the minister of public health, during a ceremony to celebrate the beginning of the construction of the new Hospital Obrero in 1938:

> Incorporated into the concert of nations that proclaim health as the most precious gift of life and social welfare as the best guarantee of peace and prosperity, and making of the defense of these principles a function of the state, Peru abandons the old constraints that limited the exercise of public health, invigorates the economic resources of the nation, oversees and modernizes institutions, stimulates the always necessary private initiative, erects the state as responsible for the rights of the humble and as the undisputed arbiter of labor relations, and, finally, faces up to the most basic, the most compelling and the most burning of our problems: to redeem

ourselves from the disease that unjustly and mercilessly oppresses us; to provide the regulated comfort and protection of social order within the realm of our healthy and necessary labor activities.[80]

Social order, and, more important, social progress, Almenara suggested, would result from a successful governmental regulation of the sphere of labor.

MAKING HEALTHY WORKERS

As the above suggests, the creation of the Seguro Social reflected rationalities of government, that is, the understanding that the state had a role to play in shaping society and more specifically in protecting and "improving" workers and their mediate and immediate environment in order to enable them to develop as agents of progress. It was an understanding that was reflected and reproduced in the ways in which the Seguro Social promoted itself, as can be seen from a booklet that is likely to have been distributed to workers in order to convince them of the benefits of the Seguro Social and of the dangers of remaining outside the Seguro Social's reach. This always highly gendered message was rendered graphically on the booklet's cover, which portrayed a dramatic image of a distressed woman cradling a child in her arms beneath a menacing and oversized dagger flanked by dramatic lettering and colors suggesting the opposition between "Anxiety—lack of foresight of the future" and "Seguro Social—tomorrow's well-being." The booklet's key function appears to have been to address the key critiques or perceived fears that the Seguro Social engendered, since it began by listing a series of points that it proceeded to discuss in some detail.[81] First, it addressed the critique that the Peruvian Seguro Social was a poor copy of other laws by stating boldly that the Peruvian law was superior to all others: "The Peruvian social security law provides greater benefits than foreign laws and there is no country in the American continent that is capable of offering greater benefits."[82] It proceeded to address the probably widely held belief that the new monies would be misspent, noting that the funds raised by the new contributions would be "untouchable" and could only be used for "assistance and first aid and the construction of hospitals, sanatoriums, maternity hospitals, clinics, and above all worker housing." Moreover, the Caja Nacional de Seguro Social, the entity charged with overseeing the investment, would be independent, while workers themselves would intervene in the management of its resources and help oversee the provision of services.

The booklet went on to address the argument that workers should not be expected to contribute part of their wages in order to fund the Seguro Social and argued that the worker contribution was not only universally accepted, it was also in their interest. The booklet noted that this tripartite funding was normal: "In all countries where social security is in operation, workers, employers and the state contribute a quota."[83] In any case, workers paid the smallest of the three contributions, with the state being the largest contributor. Moreover, whereas the worker, understood in this and other documents to be primarily if not exclusively male, paid for himself and the employer for his workers, the state paid for "the whole/integrity of [*integridad*] the country's workers" (that is, all workers and the integrity of workers).[84] More important, however, was the fact that for a small payment of a few centavos per day, which corresponded to less than "what is spent in bars or on matches and cigarettes," the worker obtained not only medical attention and money in case of illness, a pension if he became disabled, a "decent" burial, and help for the surviving spouse and children, but also dignity and "peace of mind over his home and security for the future."[85] In other words, the booklet stressed not only the material benefits of the Seguro Social but also its moral benefits: rather than waste money getting drunk in a bar, workers would now be contributing directly to their moral ennoblement and the well-being of their families through their contributions to the Seguro Social. In short, the Seguro Social protected the workers' welfare but also improved them morally. It civilized them and made them better husbands, fathers, workers, and citizens.

This "civilizing" dimension to the Seguro Social was restated more forcefully later in the booklet, in a passage that reprised the argument that workers stood to gain the most from participating in the scheme but that, at the same time, framed this participation within a project of governmentality. The booklet suggested that social assistance provided by the state transformed private benevolence into an obligation, "transforming the moral into the juridical." But the social security legislation went beyond this by making workers "the makers of their own destiny" as it helped to develop in them habits such as thrift and foresight. It was the responsibility of the worker to improve himself, but, the booklet stressed, such an improvement would be possible thanks to a new conception of labor policy. Indeed, it was no longer sufficient to address a problem when it occurred. Now, the state sought to reduce the occurrence of problems as well as their consequences: "It is not enough to cure those afflicted with tuberculosis; it is important that we stop workers from becoming infected. It is not enough to assist mothers when they give birth; it is necessary to correct the problems that arise in pregnancy, to look after the life of the child and to help it and its mother for a while." The state would be able to do this by providing "hospitals, clinics and . . . sanitation; by giving workers cheap and hygienic housing."[86] The state would not limit its intervention to treating disease: it would act upon workers' immediate and mediate environments in order to stop disease from developing in the first place.

The assumption that undergirded these arguments was that although workers were a valuable resource they were also physically and morally deficient and that it was up to the state, through the Seguro Social, to fashion healthy and "civilized" workers capable of, and ready for, labor. That this assumption was explicitly stated in a document ostensibly aimed at workers speaks volumes about the extent to which such beliefs were understood to be self-evident. The booklet stated unequivocally: "Lack of foresight [in health issues] is a general phenomenon in Peru."[87] Its origins were located in both the climate and the legacy of colonialism, characterized by a "paternal" government that substituted personal foresight. These "influences" were most clearly recognizable among the working classes: "Our workers spend what they earn, and pay no attention to the fact that with time their capacity to work diminishes."[88] The situation was dire in the cities, where mutual aid associations were rare and few workers owned their own homes, but it was far worse in the countryside, where beggars were plentiful. But above all, it was the Indian who presented the most extreme case, a point I will return to below: "Of our indigenous race there is nothing to say. During a feast to honor the village saint it spends all it has. Its lack of foresight is such that it has been necessary to maintain the [indigenous] communities as the only means for the indigenous to preserve their patrimony." It followed that no country was in greater need of a social security law than Peru, "[a] tropical country, [where] life is shorter. Because of the physical conditions, our productive capacity is rapidly used up. Diseases, [poor] nutrition, reduce our productive efficiency."[89] The provision of social security for workers, such a diagnosis implied, was imperative in order that the productive capacity of labor could be harnessed.

As the above suggests, the architects of the Seguro Social understood social insurance as a technology of government. The environmental and sociobiological determinism implicit in the arguments used to justify the establishment of the Seguro Social was clearly instrumental: it provided the justification for new social legislation. Given the harsh climatic conditions and the evident deficiencies of the Peruvian population, the booklet discussed above seemed to suggest, it was only normal for the state to take on the responsibility of providing a corrective environment. But this instrumentality reveals more broadly the ways in which elites in early twentieth-century Peru understood state formation as a project of governmentality that aimed at national redemption and uplift and that necessarily involved the "improvement" of the population. It is in this light that the Seguro Social needs to be understood primarily: as a part of a broader attempt to make proper workers by, as George Steinmetz has put it, producing a "habitus of self-discipline" among the working class.[90] It was an attempt informed by increasingly governmental understandings of the social and by the belief that scientific and social scientific knowledge could produce effective social intervention. The Seguro Social was conceived not simply as a way of making available to workers social protection in the shape of hospitalization or a sickness pension. It was also aimed at inculcating values and behaviors in workers that would transform what Rebagliati and others clearly viewed as physically and morally deficient workers into productive workers capable of contributing effectively to the broader project of national redemption and uplift through industrialization that these elites had in mind.

These ideas, regarding the governmental role of the state in protecting and improving the physical and moral makeup of workers for the greater benefit of the nation, were contained in the various speeches and newspaper editorials that accompanied the inauguration of the Hospital Obrero in late 1940, attended by foreign dignitaries, including Salvador Allende, then Chile's minister of public health. In his speech, Rebagliati framed the idea that the hospital, and the Seguro Social more broadly, was engaged in a struggle for the improvement of human capital in a consideration of the broader context provided by the Second World War: "It is, of course, noteworthy that while other countries destroy each other and their men expend their energies and their lives in the heat of war, our countries, the countries of America, persist in their tradition of concord and they emulate and compete with each other in order to defend their human capital and achieve the wellbeing of their citizens."[91] President Manuel Prado, recently elected, meanwhile, emphasized the fact that the Seguro Social, although begun by Benavides, was an important element of his own government's policy, which "not only aspires to resolve our new problems that derive from the current world conditions, but also those that, in a permanent way, are related to welfare, security and the protection of workers."[92] The following day *La Crónica* ran an editorial praising the opening of the Hospital Obrero, which would help "the working man to regain his health" and reflected on the fact that the state "has answered more than satisfactorily growing needs that cannot be put off." The editorial then went on to discuss the dangers represented by the low birth rate and high death rate and the need to address population growth, or rather, the lack of it.[93]

The difference that the Hospital Obrero made to the health and welfare of workers is beyond the scope of this study. Unfortunately, I have been unable to find much documentary evidence of how those that the Hospital Obrero was supposed to serve viewed its inauguration. But it is interesting to note that one of the few commentaries available, an editorial in labor periodical *La Voz del Obrero*, emphasized the ways in which the Hospital Obrero represented a new era of medical attention for workers, who would no longer need to depend on charity:

> The medical attention that workers received in the hospitals of the Beneficence, as acts of charity, which is depressing and degrading, is to become a thing of the past. Workers will have access to medical attention and to some of their wages in the Seguro Social, they will no longer ask for charitable medical attention, but will turn to the Seguro to request what by right is owed to them; they will no longer receive charity, they will no longer feel ashamed or afraid for the future of their loved ones.[94]

The editorial could well have been another piece of government propaganda. Still, it expressed the belief, likely shared by some workers, that the Hospital Obrero represented not merely a bulwark against the rise of communism, but rather another site, along with the restaurantes populares and barrios obreros, where values important to the self-fashioning of workers, in this case dignity, could be performed and reinforced. At the same time, this editorial provides further evidence of how the rationalities of government of the architects of the labor state were shared by those they sought to governmentalize.

THE EXCLUSION OF THE INDIAN

As I have suggested so far, in order to understand the motivations for the establishment of the Seguro Social we need to take seriously the rationalities of government that shaped its creation and design. The creation of the Seguro Social may have been prompted by political calculation, that is, by the belief that such a measure would weaken the political appeal of APRA and the Peruvian Communist Party among labor, as many contemporaries believed and several historians have repeated. But, as the analysis above suggests, political imperatives mobilized a far more complex and deep-seated set of beliefs and assumptions. On the one hand, the Seguro Social reflected a particular understanding of the project of governmentality that the state ought to assume in ordering and shaping labor and society more generally—a highly gendered understanding, as I have shown, that identified, indeed created, an equivalence between progressive governmental labor policy and "modernity" and that envisioned the primary function of the state through agencies such as the Seguro Social to be the protection and improvement of workers in order to enhance their contribution to the nation. But the Seguro Social also reflected a broader set of beliefs regarding the character of Peruvian society that were expressed through the exclusions that it established. These exclusions could be seen as corresponding to what Pierre Bourdieu calls "classification struggles": the establishment or reinforcement of "distinction among elements that might otherwise emerge as a social group."[95]

Certainly, the Seguro Social law established that persons covered by Law 4916, that is, white-collar workers, were excluded from eligibility.[96] By creating a further source of differentiation, through a legal classification, between obreros and empleados, Law 8433 arguably drove yet another wedge (in addition to the empleado Law 4916, which excluded manual or blue-collar workers) between two potential allies in a common struggle against the capitalist class. However, as David Parker has shown, distinctions between obreros and empleados were not merely, or indeed primarily, imposed from above or a consequence of legislative "divide-and-rule" strategies. They expressed internalized beliefs about the differences between two different types of workers that hinged as much on factors such as cultures of consumption, "respectability," "decency," and, indeed, "race" as on whether the labor each performed was primarily manual or "intellectual."[97] There is little to suggest that the exclusion of white-collar workers from the Seguro Social's coverage was challenged in any way. Indeed, a fully separate Seguro Social del Empleado (Employee or White-Collar Social Security Law) was decreed in 1948.[98] The exclusion of white-collar workers from Law 8433 reflected, then, not a political strategy but rather widely held and largely unchallenged assumptions about the fundamental differences and incommensurability between obreros and empleados.

However, the primary exclusion established by the Seguro Social was not that of empleados but rather that of the indigenous. Yet, crucially, "Indians" were excluded not by virtue of their ethnicity but by virtue of how the term "worker" came to be defined for the purposes of the Seguro Social. The definition of the term was far from straightforward. Indeed, some of the early critiques of the Seguro Social focused on the contested term "worker." In early 1937, *La Crónica* published a series of articles that reprised many of the concerns discussed above. It asked, "Can a low-yielding country [*un país de pobre rendimiento*] in the sphere of labor, such as ours, given that most of its resources are yet to be exploited, sustain the extraction of millions of soles each year to fund the Seguro Social?"[99] The newspaper seemed thus to suggest that Peru was not ready for the Seguro Social because it could not sustain its cost. But it was also unready for another reason. *La Crónica* argued that Peru's *population* was unsuitable for such a law: "The law's complexity is at odds with the average level of culture of the Peruvian worker. We must not forget that there are four million illiterate Indians who labor on the Andean ridges and whom it will be impossible to include in the Seguro Social because they have no knowledge of it and because of their traditional inertia."[100] The newspaper restated this belief in another article: "We recognize that the Seguro Social is of benefit to societies that are ready to implement it, but we proclaim with equal sincerity that Peru, because of its peculiar labor systems, because of the psychology and characteristics of Andean workers, of the coastal *yanacón* (a type of sharecropper), of the age-old *mitayo* (corvée laborer), because of our topographic, ethnic, and social difficulties, because of the limited economic capacity of employers, was not and is not ready to implement a social security system."[101]

Rebagliati responded to these comments, which appear to have formed a key aspect of objections formulated by the Arequipa Chamber of Commerce to the Seguro Social, by arguing in a way that reproduced an older indigenista critique (which placed blame for the Indians' supposed backwardness on their Andean exploiters—the so-called gamonales): "The law does not exclude people because of social condition, but because of work conditions; thus, once the conditions disappear that place the indigenous population beyond the reach of social rights, more as a consequence of the sordidness of those who oppress it than because of the absence of the law, the Seguro will extend its protection to them."[102] As this suggests, Rebagliati did not dispute that Indians were backward. He simply rejected the notion that Indians were inherently unsuitable for such a law. He argued that the Seguro Social did not yet cover them because it needed to be established gradually, "in accordance with the aim to adapt its implementation in the country depending on the industrial development, the geographic conditions, and the feasibility of establishing the services offered by the Seguro in its different regions." But, crucially, for Rebagliati, the incorporation of Indians into the Seguro Social hinged not so much on the capacity of the state to provide the services that the Seguro Social envisaged but rather on when (indeed, whether) the Indian became a worker: "When the indigenous population . . . enters industrial life, it will be incorporated into the Seguro, but it is and must remain excluded as long as the Indian does not qualify as a worker [*no asume el contenido de trabajador*], [as long as] he remains a serf, he is exploited as a 'pongo,' sold as livestock by the gamonales, dispossessed by the 'truk-system' (the exchange of labor for commodities) or remains a victim of peonage, in the sense of forced unpaid labor, in order to pay suspicious and fraudulent debts."[103]

In other words, the Seguro Social would extend to Indians when Indians became workers. Rebagliati's response to the objections of the Arequipa Chamber of Commerce reveals the extent to which the Seguro Social was narrowly associated with a particular idea of what constituted a worker. Indeed, a document written by Rebagliati made explicit the cases in which the law applied: "in transport industries, only when it takes place by mechanic traction; in agriculture, only if nonhuman engines are used and only with regard to the employees exposed to the danger of machinery; in the docks, only if they operate mechanical apparatus not moved by men; in the livestock haciendas, only if the driving force is nonhuman; in the mines, quarries, and deposits of coal, oil, borax, nitrate, guano and similar substances, if they employ more than thirty-five operatives."[104] In other words, according to this definition, it was workers' exposure to mechanization that qualified them as workers. In another document, probably the first serious statistical study undertaken by the Caja del Seguro Social, the definition was somewhat different: "The category 'worker' refers to people who perform manual labor [*trabajan manualmente*] in workshops, factories, or in their homes for the benefit of an employer (dependents) and also those who perform similar labor for their own benefit (independents)."[105] According to this definition, the location of work (the workshop, the factory, even the home) was determinative of the worker's status as a worker. Both these definitions reveal how the idea of what constituted a worker was associated largely with forms of labor and locations of work that, in the Peruvian context, were construed as necessarily nonindigenous.[106]

That Rebagliati understood the Seguro Social as extending to Indians *qua workers* and not to Indians *qua Indians* reflects the idea that Indians were, by definition, *not workers* and workers were by definition *not Indians*. This idea was consistent with the belief in 1930s Peru that Indianness was inimical to progress; it was a condition that needed to be overcome, indeed eliminated. An article in the Seguro Social mouthpiece *Informaciones Sociales* titled "The Indian in the Seguro Social" established in no uncertain terms the belief that the extension of the Seguro Social to the Indian, when it came, would have as its primary objective not the provision of social insurance to Peru's indigenous population but rather its "redemption," that is, its de-Indianization. The article noted that indigenous people, even when in contact with "advanced forms of culture," maintained customs "particularly in domestic life, which are a real obstacle to their incorporation into our civilization." The Seguro Social would help them "to elevate their lives." Although naturally suspicious, the Indians would have no choice, once confronted by the deeds of the Seguro Social in the fields of social insurance and medical care and by its capacity to eradicate the diseases that profoundly affected their people, but to "turn definitively and unreservedly toward modern civilization." In short, the article concluded, "the Seguro Social, therefore, assumes its role in the redemption of the Indian."[107] In other words, the Seguro Social would extend not to the indigenous but to "redeemed" Indians, that is, to de-Indianized workers.

The inclusion of discussion articles on the so-called Indian question or that tackled Peru's "racial future" in *Informaciones Sociales* confirms that the "question" of Peru's Indian "masses" and their place in a modern Peru that was reflected in the exclusions of Seguro Social was very much in the minds of Rebagliati and his collaborators even as they claimed to be focusing on "workers." To judge from the different points of view expressed in these articles, the solution to the "Indian question" was not evident. In an article entitled "The Indian Problem," Alejandro Vega argued strongly in favor of the Indian's potential: "Give the Peruvian aborigine culture, land to cultivate, and adequate guidance to his muscular effort and you will make of him a conscientious, enthusiastic, and useful element." Vega rejected the racial pessimism of the influential Peruvian philosopher Alejandro Deustua, who, following Spengler, believed that Indians had degenerated and that "the country can do nothing for them." For Vega, who drew on the ideas of liberal and progressive intellectuals such as Manuel Vicente Villarán, José Antonio Encinas, Uriel García, and Hildebrando Castro Pozo, given a corrective environment, in the shape of rural schools, roads, and markets, the Indian's potential (clearly evident in past achievements in the Incan and colonial periods) as a worker would be recovered: "When the Indian is placed among a network of communication, he will regain the sense of his life and the historic force of his race." In this way, Vega conceived and presented the Indian's redemption as a project that the state should undertake for the benefit of Peru as a whole.[108]

Alongside this arguably "progressive" view, the journal published a lecture given by Pedro J. M. Larrañaga, "because we consider it to be worthy of diffusion." Perhaps aware that the title of his talk, "The Economic Bases of Our Racial Future," might have led some to believe that he was in fact a racist, Larrañaga began by stressing that he did not make "common cause" with "the present exaggerated racist thesis that occupies the European scene and that has infected some people in our continent," that he grouped races according to their geographical origins and not intrinsic value, and that he considered that even "our oldest families" (he was addressing a gathering of elite ladies and gentlemen at the Sociedad "Entre Nous") were a product of mestizaje. Larrañaga then, however, warned that South America was becoming an "Asiatic region." The problem, as far as Larrañaga was concerned, was straightforward. How to attract to Peru "the best of the white race?" Studies, he argued, demonstrated that Europeans moved to areas that offered industrial employment. It followed that Peru, and in particular the Peruvian coast, needed to develop industrially in order to attract white immigrants:

> A democratic American country must make this decision at some point: what color does it want to be—what slant does it desire for its population: European, Asiatic, or African? And the answer cannot be provided by the Ministry of Government, or the Ministry of Foreign Affairs, but by the Ministry of Development. If it wants to be white, it must provide work and opportunities for whites who wish to emigrate: that is to say, it must industrialize in those regions where the temperate climate is favorable to the immigrant race and where the land possesses the basic resources for industry.[109]

Larrañaga was not interested in either the Andes or the Amazon, which he saw as unsuitable for European occupation: "To consider seriously an ethnic interchange with that region is a waste of time."[110] For Larrañaga as for many others as I have shown, industrialization and racial whitening were mutually constitutive and would allow Peru, or, rather, coastal Peru, to become "Modern Peru, the New Industrial California of the South!"[111]

These texts illustrate the type of ideas that circulated in 1930s Peru regarding the "Indian question." Given that the architects of the Seguro Social considered them worthy of discussion it is fair to assume that these texts informed their own thinking. Although the views examined here expressed different, indeed conflicting, types of racial or racist beliefs, they shared common racialized assumptions regarding the role that the state had to play in addressing the social and economic development of Peru. In both these views social and economic development, or "progress," was understood primarily as a project of racial improvement: in the first case by "improving" the Indian through the correction of the degenerative environment, in effect, by "de-Indianizing" the Indian; in the second, by fully realizing the potential of the Peruvian coast through the infusion of racially superior European immigrants. However, neither project, like the Seguro Social itself, had a place for the Indian *qua Indian* in the envisioned Peruvian nation, for the simple reason that both authors assumed that Indianness was incommensurable with progress. More specifically, these texts reveal how the idea (discussed extensively in the first chapter) that Indian labor was incommensurable with indus-

trial progress (or commensurable to the extent that in performing industrial labor Indians ceased to be Indian) informed the thinking of the
architects of the Seguro Social. For Rebagliati and others, although Indians performed a form of labor, it was a form of labor that, given Indian
"culture" and the Indian environment, was fundamentally distinct from
the labor performed by workers and, because it was not conducive to
progress, did not qualify them as workers and therefore excluded them
from the Seguro Social.

CONCLUSION

Shortly after the inauguration of the Hospital Obrero, the focus of the
Seguro Social began to shift. A document from 1942 pointed to a growing
awareness among the architects of the Seguro Social that the need for
social security was far greater in nonurban areas than they had realized.
Following a nationwide statistical study, researchers at the Seguro Social
had reached the conclusion that "of the 500,000 insured, more than 70
percent are agricultural workers, a remarkable situation, because awareness of this fact represents, in relation to the Seguro, the possibility of
extending its benefits to the waged sector that most needs them, because
in contrast to what once was assumed, diseases spread in rural contexts
with equal or greater virulence than in urban contexts, given that they are
helped by deficient nutrition, housing, hygiene, and medical assistance."[112]
The document argued the need for a significant expansion in hospital care
and set out an ambitious program of construction of twelve new hospitals,
thirty polyclinics, fifty rural "postas," and ten "roving outpatient departments." In this way, the Seguro Social would reach this 70 percent of the
insured who were not urban workers or based in Lima. This expansion
responded to a growing realization that it was not enough to treat the sick.
The purpose of the Seguro Social was to prevent illness by acting upon
those susceptible to illness: "Until recently the role of hospitals was limited to the occasional treatment of sick or indigent patients who came
through their doors. Today that practice is replaced by the idea of search-
ing out the ill, by immediate examination and treatment and intensive
prophylaxis, which guard against the failure of late treatment and prevent
losses in productive capacity."[113] This document points to some of the
tensions at the heart of the Seguro Social and social reform in Peru more
generally. On the one hand, armed with their increasingly sophisticated
data, social reformers could see that the problems the Seguro Social pur-

ported to address clearly surpassed the category "worker" that they had been focused on. On the other, they continued to see social reform in terms of how its action upon those considered "productive" would create a desired outcome.

The idea that men and women other than those considered "productive" deserved to have access to social security, or rather, that it was the duty of the state to protect only those considered productive, changed very slowly in the later part of the twentieth century and, in turn, helped to change the notion of who was productive and who was not. In the 1950s, Federico More published an article that claimed that Peru did not really have a Seguro Social because a vast number of professionals, such as physicians, lawyers, writers, musicians, and painters, as well as prostitutes, were excluded from either the Seguro Social Obrero or the Seguro Social del Empleado: "The number of workers outside the Seguro is probably larger than the number covered by the Seguro."[114] In the 1960s, President Fernando Belaúnde spoke of the need to extend the coverage of the medical services offered by the Seguro Social: "We all know that there is a problem of concentration of the medical profession in the urban centers and that it is very difficult to extend these services to remote and isolated areas."[115] He believed the roads that his government was building would help change that situation. In the 1970s, in the context of Velasco's "revolutionary government of the armed forces," Teodosio Arístides Palomino Ramírez argued for the need to extend social security to Peru's indigenous peoples:

> Today, more than ever, we need to include, to consider that great defenseless mass in Peru; I am referring to the campesinos of the Sierra and the Selva, to those people who silently work tilling the land, transforming our wild geography to expand the habitable areas. We need, more than ever, to incorporate that great mass of rural workers [*trabajadores del campo*] who for many years were forgotten, by a government that only used them as objects of vile humiliation and exploitation; they are Peruvians like us . . . except that whereas we have access to social security, to well-equipped clinics, to hospitals with the proper instruments, they, those sad campesinos, do not have schools where they can educate themselves, or hospitals where they can prevent or treat their diseases.[116]

Significantly, in keeping with the class-focused rhetoric of the Velasco period, Palomino Ramírez argued that it was as "campesinos" and "rural workers" that Peru's indigenous people deserved to be incorporated into the Seguro Social.

These changing perspectives of who was insurable, of who deserved the protection of the state, point to the ways in which the creation of the Seguro Social reflected how ideas of labor were racially constituted in early twentieth-century Peru, and, indeed, later in the century. The racial constitution of labor had important implications for the broader project of governmentality that the Seguro Social reflected and contributed to. The Seguro Social corresponded to a project of governmentality that projected an industrial future as the solution to an indigenous present. As this project of governmentality began to shape state intervention in society, via its instantiation in state agencies and legislation such as the Seguro Social, the racialized assumptions at its heart inevitably were reflected in labor policy. The Seguro Social was clearly more than a simple attempt to coopt labor. It expressed the genuine belief among sectors of the Peruvian elite that the state had a role to play in addressing the problems of modern society. Specifically, it expressed the belief that the state could and should protect and "improve" labor by addressing its susceptibility to disease and its mediate and immediate environment, which fostered disease. In so doing, the state contributed to the broader project of national redemption through industrialization by fashioning the type of labor required for this project. The exclusion of Indians qua Indians from the Seguro Social, and by extension from the project of national redemption, reflected the fact that by definition national redemption was understood as a project of racial improvement that necessarily involved the de-Indianization of Peru.

CONCLUSION

In recent years, Peru appears to have bucked the regional trend toward the ethnicization of politics, a process that has been most visible in neighboring Andean countries. The "ethnic awakening" in Bolivia or Ecuador, a new beginning, some argue, for the historically marginalized, has no parallels in Peru. Yet, the absence of strong indigenous movements in Peru is puzzling.[1] Race and racism structure Peruvian history and society profoundly, as Peru's recent "time of fear" illustrated tragically. Shining Path was not an indigenous movement, and the war that it initiated was not a "race war." But the war reflected, reproduced, and indeed, deepened, Peru's racial cleavages. As Peru's Truth and Reconciliation Commission (TRC) concluded, the war, which produced some seventy thousand victims, "reproduced in large measure the ethnic and social rifts that affect the whole of Peruvian society."[2] The war magnified what Peruvians experience on an everyday basis: the ways in which race and racism order Peruvian society and naturalize that ordering. However, scholars have begun only recently to examine seriously the role that race and racism play in structuring Peruvian society. This book is a contribution to this effort and to broader considerations of race, labor, and the state. I have sought to suggest new ways of thinking about the relationship between race and nation-state formation through an examination of the formation of the Peruvian state from the perspective of labor policy. My principal aim has been to show that the study of labor policy in early twentieth-century Peru provides valuable insight into the ways in which race and racism have shaped state formation and, in turn, Peru's "durable inequalities."[3]

I have argued in this book that racism and ideas about race were constitutive of what I have called the labor state. As several scholars have shown, racism, as a normalized idea and behavior, is central to the exclusionary character of nation building in Peru. Gonzalo Portocarrero has suggested that racism hinders the capacity of Peruvians to "construct a memory, a narrative that creates a national *we*, a common history through which Peruvians can recognize themselves as equal while diverse."[4] For Marisol de la Cadena, racism in Peru is "discreet" or "silent" because it is institutional, hegemonic, legitimizing, normalized.[5] As Romeo Grompone suggests, racism in Peru "is strengthened by what is silenced, veiled, not said and yet, at the same time, known by everyone."[6] In sum, as many scholars recognize, racism in Peru structures social hierarchies and shapes social policies because, by racializing culture and culturalizing race (by making ideas of racial and cultural superiority/inferiority mutually reinforcing), it constructs the nonwhite "other" (the indigenous, the mestizo, the Afro-Peruvian, the *chino*) as the depository and agent of poverty, cultural backwardness, and national failure. Racism leads Peruvians to perceive socioeconomic and political inequalities as both inevitable and, in some cases, desirable because, perversely, by putting everyone in his or her place, racism constructs a "normalized" order that, given the racial and cultural aptitudes of every Peruvian, is optimal. The purpose of this book has been to give historical substance to these interpretations.

The argument, central to the broader argument of this book, that a labor state existed in early twentieth-century Peru may come as a surprise to many. After all, how could a labor state exist in a country where "workers" were a small minority of the laboring population? I have shown, first, that several factors, and not just the elite's attempt to coopt labor or neutralize political forces of the Left, shaped the labor state, manifested in state "agencies" such as the Sección del Trabajo, the barrios obreros, the restaurantes populares, the Seguro Social, and the broader "social politics" that the governments of the 1920s and 1930s sought to implement. I subscribe to Daniel Rodgers's contention that "no piece of social politics . . . can claim a tidy lineage, a monocausal raison d'être, or, least of all, tidy effects. The field of social politics is too large for any one site of explanation, or single set of characters, to command it all. Its processes, too, are multiple: compassion, outrage, exposure, publicization, agitation, mobilization, invention, lobbying, pacification, preemption, calculation, bargaining, compromise, enforcement, administration and manipulation."[7] By paying attention to the various discourses, from above and below, from the Left and the Right, that shaped the creation, implementation, negotiation, resistance to, and rejection of the state agencies and the labor policies more generally, I hope to have provided a sense of how in Peru too, as in the North Atlantic economies studied by Rodgers and the scholars that he has drawn upon, social politics "was too large for any one site of explanation, or single set of characters, to command it all."

Certainly, as the analysis of the state agencies in the preceding chapters shows, a conflation of forces shaped early twentieth-century Peruvian social politics, and more concretely Peruvian labor policy. I have challenged the idea that all labor policy was reactive to, a product of, or a straightforward consequence of elite responses to labor unrest. Elites, I have shown, played a key role in devising and introducing labor policy. Their motives were multiple: they were shaped by transnational processes and they reflected apparently conflicting ideas of labor. In particular, I have argued that two key ideas of labor, themselves influenced by a conflation of political and social thought (specifically, social Catholicism and positivism) shaped labor policy: the idea that labor, because it was associated with industrialization, was an agent of progress and the idea that labor, because it was associated with militancy and dangerous social doctrines, was a source of danger. The labor state was the product of these ideas and reflected the increasingly hegemonic view that the purpose of the state was to protect and "improve" labor in order to enable and enhance labor's contribution to Peru march toward civilization. At the same time, I have argued that workers too shaped the labor state, which they came to see as an expression of their own aspirations.

In invoking the idea of a labor state I have mobilized theoretical insights from a growing literature that examines the cultural formation of states and particularly from the literature inspired by Foucault's work on governmentality. I have approached the labor state not merely, or indeed primarily, as a bureaucratic apparatus, but rather as a form of power shaping labor relations. In this sense, I have approached the agencies of the labor state analyzed in this book, the Sección del Trabajo, the barrios obreros, the restaurantes populares, and the Seguro Social as elements in a project of governmentality manifested in the labor state; that is, as agencies expressive of rationalities of government (and discipline) and as technologies of government. I have argued that the purpose of these agencies was indeed, in part, to undermine labor militancy and the appeal of the parties of the Left by providing labor with goods and services: mediation in labor disputes, adequate housing, cheap nutrition, and social insurance. However, their purpose was also, and perhaps primarily, to act upon workers both physically and morally and upon workers' mediate and immediate environments in order to protect and "improve" labor, that is, in order to enable workers to fulfill their role as agents of progress. Ultimately, of course, as the various chapters show, these agencies, or "weapons of the strong," proved rather blunt and were largely unsuccessful in their attempt to either discipline, protect, or "improve" labor.

However, the key contribution of this book arises from the attempt to show that race and racism undergirded the multiple processes shaping social politics in early twentieth-century Peru. The labor state, I have argued, reflected and reinforced racialized understandings of labor, and, in turn, a process of nation-state formation that reproduced the exclusion of the indigenous from conceptions of national progress. Peruvian elites, I have suggested, identified industrialization with "civilization." As a consequence, they came to see labor as a force that needed to be harnessed in order to transform Peru into an industrialized and civilized nation; this was the allure of labor. Labor policy, therefore, was profoundly influenced by this understanding. Labor was to be "improved" so that it could better fulfill its civilizing function. However, labor was understood in racialized terms: specifically in terms that excluded the indigenous from the sphere of labor. Constitutional arrangements, labor legislation, and labor policy reflected and reinforced this exclusion by creating incommensurable constitutional and legislative regimes for labor and for the indigenous. These regimes allowed for Indians to become workers, but in so doing Indians necessarily ceased being Indian. In this way, the indigenous were excluded from the project of governmentality manifested in the labor state. At the same time, the indigenous remained immanent to the labor state insofar as they were identified as incommensurable with the achievement of progress. Progress became in this way synonymous with the de-Indianization of Peru.

Through such arguments, this book contributes to a broader discussion on the extent to which biopolitical projects of governmentality, in liberal, neoliberal, or indeed illiberal (colonial or authoritarian) societies, serve to reproduce forms of differentiation among populations. My analysis echoes in some ways Aiwha Ong's discussion of how "graduated sovereignty" operates in modern Southeast Asia. Through case studies of the implementation of neoliberal reforms in Malaysia and Indonesia, Ong has explored "the differential treatment of populations—through schemes of biopolitical disciplining and pastoral care—that differently insert them into processes of global capitalism. These gradations of governing may be in a continuum, but they overlap with pre-formed racial, religious, and gender hierarchies, and further fragment citizenship for people who are all, nominally speaking, citizens of the same country."[8] In an analogous manner, the Peruvian labor state reflected, and, in turn, served to reassert, pre-existing racial structures that determined that some sectors of the population were deemed amenable to governmental rule (to techniques of self-governing) while others were not (and were therefore, in effect, excluded from conceptions of national progress). My analysis also resonates with Giorgio Agamben's distinction between political life and "bare life." As is well known, Agamben builds on Foucault's work on biopower and on Carl Schmitt's discussion of the state of exception to argue that "in modern biopolitics, sovereign is he who decides on the value of or the nonvalue of life as such."[9] Agamben's suggestion that biopolitics operates through the reduction of certain categories of people to "bare life," to a "life devoid of value," or to a "life not worth living," or indeed to the status of *homo sacer*, he who can be killed with impunity, helps account for the rationalities and practices that undergirded the exclusion of the indigenous from the Peruvian labor state. Indeed, as I have suggested throughout, the evacuation of the indigenous from the sphere of labor, and, therefore, from conceptions of national progress, reflected the belief that theirs was a life devoid of value, a bare life not suitable for transforming Peru into a modern industrial nation.

Beyond their theoretical possibilities, the arguments I develop in this book have implications for how we understand Peru's twentieth-century history more generally. Research on the social politics of later periods along the lines pursued here is necessary. But I strongly suspect that my general argument holds for the rest of the twentieth century. The Peruvian governments of the twentieth century, military or civilian, conservative or progressive, excluded the indigenous from their projects of nation-state formation because they all viewed the indigenous as incompatible with progress. Of course, most governments used discourses of "inclusion" and several implemented policies that, through education, health provision, or military conscription, sought to "incorporate" the indigenous into economic and even, by the 1980s, political citizenship. But they all, including General Velasco's "progressive" military regime, reproduced the idea that inclusion or incorporation implied the *overcoming* of indigeneity, and therefore, reproduced the idea central to social politics in the early twentieth century, traced in this book, that indigeneity was incommensurable with civilization and progress. Today, in what appears to be an ironic twist, given the supposedly indigenista roots of APRA, but which is in fact, as I showed in the second chapter, a historically consistent move, President Alan García and his acolytes accuse the indigenous of undermining his neoliberal revolution. According to García, Indians, their customs, and those who represent or allegedly manipulate them (NGOs primarily) are "dogs in the manger," obstacles to progress.

This persistent idea about the incommensurable nature of indigeneity and progress is a dangerous racist fiction and needs to be understood to be so. In my view, it is key to understanding the character of the violence that Peru experienced in the 1980s and 1990s. The report of the Truth and Reconciliation Commission revealed that the number of victims was close to seventy thousand; a figure almost twice as high as previous estimates. Significantly, the report noted, during the twenty years of armed conflict, there existed a "prominent relationship between a situation of poverty and social exclusion and the likelihood of becoming a victim of violence." About 85 percent of victims were concentrated in highland and *selva* departments (Ayacucho, Junín, Huánuco, Huancavelica, Apurímac, and San Martín), while Ayacucho alone accounted for 40 percent of all victims. Seventy-nine percent of victims lived in rural areas, and 59 percent were engaged in agricultural activities (in contrast to national averages of 29 percent and 28 percent respectively, according to the 1993 national census). Similarly, 75 percent of victims were Quechua speakers or speakers of other indigenous languages (in contrast to a national average of only 16 percent). Finally, 68 percent of victims had not received any secondary education (in contrast to a national average of 40 percent). In other words, most victims were poor, lived in rural areas, were speakers of an indigenous language, and had received very limited formal education. The report concluded that the violence superimposed itself on, and reproduced, deep class, ethnic, and gender inequalities that separate those who are included from those who are excluded in the nation-state.

For Salomón Lerner, the president of the TRC, the report revealed that Peru is "a country where exclusion is so absolute that tens of thousands of citizens can disappear without anyone in integrated society, in the society of the nonexcluded, noticing a thing."[10] But how do we account for this? As the TRC report suggested, and as I hope to have shown from a particular vantage point in this book, part of the explanation is to be found in how race and racism have shaped nation-state formation in Peru. Historically, the indigenous in Peru have been seen not only as marginal to the nation-state but as an obstacle to the pursuit of progress. This was a perception that reflected less an understanding of the actual labor performed by the indigenous (which some, not least Andean landlords who relied on indigenous labor, reluctantly recognized as valuable) than the quasi-ontological status assigned to the indigenous as a nonproductive being. The indigenous in Peru represented an obstacle to progress in Peru because of their nonproductivity, their incommensurability with labor. It followed that little could be expected from the indigenous. The indigenous could only become productive by ceasing to be indigenous: by becoming nonindigenous, that is, by becoming a mestizo, perhaps, or a worker. Marisol de la Cadena argues that the process of self-de-Indianization was a form of cultural resistance.[11] But, of course, self-de-Indianization was a resistance strategy that arose within a dominant culture of de-Indianization. In contrast to the United States or Argentina and Chile, in Peru the indigenous were not physically erased from the national fabric. But they have continuously been subjected to a cultural erasure and, today as in the past, are valued qua Indians only in so far as they can be reduced to archeological or museum pieces.

The cultural erasing, or evacuation, of the indigenous from conceptions and projects of Peruvian nationhood and "progress" helps to explain both the exclusionary processes of nation-state formation that shaped the twentieth century and the disproportionate impact that the armed conflict of the 1980s and early 1990s had on the indigenous. Indians qua Indians could not contribute to progress: it followed that they had to be de-Indianized to be made productive. Efforts could be, and were, directed at de-Indianization (through "education," etc.), but those who did not de-Indianize, because they refused to do so or because resources to implement the process of de-Indianization were lacking, could be, and indeed came to be seen as in need of being, erased from the purview of the nation-state. The historical marginalization of the indigenous, in this sense, is best understood not as a lack or failure of the Peruvian nation-state but as its necessary and constitutive condition. Similarly, the indigenous could be killed with impunity by either the Shining Path or the armed forces not because the state failed to protect them but precisely because their status as indigenous, as nonproductive and culturally erasable entities, indicated that they were unprotected and disposable. The armed conflict laid bare not the failures of the Peruvian nation-state but its historically constituted character and the racist fictions that undergird Peru's "durable inequalities." The allure of labor, and its subsequent manifestations (currently the allure of neoliberalism, perhaps), expresses the impossibility of imagining the indigenous as subjects and agents of Peruvian history.

NOTES

NOTES TO INTRODUCTION

1. Alayza Paz Soldán, *La industria moderna*, 16. Unless otherwise stated, all translations from the Spanish are my own.

2. In 1931, with a population of around six million, Peru remained an overwhelmingly rural country. The largest city, Lima (including the nearby port of Callao), had a population of 370,000. Peru's ten largest provincial cities barely mustered a combined population of 250,000. Gurney, *Report on the Economic Conditions in Peru*. In fact, most Peruvians, around 60 percent in 1876 and 63 percent in 1940, were employed in agricultural activities (as registered by the only two national censuses conducted in the period), and some of these took place in urban settings. According to the 1940 census, employment in "manufacturing" accounted for 15 percent of total employment (if we add "communication," "transportation," and "mining," the total rises to 19 percent), more or less the same as employment in the service sector ("government," "services," and "commerce" combined), and only a quarter of the population employed in agriculture. Moreover, probably about half of the 360,000 workers employed in manufacture in 1940 were not industrial workers, but rather handloom weavers, whose principal economic activity was agricultural. According to a 1954 estimate, out of a total of 500,000 persons employed in manufacturing, 235,000 were women producing textiles on hand looms. Burgess and Harbison, *Casa Grace in Peru*, 14.

3. *Industria* 1, no. 1 (11 December 1915).

4. *Industria Peruana* 1, no. 1 (November 1931). The similarities in composition between this image and the photograph on the cover of Marisol de la Cadena's *Indigenous Mestizos*, where the position/role of the worker is assumed by an indigenista intellectual, are striking. Whether Rossell drew

inspiration from the photograph is unknown. It seems worth noting that the interaction between the intellectual and the Indian in the photograph is far more limited than that between the worker and Indian in the drawing. See de la Cadena, *Indigenous Mestizos*.

5. See Bonnell, *Iconography of Power*. See also, for a later period and a different regime, Evans and Donald, *Picturing Power*.

6. Two important exceptions that sit outside this dichotomous view are David Nugent's study of nation-state formation in Chachapoyas and David Parker's history of Lima's middle class, both of which have influenced my thinking about Peruvian history. See Nugent, *Modernity at the Edge of Empire*; and Parker, *The Idea of the Middle Class*.

7. See Poole, *Vision, Race and Modernity*; de la Cadena, *Indigenous Mestizos*.

8. In so doing, I build on several historians' exploration of the interplay of nation-building and statecraft in nineteenth-century Peru. See, among others, Gootenberg, *Between Silver and Guano* and *Imagining Development*; Mallon, *Peasant and Nation*; Thurner, *From Two Republics to One Divided*; Walker, *Smoldering Ashes*; García-Bryce, *Crafting the Republic*; Méndez, *The Plebeian Republic*.

9. Denis Sulmont, for example, has called the social measures of the 1930s "right-wing populism." Baltazar Caravedo sees the measures as a product of a "neutralizing alliance" between the state and a new industrial bourgeoisie. Julio Cotler views the measures as a way of "undermining the citizenship's support for APRA." Adám Anderle stresses the "political dividends" that resulted from the measures. See Sulmont, *El movimiento obrero*, 167–69; Caravedo Molinari, *Burguesía e industria*, 129–31; Cotler, *Clases, estado y nación*, 252; Anderle, *Los movimientos políticos*, 284.

10. See, for two pioneering examples, James, *Resistance and Integration*, and French, *The Brazilian Workers' ABC*. On "classic" populism, see Knight, "Populism and Neo-Populism."

11. Donzelot, *L'invention du social*.

12. This literature has been useful in helping me to locate the Peruvian case within a broader global context. Rodgers's magisterial *Atlantic Crossings*, with its attention to the transnational dimension of social politics, has proved particularly useful, but I have also benefited from, among others, Steinmetz, *Regulating the Social*; Pedersen, *Family, Dependence, and the Origins of the Welfare State*; Kotkin, *Magnetic Mountain*; Skocpol, *Protecting Soldiers and Mothers*; Lindenmeyr, *Poverty Is Not a Vice*; Hong, *Welfare, Modernity, and the Weimar State*; Quine, *Italy's Social Revolution*; Horne, *A Social Laboratory for Modern France*; Swenson, *Capitalists against Markets*.

13. Foucault, *The Birth of Biopolitics*, 186. Orloff's "Social Provision and Regulation" is a useful overview of this literature. On culturalist approaches to the state (Foucauldian or otherwise), see, among others, Abrams, "Notes on the

Difficulty of Studying the State"; Corrigan and Sayer, *The Great Arch*; Stein-metz, *State/Culture*; Mukerji, *Territorial Ambitions*; Adams, *The Familial State*; Coronil, *The Magical State*; Scott, *Seeing Like a State*; Carroll, *Science, Culture, and Modern State Formation*; Hansen and Stepputat, *States of Imagination*; Das and Poole, *Anthropology in the Margins of the State*; Krohn-Hansen and Nustad, *State Formation*; Sharma and Gupta, *The Anthropology of the State*; Trouillot, "The Anthropology of the State"; Mitchell, *Rule of Experts*. A pioneering volume in the context of Latin American history is Joseph and Nugent, *Everyday Forms of State Formation*.

14. Foucault, *Security, Territory, Population*, 105.
15. Although, admittedly, these studies often invoke Foucault and his oeuvre if not governmentality as such. See, among others, Lavrin, *Women, Feminism, and Social Change*; Besse, *Restructuring Patriarchy*; Weinstein, *For Social Peace in Brazil*; Klubock, *Contested Communities*; Rosemblatt, *Gendered Compromises*; Hutchison, *Labors Appropriate to their Sex*; Snodgrass, *Deference and Defiance in Monterrey*; Farnsworth-Alvear, *Dulcinea in the Factory*; Tinsman, *Partners in Conflict*; Dore, *Myths of Modernity*; Ehrick, *The Shield of the Weak*; Guy, *Women Build the Welfare State*. See also Dore and Mo-lyneux, *Hidden Histories*.
16. Clark, *The Redemptive Work*; Gould, *To Die in This Way*; Chomsky, *West Indian Workers*; Dávila, *Diploma of Whiteness*; Weiner, *Race, Nation and Market*; Bronfman, *Measures of Equality*.
17. Foucault, *Security, Territory, Population*, 346.
18. Miller and Rose, *Governing the Present*.
19. As Foucault argues, "it is not a matter of imposing a law on men, but of the disposition of things, that is to say, of employing tactics rather than laws, or, of as far as possible employing law as tactics; arranging things so that this or that end may be achieved through a certain number of means." *Security, Territory, Population*, 99.
20. Although my analytical approach is different, this argument echoes Kevin Middlebrook's interpretation of how top-down and bottom-up forces shaped Mexico's own labor state. See *The Paradox of Revolution*.
21. Miller and Rose, *Governing the Present*, 17.
22. In foregrounding these questions, my approach builds upon, and at same time complicates, interpretations in several studies of Peruvian labor history such as Sulmont, *El movimiento obrero*; Blanchard, *The Origins of the Peruvian Labor Movement*; and, though its focus is broader than the history of labor, Stein, *Populism in Peru*.
23. See, among others, Burchell, Gordon, and Miller, *The Foucault Effect*; Rose, *Powers of Freedom*; Dean, *Governmentality*; Miller and Rose, *Governing the Present*. Useful examples of applications of the governmentality approach to history, geography, and anthropology include Prakash, *Another Reason*;

Joyce, *The Rule of Freedom*; Hannah, *Governmentality and the Mastery of Territory*; Legg, *Spaces of Colonialism*; Li, *The Will to Improve*; Ong, *Neoliberalism as Exception*. For an application of the governmentality approach to a Latin American case, see Poblete, "Governmentality and the Social Question." In the case of Peruvian scholarship, the governmentality approach has had, as yet, a limited impact. See, however, David Nugent's innovative discussion of APRA's project of subaltern governmentality. Nugent, "Governing States."

24. Foucault acknowledges as much: "We should not see things as the replacement of a society of sovereignty by a society of discipline, and then of a society of discipline by a society, say, of government. In fact, we have a triangle: sovereignty, discipline and governmental management, which has population as its main target and apparatuses of security as its essential mechanism." *Security, Territory, Population*, 108.

25. Scott, "Colonial Governmentality"; Dean, *Governmentality*, chap. 7. As a number of scholars suggest, governmentality has proved to be perfectly compatible with highly illiberal projects of rule, particularly in its neoliberal iteration. See Agamben, *Homo Sacer*, Butler, *Precarious Life*, Ong, *Neoliberalism as Exception*, and Brown, "Neoliberalism and the End of Liberal Democracy" and "American Nightmare."

26. Stoler, *Race and the Education of Desire*, 86, 88.

27. In thinking about how labor was racialized in the Peruvian context, I have drawn on insights gleaned from Cooper, *Decolonization and African Society*, and Lieberman, *Shifting the Color Line*, and more generally on the literature on racialization and race formation in Latin America and Peru. See, among others, Mörner, *Race and Class*; Graham et al., *The Idea of Race*; Stepan, *The Hour of Eugenics*; Wade, *Race and Ethnicity*; Appelbaum, McPherson, and Rosemblatt, *Race and Nation*. On Peru, see Nugent, *El laberinto de la choledad*; Manrique, *La piel y la pluma*; Poole, *Vision, Race, and Modernity*; de la Cadena, *Indigenous Mestizos*; Portocarrero, *Racismo y mestizaje*.

28. See, among others, Graham et al., *The Idea of Race*; Appelbaum, McPherson, and Rosemblatt, *Race and Nation*; Larson, *Trials of Nation Making*; Dawson, *Indian and Nation*; O'Connor, *Gender, Indian, Nation*; Canessa, *Natives Making Nation*; Gould, *To Die in This Way*; Grandin, *The Blood of Guatemala*. On Afro-Latin Americans in Brazil and Cuba: Skidmore, *Black into White*; Dávila, *Diploma of Whiteness*; Lesser, *Negotiating National Identity*; de la Fuente, *A Nation for All*; Bronfman, *Measures of Equality*.

29. Davies, *Indian Integration*; Jacobsen, *Mirages of Transition*; Nugent, *Modernity at the Edge of Empire*; Wilson, "Indian Citizenship"; Cueto, *El regreso de las epidemias*; Contreras, "Maestros, mistis y campesinos"; Fonseca Ariza, *Misioneros y civilizadores*; Rénique, *La batalla por Puno*. To be sure, as several historians have shown, along with Indians other groups such as

women or criminals were similarly deemed amenable to redemption. However, as happened with the indigenous, civilizing interventions were more likely to reproduce social hierarchies than challenge them. See Mannarelli, *Limpias y modernas*; Muñoz Cabrejo, *Diversiones públicas*; Aguirre, *The Criminals of Lima*.

30. See, among others, Stern, *Peru's Indian Peoples*; Spalding, *Huarochirí*; Flores Galindo, *Buscando un Inca*; and Silverblatt, *Modern Inquisitions*.

31. Portocarrero, *De Bustamante a Odría*; Collier, *Squatters and Oligarchs*; Stepan, *The State and Society*; Lowenthal, *The Peruvian Experiment*; Tovar, *Velasquismo y movimiento popular*; Mayer, *Cuentos feos*; Stern, *Shining and Other Paths*; Conaghan, *Fujimori's Peru*; Carrión, *The Fujimori Legacy*.

32. I borrow the idea of the racial state from Goldberg, *The Racial State*.

NOTES TO CHAPTER 1: RACIALIZING LABOR

1. *Memoria que el Ministro de Gobierno y Policía presenta al Congreso Ordinario de 1913* (Lima: Tipografía Opinión Nacional, 1913), ix–x.

2. See Blanchard, *The Origins of the Peruvian Labor Movement*. Official strike statistics for this period do not exist. See, however, Zitor, *Historia de las principales huelgas*, and Iziga Nuñez, *Sociología de la clase obrera peruana*, 93–94, 156–58.

3. Rodgers, *Atlantic Crossings*, 51.

4. As Frederick Cooper notes: "Accepting Africans as urban laborers, in need of trade unions, wage setting machinery, social security and collective bargaining agreements, and conceiving of Africans as peasants unable and unwilling to work for wages unless coerced implied very different conceptions of the state, of production, and of the laborer." Cooper, *Decolonization and African Society*, 165–66.

5. To be sure, Peru was not unique in this respect. Historians have shown that ideas about race played a key role in constituting ideas about labor in places as diverse as the United States in the eighteenth and nineteenth century, postemancipation Jamaica, and colonial West Africa. David Roediger, for example, examines the process whereby whiteness came to be associated with modern industrial wage labor, while blackness came "to embody the preindustrial past that [the white working class] scorned and missed" in the United States in the eighteenth and nineteenth centuries. Thomas Holt discusses how changing colonial ideas of former slaves' capacity to perform disciplined free wage labor shaped the nature of "freedom" in postemancipation Jamaica. Frederick Cooper, meanwhile, explores the ways in which "the notion of an 'African worker'" as "two concepts incompatible with each other" came to be challenged in French and British colonial Africa. See Roediger, *The Wages of Whiteness*, 97; Holt, *The Problem of Freedom*; Cooper, *Decolonization and African Society*.

6. On the new professional sectors, see Proyecto Historia UNI, *Construyendo el Perú*; and Cueto, *Excelencia científica*.

7. The historical study of philanthropy remains limited in the Peruvian context. See, however, the relevant articles in Portocarrero and Sanborn, *De la caridad a la solidaridad*.

8. Steinmetz, *Regulating the Social*.

9. Miro Quesada, "El contrato del trabajo," in Miro Quesada, *Albores de la reforma social*, 50.

10. Elmore, lecture, "Academia peruana de legislación y jurisprudencia."

11. *Memoria que el Ministro de Gobierno y Policía presenta al Congreso Ordinario de 1916* (Lima: Imprenta del Estado, 1916), xiv; *La Crónica*, 1 September 1916.

12. Perhaps naturally, workers rejected the idea that foreigners were responsible for rising militancy. An article in *La Protesta*, an anarchist periodical, noted: "To accuse foreigners, few of whom come to this city, of being the sole cause of anarchist propaganda is to attempt to hide, in the most inept way, the failure to combat our ideals." Indeed, anarchists claimed, there were perfectly good and obvious reasons for the rise in militancy: "The social question has been debated in Peru for three decades not because we ape others but because since then capitalism has begun to demonstrate, among us, its monopolizing tendencies and its merciless profiteering." *La Protesta* 5, no. 49 (August 1916) and 1, no. 11 (December 1911), quoted in Pareja, *Anarquismo y sindicalismo*, 53, 54.

13. Miro Quesada, "La moderna crisis social," in Miro Quesada, *Albores de la reforma social*, 21–22.

14. Elmore, Inaugural lecture.

15. Parker, "Peruvian Politics and the Eight-Hour Day."

16. Ulloa y Sotomayor, *¿Conviene establecer una Dirección del Trabajo?*, n.p.

17. Parker, "Peruvian Politics and the Eight-Hour Day," 423.

18. As David Rock notes, social Catholicism argued that "government was fully entitled to act against those 'imbued with bad principles [who] are anxious for revolutionary changes. . . . The state should intervene [against these disturbers], to save the workmen from their seditious acts, and to protect lawful owners from spoliation.'" Rock, "Intellectual Precursors."

19. Cabré, *Conferencia dada al "Circulo de Obreros Católicos."*

20. Belaúnde, *La realidad nacional*, 150–51.

21. On the influence of positivism in Latin America, see Hale, "Political Ideas and Ideologies."

22. See Cueto, *El regreso de las epidemias*; Parker, "Civilizing the City of Kings"; Wilson, "Indian Citizenship"; Contreras, "Maestros, mistis y campesinos"; Aguirre, *The Criminals of Lima*; Muñoz Cabrejo, *Diversiones públicas*;

Mannarelli, *Limpias y modernas*; Drinot, "Moralidad, moda y sexualidad"; Drinot, "Madness, Neurasthenia and 'Modernity.'"

23. Miro Quesada, "La moderna crisis social," in Miro Quesada, *Albores de la reforma social*, 21–22.

24. Li, *The Will to Improve*; Miller and Rose, *Governing the Present*.

25. *Ilustración Obrera*, 13 October 1917.

26. Angulo de Puente Arnao, *Legislación obrera*, 34.

27. *Mundial* 2, no. 68 (2 September 1921). Valdez Tudela, "El problema social," 29.

28. Corpancho, *El problema obrero*, 52.

29. In his recent pioneering study of criminality and prison life in early twentieth-century Lima, Carlos Aguirre suggests that workers were seen and saw themselves as distinct from, and, indeed, superior to, Lima's "dangerous classes." He notes that "the world of labor and the world of crime became, in the eye of experts, discrete territories, each with its own problems and peculiar relationship with the social order," while "workers began to distance themselves from criminals and, to a certain extent, internalized the discourse on honesty and working habits disseminated by the state, the school, the church and even the union." Aguirre, *The Criminals of Lima*, 16. While I endorse this interpretation insofar as I share Aguirre's insistence on the importance of certain values to the self-fashioning of workers, I believe that it needs to be reframed in the context of the discussion in this section. What redeemed, indeed, exalted workers in the eyes of social reformers was their identification with "progress." But elites never ceased to view workers as a potential source of danger to the social order.

30. *La Industria* 1, no. 8 (15 August 1916).

31. *La Industria* 1, no. 1 (11 December 1915).

32. *La Industria* 2, no. 19 (30 May 1917).

33. Rodríguez, "Coaliciones y huelgas."

34. *La Prensa*, 19 January 1918.

35. Coronado, "Génesis, evolución y estado actual de la Legislación Social Peruana."

36. *Peru To-Day* 4, no. 11 (February 1913): 586.

37. Santistevan, *La huelga en el Perú*, 35–44.

38. Blanchard, *The Origins*, 39.

39. Genaro F. Salmon, *Anales de la inspección de trabajo de mujeres y niños del Concejo Provincial de Lima* (Lima, 1924), cited in Miller, "La mujer obrera," 23.

40. Nuñez Borja, *Legislación social peruana*, 112–18. For an analysis of the law with special reference to its impact on children, see Portocarrero Grados, *El trabajo infantil*.

41. Rodgers, *Atlantic Crossings*, 239.
42. Steinmetz, *Regulating the Social*, 168.
43. In *Las memorias de la Ciudad de Lima* (Lima, 1925), 174, cited in Miller, "La mujer obrera," 23.
44. Valdez Tudela, "Nuestra realidad social," 5.
45. Miro Quesada, "La moderna crisis social," in Miro Quesada, *Albores de la reforma social*, 27–28.
46. Miro Quesada, *El contrato de trabajo*, 51–52.
47. Miro Quesada, "El riesgo profesional aplicado al Perú," in Miro Quesada, *Albores de la reforma social*, 43.
48. *Memoria que presenta el Ministro de Justicia, Culto e Instrucción al Congreso Ordinario de 1903* (Lima: Imprenta Torres Aguirre, 1903), 16.
49. Diez Canseco, *Seguro obligatorio*, 19.
50. Hutchison, *Labors Appropriate to Their Sex*, 230.
51. Douglas, *Purity and Danger*.
52. Hutchison, *Labors Appropriate to Their Sex*, 58.
53. AGN/MF/RC/6:121, Inspector General del Trabajo to Jefe de la Sección del Trabajo, 29 December 1932.
54. AGN/PL/3.9.5.1.15.1.1.22, Sección del Trabajo to Prefecto, 27 January 1939.
55. Ulloa Sotomayor, *La organización social y legal*, 233.
56. Echegaray and Silva, *Legislación del trabajo*, 73.
57. Rodgers, *Atlantic Crossings*, 235.
58. Mitchell, *Colonising Egypt*, 76.
59. On the concept of racialization in the Latin American context see Appelbaum, Macpherson, and Rosemblatt, *Race and Nation in Modern Latin America*, especially the introduction, where racialization is defined as "the process of marking human differences according to hierarchical discourses grounded in colonial encounters and their national legacies," 2.
60. Biernacki, *The Fabrication of Labor*, 486.
61. Ibid., 347.
62. *Economista peruano* 2, no. 24 (28 February 1911).
63. Bourdieu, "Rethinking the State," 69.
64. See AGN/Tierras de Montaña/legajo 47, cuaderno 01699, expediente No. 1877, "Expediente relativo al informe que en el proyecto de ley reglamentando las relaciones entre los Patrones y Obreros solicita la H. Cámara de Diputados," 31 August 1903. I am grateful to Walter Huamaní for sharing this document. On Vidaurre's legislative activity, see Blanchard, *The Origins*, chap. 3.
65. Alejandro Garland to Director de Fomento, 2 January 1904, in Dirección de Fomento, Sección de Industrias, "Expediente relativo al informe que en el proyecto de ley reglamentando las relaciones entre los Patrones y Obreros solicita la H. Cámara de Diputados," 31 August 1903.

66. Ulloa Sotomayor, *La organización social*. Ulloa became foreign minister in the 1930s. The review, signed I.S.V., was published in *La Crónica*, 10 October 1916.

67. Ulloa Sotomayor, *La organización social*, 4.

68. Ulloa Sotomayor argued that blacks and Chinese were bound to disappear, "because now that their entry to the country has been stopped and given their low rate of reproduction they will cease to be an ethnic danger." He regretted the fact that the white worker "energetic, dedicated, intelligent, neat, punctual . . . the best type of worker of all" is "almost imperceptible among the working masses." He regretted that immigration programs had not been more successful. Like many others, as I discuss below, Ulloa Sotomayor believed that "the positive influence the white foreigner would have had and would have on his work colleagues, would have modified many of the pernicious habits of the national worker and would have elevated his moral and social level." Ibid., 4, 19–20. On other contemporary ideas about Afro-Peruvians' aptitude for work, see Oliart, "Images of Gender and Race," 61–62. Naturally, such ideas drew on much older views of the Peru's indigenous peoples. See, among others, Pablo Macera's essays "El indio y sus intérpretes peruanos del siglo XVIII" and "El indio visto por los criollos y españoles," in Pablo Macera, *Trabajos de historia*, vol. 2.

69. Alayza Paz Soldán, *La industria moderna*, 42.

70. On racial ideologies in early twentieth-century Peru, see, among others, Marcone, "Indígenas e inmigrantes"; Oliart, "Images of Gender and Race"; Portocarrero, "El fundamento invisible"; Poole, *Vision, Race, and Modernity*; Manrique, *La piel y la pluma*; de la Cadena, *Indigenous Mestizos*.

71. De la Cadena, *Indigenous Mestizos*.

72. The literature on this topic is vast. See, among others, Graham el al. *The Idea of Race*; and Wade, *Race and Ethnicity*. For a more recent interpretation, see Earle, *The Return of the Native*.

73. Stepan, *The Hour of Eugenics*.

74. Ulloa Sotomayor, *La organización*, 10. On "hard" and "soft" inheritance see Wade, *Race, Nature, and Culture*, chap. 3.

75. Ulloa Sotomayor, *La organización*, 12.

76. Ibid., 14–15.

77. Portocarrero, "El fundamento invisible."

78. Kristal, *Una visión urbana de los Andes*.

79. Needless to say, the protection of the Indian and the exaltation of a noble Inca past were the central tenets of *indigenismo* in Peru. On this point, see Méndez, "Incas Sí, Indios No."

80. Naturally, this was not an exclusively Peruvian phenomenon. Elite ideas about the redemptive and racially improving character of labor are to be found throughout Latin America in this period. See, among others, Clark, *The Re-*

demptive Work; Grandin, *The Blood of Guatemala*, especially chap. 6; and Weiner, *Race, Nation, and Market*, especially chap. 2. See also, Jeffrey L. Gould's study of Nicaragua, which suggests that the erasure of indigenous culture operated, in part, through forced and largely successful labor drafts, despite a history of resistance. Gould, *To Die in This Way*. For a somewhat different approach, see Wolfe, "Those That Live by the Work of Their Hands."

81. Luis Esteves, *Apuntes para la historia económica del Perú* (Lima: Imprenta Huallaga, 1882), 41, quoted in Gootenberg, *Imagining Development*, 194.

82. See Luna, "Etat, civilismo et société nationale au Pérou."

83. *La Prensa*, 1 January 1918.

84. *Economista peruano* 2, no. 21 (30 November 1910): 256–57, and continued in 2, no. 23 (31 January 1911).

85. *Boletín de la Sociedad Nacional de Agricultura* 5, no. 1 (July 1900): 3–4.

86. On this point, see Marcone, "Indígenas e inmigrantes", García Jordán, "Reflexiones sobre el Darwinismo social," and Contreras, "¿Inmigración o autogenia?"

87. *Boletín de Minas, Industrias y Construcciones* 3, no. 8 (31 July 1887): 51–54.

88. *El Agricultor Peruano* 10, no. 212 (14 December 1907): 3.

89. *La Agricultura* 5, no. 55 (1920): 12–13.

90. Ibid.

91. To be sure, as I have noted above, such ideas circulated prior to the 1920s. In 1906, for example, Luis Pesce argued that Indians could become productive if put to work alongside foreign migrants: "The Indians from the highlands, when redeemed and transplanted to the coast and the jungle as part of a well conceived plan of internal migration, are the best, indeed the only, elements called upon to undertake everyday agricultural labor in Peru; in fact, they are a constituent part, next to the European worker and capitalist, of the great task of exploiting the natural wealth of the country." Pesce, *Indígenas e inmigrantes*, 37.

92. *La Agricultura* 5, no. 55 (1920): 12–13.

93. *La Agricultura* 5, no. 58 (1920): 16–18.

94. Ibid.

95. *Boletín de la Sociedad Nacional de Agricultura* 4, no. 21 (March 1920): 475.

96. Ibid., 480.

97. *El Nacionalista* 1, no. 10 (September 1932): 4.

98. On Asian labor on Peru's coastal plantations, see, among others, Macera, *Cayaltí*; and Gonzales, *Plantation Agriculture*.

99. Quoted in Macera, *Cayaltí*, 196.

100. On enganche and the proletarianization of Andean labor see, among others, Klarén, *Modernization, Dislocation and Aprismo*; Gonzales, *Plantation Agriculture*; Flores Galindo, *Los mineros de Cerro de Pasco*; Mallon, *Defense of Community*. On cotton, see, Peloso, *Peasants on Plantations*.

101. Alayza Paz Soldán, *El problema del indio*, 5.

102. Ibid., 10.

103. Ibid., 62.

104. Eloy Gregorio Parra, "Industrializar el Perú es la fase final de la solución del problema del indio," *La Revista* 4, no. 153 (7 August 1930): 19.

105. Ferrero, "Destino racial del Perú."

106. "El Perú será fuerte cuando el indio sea apto," *Industria Peruana* 3, no. 12 (July 1933): n.p.

107. On Mariátegui's views on Peru's indigenous population, see Valderrama, "Los planteamientos"; Manrique, "Mariátegui"; and Leibner, *El mito del socialismo indígena*.

108. For the context in which Mariátegui expressed these views, see Flores Galindo, "La agonía de Mariátegui"; and Becker, "Mariátegui."

109. Mariátegui, "El problema," 31.

110. Ibid., 28.

111. Ibid., 31–32.

112. Haya de la Torre, *El anti-imperialismo*, 135.

113. Ibid., 137.

114. Meneses, *Por el APRA*, 40.

115. Ibid., 43. The acknowledgment of Haya de la Torre as the source of the quoted sentence within this passage is in the original.

116. Goldberg, *Racial State*, 2.

117. In some ways, my argument complements Charles Bergquist's contention that the importance of "workers," a term that he also problematizes, to the political history of Latin America, which far outstripped their demographic significance, owed to their strategic position in export sectors. In Peru, I argue, the importance of workers to the political history of the country owes in part to their strategic position in export sectors (sugar, cotton, copper, oil, fishmeal, etc.) as others have shown, but also, and perhaps primarily, to the pervasive racialized valorization of workers over Indians. See Bergquist, *Labor in Latin America*.

118. See, among others, Chevalier, "Official Indigenismo"; Davies, *Indian Integration in Peru*; de la Cadena, *Indigenous Mestizos*; Contreras, "Maestros, mistis y campesinos."

119. Goldberg, *Racial State*, 9.

NOTES TO CHAPTER 2: CONSTITUTING LABOR

1. For an analysis of these strikes, see Klarén, *Modernization, Dislocation and Aprismo*, chap. 2.

2. AGN/MF/RC/1:14, Sección del Trabajo del Ministerio de Fomento to los obreros en huelga, 1 October 1920.

3. See, for example, Sulmont, *El movimiento obrero en el Perú*.

4. *Mensaje del presidente del Perú, Augusto Bernardino Leguía Salcedo, ante el congreso, 28 de julio 1920.* Most presidential speeches, including this one, are available on the website of the Peruvian Congress. See http://www.con greso.gob.pe/museo.htm.

5. Joll, *The Anarchists,* 217.

6. The events are studied in detail in Blanchard, *The Origins of the Peruvian Labor Movement.*

7. Leguía's regime "is still a period of myths, polarized opinions, and even opportunistic speculation." Irurozqui, "El Perú de Leguía," 98.

8. Peter Klarén, for example, notes that Leguía embarked on a "new program of national modernization and reform" and that the Patria Nueva "included a stronger, interventionist state," while Manuel Burga and Alberto Flores Galindo have suggested that Leguía "understood the need to develop the apparatus of the state." Carlos Contreras and Marcos Cueto similarly argue that "the Patria Nueva meant the modernization of the state . . . , export taxes were raised, the state bureaucracy was increased, foreign loans were obtained, and technical agreements, particularly with U.S. agencies and experts, were signed, to modernize health, education, agricultural technology and other public activities." Gonzalo Portocarrero, meanwhile, stresses the acceleration of a process that had been initiated earlier: "the state, led by Leguía, starts to develop assertively the function of promoter and accelerator of progress that had begun to emerge in the previous period." See Klarén, *Peru,* 242; Burga and Flores Galindo, *Apogeo y crisis de la República Aristocrática,* 205; Contreras and Cueto, *Historia del Perú contemporáneo,* 190; Portocarrero, "Ideologías, funciones del estado y políticas económicas," 14.

9. Stein, *Populism in Peru.*

10. Ruiz Zevallos, *La multitud, las subsistencias y el trabajo,* 213. The Partido Popular Cristiano (Christian Popular Party) or PPC, a Christian Democratic Party, was established in the mid-1960s.

11. As James Ferguson suggests in his study of development projects in Lesotho, "what is expanded is not the magnitude of the capabilities of 'the state,' but the extent and reach of a particular kind of exercise of power." *The Anti-Politics Machine,* 274.

12. Manzanilla, *Discursos parlamentarios,* 176–79; Manzanilla, *Elecciones políticas y municipales,* 122; see also Blanchard, *The Origins of the Peruvian Labor Movement,* 37.

13. Angulo Puente Arnao, *Legislación obrera,* 57–61; Núñez, *Legislación social peruana,* 72–75.

14. The short Billinghurst presidency and its prolabor measures are discussed in Blanchard, "A Populist Precursor"; and Huiza, "From the República Aristocrática to Pan Grande."

15. The statutes of the secciones obreras are included in *Memoria que el Minis-*

tro de Gobierno y Policia presenta al Congreso Ordinario de 1913 (Lima: La Opinión Nacional, 1913), 41–45; and reproduced in Angulo de Puente Arnao, *Legislación obrera*, 56–61.

16. On "legibility," see Scott, *Seeing Like a State*.

17. Miro Quesada, "La cuestión obrera en el Perú" [1905], in Miro Quesada, *Albores de la reforma social*, 115–19.

18. Ulloa Sotomayor, *La organización social*, 232.

19. Angulo de Puente Arnao, *Legislación obrera*, 7–9.

20. Miro Quesada, "La cuestión obrera."

21. Puente Arnao, *Legislación obrera*.

22. Ibid.

23. *Ilustración Obrera*, 16 June 1917. Despite its title, this periodical does not seem to have been written by workers. See Sánchez Ortiz, *La prensa obrera*, 50; and Machuca Castillo, *La tinta, el pensamiento, y las manos*, 138–40.

24. *Ilustración Obrera*, 23 June 1917.

25. On Zubiaga's career, see Blanchard, *The Origins of the Peruvian Labor Movement*, 41–46, 162.

26. AGN/PL/3.9.5.1.15.1.11.3, Adrián Zubiaga to Prefecto, 15 October 1914.

27. Manzanilla was, of course, referring to the Treaty of Versailles and the International Labor Office. See Manzanilla, *Discursos parlamentarios*, 176.

28. Ulloa Sotomayor, *La organización social y legal*, 232.

29. Bourdieu, "Rethinking the State," 55.

30. *Memoria que el Ministro de Fomento Dr. D. Julio R. Ego Aguirre presenta al Congreso Ordinario de 1920* (Lima: Imprenta Torres Aguirre, 1921), 26.

31. Jacobsen, *Mirages of Transition*, 345. On official indigenismo, see Chevalier, "Official Indigenismo"; Kapsoli and Reategui, *El campesinado peruano*; and Degregori et al., *Indigenismo, clases sociales y problema nacional*.

32. On this point, see Davies, *Indian Integration in Peru*, 69–77.

33. See, among others, Cueto, "Indigenismo and Rural Medicine"; Fonseca, "Protestantismo, indigenismo y el mundo andino," 282; and Poole, "Figueroa Aznar and the Cusco Indigenistas." On indigenista music, see Turino, "The Music of Andean Migrants."

34. De la Cadena, *Indigenous Mestizos*, 87.

35. The previous constitution, of 1867, had little if anything to say on social guarantees, although article 27 did establish the right to free association.

36. "La carestía de la vida," in Curletti, *Documentos parlamentarios*, 31.

37. León, *Patria Nueva*, 24.

38. FO 371/3894, Manners to Curzon, 16 October 1919.

39. AGN/3.9.5.1.15.1.16.36, Comisario de la Segunda to Subprefecto, 21 April 1919.

40. Ruiz Zevallos, *La multitud*, 207–9.

41. The hierarchical structure of the Sección del Trabajo requires some expla-

nation. The minister of development, appointed by the president, stood at the top of the ladder. This position was essentially a political sinecure: between 1919 and 1929 the position changed hands thirteen times, and with a few notable exceptions, the ministers were rarely involved in the day-to-day running of the ministry. Executive clout within the ministry resided with the directorate heads and the section chiefs (*jefe de sección*). The director was "a technical specialist who prepares the resolutions, who compiles information or orders it done, who oversees the subordinate sections, and who procures at his discretion new bureaucratic services, attending to various other ministerial tasks." Below the directors were the chiefs, who were "generally specialized in their various fields; although there are some who have not the least knowledge of them, but they have auxiliaries to do the work." Herbold Jr., "Developments in the Peruvian Administrative System," 178. Between 1919 and 1929, only two directors were responsible for the General Directorate of Development: Carlos Portella and Enrique Zegarra. The position of chief of the Sección del Trabajo appears to have changed hands more often. Peru, *La labor constructiva*, n.p. Portella appears to have moved relatively early on to head the Mining Directorate, so that much of the General Directorate of Development's policy in the 1920s must be attributed to Zegarra. Unfortunately, I have found almost no biographical data on Zegarra. However, my examination of the documentation reveals that Zegarra worked closely with the incumbent chief of the section.

42. In 1923, Roca left the Sección del Trabajo to take charge of the economics faculty at University of San Marcos, following the purge of the *germancistas* (supporters of German Leguía y Martínez) from government positions. Following the fall of the Leguía regime, he returned to head the General Directorate of Development. In the 1930s Roca helped found the Descentralist Party and was elected to congress. Temoche Benites, *Manual del sindicalista*, 58.

43. In the 1930s, together with Luciano Castillo, a progressive lawyer, Castro Pozo founded a Socialist Party, which in addition to helping to organize oil workers and sharecroppers in the northern department of Piura, provided one of the few democratic voices in congress during the Sánchez Cerro and Benavides governments. On Castro Pozo, see Franco, "Hildebrando Castro Pozo"; Apel, *De la hacienda a la comunidad*; and Leibner, *El mito del socialismo indígena*, 120–28.

44. I draw here on Raymond Craib's analysis of state formation and cartographic knowledge in Mexico. See *Cartographic Mexico*, 161.

45. Rodgers, *Atlantic Crossings*, 283.

46. In a form analogous to the development projects studied by James Ferguson in Zambia in *The Anti-Politics Machine*, Li in Indonesia in *The Will to Improve*, and Mitchell in Egypt in *Rule of Experts*, where "the politics of na-

tional development and economic growth was a politics of techno-science, which claimed to bring the expertise of modern engineering, technology, and social science to improve the defects of nature, to transform peasant agriculture, to repair the ills of society and to fix the economy," 15.

47. Curletti, *El problema industrial*, 18–19.
48. *Mundial* 2, no. 40 (28 January 1921): n.p. The article mistakes Castro Pozo's first name, giving it as Humberto rather than Hildebrando.
49. Scott, *Seeing Like a State*.
50. Nuñez, *Legislación social peruana*, 140.
51. I draw here on Chandra Mukerji's work on the naturalization of power in the state. For Mukerji the gardens at Versailles not only symbolized or represented the power of the absolutist state in seventeenth-century France, they demonstrated it by showing "political order as an extension of natural order." Mukerji, *Territorial Ambitions*, 298. This section draws more generally on my reading of Mukerji and of the work of scholars such as Patrick Carroll, Raymond Craib, and Timothy Mitchell, who have put forward similar arguments in relation to, respectively, engineering in nineteenth-century Ireland, cartography in twentieth-century Mexico, and the economy in twentieth-century Egypt. Carroll, *Science, Culture, and Modern State Formation*; Craib, *Cartographic Mexico*; Mitchell, *Rule of Experts*.
52. Carroll, *Science, Culture, and Modern State Formation*, 167.
53. Delfín Levano, "El malestar social," in *La Protesta* 8, no. 85 (first half of August, 1920), cited in Pareja, *Anarquismo y sindicalismo*, 47.
54. *El Obrero Textil* 1, no. 1 (22 November 1919).
55. Pareja, *Anarquismo y sindicalismo*, 47; Kapsoli, *Mariátegui*, 90.
56. Li, *The Will to Improve*, 231.
57. Núñez, *Legislación social peruana*, 138.
58. See, for example, AGN/MI/262/Particulares, Sociedad de Obreros "Billinghurst Confederada No 1" to Ministro de Gobierno, 1 January 1925.
59. Hill, *Report* (1923), 16; Peru, Ministerio de Fomento, *La labor constructiva*, n.p.
60. Hill, *Report*, 16.
61. *Memoria que el Ministro de Fomento, Dr. D Julio E. Ego-Aguirre presenta al Congreso Ordinario de 1920* (Lima: Imprenta Torres Aguirre, 1921), n.p.
62. F. C. Central del Perú, *Sistema de pagos y pactos con empleados y obreros 1950*, 1–7. I am grateful to Francisco Nuñez Gonzales for sharing this document with me.
63. AGN/MF/RC/9:161, "Fallo arbitral—Obreros 1919."
64. Miller, "Railways and Economic Development," 45.
65. Pévez, *Memorias*, 117.
66. Ibid., 139–40.
67. On artisans and the impact of economic liberalism in the nineteenth cen-

tury, see Gootenberg, *Between Silver and Guano,* and Garcia-Bryce, *Crafting the Republic.*

68. On artisans and the Partido Civil, see McEvoy, *Un proyecto nacional en el siglo XIX;* McEvoy, *La utopía repúblicana;* Muecke, *Political Culture in Nineteenth-Century Peru.* See also, Forment, *Democracy in Latin America.*

69. Among the earlier strikes were bakery workers (1887), Central Railway workers, typographers, and manual cigarette makers (1892), Callao dockworkers (1894), and Vitarte textile workers (1896).

70. Anarchists claimed that the mutual aid societies were archaic institutions that had nothing to offer the working class. According to Manuel Caracciolo Levano they did little more than "help the sick and bury the dead." Quote in Tejada, *La cuestión del pan,* 188.

71. In addition to Lima, anarchist groups were organized in the haciendas that surrounded Lima, particularly in the Ate and Carabayllo valleys and in several ports on the Peruvian coast. Pereda Torres, *Historia de las luchas sociales,* 115–16. See also Ramos Rau, *Mensaje de Trujillo,* 60–73.

72. Rancière, "The Myth of the Artisan."

73. Tejada, *La cuestión del pan,* 250–56. According to one article published in 1904 in *Los Parias,* "The Fatherland is the pretext used so that a few dozen ne'er-do-wells can live from the labor of others." In García Salvatecci, *El anarquismo,* 121.

74. CEDHIP, interview with Isaias Contreras.

75. Burga and Flores Galindo, *Apogeo y crisis,* 241.

76. Temoche, *Cofradías, gremios, mutuales y sindicatos,* 179–80.

77. Pareja, *Anarquismo y sindicalismo,* 1978, 62.

78. Temoche, *Cofradías, gremios, mutuales y sindicatos,* 192. The debate over the Universidades Populares González Prada confirmed the anarchists' isolation from the mainstream labor movement. On the UPGP, see Klaiber, "The Popular Universities"; Chanamé O[rbe], "Haya de la Torre y la Universidades Populares"; and Portocarrero, "José Carlos Mariátegui y las Universidades Populares González Prada."

79. Sabroso, *Replicas proletarias,* 55–57.

80. Ruth Thompson makes a similar argument for the Argentine case. See "The Limitations of Ideology."

81. AGN/MF/RC/6:119, Aumento acordado entre la Unificación y la Dirección de la Fábrica de Santa Catalina, 7 October 1920.

82. Pévez, *Memorias,* 124.

83. AGN/MF/RC/1:14, Asamblea General Obrera to Ministro Fomento, 15 February 1921.

84. See *Labor,* 29 December 1928.

85. For an analysis of "individual" white-collar grievances, see Parker, *The Idea of the Middle Class,* chaps. 4 and 5.

86. AGN/MF/RC/1:2 (Caylloma miners); AGN/MF/RC/3:61 (Negritos oil workers); AGN/MF/RC/1:4 (Casa Grande sugar workers); AGN/MF/RC/2:41 (Otuzco sharecroppers).

87. See AGN/MF/RC/2:33 (Mollendo stevedores); AGN/MF/RC/3:55 (Callao port workers); AGN/MF/RC/2:35 (Central Railway).

88. See AGN/MF/RC/2:37 (carpenters); AGN/MF/RC/2:40 (masons).

89. See AGN/MF/RC/1:7 (shoemakers); AGN/MF/RC/1:8 (printworkers); AGN/MF/RC/1:13 (bakery workers); AGN/MF/RC/1:15 (electricians).

90. See AGN/MF/RC/3:62 (pasta workers); AGN/MF/RC/3:63 (San Jacinto textile workers).

91. See AGN/MF/RC/3:54 (La Estrella); AGN/MF/RC/2:22 (Negociación Villa); AGN/MF/RC/2:27 (Santa Barbara); AGN/MF/RC/3:46 (Puente Piedra).

92. AGN/MF/RC/2:23 (tramway workers); AGN/MF/RC/2:29 (power plants).

93. AGN/MF/RC/1:6 (telephone workers); AGN/MF/RC/2:26 (hotel workers); AGN/MF/RC/2:28 (Compañia de Zarzuela); AGN/MF/RC/3:58 (Comité Pro-Derecho Indígena).

94. AGN/OL/802–258, Consuelo Salvi, Carmen Rosa Figueroa, Victoria Torres, F. Mini, Antonieta Tasso, Rosa Igobichi, and Angelica Gonzalez to Ministro de Fomento, 11 December 1920.

95. Cooper, *Decolonization and African Society*, 16.

NOTES TO CHAPTER 3: DISCIPLINING LABOR

1. AGN/MI/229/Fomento, Ministerio de Fomento to Ministro de Gobierno, 16 January 1922.

2. Rodgers, *Atlantic Crossings*, 305.

3. AGN/PL/3.9.5.1.15.1.16.38, Intendente de Policía to Prefecto, 29 October 1921.

4. AGN/PL/3.9.5.1.15.1.13.12, Lisandro Márquez and Molino Puerto Supe to Prefecto, 8 August 1920.

5. Echegaray and Silva, *Legislación del trabajo*.

6. AGN/MF/RC/1:10, Settlement, 29 January 1921.

7. AGN/MF/RC/3:46, Unificación de Campesinos de Carabayllo Alto to Sección del Trabajo, 26 February 1922.

8. agn/PL, 3.9.5.1.15.1.13.14, Federación de Mosaistas to Prefecto, 27 June 1923.

9. AGN/PL/3.9.5.1.15.1.13.14, Federación de Electricistas del Perú to Prefecto, 1 October 1923.

10. AGN/MF/RC/1:10, Unificación de Braceros de la Hacienda El Naranjal to Sección del Trabajo, 21 April 1921.

11. AGN/PL/3.9.5.1.15.1.13.18, Federación de Fideleros y Molineros to Prefecto, 26 January 1926.

12. AGN/MF/RC/1:15, Federación de Electricistas del Perú to Jefe de la Sección del Trabajo, 26 February 1921.

13. AGN/MI/221/Relaciones Exteriores, Ministerio de Relaciones Exteriores to Ministro de Gobierno, 4 January 1921.

14. Pévez, *Memorias*, 178.

15. A similar union was organized in the Cartavio hacienda in 1935. Glener Plasencia, "Aprismo, sindicalismo y movimiento obrero," 57–58.

16. *Variedades*, año 22, no. 970, 2 October 1926, n.p.

17. AGN/PL/3.9.5.1.15.1.1.13.11, Alfredo D. Torres, Unión Imprentas, to Prefect, 10 October 1919.

18. AGN/PL/3.9.5.1.15.1.1.15, Carlos Fabbri to FGP, 4 January 1924.

19. See *Labor*, 2 February 1929. The measures do not appear to have had the effect Mariátegui predicted; La Victoria workers took an active part in the labor unrest that characterized the 1930s.

20. AML (Archivo Municipal de Lima), box "Policía 1919–1923," Federación Gráfica del Perú to Alcalde del Concejo Provincial, 5 March 1923.

21. Peru, *Statistical Abstract*, 137.

22. Pévez, *Memorias*, 181–82.

23. FOPEP (Federation of Bakery Workers "Star of Peru"), 12 August 1922.

24. AGN/PL/3.9.5.1.15.1.13.18, FOPEP to Prefecto, 26 July 1926.

25. AGN/PL/3.9.5.1.15.1.13.19, Alejandro Antón to Prefecto, 28 March 1927.

26. AGN/PL/3.9.5.1.15.1.13.18, Fabrica de Tejidos de San Jacinto to Prefecto de Lima, 14 May 1926.

27. AGN/PL/3.9.5.1.15.1.16.47, Vigilante to Oficial Segundo, 26 December 1929.

28. FGP (Federación Gráfica del Perú), *Historia*, 62.

29. AGN/MF/RC/1:1, Humberto Ibañez to Director of the Sección del Trabajo, 13 March 1920.

30. AGN/MF/RC/1:1, Humberto Ibañez to Director of the Sección del Trabajo, 10 June and 21 May 1920 and 12 and 16 March 1922.

31. FGP, *Historia*, 123. The FGP used the term "Labor Office" here to refer to the Sección del Trabajo.

32. *El Obrero Gráfico*, 1 May 1923.

33. AGN/PL/3.9.5.1.15.1.13.14, Sarmiento to Prefecto, 7 September 1924.

34. AGN/PL/3.9.5.1.15.1.13.16, included in Enrique Zegarra to Prefect, 16 May 1925.

35. *La Revista del Foro* 8, no. 9 (September 1919): 199–203.

36. *La Revista del Foro* 8, no 2 (February 1921): 57–59.

37. Ibid, 59.

38. "El paro general," *La Mujer Peruana*, 28 June 1919, n.p.

39. "¡Viva la huelga!," in *Hogar* 1, no. 42 (1920): n.p.

40. "La huelga en la hacienda 'Roma,'" in *Hogar* 2, no. 65 (1921): n.p.

41. *Mundial*, 14 May 1920.

42. *Variedades*, 15 October 1921, 1597.

43. *Variedades*, 19 January 1924, n.p.; 26 January 1924, n.p; 15 March 1924, n.p. *Mundial* had a similar page, written by Federico Ortiz Rodríguez.

44. *Variedades*, 19 January 1924, n.p; 2 February 1924, n.p.

45. *Variedades*, 5 January 1924, n.p. On the Fiesta de la Planta, see Tapia, "La Fiesta de la Planta"; on the Universidades Populares, see Klaiber, "The Popular Universities"; Chanamé Orbe, "Haya de la Torre y la Universidades Populares"; and Portocarrero, "José Carlos Mariátegui."

46. AGN/PL/3.9.5.1.15.1.11.6, Inspector de Investigación to Subprefecto, 21 January 1928.

47. On Lima's carnival, see Rojas Rojas, *Tiempos de Carnaval*.

48. *Variedades*, 23 February 1924.

49. *Variedades*, 1 March 1924.

50. *Variedades*, 2 February 1924. Rafael Larco Hoyle was Víctor Larco Herrera's nephew.

51. *Variedades*, 25 October 1924.

52. *Variedades*, 25 October 1924.

53. *Variedades*, 11 June 1927.

54. *Mundial*, 10 June 1927.

55. Several historians locate the point of inflection in 1923, when Leguía's attempt to consecrate the nation to the Sacred Heart of Jesus produced student protests that were firmly repressed, resulting in the exile of a number of student leaders including, most famously, Victor Raúl Haya de la Torre. See, for example, Stein, *Populism in Peru*, 78. Others argue that the change came much earlier. According to Sulmont, "Leguía had only sporadic bouts of popular support and soon his populism gave way to a policy of systematic repression and control"; *El movimiento obrero*, 91. This general understanding of the period produces an interpretation of Leguía's labor policy that emphasizes inconsistency at best and outright betrayal at worst. A common formulation suggests that, having benefited from mass support (particularly from organized labor) in order to reach power, Leguía then turned his back on popular forces and began to draw his support from an unholy alliance of predatory foreign capital (selling Peru to U.S. monopoly capital—particularly to firms such as the Foundation Company, which "modernized" large parts of Lima and oil and mining interests) and (although the contradiction is seldom noted) an emergent industrial bourgeoisie. It was therefore inevitable that Leguía would renege on his early opening to labor and repress it actively in accordance with the interests of his new allies. The classic formulation is in Caravedo Molinari, *Clases, lucha política y gobierno*, but it is reprised in various texts, including Burga and Flores Galindo, *Apogeo y crisis*.

56. *Mensaje presentado al congreso ordinario por el Presidente de la República Augusto B. Leguía* (Lima, 1928), 114–15.

57. Peru, *Statistical Abstract*, 137.

58. Pévez, *Memorias*, 201.

59. AGN/PL/3.9.5.1.15.1.2.36, Director General de la Guardia Civil y Policía to Prefecto, 29 August 1924.

60. AGN/MI/224/Diversos, Consulado del Perú, Pará, to Director de Gobierno, 9 April 1921; AGN/MI/229/Relaciones Exteriores, Ministerio de Relaciones Exteriores to Director de Gobierno, 15 December 1921 and 21 January 1922; AGN/MI/227/Callao, Prefectura del Callao to Director de Gobierno, 20 January 1920.

61. AGN/MI/258/Relaciones Exteriores, Ministerio de Relaciones Exteriores to Ministro de Gobierno, 10 November 1925. Pavlevitch, or Pavletich as he appears in other documents and in his own writings, born in the cocaine producing area of Huánuco to a family of Croatian immigrants, played a key role in the political history of several Latin American countries, including Nicaragua, where he participated in Sandino's insurrection. With Terreros, who later returned to Peru in the early 1930s to briefly lead the Peruvian Communist Party, and Jacobo Hurwitz, a Peruvian born to German Jewish immigrants, Pavletich set up an APRA cell in Mexico City in 1927. See Bergel, "Nomadismo Proselitista."

62. AGN/MI/261A/Relaciones Exteriores, Ministerio de Relaciones Exteriores to Ministro de Gobierno, 12 July 1926.

63. AGN/MI/248/Relaciones Exteriores, Ministerio de Relaciones Exteriores to Director de Gobierno, 7 March 1924.

64. AGN/MI/228/Lambayeque, Prefectura de Lambayeque to Director de Gobierno, 28 September 1922.

65. AGN/MI/238/La Libertad, Prefectura de La Libertad to Director de Gobierno, 6 July 1923.

66. AGN/MI/267A/Diversos, Dirección General de la Guardia Civil y Policía, 5 October 1926.

67. See Skuban, *Lines in the Sand*.

68. *Variedades*, 10 January 1925, 4.

69. AGN/MI/236/Callao, Prefecto del Callao to Subprefecto, 28 April 1923.

70. AGN/MI/231/Diputados, Gobernación de Tinyahuarco to Subprefecto de Cerro de Pasco, 12 March 1922.

71. AGN/MI/231/ Diputados, Secretaría de la Cámara de Diputados to Ministro de Gobierno, 3 January 1922.

72. AGN/MI/267A/Diputados, Cámara de Diputados to Ministro de Gobierno, 7 January 1926.

73. AGN/MI/228/La Libertad, Prefectura de La Libertad to Director de Gobierno, 7 March 1922.

74. AGN/MI/278/Lima, Prefectura de Lambayeque to Director de Gobierno, 23 October 1928.

75. AGN/PL/3.9.5.1.15.1.13.20, Fabrica de Tejidos La Unión to Prefecto de Lima, 5 December 1929.

76. AGN/PL/3.9.5.1.15.1.13.15, Samuel Vásquez and Federación de Chauffeurs to Prefecto, 17 November 1925.

77. AGN/PL/3.9.5.1.15.1.16.44, Arturo Sabroso and Secretario General, FOLL, to Intendente, 15 January 1927.

78. AGN/PL/3.9.5.1.15.1.16.44, Subprefecto to Prefecto, 28 January 1927.

79. AGN/MI/264/Particulares, CAUU to Ministro de Gobierno y Policía, 5 May 1926; AGN/MI/261/Particulares, ASU to Presidente de la República, 18 September 1925.

80. AGN/MI/268/Huaraz, Manifiesto de la CAUU a la clase trabajadora de la República, 1 April 1927.

81. AGN/MI/278/Lima, Prefectura de Lima to Director de Gobierno, 10 May 1928.

82. AGN/MI/290/Particulares, CAUU to Ministro de Gobierno, 7 June 1929. The mutual aid societies did on occasion use their positions of influence to what could be considered positive effect. In June 1929, the CAUU requested the minister of government's intervention to curb the excesses of district governors and landlords in Santiago de Chuco, who extorted "free services" and "*fainas* [faenas-labor tasks], that is to say four days of unpaid work, as well as coerced enganche for the coast, offering or imposing derisory wages." In July 1930, it protested at the 25 percent increase in the price of fares on the Lima to Callao tramway, owned by the Empresas Electricas Asociadas. The CAUU pointed out that such an increase was unacceptable given the country was facing "the deepest crisis." It noted that the "proletarian class" had moved to the new out-of-town neighborhoods in order to find affordable housing: "The interests of these neighbors and modest landlords would be deeply undermined if some streetcar routes are eliminated, if the number of buses is reduced or if the price of tickets is raised EVEN IF ONLY BY A MINIMUM AMOUNT, as the Empresas Electricas Asociadas are trying to do." Despite such measures, the mutual aid organizations came to be seen as mere lackeys of the regime, and following the collapse of the Patria Nueva, they became one of the main targets of anti-Leguía attacks. AGN/MI/290/Particulares, CAUU to Ministro de Gobierno, 27 June and 19 August 1929.

83. Cotler, *Clases, estado y nación*, 190–91.

84. *Variedades*, 16 October 1926, n.p.

85. *Variedades*, 19 July 1924, 1760.

86. *Variedades*, 9 August 1924, 1948.

87. *Variedades*, 6 September 1924, 2204.

88. Quoted in Burga and Flores Galindo, *Apogeo y crisis*, 215.

89. *Variedades*, 18 October 1924, n.p.

90. Cited in Kristal, *Una visión urbana de los Andes*, 181.

91. Pereyra Chávez, "Los campesinos y la conscripción víal."

92. *Ciudad y Campo y Caminos* 8 (July 1925): 39.

93. *Ciudad y Campo y Caminos* 38 (March–April 1928): 41.

94. AGN/PL/3.9.5.1.15.1.1.18, Erasmo Roca to Prefecto, 21 October 1930.

95. *Boletín Oficial de la Dirección General de Fomento* 1–2 (1933): 78.

96. In April 1931 he requested that the prefecture forward data on worker accidents and a month later asked for information on strikes. The following month, similar letters were sent out to prefectures in the rest of the country. AGN/PL/3.9.1.15.1.1.18, Erasmo Roca to Prefecto, 15 April 1931 and AGN/PL/3.9.5.1.15.1.1.19, Erasmo Roca to Prefecto, 19 May 1931; ADC/6, Ministerio de Fomento to Prefecto del Cuzco, 19 May 1931.

97. AGN/MF/RC/4:70, Chávez Fernández to Director de Fomento, 14 August 1930.

98. Rodgers, *Atlantic Crossings*, 418.

99. AGN/MI/311/Lima, Prefecto del Departamento to Director de Gobierno, 26 May 1931.

100. Castillo even advertised his services in Mariátegui's *Labor*: "Luciano Castillo —Lawyer—Specializes in the legal defense of employees and workers." *Labor*, 24 November 1928, 6.

101. Costa y Cavero, *Los reclamos de los trabajadores*.

102. On the strikes in the mining centers, see Flores Galindo, *Los mineros de la Cerro de Pasco*; and Mallon, *The Defense of Community*. On the general strike, see Martínez de la Torre, *Apuntes para una interpretación marxista*, vol. 1, 130–90; Dawson, "Politics and the Labour Movement," chap. 7.

103. *La Tribuna*, 31 May 1931.

104. On the Trujillo revolution, see Giesecke, "The Trujillo Insurrection"; and García-Bryce, "A Revolution Remembered."

105. In late 1932, for example, in requesting authorization to hold sessions, the brewery workers' union stressed: "Our union is more humanitarian than struggle-based [*de lucha*], because it is some time now since we separated from the CGTP." AGN/PL/3.9.5.1.15.1.11.8, Unificación de Obreros Cerveceros Backus y Johnston to Prefecto, 24 December 1932.

106. AGN/PL/3.9.5.1.15.1.11.11, Jefe de la Brigada de Asuntos Sociales to Jefe General, 24 January 1934.

107. AGN/PL/3.9.5.1.15.1.1.19, Manuel Vigil to Prefecto, 21 September 1932.

108. AGN/PL/3.9.5.1.15.1.1.19, Manuel Vigil to Ministro de Gobierno, 25 October 1932.

109. *Boletín de la Dirección General de Fomento* 3, no. 11 (1935): 35–36.

110. *Boletín de la Dirección General de Fomento* 3, no. 11 (1935): 76. According to the British minister, the office was set up "in order to avoid unnecessary complications arising from the inefficient defence by attorneys pleading the cause of a laborer." FO 371/18721, Forbes to Hoare, 26 July 1935. Later, in

1942, the directorate was transferred to the Ministry of Justice and, finally, in 1949, President Odría created the Ministry of Labor and Indian Affairs. Herbold, "Developments in the Peruvian Administrative System," 152–58, 334–35; Payne, *Labor and Politics in Peru*, 57.

111. The 1933 constitution and the constituent congress that created it is the subject of Balbi and Madalengoitia, *Parlamento y lucha política*. Unfortunately, the authors have little to say about the constitution's provisions with regard to labor.

112. *Libertad*, 3 January 1931.

113. Herbold, "Developments," 155.

114. Peru, *La labor*, n.p.

115. The inspectorate in Arequipa had a yearly budget of 1,000 soles. *El Comercio*, 24 November 1931. In July 1932, the labor inspector in Arequipa begged the prefect to return a booklet that contained the laws and regulations that governed the inspectorate. It was his only copy. More revealing, and ironic, is the fact that, in late 1933, the same inspector wrote to a local labor union to request its assistance. He pointed out that he had not been paid for eight months and hoped the union would help him. ADA/108, Inspección Regional del Trabajo to Prefect of Arequipa, 5 July 1932; ADA/110, Jefe de la Brigada to Sargento Mayor, 10 December 1933.

116. ADC/11, L. Boza to Prefecto del Cuzco, 11 March 1936. In the provinces, and particularly in Arequipa (traditionally hostile to Lima), the inspectorates were perceived as impositions from Lima, and, as such, were strongly opposed by both workers and employers. A project to replace the inspectorate with a regional labor delegation based in Arequipa was warmly greeted by the Arequipa daily *Noticias*, 11 and 12 May 1934.

117. Martínez de la Torre, *Apuntes para una interpretación marxista*, vol. 3, 85, 124.

118. *La Tribuna*, 14 June and 13 July 1931.

119. *Boletín de la Dirección General de Fomento* (1935): 38–39.

120. AGN/PL/3.9.5.1.15.1.11.11, FTTP to Prefecto, 10 December 1934.

121. AGN/PL/3.9.5.1.15.1.11.14, Federación de Motoristas to Prefecto, 18 May 1936.

122. See AGN/MF/RC/4:73; AGN/MF/RC/5:97; AGN/MF/RC/8:150; AGN/MF/RC/16:233; and AGN/MF/RC/4:86.

123. See AGN/MF/RC/10:167 and AGN/MF/RC/11:178.

124. AGN/MF/RC, 5:106, Representatives of industriales to President of the Tribunal Arbitral, 30 August 1931.

125. AGN/MF/RC, 5:106, Representatives of industriales to President of the Tribunal Arbitral, 30 August 1931.

126. AGN/MF/RC, 5:106, Representatives of industriales to President of the Tribunal Arbitral, 10 September 1931.

127. AGN/MF/RC, 5:106, Gutiérrez to Tribunal Arbitral, 4 September 1931.

128. AGN/MF/RC/4:70, SC Silva to Jefe de la Sección del Trabajo, 8 July 1930.

129. ADA/112: Gerente Hilton and Fabrica el Huaico to Prefect, 22 November 1933.

130. AGN/MF/RC/7:134, Pedro Alvarado, Secretario General, Sindicato Textil de San Jacinto to Presidente del Tribunal Arbitral, 10 March 1930.

131. See Drinot, "Fighting for a Closed Shop"; and Drinot, "Hegemony from Below."

132. *El Obrero Gráfico*, 4 September 1940.

NOTES TO CHAPTER 4: DOMESTICATING LABOR

1. *Acción Social y Obras por la Junta Departamental de Lima Pro-Desocupados, 1931–1934* (Lima: Imprenta Torres Aguirre, 1935), n.p.

2. Scott, *Weapons of the Weak*.

3. In nineteenth-century Paris, for example, bourgeois promoters of the "cité ouvrière" argued that "removed from the environment where they became 'envious, greedy, revolutionary, skeptical and eventually communist,' in a single step workers could be placed in healthful surroundings, tied to the political order, and separated from the unregenerate and criminal elements who populated congested areas of the city." Similarly, in "Red Vienna," socialist municipal authorities intended the "peoples' palaces" they were building "to be more than better housing. They were to provide the all-important environment in which the worker family would be socialized so as to become *ordentlich* and be educated by an emerging party culture in the direction of 'nueue Menschen.'" In colonial Bombay, the City Improvement Trust was charged with replacing "the squalor and overcrowding that characterized the hovels of the poor . . . by new sanitary housing, designed to improve the working class morally and display the benevolence of the city's rulers." In early twentieth-century Spain, reforming elites believed that adequate housing would successfully wean male workers off alcohol and lead to the constitution of families that would contribute to the regeneration of the Spanish "race." See Shapiro, "Paris," 56; Gruber, *Red Vienna*, 63; Kidambi, "Housing the Poor in a Colonial City," 58; Campos Marín, "Casas para obreros." In Latin America too, such views shaped social housing policies. In Colombia, for example, Carlos Ernesto Noguera argues, projects to build hygienic houses for workers corresponded to a "medico-political" strategy to instill bourgeois values and "urbanity," a specific form of being-in-the-city, in the working classes of Bogotá and Medellín. Noguera, *Medicina y política*, 127–49.

4. Rodgers, *Atlantic Crossings*, 399.

5. The 1930s "revolutionary" crisis and the labor movement is examined in Deustua and Flores Galindo, "Los comunistas y el movimiento obrero"; Caravedo Molinari, *Clases, lucha política y gobierno*; Quijano, *El Perú en la*

crisis de los años treinta; Balbi, *El Partido Comunista y el* APRA; Stein, *Populism in Peru*; Anderle, *Los movimientos políticos en el Perú*; Pareja Pflucker, *El movimiento obrero peruano*; Derpich and Israel, *Obreros frente a la crisis*. The economics of the period are examined in Thorp and Londoño, "The Effect of the Great Depression."

6. On incorporation, see Collier and Collier, *Shaping the Political Arena*.

7. Portocarrero, *De Bustamante a Odría*, 49.

8. James, *Resistance and Integration*, 34.

9. Quoted in López Soria, *El pensamiento fascista*, 101.

10. Although this rhetoric resonated with Italian corporatism, so did the rhetoric of interwar social politics in most countries in Latin America, Europe, and in the United States. As Orazio Ciccarelli has shown, Benavides "obviously had no intellectual commitment to fascism," in contrast to what contemporary critics claimed and some historians maintain. See Ciccarelli, "Fascism and Politics," 432.

11. *El General Benavides a la Nación, Mensaje del 25 de Marzo de 1939* (Lima: Oficina de Informaciones del Perú, [1939]), 4.

12. Ibid., 55.

13. Ibid., 56–57.

14. For a useful conceptual discussion on populism, see Knight, "Populism and Neo-Populism in Latin America."

15. As Daniel James suggests, Argentine workers were drawn to Peronism because of the concrete material gains that resulted from "incorporation" but also because it entailed "an expanded notion of the meaning of citizenship and the workers' relations with the state, and a 'heretical' social component which spoke to working-class claims to greater social status, dignity within the workplace and beyond, and a denial of the elites' social and cultural pretensions." But crucially, this was no mere instrumental relationship: Peronism was shaped by its constituent forces. As James pithily notes, "Peronism in an important sense defined itself, and was defined by its working-class constituency as a movement of political and social opposition, as a denial of the dominant elite's power, symbols and values." It was the Argentine working class that gave Peronism its political purchase. James, *Resistance and Integration*, 263, 34; For the Brazilian case, see French, *The Brazilian Workers' ABC*.

16. Ramón Joffré, *La muralla y los callejones*; Lossio, *Acequias y gallinazos*.

17. Cueto, *El regreso de las epidemias*.

18. See Muñoz Cabrejo, *Diversiones públicas*.

19. See, for example, Meade, *Civilizing Rio*; Outtes, "Disciplining Society through the City"; Overmyer-Velázquez, *Visions of the Emerald City*.

20. Rodgers, *Atlantic Crossings*, 160.

21. On housing policy in this period, see Ludeña Urquizo, *Lima: Städtebau und*

Wohnungswesen; Parker, "Civilizing the City of Kings"; Proyecto Historia UNI, *Construyendo el Perú*; Ludeña Urquizo, *Lima: Historia y urbanismo*; Cabello Ortega, "Urbanismo estatal en Lima Metropolitana." On the pathologization of workers' dwellings, see also Callirgos, "Reinventing the City of Kings," 199–213.

22. *La Colmena—Sociedad anónima de construcciones y ahorros* (Lima: Tipografía de El País, 1900), 1.

23. For a useful discussion of Paulet's and León García's proposals for worker housing in the 1900s, see Callirgos, "Reinventing the City of Kings," 214–28.

24. Parker, "Civilizing the City of Kings," 163–64.

25. *La Crónica*, 16 December 1918.

26. *La Crónica*, 10 October 1916.

27. *Variedades* 17, no. 716 (19 November 1921).

28. Davila Cardenas, *La función del Estado*, n.p.

29. *Ciudad y Campo* 1 (July 1924): 11.

30. Description of callejón taken from Stein, *Populism in Peru*, 67. A detailed description of the various forms of housing in Lima in this period is Calderón, *La casa limeña*, 41–71.

31. *Variedades* 17, no. 708 (1 October 1921): 1495–96.

32. AGN/MF/Gremios 1:18, Moisés Azana et al. to Augusto Leguía, 25 October 1921.

33. See Tejada, "Malambo"; and del Aguíla, *Callejones y mansiones*. An analysis of one particular callejón is Dreifuss Serrano, "Ciudad y vivienda colectiva republicana."

34. Alexander, *Estudio sobre la crisis de la habitación*.

35. Ibid., 51.

36. Ludeña Urquizo, *Lima: Stadtebau und Wohnungswesen*, 125–46.

37. *Lima, 1919–1930* ([Lima]: no publisher, [1935?]), 29.

38. See *Ciudad y Campo y Caminos* 5, no. 37 (January–February 1928): 38–39; and 6, no. 43 (January–February 1929): 41–43.

39. *La Prensa*, 19 March 1928.

40. *Lima, 1919–1930*, 200.

41. *Variedades* 23, no. 986 (22 January 1927): n.p.

42. *Mundial* 7, no. 331 (15 October 1926).

43. *Mundial* [8], no. 421 (6 July 1928).

44. Stein, *Populism*, 51, 65.

45. *Alma Obrera* 1, no. 1 (2 April 1931): 14; and 1, no. 2 (11 April 1931): 10–11.

46. *Alma Obrera* 1, no. 2 (11 Apr. 1931): 11.

47. As Mark Swenarton has shown, during the parliamentary debates in the U.K. House of Commons on the Housing Bill in 1919, one member of parliament argued that "present housing conditions are the real, and in fact the only, reasons for social unrest," while others suggested that "it was bad

housing that drove a man to thoughts of Bolshevism, and that the answer to unrest was to provide a man with a 'real home.'" In Ireland, by the 1910s even conservative voices had begun to associate labor militancy with poor housing conditions, with the *Irish Times* noting that "the condition of the Dublin slums is responsible not only for disease and crime but for much of our industrial unrest" and adding "if every unskilled laborer in Dublin were the tenant of a decent cottage of three or even two rooms, the city would not be divided into two hostile camps." Such concerns produced debates among architects, urban planners, and politicians regarding the appropriate form or design of worker housing. In 1930s Argentina, for example, conservatives rejected multifamily housing on the grounds that the clustering of workers aided the spread of revolutionary ideas and favored instead single-family housing. Meanwhile, socialists argued that multifamily housing helped "to create communities based on equality and solidarity." In 1940s Brazil, the Realengo housing estate in Rio de Janeiro was designed according to principles that reflected the political anxieties and social engineering ideas of social reformers and not according to the needs of the tenants. As a consequence, as soon as the tenants could afford to make alterations, many aspects of the houses were changed, such as the small kitchens that prevented the sort of socialization that workers favored but social reformers feared. Swenarton, *Homes Fit for Heroes*, 85; McManus, "Blue Collars, 'Red Forts,' and Green Fields," 42; Aboy, "'The Right to a Home,'" 501; Mangabeira, "Memories of Little Moscow (1943–64)," 279.

48. FO 371/18720, Forbes to Simon, 25 April 1935.
49. *Memoria de la Junta Departamental de Lima Pro-Desocupados, 1942, 1943 y 1944* (Lima: Tipografía Peruana, 1946), n.p.
50. *El Comercio*, 5 April 1933.
51. *Memoria al 31 de diciembre de 1934 de la Junta Departamental de Lima Pro-Desocupados* (Lima: Imprenta Torres Aguirre, 1935), xxv; *Memoria de la Junta Departamental de Lima Pro-Desocupados, 1935–1936* (Lima: Imprenta Torres Aguirre), 1937, xix; *Memoria de la Junta Departamental de Lima Pro-Desocupados, 1937–1938* (Lima: Sanmartí, 1939), xxiv; *Memoria de la Junta Departamental de Lima Pro-Desocupados, 1939, 1940, y 1941* (Lima: Empresa Gráfica T. Scheuch, 1943), 23.
52. *Variedades*, 5 August 1931.
53. *Memoria 1934 Junta Departamental de Lima*, 2–5.
54. For a discussion of the ways in which architects and planners in the early twentieth century came to see the interiors as well as the exteriors of buildings as means to compel certain forms of behavior, see Jerram, *Germany's Other Modernity*, chap. 3.
55. *El Comercio*, 30 March 1931, cited in *Origen y legislación comparada sobre los Impuestos para Desocupados* ([Lima]: n.p., n.d.).

56. Although the juntas were essentially top-down initiatives, they also were responses to pressure from below. As the depression began to impact on workers, several groups proposed job creation schemes to government authorities. In January 1931, for example, unemployed workers in Arequipa, stressing that their patience was at an end, demanded that construction on the highway linking Arequipa to Puno start straight away. In May 1931, a group of self-described "unemployed professionals" from Callao suggested two measures: the repair of the Compañía Peruana de Vapores's ships and the painting and sanitation of the city's houses, which, by their calculations, would provide employment to five hundred or six hundred men. In some ways, the public works initiatives of both the Leguía and Sánchez Cerro governments, including sanitation projects and road building in Lima, colonization projects in the *montaña* (i.e., jungle) and worker housing, later consolidated under the aegis of the juntas pro-desocupados, were shaped by such demands. See *Noticias*, 27 January 1931; AGN/MI/309/ Callao, Domingo Huamán et al. to Prefecto del Callao, 12 May 1931; *Variedades*, 1 October 1930 and 11 February 1931.

57. *Boletín de Trabajo y Previsión Social* 1, no. 1 (1935): n.p.

58. Stein, *Populism*, 80.

59. Derpich, Huiza, and Israel, *Lima años 30*, 32–35.

60. Thorp and Bertram, *Peru*, 151–54.

61. Basadre and Ferrero, *Historia de la Cámara de Comercio*, 166.

62. PRO/FO 371/18720, Forbes to Simon, 25 April 1935.

63. *Ciencia, Industria y Maquinas* 1, no. 4. March 1938, 250–52.

64. Basadre, *Historia de la República*, vol. 11, 89–91.

65. ADA/105, Comité de Trabajadores Desocupados de Oficios Diversos to Prefect, 11 June 1931.

66. ADL/CPT/LCO, Concejo Provincial de Trujillo to Director de Fomento, 17 April 1931.

67. ADA/107, several unemployed workers to Prefect of Arequipa, 19 September 1932; *El Pueblo*, 21 September 1932.

68. *La Tribuna*, 23 May 1931.

69. *La Tribuna*, 17 May 1931.

70. See, for example, *El Comercio*, 8 May 1932.

71. ADA/106, Subprefect of Islay to Prefect of Arequipa, 4 October 1932.

72. AGN/JP/4.1.24, Junta Departamental de Lima to Comisión Distribuidora, 16 April 1932.

73. ADA/108, reproduced in Junta Departamental de Arequipa to Prefecto de Arequipa, 22 July 1932.

74. *La Tribuna*, 7 November 1931.

75. AGN/MI/342/Lima, Junta Departamental de Lima to Prefecto de Lima, 15 January 1934.

76. *El Socialista*, 20 July 1934.

77. *La Tribuna*, 12 August 1931.

78. *La Tribuna*, 4 June 1931.

79. *La Tribuna*, 20 November 1931.

80. ADA/108, Unión Revolucionaria to Alcalde de Arequipa, 23 April 1932.

81. ADA/108, Junta Desocupados to Presidente Club Unión Sanchezcerrista, 2 May 1932.

82. Riva Agüero, *Discursos en las fiestas del Aniversario Patrio*, 25.

83. *La Tribuna*, 2 July 1931.

84. *La Tribuna*, 5 July 1931.

85. *La Tribuna*, 9 July 1931.

86. *El Socialista*, 30 April 1932.

87. APRA, 7 January 1932.

88. *La Tribuna*, 18 June 1934.

89. *La Tribuna*, 20 June 1934.

90. *La Tribuna*, 23 June 1934.

91. *La Tribuna*, 22 June 1934.

92. *La Tribuna*, 30 June 1934.

93. Ruiz Blanco, "Las casas para obreros."

94. Ludeña Urquizo, *Lima*, 212–40.

95. Ibid., 256–71.

96. See Ruiz Blanco, "Vivienda colectiva en Lima"; Ludeña Urquizo, *Lima*, 271– 91.

97. *Revista del Ministerio de Fomento y Obras Públicas* 1, no. 1 (June 1937): 4.

98. *La Crónica*, 17 January 1937.

99. Ibid.

100. Ibid.

101. Crupi, "Nation Divided, City Divided."

102. Ibid., 174.

103. *La Crónica*, 13 March 1937.

104. *Revista del Ministerio de Fomento y Obras Públicas* 1, no. 1 (June 1937): 3.

105. *La Crónica*, 17 January 1937.

106. *Revista del Ministerio de Fomento y Obras Públicas* 1, no. 1 (June 1937): 4.

107. *La Crónica*, 24 January 1937.

108. *La Crónica*, 14 February 1937.

109. *Mundo Peruano* 2, nos. 24–25 (December–January 1936–37): 16.

110. *Cascabel*, 11 December 1937.

111. Federico Recavarren, quoted in *Revista del Ministerio de Fomento y Obras Públicas* 1, no. 1 (June 1937): 35.

112. Ibid., 33–34.

113. Ibid., 3.

114. Ibid.

115. *La Crónica*, 17 January 1937.

116. Blau, *The Architecture of Red Vienna*, 345.

117. In interwar Britain, Swenarton has suggested, "the state hoped to instill in the population ideas favorable to the status quo" through the design of houses "fit for heroes." In a different context, architectural design was intended to undermine the status quo; in "Red Vienna," Gruber argues, the imposing architecture of worker apartment buildings such as Karl-Marx Hof and Karl-Seitz-Hof "contributed to a sense of political power among the workers," although this power, Gruber concedes, was more apparent than real. Even in the Soviet Union, the aesthetics of buildings were considered important. As Stephen Kotkin notes, "For the Soviet authorities, no less than for ordinary people, their buildings had to 'look like something,' had to make one feel proud, make one see that the proletariat (not literally) would have *its* attractive buildings." In all these contexts, authorities and ordinary people recognized that architectural design could instill values, either conservative or revolutionary. See Swenarton, *Homes Fit for Heroes*, 195; Gruber, *Red Vienna*, 65; Kotkin, *Magnetic Mountain*, 119.

118. García y García, *La mujer y el hogar*, 29.

119. Ibid., 49.

120. Merino Schroder, *La vivienda barata*, 13.

121. Valega, "La habitación," *Arquitecto Peruano* 14, no. 160 (1950): n.p.

122. Palacios, *Encuesta sobre presupuestos*, 108–9.

123. Ibid., 195–96.

124. Ibid., 138.

125. Ibid., 198.

126. Crupi, "Nation Divided, City Divided," 173.

127. Rodgers, *Atlantic Crossings*, 382, 390–91.

128. Oficina Nacional de Planeamiento y Urbanismo, *Plan piloto de Lima* (Lima: Empresa Gráfica Scheuch, [1950]), 13.

129. Cordova, *La vivienda en el Perú*, 143.

130. Matos Mar, *Desborde popular*. On the formation of Lima's barriadas, see Calderón Cockburn, *La ciudad ilegal*.

131. Dennis, "Room for Improvement?," 665.

132. Amrith, *Decolonizing International Health*, 11.

133. Jerram, *Germany's Other Modernity*, 109.

NOTES TO CHAPTER 5: FEEDING LABOR

Testimony of Andrés Delgado in Taller de Testimonio, *Habla la ciudad*, 25–26, emphasis added. Delgado uses the term *comedores populares* to refer to the *restaurantes populares*.

1. AGN/MI/327/Particulares, Comisión Ejecutiva de los restaurantes populares to Director de Gobierno, 17 June 1932.

2. FO 371/19800, Wilson to Eden, 21 April 1936.

3. See Appadurai, "How to Make a National Cuisine." For a pioneering work in the Latin American context, see Pilcher, *¡Que vivan los tamales!* As Gary Alan Fine suggests, "The connection between identity and consumption gives food a central role in the creation of community, and we use our diet to convey images of public identity." Quoted in Belasco, "Food Matters," 2. Of course, philosophers, psychoanalysts, sociologists, and anthropologists have studied the interconnection between food and culture for some time now. In 1910, Georg Simmel noted that "communal eating and drinking, which can even transform a mortal enemy into a friend for the Arab, allows us to overlook that one is not eating and drinking 'the same thing' at all, but rather totally exclusive portions, and gives rise to the primitive notion that one is thereby creating common flesh and blood." See Simmel, "Sociology of the Meal," 131. For a sample of studies on the interplay of national identity and food, see Counihan and Van Esterik, *Food and Culture.*

4. See Kamminga and Cunningham, *The Science and Culture of Nutrition*; and Smith and Phillips, *Food, Science, Policy and Regulation.*

5. Vernon, *Hunger,* 3.

6. In the United States, Harvey Levenstein has argued, social reformers drew inspiration from the German *Volksküchen* to create "people's kitchens," later rebranded "New England kitchens," in order to "revolutionize the diets of the working class." Focusing on the early years of the Soviet Union, Mauricio Borrero has suggested the Bolsheviks believed that "not only would state cafeterias and communal kitchens inculcate collectivist values among the population, but they would also utilize scarce food resources in the most efficient manner." In 1940s Mexico, Sandra Aguilar-Rodriguez has shown, the public dining halls created during the Ávila Camacho administration were similarly intended to convey certain values and shape habits and behavior: "Eating at the halls was described as an act of patriotism through which responsible citizens would remain healthy and strong to work for the nation. Furthermore, the halls would free women to do paid work in or out of their homes." In interwar Britain, the cafeteria of the Pioneer Health Centre in Peckham, south London, later the model for public dining halls called national restaurants and, once rebranded, British restaurants, was similarly conceived as an agent of moral improvement. As James Vernon argues: "As the focal point of the community and its forms of civility and sociability, the cafeteria encapsulated the guiding principle of the Centre, namely self service as 'technique or mechanism of health' capable of 'engendering responsibility . . . [and] enhancing awareness as well as increasing freedom of action.' " Levenstein, *Revolution at the Table*, 49; Borrero, "Communal Dining and State Cafeterias," 163, and Borrero, "Food and the Politics of Scarcity"; Aguilar-Rodriguez, "Cooking Modernity," 187; Vernon, *Hunger,*

185. On communal eating in the United States, both self-organized and state-directed, during the Great Depression, see Levenstein, *Paradox of Plenty*.

7. The events are studied in detail in Blanchard, *The Origins of the Peruvian Labor Movement*. In the late 1970s, Rosemary Thorp and Geoffrey Bertram challenged the widely held belief that increases in food prices were linked to the expansion of export crops such as cotton and sugar, by arguing that the land devoted to foodstuffs remained constant during the first decades of the twentieth century. More recently, Augusto Ruiz Zevallos has suggested that previously unexamined sources confirm that the percentage of land devoted to foodstuffs fell in the period. Thorp and Bertram, *Peru, 1890–1977*; and Ruiz Zevallos, *La multitud*.

8. Ruiz Zevallos, *La multitud*, 207–9.

9. On the contemporaneous food riots in the United States, see Levenstein, *Revolution at the Table*, 109.

10. Peloso, "Succulence and Sustenance," 54–59.

11. Ruiz Zevallos, *La multitud*, 150.

12. Vernon, *Hunger*, chap. 3.

13. *La Razón*, 10 May 1919, cited in Ruiz Zevallos, *La multitud*, 162.

14. Horowitz, Pilcher, and Watts, "Meat for the Multitudes," 1059.

15. Pilcher, *The Sausage Rebellion*.

16. On anti-Asian racism see, McKeown, "Inmigración china al Perú"; Fukumoto, *Hacia un nuevo sol*; Rodríguez Pastor, *Herederos del Dragón*; and Bracamonte, "La modernidad de los subalternos."

17. *El Obrero Textil*, 6 December 1919.

18. *El Obrero Textil*, 13 January 1920.

19. Although, naturally, not all members of the Lima working class espoused racist views of Asians (as I show below, anarchists explicitly rejected the racism), there is considerable evidence that such feelings were widespread among urban workers in Lima.

20. Quoted in Muñoz Cabrejo, *Diversiones públicas*, 168. On the development of Chinese restaurants, or *chifas*, as they are known in Peru, see Rodríguez Pastor, *Herederos del Dragón*, 213–66.

21. On the association of Chinese immigrants and disease, see Rodríguez Pastor, "La calle del Capón"; and Cueto, *El regreso de las epidemias*, esp. chap. 1.

22. *El Comercio*, 31 January 1901 (evening ed.).

23. *El Comercio*, 12 July 1901 (evening ed.).

24. French and Phillips, "Sophisticates or Dupes?," 444.

25. Levenstein, *Revolution at the Table*, 104.

26. Muñoz, *Diversiones públicas*, 168–69.

27. *Variedades* 5, no. 60 (24 April 1909): 174.

28. *Variedades* 5, no. 62 (8 May 1909): 227. The destruction of the Callejón Otaiza is discussed in, among others, Rodríguez Pastor, "La calle del Capón."

29. *Mundial*, 16 November 1928.

30. *Los Parias* 6, no. 48 (June 1909).

31. *Los Parias* 4, no. 43 (September 1908).

32. *Cascabel*, 18 May 1935.

33. Ibid.

34. Kamminga and Cunningham, "Introduction," 2.

35. De la Puente, *Alimentación del obrero*, 21.

36. Levenstein, *Revolution at the Table*, 47.

37. De la Puente, *Alimentación del obrero*, 22.

38. Ibid., 23.

39. Ibid., 11.

40. Ibid., 30.

41. See Fonseca Ariza, "Antialcoholismo y modernización."

42. *Mundial*, 21 October 1927.

43. Bedoya, "Balance alimenticio," 54.

44. Rose Ugarte, *La situación alimenticia*, xiv.

45. Bedoya, *Estudio preliminar de alimentación*, 13.

46. Guzmán Barrón and López Guillén, *La deficiencia de proteínas*.

47. See Palacios, *Encuesta sobre presupuestos familiares*.

48. Derpich, Huiza, and Israel, *Lima años 30*, 52.

49. Palacios, *Encuesta sobre presupuestos familiares*, 168–69, 192.

50. Bedoya, "Balance alimenticio," 54.

51. As was the case in May 1909, when a mob of hundreds of urban workers attacked Chinese businesses and individuals in the city. See Ruiz Zevallos, *La multitud*, 103–21.

52. This is not to say that the food prepared in Asian restaurants was necessarily healthy or nutritious. It is likely that in many cases it was not. But then, it was also probably no more unhealthy or nonnutritious than that offered in restaurants owned by Peruvians.

53. To get a sense of the value that this represented, we may consider the fact that according to a 1938 menu from Santiago Cordova's Restaurant El Morro Solar in Chorrillos 0.30 soles bought a customer a single dish of steak and rice, whereas a customer in the restaurant popular would get a full three-course meal for the same amount. "Menú del día," 9 November 1938, Restaurant el Morro Solar (Lima: Librería e Imprenta El Misti). Copy of menu in author's possession.

54. Ugarteche, *Sánchez Cerro*, 31–36.

55. Peru, Ministerio de Salud Pública, Trabajo y Previsión Social, Dirección de Previsión Social, *Acción social del estado en el Perú* (Lima: n.p., 1938), 6. These restaurants were aimed at obreros, or blue-collar workers. A white-collar restaurant was created in the early 1940s, but its existence was short-lived in part because empleados, white-collar workers, resented the fact that

blue-collar workers also made use of the restaurant. See Parker, *The Idea of the Middle Class*, 205. Evidence suggests that poorer empleados made use of the obrero restaurants on a regular basis (see below).

56. [Gerbi], *El Perú en marcha*, 305. On the Unión Revolucionaria's "fascist" turn, see Molinari Morales, *El fascismo en el Perú*.

57. Quoted in Junta Departamental de Lima Pro-Desocupados, *Memoria del 1 de enero de 1935 al 31 de diciembre de 1936* (Lima, 1936), xlviii.

58. *Cascabel*, 3 August 1935.

59. *Boletín del Partido Unión Revolucionaria* (Abancay), no. 1, August 1936.

60. Cox, *Ideas económicas del Aprismo*, 44.

61. AGN/PL/3.9.5.1.15.1.16.56, "Partido Aprista Peruano, Cooperativa de Comedores, Economía del Comedor, N. 9," [15 October 1934].

62. *La Tribuna*, 7 April 1934.

63. Ibid.

64. *La Tribuna*, 23 June 1934.

65. *La Tribuna*, 26 June 1934.

66. *La Tribuna*, 21 June 1934.

67. AGN/PL/3.9.5.1.15.1.16.56, "Partido Aprista Peruano, Cooperativa de Comedores, Economía del Comedor, N. 9," [15 October 1934].

68. *La Tribuna*, 22 October 1941.

69. *La Voz del Obrero*, no. 19 (19 May 1937).

70. Peru, Ministerio de Salud Pública, Trabajo y Previsión Social, Dirección de Previsión Social, *Acción social del estado en el Perú* (Lima: n.p., 1938), 6.

71. Vernon, *Hunger*, 160

72. Ibid., 161.

73. Available sources say little about who were the ideological architects of the restaurants, although what evidence exists suggests that Edgardo Rebagliati, a lawyer who, as discussed in the next chapter, played a central role in the creation of Peru's social security system, was a key figure. Along with Manuel B. Llosa, Peru's foreign minister, Rebagliati signed the introduction to the book.

74. This may have had some results. In 1937, the Chilean National Nutrition Council established restaurantes populares with identical goals to the Peruvian restaurants. See Huneeus and María Paz Lanas, "Ciencia política e historia."

75. Vernon, *Hunger*, 166.

76. Ibid., 168.

77. Lack of space prevents a discussion of the gendered dimension of the conferment of values in the restaurantes populares. However, the presence of "family-only" dining areas and the provision of free meals to children suggest that the intellectual architects of the restaurants also hoped to contribute to strengthening traditional gender roles and to the state's maternalist

policies. On maternalist policies in this period, see Mannarelli, *Limpias y modernas.*

78. *Cascabel*, 2 November 1935.

79. Ibid.

80. See Junta Departamental de Lima Pro-Desocupados, *Memoria del 1 de enero de 1942 al 31 de diciembre de 1944* (Lima, 1946), 5.

81. *La Voz del Obrero*, 19 May 1937.

82. Ibid. Note the change in stress from Chinese to Japanese restaurants, a reflection of broader anti-Japanese sentiments in the late 1930s born out of fears regarding Japanese militarism and the belief that Peru's Japanese community were preparing the way for an invasion. (Emphasis added).

83. *La Voz del Obrero*, 12 August 1936.

84. Léon de Vivero, *Avance del imperialismo fascista*, 31–32.

85. See *La Voz del Obrero*, 12 October 1940.

NOTES TO CHAPTER 6: HEALING LABOR

1. *Cascabel*, 17 August 1935.

2. *Labor*, 15 January and 2 February 1929.

3. *El Trabajador*, 17 October 1930, quoted in Martínez de la Torre, *Apuntes para una interpretación marxista*, vol. 3, 93.

4. Partido Socialista del Perú, *Primer manifiesto*, 12.

5. In the mid-1990s, Philip Nord identified a shift in studies of the history of social welfare in France. In explaining the advent of welfare reform, he noted, historians had tended to emphasize social defense, that is, the notion that "the forward progress of labor put such a scare into the bourgeois Republic that its more enlightened partisans seized on meliorative measures as a means of dampening protest." But historians, Nord noted, were beginning to move on from such perspectives to consider the cultural constitution of social welfare in various countries. As Janet Horne suggests, "To examine a nation's welfare state is also to open wide the history of that nation's value systems—to investigate, for instance, not only the political pressures but also the religious, philosophical, and cultural influences exerted on policy makers." In the 1980s, pioneering feminist historians showed how welfare systems at once reflected and helped constitute gendered social orders. More recently, historians influenced by gender perspectives have pointed to the important role played by women in shaping early social policy and how the very terms of debate and the policies that informed and produced social reform were gendered. Political scientists such as Robert Lieberman and historians such as Frederick Cooper have shown that race and racism similarly shaped social welfare in the United States and colonial British and French Africa respectively in ways that perpetuated a racialized social order. Others, such as Peter Swenson, have challenged the assump-

tion that capitalists were instinctively opposed to welfare reform. See Nord, "The Welfare State in France," 823; Horne, *A Social Laboratory for Modern France*, 2; Lieberman, *Shifting the Color Line*; Cooper, *Decolonization and African Society*; Swenson, *Capitalists against Markets*. The relevant literature on the gendering of welfare state historiography is too vast to cite here, but see Koven and Michel, "Womanly Duties"; Gordon, "Social Insurance and Public Assistance"; Pedersen, *Family, Dependence, and the Origins of the Welfare State*. On the gendered character of welfare in a contemporary context, see O'Connor, Orloff, and Shaver, *States, Markets, Families*. On the gendered character of state formation, see Brown, *States of Injury*, chap. 7. For a useful overview see Hacker, "Bringing the Welfare State Back In."

6. Kotkin, *Magnetic Mountain*, 19–20.

7. Weinstein, *For Social Peace in Brazil*; Klubock, *Contested Communities*; Rosemblatt, *Gendered Compromises*; Hutchison, *Labors Appropriate to Their Sex*; Ehrlick, *The Shield of the Weak*; Guy, *Women Build the Welfare State*.

8. Hacker, "Bringing the Welfare State Back In," 127.

9. *Mundo Peruano* 2, nos. 13–14 (January–February 1936): 55.

10. *Mundo Peruano* 2, nos. 17–18 (May–June 1936): 5.

11. See Cueto, *El regreso de las epidemias*.

12. Paz Soldán, *La asistencia social en el Perú*, [46].

13. *Mundial*, 4 February 1921.

14. *Mundial*, 6 November 1925.

15. *La Crónica Médica* 47 (1930): 178–85.

16. *La Crónica Médica* 49, no. 824 (1932): 69–71; *La Crónica Médica* 51, no. 484 (1934): 105–107; *Revista Médica Peruana* 5, no. 53 (1933): n.p.; *Revista Médica Peruana* 7, no. 84 (1935): 941–58.

17. *Suplemento*, 3 June 1933.

18. *Cascabel*, 20 July 1935.

19. *Cascabel*, 1 June 1935.

20. On the tensions between private charity and state welfare, see, on the United States, Skocpol, *Protecting Soldiers and Mothers*; on Germany, Steinmetz, *Regulating the Social*, and Hong, *Welfare, Modernity, and the Weimar State*; on Italy, Quine, *Italy's Social Revolution*; on Russia and the Soviet Union, Lindenmeyr, *Poverty Is Not a Vice*, Kotkin, *Magnetic Mountain*, and Caroli, "Bolshevism, Stalinism and Social Welfare."

21. Like Luciano Castillo (see chapter 3), Rebagliati advertised his services as a labor lawyer in Mariátegui's *Labor*. See 24 November 1928, 6.

22. *Revista de Seguros* 1, no. 1 (November 1932): 7–12.

23. *Revista de Seguros* 3, no. 31 (May 1935): 1.

24. Rebagliati, "La previsión social en Chile."

25. Rosemblatt, "Charity, Rights, and Entitlement," 571.

26. FO/371/19801, Forbes to Eden, 14 October 1936.
27. PC/B3/60, Peruvian Corporation (Lima) to Cecil, 19 June 1936.
28. Rodgers, *Atlantic Crossings*, 226–27.
29. Despite the evident transnational inspiration, in tracing the genealogy of the Seguro Social he designed, Rebagliati pointed to three local legislative proposals. These included a 1931 proposal put forward by the Public Beneficence Society, a proposal by Representative Gerardo Balbuena, and, finally, the "Labor Code Project" prepared by Representative Manuel Bustamante de la Fuente in 1934. Rebagliati, *La previsión social en el Perú*, 13.
30. García Rosell, *Comentarios al proyecto de seguros sociales*.
31. Rodgers, *Atlantic Crossings*, 443.
32. FO 371/19801, Forbes to Eden, 14 October 1936.
33. PC/B3/60, Peruvian Corporation (Lima) to Cecil, 19 June 1936; Basadre and Ferrero, *Historia de la Cámara de Comercio*, 197–98.
34. PC/B3/60, Peruvian Corporation (Lima) to Cecil, 19 June 1936.
35. Eguiguren, *El usurpador*, 146–47.
36. See Haya de la Torre, *Política aprista*, 20–22.
37. Seoane, *Obras apristas*, 17–18.
38. PC/B3/60, Hixson to Cecil, 7 November 1936.
39. Ibid. This labor resistance corresponds to a broader transnational pattern. As Rodgers notes: "Nowhere in the North Atlantic economy before 1914 were labor organizations either the authors of social insurance schemes or a significant political force in their adoption. If the unions eventually signed on to measures that had their origins in the chancellery offices or middle-class reform associations, it was never without resistance or objection." *Atlantic Crossings*, 258.
40. *Chan-Chan*, 6 December 1936.
41. *La Tribuna*, 6 November 1943.
42. *Industria Peruana* 5, no. 7 (July 1935): 290–91.
43. Rodgers, *Atlantic Crossings*, 436.
44. *Industria peruana* 5, no. 12 (December 1935): 479.
45. Letter reproduced in *Industria Peruana* 6, no. 2 (February 1936): 72–73.
46. PC/B3/60, Peruvian Corporation to Cecil, 19 June 1936.
47. *La Nueva Economía* 1, no. 4 (April 1935): 123–24.
48. *La Nueva Economía* 1, no. 10 (October 1935): 339.
49. Stepan, *The Hour of Eugenics*.
50. Rodgers, *Atlantic Crossings*, 256.
51. *La Nueva Economía* 2, no. 21 (September 1936): 266.
52. Mitchell, *Rule of Experts*, 50.
53. Sulmont, *El movimiento obrero*, 168, n. 29.
54. Bustíos Romaní, *La salud pública*, 373.
55. See Baldeón, "La transición truncada."

56. PC/B3/60, Hixson to Kennedy, 23 December 1936.

57. Ibid.

58. Similarly, the fact that business resistance to the Seguro Social subsided had much to do with the fact that, as a consequence of the revisions to the Seguro Social, its actual economic cost was not that great for the larger employers, some of which already provided some form of social benefits to their workers. Although the Seguro Social represented an increase in the Peruvian Corporation's expenditure, for example, it also generated savings in a number of areas including pensions, sickness and death payments, and medical services. In the end the net cost to the company was a mere 75,000 soles in 1937. PC/B3/60, Cecil to Kennedy, 24 February 1937.

59. Swenson, *Capitalists against Markets*, 243.

60. *Informaciones Sociales* 1, no. 1 (July 1937).

61. Ibid., [2]; For a pioneering discussion of the formation of the patriarchal state and social policy in the Peruvian context, see Mannarelli, *Limpias y modernas*.

62. *Informaciones Sociales* 1, no. 1 (July 1937): 2, 3−4.

63. *Informaciones Sociales* 1, no. 2 (August 1937): 235−36.

64. Ibid.

65. *Informaciones Sociales* 1, no. 1 (July 1937): 3−4.

66. Ibid., 4.

67. "Circular enviada por la Caja Nacional de Seguro Social a los Trabajadores," 22 May 1937, reproduced in *Informaciones Sociales* 1, no. 2 (August 1937): 325−27, quotations from 326.

68. "Circular enviada por la Caja Nacional de Seguro Social a los Patronos," 18 June 1937, reproduced in *Informaciones Sociales* 1, no. 2 (August 1937): 328−30, quotations from 328, 329.

69. Caja Nacional de Seguro Social, *Cartilla de Divulgación*, 3.

70. Rebagliati, *La previsión social.*

71. Ibid., 16.

72. Caja Nacional de Seguro Social, *Cartilla de Divulgación*, 5.

73. Rebagliati, *La previsión social*, 5. *Mita* refers to an Inca form of tribute or corvée labor later adopted and adapted by the Spanish colonial state and used, most famously, to provide workers to the silver mine of Potosí.

74. Caja Nacional de Seguro Social, *Cartilla de Divulgación*, 5.

75. Muñoz Puglisevich, "El Seguro Social Obligatorio."

76. See Prakash, *Another Reason.*

77. Caja Nacional de Seguro Social, *Cartilla de Divulgación*, 3.

78. Gordon, "Social Insurance and Public Assistance," 31−35.

79. Caja Nacional de Seguro Social, *Cartilla de Divulgación*, 4−5.

80. "Discurso del Dr Guillermo Almenara," in Ministerio de Salud Pública, Tra-

bajo y Previsión Social, *Boletín de la Dirección de Salubridad Pública* (Lima, 1938), n.p.

81. *Ley No. 8433 Angustia—imprevisión social, Seguro social—bienestar del mañana* [Lima: Sanmartí y Cia, 1937].

82. Ibid., n.p.

83. Ibid.

84. Ibid.

85. Ibid.

86. Ibid.

87. Ibid.

88. Ibid.

89. Ibid.

90. Steinmetz, *Regulating the Social*, 121.

91. *La Crónica*, 9 December 1940.

92. Speech reproduced in *Industria Peruana* 10, no. 12 (December 1940): 507.

93. *La Crónica*, 10 December 1940.

94. *La Voz del Obrero*, 8 December 1940.

95. Bourdieu, "Rethinking the State," 91.

96. On the provisions of Law 4916, see Parker, *The Idea of the Middle Class*, chap. 5.

97. Ibid.

98. Bustíos Romaní, *La salud pública*, 373–77.

99. *La Crónica*, 8 January 1937.

100. *La Crónica*, 15 January 1937.

101. *La Crónica*, 27 February 1937.

102. *La Crónica*, 20 January 1937.

103. Ibid.

104. Rebagliati, *La previsión social*, 8.

105. Caja Nacional del Seguro Social, *Estadística del trabajo*, 7.

106. There are interesting parallels between the exclusions of the Seguro Social and the exclusion of African Americans from the 1935 Social Security Act in the United States. As Lieberman argues, those exclusions were achieved "through different institutional means—in some cases by excluding the occupations in which most African Americans worked, in others by drawing strict eligibility standards that most African Americans could not meet, and in still others by preserving local autonomy and passing altogether on matters of inclusion and exclusion" (*Shifting the Color Line*, 25). Citing problems arising from the "administrative feasibility" of collecting payroll taxes from workers not in industrial and commercial employment, the architects of the U.S. Social Security Act succeeded in excluding agricultural and domestic workers from eligibility for the social insurance programs, old-age insur-

ance, and unemployment insurance. In so doing, they removed more than five million workers from old-age and unemployment coverage; this meant that more than half of the African American workers in the United States would not be eligible. Lieberman sees these exclusions as arising from southern resistance to the economic independence that the act would have granted African Americans: "Any welfare policy that gave the Southern farm workers sources of income independent of the planter elite and the political institution that it dominated had the potential to undermine the rigid racial and class structures of the South" (27). Because legislators had to bring the southern congressmen on board for the law to pass, the exclusions were written into the act. As a consequence, Lieberman concludes, the 1935 Social Security Act illustrates how "the racial structure of American society and politics, embedded as it was in class and regional conflict, and reflected in structures of political power, shaped the institutional development of the American welfare state" (65).

107. "El Indio en el Seguro Social," *Informaciones sociales* 1, no. 5 (November 1937): 545–46.

108. Alejandro Vega, "El problema indígena," *Informaciones sociales* 2, no. 10 (October 1938): 1075–81.

109. Pedro J. M. Larrañaga, "Bases económicas de nuestro porvenir racial," *Informaciones sociales* 3, no. 11 (November 1939): 1165–66.

110. According to Larrañaga, "All the European colonos we have taken to the *montaña* [the jungle] have left, or if they stay, they degenerate to the level of the jungle Indians [*los chunchos*]. In the high Andean mining zone few whites can resist the altitude and harshness of mine labor." "Bases económicas," 1166.

111. Ibid., 1169.

112. Caja Nacional del Seguro Social Obrero, *La aplicación del Seguro Social.*

113. Ibid.

114. More, "¿Existe Seguro Social en el Perú?" 11.

115. Belaúnde Terry, "La salud pública y la Seguridad Social," 41.

116. Palomino Ramírez, "La Seguridad Social y la economía popular."

NOTES TO CONCLUSION

1. For a recent literature that challenges this view of "elusive" indigenous politics in Peru, see García, *Indigenous Encounters* and *Making Indigenous Citizens*; and Green, *Customizing Indigeneity.*

2. From www.cverdad.org.pe, vol. 8 of *Report of the Truth and Reconciliation Commission* (2003), 159.

3. Tilly, *Durable Inequality.*

4. Portocarrero, "Memorias del velasquismo," 252.

5. De la Cadena, "Silent Racism."

6. Grompone, "Tradiciones liberales," 508.

7. Rodgers, *Atlantic Crossings*, 25.

8. Ong, "Graduated Sovereignty," 62.

9. Agamben, *Homo Sacer*, 142.

10. See www.cverdad.org.pe/informacion/discursos/en_ceremonias05.php.

11. De la Cadena, *Indigenous Mestizos*.

BIBLIOGRAPHY

ARCHIVES

Archivo General de la Nación (AGN)
    Expedientes Oficiales (OL)
    Gremios, Ministerio de Fomento (MF)
    Manuel Bustamante papers (Bust)
    Ministerio del Interior (MI)
    Prefectura de Lima (PL)
    Reclamos Colectivos (RC), Ministerio de Fomento (MF)
    Tierras de Montaña (TM)

Archivo Departamental de Arequipa (ADA)
    Prefectura

Archivo Departamental del Cuzco (ADC)
    Prefectura

Archivo Municipal de Lima (AML)

Centro de Divulgación de Historia Popular (CEDHIP)
    Labor history interviews

Documentation Center, Social Sciences Faculty, Pontificia Universidad Católica del Perú
    Arturo Sabroso papers
    Minute books, Federación de Obreros Panaderos "Estrella del Perú" (FOPEP)

National Archives, United Kingdom
    Foreign Office papers (FO)

University College Library, United Kingdom
    Peruvian Corporation papers (PC)

NEWSPAPERS, JOURNALS, AND MAGAZINES

Alma Obrera

APRA

Arquitecto Peruano

Boletín de la Dirección de Salubridad Pública

Boletín de la Sociedad Nacional de Agricultura

Boletín de Minas, Industrias y Construcciones

Boletín de Trabajo y Previsión Social

Cascabel

Chan-Chan

Ciencia, Industria y Maquinas

Ciudad y Campo [some issues *Ciudad y Campo y Caminos*]

Economista Peruano

El Agricultor Peruano

El Comercio

El Derecho

El Nacionalista

El Obrero Gráfico

El Obrero Textil

El Pueblo (Arequipa)

El Socialista

El Trabajador

Hogar

Ilustración Obrera

Industria

Industria Peruana

Informaciones Sociales

La Abeja

La Agricultura

Labor

La Crónica

La Mujer Peruana

La Nueva Economía

La Prensa

La Razón

La Revista

La Revista del Foro

La Sanción

La Tribuna

La Voz del Obrero

Libertad

Los Parias
Mundial
Mundo Peruano
Noticias (Arequipa)
Peru To-Day
Revista de Economía y Finanzas
Revista del Ministerio de Fomento y Obras Públicas
Suplemento
Variedades

BOOKS AND ARTICLES

Aboy, Rosa. " 'The Right to a Home': Public Housing in Post World-War II Buenos Aires." *Journal of Urban History* 33, no. 3 (2007): 493–518.

Abrams, Philip. "Notes on the Difficulty of Studying the State." *Journal of Historical Sociology* 1, no. 1 (1988): 58–89.

Adams, Julia. *The Familial State: Ruling Families and Merchant Capitalism in Early Modern Europe*. Ithaca: Cornell University Press, 2005.

Agamben, Giorgio. *Homo Sacer: Sovereign Power and Bare Life*. Stanford: Stanford University Press, 1998.

Aguilar-Rodriguez, Sandra. "Cooking Modernity: Nutrition Policies, Class, and Gender in 1940s and 1950s Mexico City." *The Americas* 64, no. 2 (2007): 177–205.

Aguirre, Carlos. *The Criminals of Lima and Their Worlds: The Prison Experience, 1850–1935*. Durham: Duke University Press, 2005.

Alayza Paz Soldán, Francisco. *La industria moderna: Disertación del director de la Escuela Nacional de Artes y Oficios el día de clausura del año escolar*. Lima: Imprenta Torres Aguirre, 1927.

——. *El problema del indio en el Perú: Su civilización e incorporación en la nacionalidad*. Lima: Imprenta Americana, 1928.

Albert, Bill. "The Creation of a Proletariat on Peru's Coastal Sugar Plantations, 1880–1920." In *Proletarianization in the Third World: Studies in the Creation of a Labor Force under Development Capitalism*, edited by Barry Munslow and Henry Finch, 99–120. London: Routledge, 1984.

Alexander, Alberto. *Estudio sobre la crisis de la habitación en Lima*. Lima: Imprenta Torres Aguirre, 1922.

Aljovín, Carlos. *Caudillos y constituciones: Perú, 1821–1845*. Lima: Fondo de Cultura Económica/Pontificia Universidad Católica del Perú/Instituto Riva-Agüero, 2000.

Amrith, Sunil. *Decolonizing International Health: India and Southeast Asia, 1930–1965*. Houndmills, United Kingdom: Palgrave, 2006.

Anderle, Adam. *Los movimientos políticos en el Perú entre las dos guerra mundiales*. Havana: Casa de las Américas, 1985.

Angulo de Puente Arnao, Juan. *Legislación obrera, anotada y concordada*. Lima: Litografía e Imprenta T. Scheuch, 1917.

Apel, Karin. *De la hacienda a la comunidad: La sierra de Piura, 1934–1990*. Lima: Instituto de Estudios Peruanos, 1996.

Appadurai, Arjun. "How to Make a National Cuisine: Cookbooks in Contemporary India." *Comparative Studies in Society and History* 30, no. 1 (1988): 3–24.

Appelbaum, Nancy P., Anne S. Macpherson, and Karin Alejandra Rosemblatt, eds. *Race and Nation in Modern Latin America*. Chapel Hill: University of North Carolina Press, 2003.

Balbi, Carmen Rosa. *El Partido Comunista y el APRA en la crisis revolucionaria de los años treinta*. Lima: G. Herrera, 1980.

Balbi, Carmen Rosa, and Laura Madalengoitia. *Parlamento y lucha política: Perú, 1932*. Lima: Centro de Estudios y Promoción del Desarrollo, 1980.

Baldeón, Edson. "La transición truncada: Las elecciones de 1936 y la participación aprista." In *Historia de las elecciones en el Perú: Estudios sobre el gobierno representativo*, edited by Cristóbal Aljovín de Losada and Sinesio López, 455–82. Lima: Instituto de Estudios Peruanos, 2005.

Basadre, Jorge. *Historia de la Republica*. Lima: Editorial Universitaria, 1964.

Basadre, Jorge, and Raúl Ferrero. *Historia de la Cámara de Comercio de Lima*. Lima: Imprenta de Santiago Valverde, 1963.

Bauer, Arnold J. *Goods, Power, History: Latin America's Material Culture*. Cambridge: Cambridge University Press, 2001.

Becker, Marc. "Mariátegui, the Comintern, and the Indigenous Question in Latin America." *Science and Society* 70, no. 4 (2006): 450–79.

Bedoya, Jaime A. "Balance alimenticio de Lima, Callao, y Balnearios." *Revista Médica Peruana* 14, no. 158 (February 1942): 53–54.

Bedoya, Jaime A. *Estudio preliminar de alimentación de las familias de los alumnos de las escuelas fiscales del distrito del Rímac*. Lima: n.p., 1943.

Belaúnde, Víctor Andrés. *La realidad nacional*. Lima: Editorial Horizonte, 1991.

Belaúnde Terry, Fernando. "La salud pública y la seguridad social." *La Reforma Médica* 52, no. 643 (1966): 41–43.

Belasco, Warren. "Food Matters: Perspectives on an Emerging Field." In *Food Nations: Selling Taste in Consumer Societies*, edited by Warren Belasco and Philip Scranton, 2–23. New York: Routledge, 2002.

Bergel, Martín. "Nomadismo Proselitista y revolución: Una caracterización del primer exilio aprista (1923–1931)." *Estudios Interdisciplinarios de América Latina y el Caribe* 20, no. 1 (2009): 41–66.

Bergquist, Charles. *Labor in Latin America: Comparative Essays on Chile, Argentina, Venezuela and Colombia*. Stanford: Stanford University Press, 1986.

Besse, Susan K. *Restructuring Patriarchy: The Modernization of Gender Inequality in Brazil, 1914–1940*. Chapel Hill: University of North Carolina Press, 1996.

Biernacki, Richard. *The Fabrication of Labor: Germany and Britain, 1640–1914.* Berkeley: University of California Press, 1995.

Blanchard, Peter. *The Origins of the Peruvian Labor Movement, 1883–1919.* Pittsburgh: Pittsburgh University Press, 1982.

———. "A Populist Precursor: Guillermo Billinghurst." *Journal of Latin American Studies* 9, no. 2 (1977): 251–73.

Blau, Eve. *The Architecture of Red Vienna, 1919–1934.* Cambridge: MIT Press, 1999.

Bonnell, Victoria E. *Iconography of Power: Soviet Political Posters under Lenin and Stalin.* Berkeley: University of California Press, 1997.

Borrero, Mauricio. "Communal Dining and State Cafeterias in Moscow and Petrograd, 1917–1921." In *Food in Russian History and Culture*, edited by Musya Glants and Joyce Toomre, 162–76. Bloomington: Indiana University Press, 1997.

———. "Food and the Politics of Scarcity in Urban Soviet Russia, 1917–1941." In *Food Nations: Selling Taste in Consumer Societies*, edited by Warren Belasco and Philip Scranton, 258–76. New York: Routledge, 2002.

Bourdieu, Pierre. "Rethinking the State: Genesis and Structure of the Bureaucratic Field." In *State/Culture: State Formation after the Cultural Turn*, edited by George Steinmetz, 53–75. Ithaca: Cornell University Press, 1999.

Bracamonte, Jorge. "La modernidad de los subalternos: Los inmigrantes chinos en la ciudad de Lima, 1895–1930." In *Estudios culturales: Discursos, poderes, pulsiones*, edited by Santiago López Maguiña et al., 167–88. Lima: Red para el desarrollo de las ciencias sociales en el Perú, 2001.

Bronfman, Alejandra. *Measures of Equality: Social Science, Citizenship, and Race in Cuba, 1902–1940.* Chapel Hill: University of North Carolina Press, 2004.

Brown, Wendy. "American Nightmare: Neoliberalism, Neoconservatism, and De-Democratization." *Political Theory* 34, no. 6 (2006): 690–714.

———. "Neoliberalism and the End of Liberal Democracy." *Theory and Event* 7, no. 1 (2003): n.p.

———. *States of Injury: Power and Freedom in Late Modernity.* Princeton: Princeton University Press, 1995.

Burchell, Graham, Colin Gordon, and Peter Miller, eds. *The Foucault Effect: Studies in Governmentality.* Chicago: University of Chicago Press, 1991.

Burga, Manuel, and Alberto Flores Galindo. *Apogeo y crisis de la República Aristocrática.* In *Obras completas*, vol. 2, by Alberto Flores Galindo. Lima: SUR, 1994.

Burgess, Eugene Willard, and Frederick Hariss Harbison. *Casa Grace in Peru.* Washington: National Planning Association, 1954.

Bustamante de la Fuente, Manuel. *Proyecto de Código del Trabajo.* Lima: Imprenta Torres Aguirre, 1934.

Bustíos Romaní, Carlos. *La salud pública, la seguridad social y el Perú demoliberal (1933–1968).* Lima: Concytec, 2005.

Butler, Judith. *Precarious Life: The Powers of Mourning and Violence*. London: Verso, 2004.

Cabello Ortega, Luis. "Urbanismo estatal en Lima metropolitana: Las urbanizaciones populares, 1955–1990." *Ur[b]es* 3 (2006): 83–110.

Cabré, Francisco. *Conferencia dada al "Circulo de Obreros Católicos" en el cine Arequipa el día 27 de enero de 1918*. Arequipa: Tipografía Cáceres, 1918.

Caja Nacional de Seguro Social. *Cartilla de divulgación del seguro social obligatorio leyes 8433 y 8509*. Lima: Sanmartí, 1937.

———. *Estadística del trabajo*. Lima: Caja Nacional del Seguro Social, 1939.

Caja Nacional del Seguro Social Obrero. *La aplicación del seguro social en el Perú*. Lima: Sanmartí, 1942.

Calderón, Gladys. *La casa limeña: Espacios habitados*. Lima: Syklos, 2000.

Calderón Cockburn, Julio. *La ciudad ilegal: Lima en el siglo XX*. Lima: Universidad Nacional Mayor de San Marcos, 2005.

Callirgos, Juan Carlos. "Reinventing the City of Kings: Postcolonial Modernizations of Lima, 1845–1930." Ph.D. dissertation, University of Florida, 2007.

Campos Marín, Ricardo. "Casas para obreros: Un aspecto de la lucha antialcohólica en España durante la Restauración." *Dynamis* 14 (1994): 111–30.

Canessa, Andrew. *Natives Making Nation: Gender, Indigeneity, and the State in the Andes*. Tucson: University of Arizona Press, 2005.

Caravedo Molinari, Baltazar. *Burguesía e industria en el Perú, 1933–1945*. Lima: Instituto de Estudios Peruanos, 1976.

———. *Clases, lucha política y gobierno en el Perú, 1919–1933*. Lima: Retama Editorial, 1977.

Caroli, Dorena. "Bolshevism, Stalinism and Social Welfare (1917–1936)." *International Review for Social History* 48 (2003): 27–54.

Carrión, Julio. *The Fujimori Legacy: The Rise of Electoral Authoritarianism in Peru*. University Park: Pennsylvania State University Press, 2006.

Carroll, Patrick. *Science, Culture, and Modern State Formation*. Berkeley: University of California Press, 2006.

Chanamé O[rbe], Raúl. "Haya de la Torre y la universidades populares." In *Vida y obra de Víctor Raúl Haya de la Torre*, 1–92. Lima: Cambio y Desarrollo, 1990.

Chevalier, François. "Official Indigenismo in Peru in 1920: Origins, Significance, and Socioeconomic Scope." In *Race and Class in Latin America*, edited by Magnus Mörner, 184–96. New York: Columbia University Press, 1970.

Chomsky, Aviva. *West Indian Workers and the United Fruit Company in Costa Rica, 1870–1940*. Baton Rouge: Louisiana State University Press, 1996.

Ciccarelli, Orazio. "Fascism and Politics during the Benavides Regime, 1933–1939: The Italian Perspective." *Hispanic American Historical Review* 70, no. 3 (1990): 405–32.

Clark, Kim. *The Redemptive Work: Railway and Nation in Ecuador, 1895–1930*. Wilmington, Del.: SR Books, 1998.

Collier, David. *Squatters and Oligarchs: Authoritarian Rule and Policy Change in Peru*. Baltimore: Johns Hopkins University Press, 1976.

Collier, Ruth Berins, and David Collier. *Shaping the Political Arena: Critical Junctures, the Labor Movement, and Regime Dynamics in Latin America*. Princeton: Princeton University Press, 1991.

Conaghan, Catherine M. *Fujimori's Peru: Deception in the Public Sphere*. Pittsburgh: University of Pittsburgh Press, 2005.

Contreras, Carlos. "Maestros, mistis y campesinos en el Perú rural del siglo XX." In *El aprendizaje del capitalismo: Estudios de historia económica y social del Perú*, 214–72. Lima: Instituto de Estudios Peruanos, 2004.

———. "¿Inmigración o autogenia? La política de población en el Perú." In *El aprendizaje del capitalismo: Estudios de historia económica y social del Perú*, 173–213. Lima: Instituto de Estudios Peruanos, 2004.

Contreras, Carlos, and Marcos Cueto. *Historia del Perú contemporáneo*. Lima: Red para el desarrollo de la ciencias sociales en el Perú, 1999.

Cooper, Frederick. *Decolonization and African Society: The Labor Question in French and British Africa*. Cambridge: Cambridge University Press, 1996.

Cordova, Alberto. *La vivienda en el Perú: Estado actual y evaluación de las necesidades*. Lima: Casa Nacional de Moneda, 1958.

Coronado, Pedro P. "Génesis, evolución y estado actual de la Legislación Social Peruana." *Revista de la Facultad de Ciencias Económicas* no. 9 (1937): 87–115.

Corpancho, Clorinda. *El problema obrero y el socialismo*. Lima: Imprenta Moderna, 1913.

Coronil, Fernando. *The Magical State: Nature, Money and Modernity in Venezuela*. Chicago: University of Chicago Press, 1997.

Corrigan, Philip, and Derek Sayer. *The Great Arch: English State Formation As Cultural Revolution*. Oxford: Blackwell, 1985.

Costa y Cavero, Ramón. *Los reclamos de los trabajadores ante el Ministerio de Fomento*. Lima: Tipografía La Equitativa, 1931.

Cotler, Julio. *Clases, estado y nación en el Perú*. 1978; Lima: Instituto de Estudios Peruanos, 1992.

Counihan, Carole, and Penny Van Esterik, eds. *Food and Culture: A Reader*. London: Routledge, 1997.

Cox, Carlos M. *Ideas económicas del aprismo*. Lima: Editorial Cooperativa Aprista Atahualpa, 1934.

Craib, Raymond B. *Cartographic Mexico: A History of State Fixations and Fugitive Landscapes*. Durham: Duke University Press, 2004.

Crupi, Thomas. "Nation Divided, City Divided: Urbanism and Its Relation to the State, 1920–1940." In *Construyendo el Perú*, vol. 2, *Aportes de ingenieros y arquitectos*, 155–77. Lima: Universidad Nacional de Ingeniería, 2001.

Cueto, Marcos. *Excelencia científica en la periferia: Actividades científicas e investigación biomédica en el Perú, 1890–1950*. Lima: Grade/Concytec, 1989.

------. "Indigenismo and Rural Medicine in Peru: The Indian Sanitary Brigade and Manuel Núnez Butrón." *Bulletin of the History of Medicine* 65 (1991): 22–41.

------. *El regreso de las epidemias: Salud y sociedad en el Perú del siglo XX.* Lima: Instituto de Estudios Peruanos, 1997.

Curletti, Lauro A. *Documentos parlamentarios.* Lima: Imprenta Torres Aguirre, 1922.

------. *El problema industrial en el valle de Chicama.* Lima: n.p., 1921.

Das, Veena, and Deborah Poole, eds. *Anthropology in the Margins of the State.* Santa Fe: School of American Research Press, James Currey, 2004.

Daunton, M. J. *House and Home in the Victorian City: Working-Class Housing, 1850–1914.* London: Edward Arnold, 1983.

Davies, Thomas. *Indian Integration in Peru: A Half Century of Experience, 1900–1948.* Lincoln: University of Nebraska Press, 1970.

Dávila, Jerry. *Diploma of Whiteness: Race and Social Policy in Brazil, 1917–1945.* Durham: Duke University Press, 2003.

Davila Apolo, Diana. "Talara, los petroleros, y la huelga de 1931." B.A. thesis, Pontificia Universidad Católica del Perú, 1976.

Davila Cardenas, E. S. *La función del Estado al frente del problema de la habitación.* Lima: La Opinión Nacional, 1921.

Dawson, Alan. "Politics and the Labour Movement in Lima, 1919–1931." Ph.D. dissertation, University of Cambridge, 1981.

Dawson, Alexander S. *Indian and Nation in Revolutionary Mexico.* Tucson: University of Arizona Press, 2004.

Dean, Mitchell. *Governmentality: Power and Rule in Modern Society.* London: Sage, 1999.

Degregori, Carlos Ivan, Mariano Valderrama, Augusta Alfageme, and Marfil Francke Ballve. *Indigenismo, clases sociales y problema nacional: La discusión sobre el problema indígena en el Perú.* Lima: Centro Latinoamericano de Trabajo Social, 1981.

de la Cadena, Marisol. *Indigenous Mestizos: The Politics of Race and Culture in Cuzco, Peru, 1919–1991.* Durham: Duke University Press, 2000.

------. "Silent Racism and Intellectual Superiority in Peru." *Bulletin of Latin American Research* 17, no. 2 (1998): 143–64.

del Aguíla, Alicia. *Callejones y mansiones: Espacios de opinión pública y redes sociales y políticas en la Lima del 900.* Lima: Pontificia Universidad Católica del Perú, 1997.

de la Fuente, Alejandro. *A Nation for All: Race, Inequality, and Politics in Twentieth-Century Cuba.* Chapel Hill: University of North Carolina Press, 2001.

de la Puente, Ignacio. *Alimentación del obrero: Conferencia leída en el Ateneo de Lima el 22 de julio de 1899.* Lima: Oficina Tipográfica de "El Tiempo," 1899.

Dennis, Richard. "Room for Improvement? Recent Studies of Working-Class Housing." *Journal of Urban History* 21, no. 5 (1995): 660–73.

Derpich, Wilma, José Luis Huiza, and Cecilia Israel. *Lima años 30, salarios y costo de vida de la clase trabajadora.* Lima: Fundación Friedrich Ebert, 1985.

Derpich, Wilma, and Cecilia Israel. *Obreros frente a la crisis: Testimonios años 30.* Lima: Fundación Friedrich Ebert, 1987.

Deustua, José, and Alberto Flores Galindo. "Los comunistas y el movimiento obrero." In *Obras completas*, vol. 1, by Alberto Flores Galindo. 1977; Lima: SUR, 1993.

Diez Canseco, Salvador. *Seguro obligatorio contra accidentes del trabajo.* Lima: Librería escolar e imprenta de E. Moreno, 1907.

Donzelot, Jacques. *L'invention du social: Essai sur le déclin des passions politiques.* Paris: Fayard, 1984.

Dore, Elizabeth. *Myths of Modernity: Peonage and Patriarchy in Nicaragua.* Durham: Duke University Press, 2006.

Dore, Elizabeth, and Maxine Molyneux. *Hidden Histories of Gender and the State in Latin America.* Durham: Duke University Press, 2000.

Douglas, Mary. *Purity and Danger: An Analysis of Concepts of Pollution and Taboo.* London: Routledge and Kegan Paul, 1966.

Dreifuss Serrano, Cristina. "Ciudad y vivienda colectiva republicana en el Perú: El callejón de Petateros. Transformaciones." *Ur[b]es* 2 (2005): 125–44.

Drinot, Paulo. "Fighting for a Closed Shop: The 1931 Lima Bakery Workers' Strike." *Journal of Latin American Studies* 35, no. 2 (May 2003): 249–78.

———. "Hegemony from Below: Print Workers, the State, and the Communist Party in Peru, 1920–1940." In *Counterhegemony in the Colony and Postcolony*, edited by John Chalcraft and Yaseen Noorani, 204–227. London: Routledge, 2007.

———. "Madness, Neurasthenia and 'Modernity': Medico-legal and Popular Interpretations of Suicide in Early Twentieth-Century Lima." *Latin American Research Review* 39, no. 2 (2004): 89–113.

———. "Moralidad, moda y sexualidad: El contexto moral de la creación del barrio rojo de Lima." In *Mujeres, familia y sociedad en la historia de América Latina, siglos XVIII–XXI*, edited by Scarlett O'Phelan and Margarita Zegarra, 333–54. Lima: Pontificia Universidad Católica del Perú, 2006.

Earle, Rebecca. *The Return of the Native: Indians and Myth-Making in Spanish America, 1810–1930.* Durham: Duke University Press, 2007.

Echegaray, Mariano N., and Ramón Silva. *Legislación del trabajo y previsión social comentada y anotada.* Lima: Imprenta Torres Aguirre, 1925.

Eckert, Andreas. "Regulating the Social: Social Security, Social Welfare and the State in Late Colonial Tanzania." *Journal of African History* 45 (2004): 467–89.

Eguiguren, Luis Antonio. *El usurpador.* Lima: Talleres Gráficos Ahora, 1939.

Ehrick, Christine. *The Shield of the Weak: Feminism and the State in Uruguay, 1903–1933.* Albuquerque: University of New Mexico Press, 2005.

Elmore, Alberto. Inaugural lecture, Peruvian Academy of Legislation and Jurisprudence. Reproduced in "Academia peruana de legislación y jurisprudencia," *El Derecho* 11, nos. 345–46 (November–December 1906): 228–32.

Evans, Harriet, and Stephanie Donald, eds. *Picturing Power in the People's Republic of China: Posters of the Cultural Revolution.* Lanham, MD: Rowman and Littlefield, 1999.

Farnsworth-Alvear, Ann. *Dulcinea in the Factory: Myths, Morals, Men, and Women in Colombia's Industrial Experiment, 1905–1960.* Durham: Duke University Press, 2000.

Federación Gráfica del Perú. *Historia de la Federación Gráfica del Perú.* Lima: n.p., 1985.

Ferguson, James. *The Anti-Politics Machine: "Development," Depoliticization, and Bureaucratic Power in Lesotho.* Minneapolis: University of Minnesota Press, 1994.

Ferguson, James, and Akhil Gupta. "Spatializing States: Toward an Ethnography of Neoliberal Governmentality." *American Ethnologist* 29, no. 4 (2002): 981–1002.

F. C. Central del Perú. *Sistema de pagos y pactos con empleados y obreros.* Lima: n.p., 1950.

Ferrero, Raúl. "Destino racial del Perú: El mestizaje." In *Actas y trabajos científicos del XXVIII Congreso Internacional de Americanistas, 1939,* 205–6. Lima: Librería e Imprenta Gil, 1942.

Flores Galindo, Alberto. *Buscando un Inca: Identidad y utopía en los Andes.* Havana: Casa de las Américas, 1986.

———. "La agonía de Mariátegui." In *Obras completas,* vol. 2. 1980; Lima: SUR/ Fundación Andina, 1994.

———. *Los mineros de la Cerro de Pasco, 1900–1930.* In *Obras completas,* vol. 1. Lima: SUR, 1993.

Fonseca [Ariza], Juan. "Protestantismo, indigenismo y el mundo andino (1900–1930)." In *Más allá de la dominación y la Resistencia: Estudios de historia peruana, siglos XVI–XX,* edited by Paulo Drinot and Leo Garofalo, 282–311. Lima: Instituto de Estudios Peruanos, 2005.

Fonseca Ariza, Juan. "Antialcoholismo y modernización en el Perú (1900–1930)." *Histórica* 24, no. 2 (2000): 327–64.

Fonseca Ariza, Juan. *Misioneros y civilizadores: Protestantismo y modernización en el Perú (1915–1930).* Lima: Pontificia Universidad Católica del Perú, 2002.

Forment, Carlos A. *Democracy in Latin America, 1760–1900,* vol. 1, *Civic Selfhood and Public Life in Mexico and Peru.* Chicago: University of Chicago Press, 2003.

Foucault, Michel. *The Birth of Biopolitics.* Basingstoke, United Kingdom: Palgrave, 2008.

———. *Security, Territory, Population.* New York: Picador, 2009.

———. *Society Must Be Defended.* London: Penguin, 2004.

Franco, Carlos. "Hildebrando Castro Pozo: El socialismo cooperativo." In *Pensamiento político peruano, 1930–1968*, edited by Alberto Adrianzén, 155–230. Lima: Centro de Estudios y Promoción del Desarrollo, 1990.

French, John D. *The Brazilian Workers' ABC: Class Conflicts and Alliances in Modern Sao Paulo.* Chapel Hill: University of North Carolina Press, 1992.

French, Michael, and Jim Phillips. "Sophisticates or Dupes? Attitudes toward Food Consumers in Edwardian Britain." *Enterprise and Society* 4, no. 3 (2003): 442–70.

Fukumoto, Mary. *Hacia un nuevo sol: Japoneses y sus descendientes en el Perú.* Lima: Asociación Peruano Japonesa del Perú, 1997.

García, María Elena. *Indigenous Encounters in Contemporary Peru*, special issue of *Latin American and Caribbean Ethnic Studies* 3, no. 3 (2008).

———. *Making Indigenous Citizens: Identities, Development, and Multicultural Activism in Peru.* Stanford: Stanford University Press, 2005.

García-Bryce, Iñigo. "A Revolution Remembered, a Revolution Forgotten: The 1932 Aprista Insurrection in Trujillo, Peru." *A Contracorriente* 7, no. 3 (2010): 277–322.

———. *Crafting the Republic: Lima's Artisans and Nation-Building in Peru, 1821–1879.* Albuquerque: University of New Mexico Press, 2004.

García Jordán, Pilar. "Reflexiones sobre el Darwinismo social. Inmigración y colonización, mitos de los grupos modernizadores peruanos (1821–1919)." *Bulletin de l'Institut Français d' Études Andines* 21, no 2 (1992): 961–975.

García Salvatecci, Hugo. *El anarquismo frente al marxismo y el Perú.* Lima: Mosca Azul Editores, 1972.

García y García, Elvira. *La mujer y el hogar.* Lima: Librería e Imprenta Miranda, 1947.

García Rosell, Ovidio. *Comentarios al proyecto de seguros sociales: Conferencia en la Asociación Médica Peruana.* Lima: El Universal, 1936.

[Gerbi, Antonello]. *El Perú en marcha: Ensayo de geografía económica.* Lima: Banco Italiano-Lima, 1941.

Giesecke, Margarita. "The Trujillo Insurrection, the APRA Party, and the Making of Modern Peruvian Politics." Ph.D. dissertation, University of London, 1993.

Glener Plasencia, E. A. "Aprismo, sindicalismo y movimiento obrero en el valle de Chicama, 1930–1968." B.A. thesis, Universidad de Trujillo, no date.

Goldberg, David Theo. *The Racial State.* Oxford: Blackwell, 2001.

Gonzales, Michael. *Plantation Agriculture and Social Control in Northern Peru, 1875–1933.* Austin: University of Texas Press, 1985.

Gootenberg, Paul. *Between Silver and Guano: Commercial Policy and the State in Postindependence Peru.* Princeton: Princeton University Press, 1989.

———. *Imagining Development: Economic Ideas in Peru's "Fictitious Prosperity" of Guano, 1840–1880.* Berkeley: University of California Press, 1993.

Gordon, Linda. "Social Insurance and Public Assistance: The Influence of Gender in Welfare Thought in the United States, 1890–1935." *American Historical Review* 97, no. 1 (1992): 19–54.

Gould, Jeffrey L. *To Die in This Way: Nicaraguan Indians and the Myth of Mestizaje, 1880–1965*. Durham: Duke University Press, 1998.

Graham, Richard, Thomas E. Skidmore, Aline Helg, and Alan Knight. *The Idea of Race in Latin America, 1870–1940*. Austin: University of Texas Press, 1990.

Grandin, Greg, *The Blood of Guatemala: A History of Race and Nation*. Durham: Duke University Press, 2000.

Greene, Shane. *Customizing Indigeneity: Paths to a Visionary Politics in Peru*. Palo Alto: Stanford University Press, 2009.

Grompone, Romeo. "Tradiciones liberales y autonomías personales en el Perú: Una aproximación desde la cultura." In *Estudios culturales: discursos, poderes, pulsiones*, edited by Santiago López Maguiña, Gonzalo Portocarrero, Rocío Silva Santisteban and Víctor Vich, 491–514. Lima: Red para el desarrollo de las ciencias sociales en el Perú, 2001.

Gruber, Helmut. *Red Vienna: Experiment in Working-Class Culture, 1919–1934*. Oxford: Oxford University Press, 1991.

Gurney, W. R. *Report on the Economic Conditions in Peru*. London: His Majesty's Stationary Office, 1931.

Guy, Donna J. *Women Build the Welfare State: Performing Charity and Creating Rights in Argentina, 1880–1955*. Durham: Duke University Press, 2009.

Guzmán Barrón, Alberto, and Julio López Guillén, *La deficiencia de proteínas en la alimentación de los habitantes del Perú*. Lima: n.p., 1948.

Hacker, Jacob S. "Bringing the Welfare State Back In: The Promise (and Perils) of the New Social Welfare History." *Journal of Policy History* 17, no. 1 (2005): 125–54.

Hale, Charles A. "Political Ideas and Ideologies in Latin America, 1870–1930." In *Ideas and Ideologies in Twentieth Century Latin America*, edited by Leslie Bethell, 133–204. Cambridge: Cambridge University Press, 1996.

Hannah, Matthew G. *Governmentality and the Mastery of Territory in Nineteenth-Century America*. Cambridge: Cambridge University Press, 2000.

Hansen, Thomas Blom, and Finn Stepputat, eds. *States of Imagination: Ethnographic Explorations of the Postcolonial State*. Durham: Duke University Press, 2001.

Haya de la Torre, Víctor Raúl. *El anti-imperialismo y el APRA*. 1928; Lima: n.p., 1986.

———. *Política aprista*. Lima: Editorial Imprenta Amauta, 1967.

Herbold Jr., C. F. "Developments in the Peruvian Administrative System, 1919–1939: Modern and Traditional Qualities of Government under Authoritarian Regimes." Ph.D. dissertation, Yale University, 1973.

Hill, A. J. *Report on the Finance, Industry and Trade of Peru*. London: His Majesty's Stationary Office, 1923.

Holt, Thomas C. *The Problem of Freedom: Race, Labor and Politics in Jamaica and Britain, 1832–1938*. Baltimore: Johns Hopkins University Press, 1992.

Hong, Young-Sun. *Welfare, Modernity, and the Weimar State, 1919–1933*. Princeton: Princeton University Press, 1998.

Horne, Janet R. *A Social Laboratory for Modern France: The Musée Social and the Rise of the Welfare State*. Durham: Duke University Press, 2002.

Horowitz, Roger, Jeffrey M. Pilcher, and Sydney Watts. "Meat for the Multitudes: Market Culture in Paris, New York City and Mexico City over the Long Nineteenth Century." *American Historical Review* 109, no. 4 (2004): 1055–83.

Huiza, José Luis. "From the República Aristocrática to Pan Grande: Guillermo Billinghurst and Populist Politics in Early Twentieth Century Peru." Ph.D. dissertation, University of Miami, 1998.

Huneeus, Carlos, and María Paz Lanas. "Ciencia política e historia: Eduardo Cruz-Coke y el estado de bienestar en Chile, 1937–1938." *Historia* (Santiago) 35 (2002): 151–86.

Hutchison, Elizabeth Quay. *Labors Appropriate to Their Sex: Gender, Labor and Politics in Urban Chile, 1900–1930*. Durham: Duke University Press, 2001.

Irurozqui, Marta. "El Perú de Leguía: Derroteros y extravíos historiográficos." *Apuntes* 34 (1994): 85–101.

Iziga Nuñez, R. *Sociología de la clase obrera peruana*. Lima: Editorial Universitaria de San Marcos, 1994.

Jacobsen, Nils. *Mirages of Transition: The Peruvian Altiplano, 1780–1930*. Berkeley: University of California Press, 1993.

James, Daniel. *Resistance and Integration: Peronism and the Argentine Working Class, 1946–1976*. Cambridge: Cambridge University Press, 1988.

Jerram, Leif. *Germany's Other Modernity: Munich and the Making of Metropolis, 1895–1930*. Manchester, United Kingdom: Manchester University Press, 2007.

Joll, James. *The Anarchists*. London: Methuen, 1967.

Joseph, Gilbert M., and Daniel Nugent, eds. *Everyday Forms of State Formation: Revolution and the Negotiation of Rule in Modern Mexico*. Durham: Duke University Press.

Joyce, Patrick. *The Rule of Freedom: Liberalism and the Modern City*. London: Verso, 2003.

Kamminga, Harmke, and Andrew Cunningham. "Introduction: The Science and Culture of Nutrition, 1840–1940." In Kamminga and Cunningham, *The Science and Culture of Nutrition*, 1–15.

——, eds. *The Science and Culture of Nutrition, 1840–1940*. Amsterdam: Rodopi, 1995.

Kapsoli, Wilfredo, and Wilson Reategui. *El campesinado peruano: 1919–1930*. Lima: Universidad Nacional Mayor de San Marcos, 1972.

Kapsoli, Wilfredo. *Mariátegui y los congresos obreros*. Lima: Empresa Editora Amauta, 1980.

Kidambi, Prashant. "Housing the Poor in a Colonial City: The Bombay Improvement Trust, 1898–1918." *Studies in History* 17, no. 1 (2001): 57–79.

Klaiber, Jeffrey. "The Popular Universities and the Origins of Aprismo, 1921–1924." *Hispanic American Historical Review* 55, no. 4 (1975): 693–715.

Klarén, Peter. *Modernization, Dislocation and Aprismo: Origins of the Peruvian Aprista Party, 1870–1932.* Austin: University of Texas Press, 1973.

———. *Peru: Society and Nationhood in the Andes.* Oxford: Oxford University Press, 2000.

Klubock, Thomas Miller. *Contested Communities: Class, Gender, and Politics in Chile's El Teniente Copper Mine, 1904–1951.* Durham: Duke University Press, 1998.

Knight, Alan. "Populism and Neo-Populism in Latin America, especially Mexico." *Journal of Latin American Studies* 30, no. 2 (1998): 223–48.

Kotkin, Stephen. *Magnetic Mountain: Stalinism as Civilization.* Berkeley: University of California Press, 1995.

Koven, Seth, and Sonya Michel. "Womanly Duties: Maternalist Politics and the Origins of Welfare States in France, Germany, Great Britain and the United States, 1880–1920." *American Historical Review* 95, no. 4 (1990): 1076–1108.

Kristal, Efraín. *Una visión urbana de los Andes: Génesis y desarrollo del indigenismo en el Perú, 1848–1930.* Lima: Instituto Pasado y Presente, 1991.

Krohn-Hansen, Christian and Knut G. Nustad, eds. *State Formation: Anthropological Perspectives.* London: Pluto Press, 2005.

Larrañaga, Pedro J. M. "Bases económicas de nuestro porvenir racial." *Informaciones sociales* 3, no. 11 (November 1939): 1165–66.

Larson, Brooke. *Trials of Nation Making: Liberalism, Race, and Ethnicity in the Andes, 1810–1910.* Cambridge: Cambridge University Press, 2004.

Lavrin, Asunción. *Women, Feminism, and Social Change in Argentina, Chile, and Uruguay, 1890–1940.* Lincoln: University of Nebraska Press, 1995.

Legg, Stephen. *Spaces of Colonialism: Delhi's Urban Governmentalities.* Oxford: Blackwell, 2007.

Leibner, Gerardo. *El mito del socialismo indígena en Mariátegui.* Lima: Pontificia Universidad Católica del Perú, 1999.

León, Carlos Aurelio. *Patria Nueva: La reforma constitucional del 1919.* Lima: Librería e imprenta Gil, 1919.

Léon de Vivero, Fernando. *Avance del imperialismo fascista en el Perú.* Mexico City: Colección Trinchera Aprista, 1938.

Lesser, Jeffrey. *Negotiating National Identity: Immigrants, Minorities and the Struggle for Ethnicity in Brazil.* Durham: Duke University Press, 1999.

Levenstein, Harvey. *Paradox of Plenty: A Social History of Eating in Modern America.* New York: Oxford University Press, 1993.

Levenstein, Harvey. *Revolution at the Table: The Transformation of the American Diet.* New York: Oxford University Press, 1988.

Li, Tania Murray. *The Will to Improve: Governmentality, Development, and the Practice of Politics*. Durham: Duke University Press, 2007.

Lieberman, Robert C. *Shifting the Color Line: Race and the American Welfare State*. Cambridge: Harvard University Press, 1998.

Lindenmeyr, Adele. *Poverty Is Not a Vice: Charity, Society, and the State in Imperial Russia*. Princeton: Princeton University Press, 1996.

López Soria, José Ignacio. *El pensamiento fascista*. Lima: Mosca Azul Editores, 1981.

Lossio, Jorge. *Acequias y gallinazos: Salud ambiental en Lima del siglo xix*. Lima: Instituto de Estudios Peruanos, 2003.

Lowenthal, Abraham F. *The Peruvian Experiment: Continuity and Change under Military Rule*. Princeton: Princeton University Press, 1975.

Ludeña Urquizo, Wiley. *Lima: Historia y urbanismo, 1821–1970*. Lima: Ministerio de Vivienda, Construcción y Urbanización and Universidad Nacional de Ingeniería, 2004.

———. *Lima: Städtebau und Wohnungswesen. Die Intervention des Staates, 1821–1950*. Berlin: Verlag Dr. Köster, 1996.

Luna, Pablo F. "Etat, civilismo et société nationale au Pérou." *Histoire et Société de l'Amérique latine* 5 (1997), www.univ-paris-diderot.fr/hsal/hsa1971/pf197–1.html.

Macera, Pablo. *Cayaltí, 1875–1920: Organización del trabajo en una plantación azucarera del Perú*. Lima: Seminario de Historia Rural Andina, 1973.

———. *Trabajos de historia*. 4 vols. Lima: Instituto Nacional de Cultura, 1977.

Machuca Castillo, Gabriela. *La tinta, el pensamiento y las manos: La prensa popular anarquista, anarcosindicalista y obrera-sindical en Lima 1900–1930*. Lima: Universidad de San Martín de Porres, 2006.

Mallon, Florencia. *Defense of Community in Peru's Central Highlands: Peasant Struggle and Capitalist Transition*. Princeton: Princeton University Press, 1983.

———. *Peasant and Nation: The Making of Postcolonial Mexico and Peru*. Berkeley: University of California Press, 1995.

Mangabeira, Wilma. "Memories of Little Moscow (1943–64): Study of a Public Housing Experiment for Industrial Workers in Rio de Janeiro, Brazil." *Social History* 17, no. 2 (1992): 271–87.

Mannarelli, María Emma. *Limpias y modernas: Genero, higiene y cultura en la Lima del novecientos*. Lima: Ediciones Flora Tristán, 1999.

Manrique, Nelson. "Mariátegui y el problema de las razas." In *La aventura de Mariátegui: Nuevas perspectivas*, edited by Gonzalo Portocarrero, Eduardo Cáceres, and Rafael Tapia, 443–68. Lima: Pontificia Universidad Católica del Perú, 1995.

———. *La piel y la pluma: Escritos sobre literatura, etnicidad y racismo*. Lima: SUR/Centro de Información y Desarrollo Integral de Autogestión, 1999.

Manzanilla, J. M. *Discursos parlamentarios de J. M. Manzanilla, [1]916–18.* Lima: Imprenta Americana, 1919.

——. *Elecciones políticas y municipales: Discursos parlamentarios.* Lima: Imprenta A. J. Rivas Berrio, 1931.

Marcone, Mario. "Indígenas e inmigrantes durante la República Aristocrática: Población e ideología civilista." *Histórica* 19, no. 1 (1995): 73–93.

Mariátegui, José Carlos. "El problema de las razas en América Latina." In *Ideología y política*, 21–86. Lima: Amauta, 1969.

Martínez de la Torre, Ricardo. *Apuntes para una interpretación marxista de la historia social del Perú.* 4 vols. Lima: Universidad Nacional Mayor de San Marcos, 1974.

Matos Mar, José. *Desborde popular y crisis del Estado: El nuevo rostro del Perú en la década de 1980.* Lima: Instituto de Estudios Peruanos, 1984.

Mayer, Enrique. *Cuentos feos de la reforma agraria peruana.* Lima: Instituto de Estudios Peruanos/Centro Peruano de Estudios Sociales, 2009.

McKeown, Adam. "Inmigración china al Perú: Exclusión y negociación." *Histórica* 20, no. 1 (1996): 59–92.

McEvoy, Carmen. *Un proyecto nacional en el siglo XIX: Manuel Pardo y su visión del Perú.* Lima: Pontificia Universidad Católica del Perú, 1994.

——. *La utopía republicana: Ideales y realidades en la formación de la cultura política peruana (1871–1919).* Lima: Pontificia Universidad Católica del Perú, 1996.

McManus, Ruth. "Blue Collars, 'Red Forts,' and Green Fields: Working-Class Housing in Ireland in the Twentieth Century." *International Labor and Working Class History* 64 (2003): 38–54.

Meade, Teresa. *Civilizing Rio: Reform and Resistance in a Brazilian City.* University Park: Pennsylvania State University Press, 1996.

Méndez, Cecilia. "Incas Sí, Indios No: Notes on Peruvian Creole Nationalism and its Contemporary Crisis." *Journal of Latin American Studies* 28 (1996): 197–225.

——. *The Plebeian Republic: The Huanta Rebellion and the Making of the Peruvian State, 1820–1850.* Durham: Duke University Press, 2005.

Meneses, Rómulo. *Por el APRA (en la cárcel, al servicio del PAP).* Lima: Editorial Cooperativa Aprista, 1933.

Merino Schroder, M. V. *La vivienda barata en el Perú y el Banco Constructor.* Lima: Imprenta Accinelli, 1940.

Middlebrook, Kevin J. *The Paradox of Revolution: Labor, the State, and Authoritarianism in Mexico.* Baltimore: Johns Hopkins University Press, 1995.

Miller, Laura. "La mujer obrera en Lima, 1900–1930." In *Lima obrera, 1900–1930*, vol. 2, edited by Steve Stein, 11–152. Lima: Editorial Virrey, 1987.

Miller, Peter, and Nikolas Rose. *Governing the Present: Administering Economic, Social and Personal Life.* Cambridge: Polity, 2008.

Miller, Rory. "Railways and Economic Development in Central Peru, 1890–1930." In *Social and Economic Change in Modern Peru*, edited by Rory Miller, C. T. Smith, and John Fisher, 27–52. Liverpool: Institute of Latin American Studies, 1976.

Miro Quesada, Luis. *Albores de la reforma social en el Perú*. Lima: Talleres Gráficos Villanueva, 1965.

———. *El contrato de trabajo*. Lima: Imprenta de E. Moreno, 1901.

Mitchell, Timothy. *Colonising Egypt*. Berkeley: University of California Press, 1988.

———. *Rule of Experts: Egypt, Techno-Politics, Modernity*. Berkeley: University of California Press, 2002.

Molinari Morales, Tirso. *El fascismo en el Perú: La Unión Revolucionaria, 1931–1936*. Lima: Universidad Nacional Mayor de San Marcos, 2006.

More, Federico. "¿Existe Seguro Social en el Perú?" *Revista Excelsior* 19, no. 226 (November–December 1953): 11.

Mörner, Magnus, ed. *Race and Class in Latin America*. New York: Columbia University Press, 1970.

Muecke, Ulrich. *Political Culture in Nineteenth-Century Peru: The Rise of the Partido Civil*. Pittsburgh: University of Pittsburgh Press, 2004.

Mukerji, Chandra. *Territorial Ambitions and the Gardens of Versailles*. Cambridge: Cambridge University Press, 1997.

Muñoz Cabrejo, Fanni. *Diversiones públicas en Lima, 1890–1920: La experiencia de la modernidad*. Lima: Red para el desarrollo de las ciencias sociales en el Perú, 2001.

Muñoz Puglisevich, Germán. "El seguro social obligatorio en el imperio peruano de los Incas." In *Actas y trabajos científicos del XXVIII Congreso Internacional de Americanistas, 1939*. Lima: Librería e Imprenta Gil, 1942.

Noguera, Carlos Ernesto. *Medicina y política: Discurso médico y prácticas higiénicas en la primera mitad del siglo XX en Colombia*. Medellín: Fondo Editorial Universidad EAFIT, 2003.

Nord, Philip. "The Welfare State in France, 1870–1914." *French Historical Studies* 18, no. 3 (1994): 821–38.

Nugent, David. "Governing States." In *A Companion to the Anthropology of Politics*, edited by David Nugent and Joan Vincent, 199–215. Oxford: Blackwell, 2004.

———. *Modernity at the Edge of Empire: State, Individual, and Nation in the Northern Peruvian Andes, 1885–1935*. Stanford: Stanford University Press, 1997.

Nugent, Guillermo. *El laberinto de la choledad*. Lima: Fundación Ebert, 1992.

Nuñez Borja, Humberto. *Legislación social peruana*. Arequipa: Tipografía Cuadros, 1934.

O'Connor, Erin. *Gender, Indian, Nation: The Contradictions of Making Ecuador, 1830–1925*. Tucson: University of Arizona Press, 2007.

O'Connor, Julia, Ann Orloff, and Sheila Shaver. *States, Markets, Families: Gender, Liberalism and Social Policy in Australia, Canada, Great Britain and the United States.* Cambridge: Cambridge University Press, 1999.

Oliart, María Patricia. "Images of Gender and Race: The View from Above in Turn-of-the-Century Lima." M.A. thesis, University of Texas at Austin, 1994.

Ong, Aiwha. *Neoliberalism as Exception: Mutations in Citizenship and Sovereignty.* Durham: Duke University Press, 2006.

——. "Graduated Sovereignty in South-East Asia." *Theory, Culture and Society* 17, no. 4 (2000): 55–75.

Orloff, Ann Shola. "Social Provision and Regulation: Theories of States, Social Policies, and Modernity." In *Remaking Modernity: Politics, History, and Sociology*, edited by Julia Adams, Elisabeth S. Clemens, and Ann Shola Orloff, 190–224. Durham: Duke University Press, 2005.

Outtes, Joel. "Disciplining Society through the City: The Genesis of City Planning in Brazil and Argentina (1894–1945)." *Bulletin of Latin American Research* 22, no. 2 (2003): 137–64.

Overmyer-Velázquez, Mark. *Visions of the Emerald City: Modernity, Tradition, and the Formation of Porfirian Oaxaca.* Durham: Duke University Press, 2006.

Palacios, Leoncio M. *Encuesta sobre presupuestos familiares obreros realizada en la ciudad de Lima, en 1940.* Lima: Universidad Nacional Mayor de San Marcos, 1944.

Palomino Ramírez, Teodosio Arístides. "La Seguridad Social y la economía popular." In *Anales del Segundo Congreso Peruano de Derecho del Trabajo y de "Seguridad Social,"* vol. 2, 334–35. Lima: Universidad Nacional Mayor de San Marcos, 1971.

Pareja, Piedad. *Anarquismo y sindicalismo en el Perú.* Lima: Ediciones Rikchay Peru, 1978.

Pareja Pflucker, Piedad. *El movimiento obrero peruano de los años 30.* Lima: Fundación Friedrich Ebert, 1985.

Parker, David S. "Civilizing the City of Kings: Hygiene and Housing in Lima, Peru." In *Cities of Hope: People, Protests, and Progress in Urbanizing Latin America, 1870–1930*, edited by Ronn Pineo and James A. Baer, 153–78. Boulder: Westview Press, 1998.

——. *The Idea of the Middle Class: White-Collar Workers and Peruvian Society, 1900–1950.* University Park: Pennsylvania State University Press, 1998.

——. "Peruvian Politics and the Eight-Hour Day: Rethinking the General Strike." *Canadian Journal of History/Annales canadiennes d'histoire* 30 (1995): 417–38.

Partido Socialista del Perú. *Primer manifiesto y programa de reivindicaciones inmediatas, aprobadas por la Primera Conferencia Nacional del Partido.* Lima: Empresa Editorial Rímac, 1933.

Payne, James L. *Labor and Politics in Peru: The System of Political Bargaining.* New Haven: Yale University Press, 1965.

Paz Soldán, Carlos Enrique. *La asistencia social en el Perú.* Lima: Imprenta del Centro Editorial, 1914.

Pedersen, Susan. *Family, Dependence, and the Origins of the Welfare State: Britain and France, 1914–1945.* Cambridge: Cambridge University Press, 1993.

Peloso, Vincent C. *Peasants on Plantations: Subaltern Strategies of Labor and Resistance in the Pisco Valley, Peru.* Durham: Duke University Press, 1999.

———. "Succulence and Sustenance: Region, Class and Diet in Nineteenth-Century Peru." In *Food, Politics and Society in Latin America,* edited by J. C. Super and T. C. Wright, 44–64. Lincoln: University of Nebraska Press, 1985.

Pereda Torres, Rolando. *Historia de las luchas sociales del movimiento obrero en el Perú republicano, 1858–1917.* Lima: Editorial Imprenta Sudamericana, 1982.

Pereyra Chávez, Nelson E. "Los campesinos y la conscripción víal." In *Estado y mercado en la historia del Perú,* edited by Carlos Contreras and Manuel Glave, 334–50. Lima: Pontificia Universidad Católica del Perú, 2002.

Peru. *Statistical Abstract of Peru, 1923.* Lima: Dirección de Estadística, 1924.

Peru. *Los Restaurantes populares del Perú: Contribución al estudio del problema de la alimentación popular.* Santiago de Chile: Imprenta Universitaria, 1936.

Peru, Ministerio de Fomento. *La labor constructiva del Perú en el gobierno de Don Augusto Leguía.* Lima: Imprenta Torres Aguirre, 1930.

Pesce, Luis. *Indígenas e inmigrantes.* Lima: Imprenta de la Opinión Nacional, 1906.

Pévez, Juan H. *Memorias de un viejo luchador campesino.* Lima: Tarea, 1983.

Pierce, Steven. "Looking Like a State: Colonialism and the Discourse of Corruption in Northern Nigeria." *Comparative Studies in Society and History* 48, no. 4 (2006): 887–914.

Pilcher, Jeffrey M. *¡Que vivan los tamales!: Food and the Making of Mexican Identity.* Albuquerque: University of New Mexico Press, 1998.

———. *The Sausage Rebellion: Public Health, Private Enterprise and Meat in Mexico City, 1890–1917.* Albuquerque: University of New Mexico Press, 2006.

Poblete, Juan. "Governmentality and the Social Question: National Formation and Discipline." In *Foucault and Latin America: Appropriations and Deployments of Discursive Analysis,* edited by Benigno Trigo, 137–52. London: Routledge, 2002.

Poole, Deborah. "Figueroa Aznar and the Cusco Indigenistas: Photography and Modernism in Early Twentieth-Century Peru." *Representations* 38 (1992): 39–75.

———. *Vision, Race, and Modernity: A Visual Economy of the Andean Image World.* Princeton: Princeton University Press, 1997.

Portocarrero, Felipe, and Cynthia Sanborn, eds. *De la caridad a la solidaridad: Filantropía y voluntariado en el Perú.* Lima: Universidad del Pacifico, 2003.

Portocarrero, Gonzalo. *De Bustamante a Odría: El fracaso del Frente Democratico Nacional, 1945–1950.* Lima: Mosca Azul Editores, 1983.

———. "El fundamento invisible: Función y lugar de las ideas racistas en la República Aristocrática." In *Mundos interiores: Lima 1850–1950*, edited by Aldo Panfichi and Felipe Portocarrero, 219–59. Lima: Universidad del Pacífico, 1995.

———. "Ideologías, funciones del estado y políticas económicas, Perú: 1900–1980." *Debates en sociología* 9 (1983): 7–30.

———. "Memorias del velasquismo." In *Batallas por la memoria: antagonismos de la promesa peruana*, edited by Marita Hamann, Santiago López Maguiña, Gonzalo Portocarrero, and Víctor Vich, 229–56. Lima: Red para el desarrollo de las ciencias sociales en el Perú, 2003.

———. *Racismo y mestizaje*. Lima: Editorial del Congreso, 2007.

Portocarrero Grados, Ricardo. *El trabajo infantil en el Perú: Apuntes de interpretación histórica*. Lima: Radda Barnen, n.d.

Portocarrero, Ricardo. "José Carlos Mariátegui y las Universidades Populares González Prada." In *La Aventura de Mariátegui*, edited by Gonzalo Portocarrero, Eduardo Cáceres, and Rafael Tapia, 389–420. Lima: Pontificia Universidad Católica del Perú, 1995.

Prakash, Gyan. *Another Reason: Science and the Imagination of Modern India*. Princeton: Princeton University Press, 1999.

Proyecto Historia UNI. *Construyendo el Perú: Aportes de ingenieros y arquitectos*, vols. 1 and 2. Lima: Universidad Nacional de Ingeniería, 1999 and 2001.

Quijano, Aníbal. *El Perú en la crisis de los años treinta*. 1978; Lima: Mosca Azul, 1985.

Quine, Maria Sophia. *Italy's Social Revolution: Charity and Welfare from Liberalism to Fascism*. New York: Palgrave, 2002.

Ramón Joffré, Gabriel. *La muralla y los callejones: Intervención urbana y proyecto político durante la segunda mitad del siglo XIX*. Lima: Seminario Interdisciplinario de Estudios Andinos, 1999.

Ramos Rau, Demetrio. *Mensaje de Trujillo: Del anarquismo al aprismo*. Trujillo: Instituto NorPeruano de Desarrollo Económico Social, 1987.

Rancière, Jacques. "The Myth of the Artisan: Critical Reflections on a Category of Social History." *International Labor and Working Class History* 24 (1983): 1–16.

Rebagliati, Edgardo. "La previsión social en Chile." *Investigaciones sociales* 1, no. 2 (August 1937): 401–03.

———. *La previsión social en el Perú*. Lima: Biblioteca de la Caja Nacional de Seguro Social, 1937.

Rénique, Gerardo. "Race, Region, and Nation: Sonora's Anti-Chinese Racism and Mexico's Postrevolutionary Nationalism, 1920s–1930s." In *Race and Nation in Modern Latin America*, edited by Nancy P. Appelbaum, Anne S. Macpherson, and Karin Alejandra Rosemblatt, 211–36. Chapel Hill: University of North Carolina Press, 2003.

Rénique, José Luis. *La batalla por Puno: Conflicto agrario y nación en los Andes peruanos, 1866–1995*. Lima: Instituto de Estudios Peruanos/SUR/Centro Peruano de Estudios Sociales, 2004.

Riva Agüero, José de la. *Discursos en las fiestas del Aniversario Patrio de 1931*. Lima: Imprenta Torres Aguirre, 1931.

Rock, David. "Intellectual Precursors of Conservative Nationalism in Argentina, 1900–1927." *Hispanic American Historical Review* 67, no. 2 (1987): 271–300.

Rodgers, Daniel T. *Atlantic Crossings: Social Politics in a Progressive Age*. Cambridge: Harvard University Press, 1998.

Rodríguez Pastor, Humberto. "La calle del Capón, el callejón Otaiza y el barrio chino." In *Mundos interiores: Lima 1850–1950*, edited by Aldo Panfichi and Felipe Portocarrero, 397–430. Lima: Universidad del Pacífico, 1995.

——. *Herederos del Dragón: Historia de la comunidad china en el Perú*. Lima: Fondo Editorial del Congreso del Perú, 2000.

Rodríguez, J. M. "Coaliciones y huelgas." *Economista peruano* 4, nos. 47–48 (1913): 1.

Roediger, David. *The Wages of Whiteness: Race and the Making of the American Working Class*. Rev. ed. 1991; London: Verso, 2007.

Rojas Rojas, Rolando. *Tiempos de Carnaval: El ascenso de lo popular a la cultura nacional (Lima, 1822–1922)*. Lima: Instituto de Estudios Peruanos/Instituto Francés de Estudios Andinos, 2005.

Rose, Nikolas. *Powers of Freedom: Reframing Political Thought*. Cambridge: Cambridge University Press, 1999.

Rose Ugarte, Luis. *La situación alimenticia en el Perú*. Lima: Servicio Cooperativo Inter-Americano de Producción de Alimentos, 1945.

Rosemblatt, Karin Alejandra. "Charity, Rights, and Entitlement: Gender, Labor, and Welfare in Early Twentieth-Century Chile." *Hispanic American Historical Review* 81, nos. 3–4 (2001): 555–85.

——. *Gendered Compromises: Political Cultures and the State in Chile, 1920–1950*. Chapel Hill: University of North Carolina Press, 2000.

Ruiz Blanco, Manuel. "Las casas para obreros de Rafael Marquina." *Huaca* 3 (1993): 33–41.

——. "Vivienda colectiva en Lima (1535–1940)." In *Construyendo el Perú*, vol. 2, *Aportes de ingenieros y arquitectos*, 101–22. Lima: Universidad Nacional de Ingeniería, 2001.

Ruiz Zevallos, Augusto. *La multitud, las subsistencias y el trabajo: Lima, 1890–1920*. Lima: Pontificia Universidad Católica del Perú, 2001.

Sabroso, Arturo. *Replicas proletarias*. Lima: Minerva, 1934.

Sánchez Ortiz, Guillermo. *La prensa obrera, 1900–1930*. Lima: Ediciones Barricada, 1987.

Santistevan, Jorge. *La huelga en el Perú*. Lima: Centro de Estudios de Democracia y Sociedad, 1980.

Scott, David. "Colonial Governmentality." *Social Text* 43 (1995): 191–220.

Scott, James C. *Seeing Like a State: How Certain Schemes to Improve the Human Condition Have Failed*. New Haven: Yale University Press, 1998.

——. *Weapons of the Weak: Everyday Forms of Peasant Resistance*. New Haven: Yale University Press, 1987.

Seoane, Manuel. *Obras apristas, 1931 a 1948*. Lima: Ediciones Continente, 1957.

Shapiro, Ann Louise. "Paris." In *Housing the Workers, 1850–1914: A Comparative Perspective*, edited by Martin J. Daunton, 41–57. London: Leicester University Press, 1990.

Sharma, Aradhana, and Akhil Gupta. "Introduction: Rethinking Theories of the State in an Age of Globalization." In Sharma and Gupta, *The Anthropology of the State*, 1–42.

——, eds. *The Anthropology of the State: A Reader*. London: Blackwell, 2006.

Silverblatt, Irene. *Modern Inquisitions: Peru and the Colonial Origins of the Civilized World*. Durham: Duke University Press, 2004.

Simmel, Georg. "Sociology of the Meal." In *Simmel on Culture*, edited by David Frisby and Mike Featherstone, 130–136. London: Sage Publications, 1997.

Skidmore, Thomas E. *Black into White; Race and Nationality in Brazilian Thought*. New York: Oxford University Press, 1974.

Skocpol, Theda. *Protecting Soldiers and Mothers: The Political Origins of Social Policy in the United States*. Cambridge: Harvard University Press, 1995.

Skuban, William E. *Lines in the Sand: Nationalism and Identity on the Peruvian Chilean Frontier*. Albuquerque: University of New Mexico Press, 2007.

Spalding, Karen. *Huarochirí: An Andean Society Under Inca and Spanish Rule*. Stanford: Stanford University Press, 1984.

Smith, David F., and Jim Phillips, eds. *Food, Science, Policy and Regulation: International and Comparative Perspectives*. London: Routledge, 2000.

Snodgrass, Michael. *Deference and Defiance in Monterrey: Workers, Paternalism, and Revolution in Mexico, 1890–1950*. Cambridge: Cambridge University Press, 2003.

Stein, Steve. *Populism in Peru: The Emergence of the Masses and the Politics of Social Control*. Madison: University of Wisconsin Press, 1980.

Steinmetz, George. "Introduction: Culture and the State." In Steinmetz, *State/Culture*, 1–49.

——. *Regulating the Social: The Welfare State and Local Politics in Imperial Germany*. Princeton: Princeton University Press, 1993.

——, ed. *State/Culture: State Formation after the Cultural Turn*. Ithaca: Cornell University Press, 1999.

Stepan, Alfred C. *The State and Society: Peru in Comparative Perspective*. Princeton: Princeton University Press, 1978.

Stepan, Nancy Leys. *The Hour of Eugenics: Race, Gender, and Nation in Latin America*. Ithaca: Cornell University Press, 1991.

Stern, Steve, J. *Peru's Indian Peoples and the Challenges of Spanish Conquest: Huamanga to 1640*. Second edition. Madison: University of Wisconsin Press, 1993.

Stern, Steve J., ed. *Shining and Other Paths: War and Society in Peru, 1980–1995*. Durham: Duke University Press, 1998.

Stoler, Ann Laura. *Race and the Education of Desire: Foucault's* History of Sexuality *and the Colonial Order of Things*. Durham: Duke University Press, 1995.

Sulmont, Denis. *El movimiento obrero en el Perú, 1900–1956*. Lima: Pontificia Universidad Católica del Perú, 1975.

Swenarton, Mark. *Homes Fit for Heroes: The Politics and Architecture of Early State Housing in Britain*. London: Heinemann, 1981.

Swenson, Peter A. *Capitalists against Markets: The Making of Labor Markets and Welfare States in the United States and Sweden*. Oxford: Oxford University Press, 2002.

Taller de Testimonio. *Habla la ciudad*. Lima: Municipalidad de Lima Metropolitana/Universidad Nacional Mayor de San Marcos, 1986.

Tapia, Rafael. "La Fiesta de la Planta de Vitarte." *Pretextos* 3–4 (1992): 187–205.

Tejada, Luis. *La cuestión del pan: El anarcosindicalismo en el Perú 1880–1919*. Lima: Instituto Nacional de Cultura/Banco Industrial del Perú, 1988.

——. "Malambo." In *Mundos interiores: Lima 1850–1950*, edited by Aldo Panfichi and Felipe Portocarrero, 145–60. Lima: Universidad del Pacífico, 1995.

Temoche, Ricardo. *Cofradías, gremios, mutuales y sindicatos en el Perú*. Lima: Editorial Escuela Nueva, 1987.

Temoche Benites, Ricardo. *Manual del sindicalista*. Lima: Librería Studium Editores, 1989.

Thompson, Ruth. "The Limitations of Ideology in the Early Argentine Labour Movement: Anarchism in the Trade Unions." *Journal of Latin American Studies* 16, no. 1 (1984): 81–99.

Thorp, Rosemary, and Geoffrey Bertram. *Peru, 1890–1977: Growth and Policy in an Open Economy*. London: MacMillan, 1978.

Thorp, Rosemary, and Carlos Londoño. "The Effect of the Great Depression on the Economies of Peru and Colombia." In *Latin America in the 1930s: The Role of the Periphery in World Crisis*, edited by Rosemary Thorp, 81–116. Basingstoke, United Kingdom: Macmillan, 1984.

Thurner, Mark. *From Two Republics to One Divided: Contradictions of Postcolonial Nationmaking in Andean Peru*. Durham: Duke University Press, 1997.

Tilly, Charles. *Durable Inequality*. Berkeley: University of California Press, 1999.

Tinsman, Heidi. *Partners in Conflict: The Politics of Gender, Sexuality, and Labor in the Chilean Agrarian Reform, 1950–1973*. Durham: Duke University Press, 2002.

Tovar Samanez, Teresa. *Velasquismo y movimiento popular: Otra historia prohibida*. Lima: Centro de Estudios y Promoción del Desarrollo, 1985.

Trouillot, Michel-Rolph. "The Anthropology of the State: Close Encounters of a Deceptive Kind." *Current Anthropology* 42, no. 1: 125–38.

Turino, Thomas. "The Music of Andean Migrants in Lima, Peru: Demographics, Social Power, and Style." *Latin American Music Review/Revista de Música Latinoamericana* 9, no. 2 (1988): 127–50.

Ugarteche, Pedro. *Sánchez Cerro: Papeles y recuerdos de un presidente del Perú*, vol. 4. Lima: Editorial Universitaria, 1969.

Ulloa Sotomayor, Alberto. *¿Conviene establecer una Dirección del Trabajo? ¿Cómo debería organizarse?* Lima: Ernesto Villarán, 1919.

———. *La organización social y legal del trabajo en el Perú*. Lima: n.p., 1916.

Valderrama, Mariano. "Los planteamientos de Haya de la Torre y de José Carlos Mariátegui sobre el problema indígena y el problema nacional." In *Indigenismo, clases sociales, y problema nacional: La discusión sobre el "problema indígena" en el Perú*, by Carlos Ivan Degregori et al., 187–226. Lima: Ediciones Centro Latinoamericano de Trabajo Social, n.d.

Valdez Tudela, Napoleón. "Nuestra realidad social." *Revista de la Facultad de Ciencias Económicas* 16 (1939): 1–17.

———. "El problema social ante la historia y su solución en el presente." *Ciencias, Industria, y Maquinas* 1, no. 1 (1937): 28–36.

Valega, Manuel. "La habitación." *Arquitecto Peruano* 14, no. 160 (1950): n.p.

Vega, Alejandro. "El problema indígena." *Informaciones sociales* 2, no. 10 (1938): 1075–81.

Vernon, James. *Hunger: A Modern History*. Cambridge: Harvard University Press, 2007.

Vigil, Manuel A., *Legislación del trabajo*. Lima: Talleres Gráficos Hermanos Faura, 1937.

Wade, Peter. *Race and Ethnicity in Latin America*. London: Pluto Press, 1997.

———. *Race, Nature, and Culture: An Anthropological Perspective*. London: Pluto Press, 2002.

Walker, Charles. *Smoldering Ashes: Cuzco and the Creation of Republican Peru, 1780–1840*. Durham: Duke University Press, 1999.

Weiner, Richard. *Race, Nation, and Market: Economic Culture in Porfirian Mexico*. Tucson: University of Arizona Press, 2004.

Weinstein, Barbara. *For Social Peace in Brazil: Industrialists and the Remaking of the Working Class in Sao Paulo, 1920–1964*. Chapel Hill: University of North Carolina Press, 1996.

Wilson, Fiona. "Indian Citizenship and the Discourse of Hygiene/Disease in Nineteenth-Century Peru." *Bulletin of Latin American Research* 23, no. 2 (2004): 165–80.

Wolfe, Justin. "Those That Live by the Work of Their Hands: Labour, Ethnicity and Nation-State Formation in Nicaragua, 1850–1900." *Journal of Latin American Studies* 36, no. 1 (2004): 57–83.

Zitor [pseudonym]. *Historia de las principales huelgas y paros obreros habidos en el Perú, 1896–1946*. Lima: n.p., 1976.

INDEX

Acción Popular, 53

Alayza Paz Soldán, Francisco, 1–2, 7, 35, 44–45, 49

Alba, Antonio, 197

Alexander, Alberto, 133, 145

Alianza Popular Revolucionaria Americana (APRA), 6, 14, 47–48, 53, 66, 74, 102, 112, 114, 119, 124–29; campaign by, against Japanese immigrants, 190; campaign by, against Juntas Pro-desocupados, 144–47; campaign by, against restaurantes populares, 174–80; critique by, of Seguro Social, 202–3

Allende, Salvador, 219

Almenara, Guillermo, 215–16

Anarchism, 7, 30, 72–74, 99, 168, 244 n. 12

Andes, invisibilization of, 38

Angulo de Puente Arnao, Juan, 24, 56, 58

Arnaud, Leopoldo, 43

Asamblea de Sociedades Unidas (ASU), 72, 105

Barba, Carlos, 65

Barrios obreros, 5–6, 14, 147; as attempt to control population groups, 149–50; early projects of, 129–36; as expression of Benavides' social action, 148–49, as expression of rationalities of government, 124–25, 150–55; failure of, 155–58; as technologies of government, 124–25, 150–55

Belaúnde, Víctor Andrés, 23–24

Belaúnde Terry, Fernando, 14, 228

Benavides, Óscar R., 6, 54, 56, 113, 125–29, 138; food policy of, 174–90; housing policy of, 147–50, 154–55, 161; social insurance policy of, 193–208

Bergquist, Charles, 249 n. 117

Billinghurst, Guillermo, 17, 28, 54, 57, 131, 136, 155, 168, 250 n. 14

Biopolitics. See Governmentality

Biopower. See Governmentality

Bourdieu, Pierre, 33, 221

Boza, Edilberto C., 204–7

Bustamante, Luis, 102

Bustamante y Rivero, José Luis, 110

Cabré, Francisco, 23

Castillo, Luciano, 110, 143, 193, 252 n. 43

Castro Pozo, Hildebrando, 66–67, 71–72, 90, 93, 225, 252 n. 43

Chávez Fernández, Manuel, 110, 112

Civilismo. *See* Partido Civil

Collective contracts, 71, 75–76, 87–90

Comintern, 194

Comité Pro-Abaratamiento de las Subsistencias, 73, 164

Confederación de Artesanos Unión Universal (CAUU), 72, 105, 109, 166, 259 n. 82

Confederación General de Trabajadores del Perú (CGTP), 111, 193

Constitution: articles in, regarding labor (1920), 60–64, 77; articles in, regarding labor (1933), 112–13

Contreras, Isaias, 73

Corpancho, Clorinda, 25

Corporatism. *See* Social action

Cox, Carlos Manuel, 176

Curletti, Lauro, 65–66, 75, 85, 90, 93

Dammert, Alfredo, 147, 154

de la Cadena, Marisol, 5, 36, 61, 232, 237

de la Puente, Ignacio, 169–72

de Ojeda, Dagoberto, 102

Deustua, Alejandro, 36, 225

Diez Canseco, Salvador, 30

Eguiguren, Luis Antonio, 202

Elites: differentiated views by, of labor, 35–36; views of, of indigenous population, 39–46, 49, 81; views of, on industrialization, 1–4, 7; views of, on labor militancy, 93–99, 120, 124; views of, on social policy, 7–8, 19–27, 199, 215, 233; views of, on worker housing, 131; views of, on workers as agents of progress, 147–59, 180–87, 216–21

Elmore, Alberto, 20–21

Employers: reactions of, to Sección del

Trabajo, 86; reactions of, to Seguro Social, 203–4

Encinas, José Antonio, 225

Enganche. *See* Indentured labor

Esteves, Luis, 39

Ethnicity. *See* Racism

Eugenics, 37, 205–6

Federación de Obreros Panaderos "Estrella del Perú" (FOPEP), 90; dispute of, with bakery owners, 115–19

Federación Gráfica del Perú (FGP), 89, 91–93, 101, 119

Federación Obrera Local del Callao (FOLC), 74

Federación Obrera Local de Lima (FOLL), 74, 104

Federación Obrera Regional del Perú (FORP), 74, 77

Federación Regional de Trabajadores de Ica, 88

Ferrero, Raúl, 45–46, 49

Fiesta de la Planta, 96, 111

Food: APRA's policy toward, 174–80; concern with quality of, 167–68; gendering of, 165–66; historiography of, 162, 269 n. 3; racialization of, 163–69, 187–91; rise in price of, 163–64, 270 n. 7; sexualization of, 165–66. *See also* Nutrition

Ford, Henry, 27

Foucault, Michel, 8–9, 12–13, 233, 235

Gamarra, Abelardo, 166

García, Uriel, 36, 225

García Calderón, Francisco, 36, 39

García Calderón, Ventura, 36

García Rossell, Ovidio, 201

García y García, Elvira, 152, 155

Garland, Alejandro, 34–35

Gazzeri, Ernesto, 88

Gender: role of, in food policy, 164–66; role of, in historiography on social welfare in Latin America, 194–95; role of, in historiography on state formation, 8–9; role of, in housing policy, 149–55; role of, in labor policy, 28–32; role of, in public health policy, 197, 208–20

Gonzalez Prada, Manuel, 72

Governmentality, 8–15, 24–25, 53–59, 233; as in collective contracts, 75–76; as in food policy toward workers, 180–87; implications of study for, 234–35; as in Leguía's labor policy, 107–9; as in public health and social insurance policy, 216–21; as in Sección del Trabajo, 75–83; as in worker housing policy, 124–25, 150–55

Gutarra, Nicolás, 101

Haaker Fort, Roberto, 147, 154
Haya de la Torre, Agustín, 66
Haya de la Torre, Víctor Raúl, 6, 47–48, 66, 99, 101, 176, 191, 193
Hospital Obrero, 193, 207, 215, 219–21, 227
Hurwitz, Jacobo, 258 n. 61

Indentured labor, 44
Indigeneity. See Indigenous population
Indigenismo, 36, 61
Indigenous (Indian) population: as descendant of Inca civilization, 45; exclusion of, from projects of nation-state formation, 13–15, 38, 48–49, 221–27; exclusion of, from Sección del Trabajo, 81; exclusion of, from Seguro Social, 221–27; exclusion of, from sphere of labor, 13–15, 33–35; as obstacle to or incommensurable with progress, 14, 32–49, 82; physi-

cal and moral degeneration of, 35–36; redemption of, through actions of APRA, 47–48; redemption of, through actions of Leguía, 107–8; redemption of, through exposure to labor, 39–50, 248 n. 91; redemption of, through socialism, 46–47

Industry: limited size of, 1–3, 239 n. 2, perceived role of, in nation-building, 25–27, 44–47

Inspecciones Regionales del Trabajo, 110, 113, 115, 261 nn. 115–16

Joya, Glicerio, 136
Junta Departamentales Pro-Desocupados de Lima: criticisms of, 142–43; inspiration for, 138–39; organization of, 123, 136; as responses to popular pressure, 266 n. 56; role of, in operation of restaurantes populares, 174; unpopularity of, 141–42; worker housing built by, 137–38, 143–44

Labor question, 2–8, 19–27, 31–34, 49, 52, 58–61, 67, 81, 86, 94
Labor state: changes to, in 1930s, 109–20; changes to, in Oncenio, 99–109; development of, 7–15, 53–54, 86, 93; as expressed in Sección del Trabajo, 70–83; gendering of, 28–32; technification of, 64–70; workers' appropriation and redeployment of, 114–20
Labor: as agent of progress, 6, 10–14, 25, 50, 59, 75, 81–83, 86, 93, 109, 118–19, 124, 129, 233; form of, congenial to elite, 96–99; invocation by, of governmentality, 115–19; racialization of, 13–14, 32–50, 242 n. 27; 243 nn. 4–5; repression of, 99–105. See also Constitution

Larco Herrera, Víctor, 88, 95
Larco Hoyle, Rafael, 98
Larrañaga, Pedro J. M., 225–26
Leguía, Augusto B., 52–53, 61, 64–66,
    72, 75, 81, 87, 90–92; food policy
    and, 163–64; historiography and,
    250 n. 8, 257; justification by, of dic-
    tatorship, 106–8; labor policy of,
    99–109; support by, of CAUU and
    ASU, 105; views of, on indigenous
    population, 107–8; worker housing
    policy of, 133–36
Leguía y Martínez, Germán, 65, 90
León, Carlos Aurelio, 63
León García, Enrique, 131
Levano, Delfín, 69, 73–74
Levano, Manuel Caracciolo, 73, 254
    n. 70
Ley de Accidentes del Trabajo (Law
    1378), 28–32
Ley de Conscripción Víal, 61, 108
Ley sobre Trabajo de Mujeres y Niños
    (Law 2851), 28–32

Manzanilla, José Matías, 54–59, 75, 93
Mariátegui, José Carlos, 6, 23, 27, 46–
    49, 89, 96, 99, 101–2, 193
Marquina, Rafael, 147
Maurer, Augusto, 204
Meiggs, Enrique, 135
Meneses, Rómulo, 48
Merino Schroder, M. V., 155
Miller, Peter, 9, 11, 24
Miro Quesada, Luis, 19–21, 24, 29–
    30, 55–58, 93
More, Federico, 168–69, 199, 228
Mostajo, Francisco, 110
Muñoz Puglisevich, Germán, 213
Mussolini, Benito, 126

Nutrition: as field of study, 169–74; of
    Lima workers, 172–73; as matter

for state intervention, 169–74. See
    also Food

Odría, Manuel, 14
Oliveira, Pedro, 39
Oncenio. See Leguía, Augusto B.
Ortiz Rodríguez, Federico, 135–36,
    171

Palacios, Leoncio, 156–57, 172–73
Palma, Clemente, 36, 100, 106–7
Palomino Ramírez, Teodosio
    Arístides, 228–29
Pardo, José, 22
Pardo, Octavio, 40–41
Parker, David, 21–22, 130–31, 221
Partido Civil, 53, 72
Partido Comunista Peruano (PCP), 6,
    109, 111–12, 114, 119, 124–29,
    142–44, 174, 194, 207–9, 221, 258
    n. 61
Partido Popular Cristiano (PPC), 53
Pasquel, Alfonso, 198
Patria Nueva. See Leguía, Augusto B.
Patronato de la Raza Indígena, 61
Paulet, Pedro, 130
Pavlevitch, Esteban, 102, 258 n. 61
Paz Soldán, Carlos Enrique, 131, 197
Perón, Juan Domingo, 126, 263 n. 15
Peruvian Corporation, 71, 202, 204,
    208, 276 n. 58
Pévez, Juan, 71, 76
Piérola, Nicolás de, 130
Populism, 6–7, 240 n. 9, 263 n. 15
Portella, Carlos, 252 n. 41
Portocarrero, Julio, 74
Positivism, 7, 23–24, 32, 233, 244 n. 21
Prado, Manuel, 203, 220

Race. See Racism
Racialization. See Racism
Racism: toward Afro-Peruvians, 35–

37, 46, 247 n. 68; toward Chinese, 35–37, 41, 44, 164–69, 173, 187–91, 247 n. 68, 270 n. 19; expressed in differentiated impact of violence in 1980s and 1990s, 236–37; expressed in project to de-indianize Peru, 32–50; 108–9, 224, 237–38; interpretations of, 232; toward Japanese, 44, 164–69, 187–91, 270 n. 19; toward mestizos, 35–38; racialization of labor, 11–15, 32–50, 234

Ramos, Angela, 109

Rationalities of discipline. *See* Governmentality

Rationalities of government. *See* Governmentality

Rebagliati, Edgardo, 110, 199–201, 208–16, 223–27

Recavarren, Federico, 149–50

Rerum novarum. See Social Catholicism

Restaurantes populares, 5–6, 14, 55 n. 271; architects of, 272 n. 73; as elements in construction of working-class identity, 187–91; as expression of rationalities of government, 180–87, 269 n. 6; gendering of, 272 n. 77; politicization of, 174–80; as technology of government, 180–87, 269 n. 6

Revolutionary syndicalism: as complement to technification of labor state, 75; development of, 74–78; at odds with repression under Leguía, 105

Riva-Agüero, Jose de la, 143–44

Roca, Erasmo, 65–66, 72, 90, 93, 109–10; 112, 252 n. 42

Rodgers, Daniel T., 18, 29, 31, 66, 85, 101, 126, 205, 232

Roosevelt, Franklin D., 126

Roosevelt, Theodore, 205

Rose, Nikolas, 9, 11, 24

Rossell, A. G., 2

Sabroso, Arturo, 74–75, 93

Samanez Ocampo, David, interim government of, 109–11

Sánchez Cerro, Luis Miguel, 6, 109, 111, 113, 125–29, 138, 142, 162, 174

Sarmiento, Teobaldo, 92

Schrüfer, Franz, 199–201

Schwab, Charles M., 27

Sección de Asuntos Indígenas, 13, 60–61, 64

Sección del Trabajo, 5–6, 13, 52–54, 60–61; bureaucracy at, 113; employers' reactions to, 86; exclusion from, 80–81; as expressive of rationalities of government, 75–83; left-wing critique of, 113–14; opposition to, 69–70; reorganization of, in 1930s, 109–20; structure of, 251–52 n. 41; success of, 70–72; technification of, 66–69; as technology of government, 75–83; weakness of, 101, 109; workers at, 78–80, 114–15; workers' shunning of, 90–93

Secciones obreras, 54–57

Seguro Social, 5–6, 13, 193; changes in, after 1940s, 227–28; exclusion from, of indigenous population, 221–27; exclusion from, of white-collar workers, 221–22; as expression of rationalities of government, 216–21; law of, 200–201; modification of law and, 206–7; opposition to, 201–2; origins of, 196–200, 275 n. 29; parallels of, with U.S. Social Security Act, 277–78 n. 106; promotion of, 208–16; support for, 204–6; as technology of government, 216–21

Sendero Luminoso (Shining Path), 14, 232, 236–38
Seoane, Manuel, 202
Social action, of Benavides government, 126–29
Social Catholicism, 7, 22–23, 32
Socialism, 7, 22–26, 46–47, 62, 94, 99–100, 126–28, 145, 198, 202
Sociedad de Beneficencia Pública de Lima, 131, 196–99
Sociedad Nacional de Agricultura, 40
Sociedad Nacional de Industrias, 2, 25, 27
Sociedad Nacional de Minería, 34–35
Solano, Susana, 196–97
State: coproduction with labor, 76–83; historiographical approaches and, 8–9
Steinmetz, George, 19, 29, 219
Strikes, 17–18, 20, 28, 51, 52, 64, 76, 85, 124–26

Technologies of government. *See* Governmentality
Temoche Benites, Ricardo, 74
Terreros, Nicolás, 102, 258 n. 61
Tizón y Bueno, Ricardo, 89
Truth and Reconciliation Commission, 231, 236–37

Ulloa Sotomayor, Alberto, 22, 31, 35–39, 55–59
Unemployment, 139–41

Unionization, 76–78
Unión Revolucionaria, 124; food policy of, 175
Unions: control of, by employers, 88; Second Workers Congress of 1927, 100, 104; view of, as respectable, 96

Valcarcel, Luis, 36
Valdez Tudela, Napoleon, 25
Vásquez, Samuel, 102, 104
Vega, Alejandro, 225
Velasco Alvarado, Juan, 14, 228
Vernon, James, 162, 179
Vidaurre, Rosendo, 28, 33–35
Vigil, Manuel, 111–12
Villarán, Manuel Vicente, 106, 225

Welfare: historiography of, 194–95, 273–74 n. 5
Worker housing: comparative historiography and, 262 n. 3; conditions of, in 1930s, 156–57; conditions of, in 1950s, 157; conditions of, prior to 1930s, 129–36; as factor in labor militancy, 124, 129, 136–39, 264–65 n. 47; as means to "improve" workers, 149–57, 268 n. 117. *See also* Barrios obreros

Young, W. M., 78

Zegarra, Enrique, 251–52 n. 41
Zubiaga, Adrián, 57

Paulo Drinot is a senior lecturer in Latin American History at the Institute for the Study of the Americas, School of Advanced Study, University of London. He is the author of *Historiografía, identidad historiografica y conciencia histórica en el Perú* (2006), the editor of *Che's Travels: The Making of a Revolutionary in 1950s Latin America* (also published by Duke University Press, 2010), and, with Leo Garofalo, the editor of *Más allá de la dominación y la resistencia: Estudios de historia peruana, siglos XVI–XX* (2005).

Library of Congress Cataloging-in-Publication Data
Drinot, Paulo.
The allure of labor : workers, race, and the making of the Peruvian state / Paulo Drinot.
p. cm.
Includes bibliographical references and index.
ISBN 978-0-8223-5002-6 (cloth : alk. paper)
ISBN 978-0-8223-5013-2 (pbk. : alk. paper)
1. Labor policy—Peru—History—20th century. 2. Working class—Peru—History—20th century. 3. Peru—Race relations—History—20th century. 4. Peru—Politics and government—20th century. I. Title.
HD8346.D75 2011
331.10985—dc22   2010039877